The 2014 Solo and Small Firm
Legal Technology Guide

CRITICAL DECISIONS MADE SIMPLE

Sharon D. Nelson, Esq., John W. Simek and Michael C. Maschke

INTRODUCTION BY JAMES A. CALLOWAY, ESQ.

ABALAW
PRACTICE
DIVISION
The Business of Practicing Law

Facebook®, Twitter®, LinkedIn®, Google®, Pinterest®, and YouTube® are registered trademarks of their respective corporations.

Cover design by RIPE Creative, Inc.

Printed in the United States of America.

Library of Congress Cataloging-in-Publication Data
The 2014 Solo and Small Firm Legal Technology Guide: Critical Decisions Made Simple. Sharon Nelson, John Simek, and Michael Maschke: Library of Congress Cataloging-in-Publication Data is on file.

ISBN: 978-1-62722-439-0

Discounts are available for books ordered in bulk. Special consideration is given to state bars, CLE programs, and other bar-related organizations. Inquire at Book Publishing, American Bar Association, 321 N. Clark Street, Chicago, Illinois 60654.

www.ShopABA.org

Dedication

SHARON NELSON AND John Simek dedicate this book to our children, Kelly, Sara, Kim, JJ, Jason, and Jamie, and to our grandchildren, Samantha, Lilly, Tyler, Evan, Jordan, and Cash—with many more to come, we hope!

Michael Maschke dedicates this book to his family, especially MD, DD, LE, CE, EE, and LE, and, of course, the beautiful YFC. Without them life would just not be the same—and certainly not as bright and wonderful.

All three authors dedicate this book also to our friend Ross Kodner, who left us far too young. Ross wrote the introduction to this book and its "Paper LESS" chapter for years. He was an extraordinary legal technologist—the entire legal tech community mourns his passing—and we mourn the loss of our dear friend.

Contents at a Glance

Contents

About the Authors

Sharon D. Nelson, Esq.

 Sharon D. Nelson is the president of Sensei Enterprises, Inc. Ms. Nelson graduated from Georgetown University Law Center in 1978 and has been in private practice ever since. She now focuses exclusively on electronic evidence law.

Ms. Nelson, Mr. Simek, and Mr. Maschke are the co-authors of the six most recent editions of this book (2008–2013). Ms. Nelson and Mr. Simek are also co-authors of *Locked Down: Information Security for Lawyers* (American Bar Association, 2012). Additionally, Ms. Nelson and Mr. Simek are co-authors of *The Electronic Evidence and Discovery Handbook: Forms, Checklists, and Guidelines* (ABA, 2006). Ms. Nelson is a co-author of *How Good Lawyers Survive Bad Times* (ABA, 2009). Ms. Nelson and Mr. Simek's articles have appeared in numerous national publications, and they frequently lecture throughout the country on digital forensics and legal technology subjects.

Ms. Nelson is a co-host of Legal Talk Network's *The Digital Edge: Lawyers and Technology* and *Digital Detectives* podcasts. Ms. Nelson and Mr. Simek have a regular legal tech column called "Hot Buttons" in the ABA Law Practice Division magazine *Law Practice*. Ms. Nelson is a member of the American Bar Association's Cybersecurity Task Force, its Standing Committee on Technology and Information Systems, and a member of the Editorial Board of *Law Technology News*.

Ms. Nelson is currently the seventy-fifth president of the Virginia State Bar. She is past president of the Fairfax Bar Association, a director and

President-elect of the Fairfax Law Foundation, past chair of the ABA's TECHSHOW Board, and past chair of the ABA's Law Practice Management Publishing Board. She currently serves as the Vice Chair of its Education Board. She is a member of the Sedona Conference. She is a graduate of Leadership Fairfax and serves on the Governing Council of the Virginia State Bar as well as on its Executive Committee. She is the former chair of the Virginia State Bar's Unauthorized Practice of Law Committee and serves on both its Technology Committee and its Standing Committee on Finance. She also serves on the Virginia Supreme Court's Advisory Committee on Statewide E-filing. She is a member of the ABA, the Virginia Bar, the Virginia Bar Association, the Virginia Trial Lawyers Association, the Virginia Women Lawyers Association, and the Fairfax Bar Association.

John W. Simek

John W. Simek is the vice president of Sensei Enterprises, Inc. He is an EnCase-Certified forensic technologist (EnCE) and a nationally known testifying expert in the area of digital forensics.

Mr. Simek holds a degree in engineering from the United States Merchant Marine Academy and an MBA in finance from Saint Joseph's University. After forming Sensei, he ended his more than 20-year affiliation with Mobil Oil Corporation, where he served as a senior technologist, troubleshooting and designing Mobil's networks throughout the Western Hemisphere.

In addition to his EnCE designation, Mr. Simek is a Certified Handheld Examiner, a Certified Novell Engineer, Microsoft Certified Professional + Internet, Microsoft Certified Systems Engineer, NT Certified Independent Professional, and a Certified Internetwork Professional. He is also a member of the High Tech Crime Network, the Sedona Conference, the Fairfax Bar Association, the International Information Systems Forensics Association, and the American Bar Association. In addition to co-authoring the books cited in Ms. Nelson's biography, he also serves on the Education Board of the ABA's Law Practice Division and on its governing Council. He currently provides information technology support to more than 250 area law firms, legal entities, and corporations. He lectures on legal technology and digital forensics subjects throughout the United States and Canada.

He is also a co-host of Legal Talk Network's *Digital Detectives* podcast.

Michael C. Maschke

 Michael Maschke is the Chief Information Officer and a digital forensics examiner at Sensei Enterprises, Inc. He is a Certified Computer Examiner (CCE), an EnCase Certified forensic technologist (EnCE), and a Certified Information Systems Security Professional (CISSP).

Mr. Maschke holds a degree in telecommunications from James Madison University. He has significant experience with network troubleshooting, design and implementation, systems integration, and computer engineering. Prior to becoming the Chief Information Officer, Mr. Maschke oversaw Sensei's information technology department, which provided support to hundreds of area law firms and corporations.

He has spoken at the American Bar Association's TECHSHOW conference on information security and is a co-author of *Information Security for Lawyers and Law Firms* as well as *The 2012 Solo and Small Firm Legal Technology Guide: Critical Decisions Made Simple*, both published by the American Bar Association.

Acknowledgments

SADLY, WE BID FAREWELL to our good friend Ross Kodner, one of the nation's finest legal technology consultants, who died suddenly last year.

Ross's contribution to legal technology knowledge can't be overstated—his compendium of writings, his lectures, and his willingness to help one and all through the American Bar Association's Solosez listserve all contributed to his stellar reputation. His knowledge ran broad and deep. We have lightly updated his famous chapter on the Paper LESS Office and included it in this year's book—we think he'd like that.

This year, we are happy to introduce our good friend Jim Calloway as the author of the introduction to this book. Jim is the Director of the Oklahoma Bar Association's Management Assistance Program. He frequently writes and speaks on legal technology issues, Internet research, law office management and organization, and legal ethics. He is frequently on the faculty with us at ABA TECHSHOW and is Sharon's co-host on the Legal Talk Network's *Digital Edge: Lawyers and Technology* podcast.

We are very happy that our friend and colleague Jennifer Ellis is a contributing author once again. She has updated her marvelous Social Media chapter for this edition of our book. Jennifer is a social media maven par excellence. You couldn't possibly get better advice.

Thanks go to good friends Tom Mighell and Paul Unger, who generously updated their excellent "iWin: iPad for Litigators" materials as an appendix that litigators are sure to find useful.

We are thrilled to have Denise Constantine as our Manager of Book Publishing at the Law Practice Division. She has been a model of efficiency and is no doubt amazed that we pretty much always finish our manuscript on schedule. We are delighted to be working with the LP's gifted

Marketing Manager, Lindsay Dawson. You've done a superb job marketing all the LP books, Lindsay!

Kudos as well to Laura Bolesta, our Publishing Specialist. The entire publishing staff has been amazing to work with—it is always a pleasure. And we know a lot of authors who can't say that about their publishers!

We are very grateful to our good friend Dave Ries, an extraordinary litigator in Pittsburgh and a terrific self-taught technologist, who served as project manager for this book. His suggestions and thoughts enriched the final product immeasurably.

Finally, we again thank our colleagues here at Sensei, who carried the load while we were writing and were never too busy to deliberate over recommendations and offer insightful comments. We don't come to work every day; we come to play, and we really like the folks we play with. Thanks, one and all!

Mike Maschke
Sharon Nelson
John Simek

Preface to the
Seventh Edition

WHAT WE HOPE TO do with this book is simple: We want to help solo and small firm lawyers find the "sweet spot" of legal technology—the best value for the dollars. You don't need a yacht, and you won't be well served by a rowboat. But there is a happy medium—professional-grade hardware and software that doesn't cost an arm and a leg.

This guide is an annual one, so you can't go too far wrong with our advice. Some chapters will remain almost absolutely current. At worst, we'll only be several months behind the curve. Still, if you can't afford your own legal technology consultant and you are concerned about those who are selling snake oil, at least this book should provide you with a neutral view of legal technology products.

As always, the parts of this book that age quickly are the hardware specifications. We are always happy to give you our latest specs—just drop us a quick line at **sensei@senseient.com**. We've given out hundreds of updated specs over the years, so don't hesitate to write!

We do our absolute best to be vendor neutral. Readers of previous editions will be keenly aware that our advice has changed from year to year as some products excel and others . . . well . . . decline—and sometimes precipitously. We have some exciting new products to talk about this year—nothing moves as fast as technology!

This is the only book we're aware of that deals with legal technology on a collective, annual basis. We are now in our seventh edition, so we must be doing something right. We seem to have a growing, loyal readership who wants independent advice on legal technology and finds a yearly dose of that advice compelling. In this book, we provide information on and recommendations for computers, servers, networking equipment, legal software, utilities, cool gadgets for lawyers, and more. We take an in-depth look at the technologies that will be around in 2014 and provide information on how these technologies will shape the way solo and small firm decision makers think about their technology decisions.

Our recommendations are what we would do in a solo or small practice ourselves: Invest in quality technology that will have a good shelf life and serve you well—that means buying business-grade (not consumer-grade) technology. And don't expect more than the machines can give. A server can be expected to last four to five years; a workstation or laptop, three to four. That's it, folks. As the software also evolves, it demands ever more resources, and the hardware ages both physically and in its ability to handle the new software. Remember the Rule of Three in upgrading: You should be upgrading one-third of your technology each year. Sometimes you can stretch it to four, but if you try to limp along patching things with spit and promises, you are likely going to be in for a "big bang" upgrade, which is acutely painful to the average solo or small law firm. Leasing may help lessen this financial burden (at least on an annual basis), but you lose the option to change course quickly without paying penalty fees.

Be mindful of the fact that this book is written exclusively for solos and small law firms. There is no attempt to include big-firm products or solutions, though many big firm lawyers have enjoyed portions of this book. In addition, we want to stress that we have included our recommendations only, not all available products. If you don't see a product here, it is because that product is not among our usual recommendations. This is a best-of-breed selection to keep you from being confused by the veritable cornucopia of choices that exist. No one has time to wade through all the choices, so we've tried to give you limited but tested options that work.

We used to say that generally we couldn't serve as your legal technology consultant unless you were in the D.C. area, but we are now providing remote backup and disaster recovery service to law firms anywhere in the country. Today, we are moving folks to the cloud, using a data center in northern Virginia. This means we can now provide IT (information technology) support nationwide and use remote access to connect to any part of your network that is not housed in the data center. Call us if this is an option you want to explore. With all the law firm data breaches that have been reported in the last several years, our Information Security Department has been hopping, investigating data breaches and assessing and securing law firm networks. More information about our services may be found on our website, **www.senseient.com**, or you can call us at 703-359-0700 for further information. Security assessments should be an annual (at least) exercise for all law firms—and they cost less than you might think.

We are serious about our commitment to the legal profession and proud of our professional giveback through the ABA. If you have a question, we'll do our best to help. Just e-mail us at **sensei@senseient.com**. We appreciate all your comments and suggestions, as they help make each subsequent edition of this book better than the one before. Thanks, in advance, for your continuing help!

Introduction to 2014 Small Firm Technology Guide

by James A. Calloway, Esq.

"Any sufficiently advanced technology is indistinguishable from magic."
—Arthur C. Clarke, well-known science fiction author

You have to be of a certain age to recall when most lawyers thought computers were only word-processing tools for staff and when all telephones were attached to walls by cords. Now almost every type of professional office has computers at every workspace. Many of the technology tools we have today seem like magic, and the number of things one can do from a smartphone continues to amaze us all.

Solo practitioners and small law firms have great opportunities created by technology in that they can communicate and collaborate easily worldwide and can use today's powerful tools to do things that a few decades back could have been done only by a large firm with legions of associates. But rapid changes in technology also impact the entire legal profession in ways that are not at all positive.

The small law firm often cannot hire a human relations coordinator or full-time IT (information technology) staff. By necessity, the small firm lawyer cannot just practice law but also must handle several administrative duties. It has been said many times that the small firm lawyer wears many hats.

I recall once talking on the phone to a senior lawyer and hearing a happy baby gurgling in the background. He explained that his legal assistant's babysitter was sick and he had a brief due that day. "I may not be able to format that brief correctly, and I cannot type fast," he said. "But I know how to take care of a baby."

The 2014 Solo and Small Firm Legal Technology Guide may not replace a law firm having a full-time IT director, but annually it provides the bedrock information for a small firm lawyer who *is* the firm IT director, like it or not. Some of the book will be read and reread, while other portions will be skimmed or skipped depending on the immediate technology needs of the firm. But a law firm of any size today can no more avoid technology than a trial lawyer can avoid the courthouse.

I was honored to be asked to write this Introduction, particularly because the introductions to prior editions of this book had been written by my friend Ross Kodner. There was shock and sadness around the country when Ross suddenly passed away last summer. Ross was a champion of the smart use of technology in the law office. He spoke at so many legal technology conferences, CLE programs, and bar solo and small firm conferences that the total number of lawyers who have heard Ross speak about legal technology or have read his writings must be staggering. Sharon Nelson, John Simek, and I were all first recruited to speak at ABA TECHSHOW by Ross Kodner. He always loved to show small firm lawyers how technology "smarts" could improve their practices and their lives. Thanks for everything, Ross.

This is the second edition of the *Guide* released since the ABA revised its Model Rules of Professional Conduct to require that a lawyer be competent with the technology tools that lawyers must use today.

The official comment to Rule 1.1 on Competence added the language below (italics mine):

> To maintain the requisite knowledge and skill, a lawyer should keep abreast of changes in the law and its practice, *including the benefits and risks associated with relevant technology*, engage in continuing study and education and comply with all continuing legal education requirements to which the lawyer is subject.

No doubt this will be threatening to some of our fellow lawyers, and some jurisdictions may not include this provision in their version of the Rules of Professional Conduct. But to many, this aspect of competency has been obvious for some time now. Mastery of technology is clearly an important business skill for survival, and too many law firms are allowing the press of day-to-day business to delay training and planning for the future.

This guidebook is here to provide the basics of what a lawyer really needs to know about networking, encryption, or social media. But it also provides some deep expertise. It is the law office technology book for lawyers who love technology—and for those who hate it! It is a quick reference guide you can count on when someone tells you that you simply have to drop everything to purchase some gadget or software unfamiliar to you. If you need more information, you can find a huge amount of information on any topic online. But some of that online information will conflict, and some will be promotional material. A baseline understanding from a trusted source is the foundation of good research on technology tools.

Some time-challenged lawyers will simply use the examples in the book as their shopping list. But the main goal should be to learn what features of a product are useful for your situation so you will know when that 25 percent discount or a new release actually *is* a great deal.

But competency in serving clients is only one aspect of why lawyers should have a general understanding of today's technology.

Technology is harnessed today to increase efficiency in small businesses, and even though lawyers still prefer the term *profession* over the term *business*, a small law firm is a small business. We've seen whole classes of businesses become roadkill on the great information superhighway. Because of changes fueled by technology advances, there are far fewer travel agents, music stores, bookstores, and newspapers. It can be hard to conceive that the virtually ubiquitous access to free, instant photographs caused Kodak to declare bankruptcy at the beginning of 2012.

As I write, Kodak has emerged from bankruptcy with a new focus on digital imaging for businesses—we must all reinvent ourselves.

No serious observer can dismiss the well-documented impending challenges to the legal profession, including the online delivery of legal services by non-lawyers. These services directly compete with the small law firm providing general legal advice and services to individuals and small businesses.

The lawyer wearing a CEO hat should recognize that some changes are inevitable. With most types of businesses, the need for improvements to increase efficiency is simply a part of doing business today—not that technology tools trump the traditional and critical skills that successful lawyers have.

Knowledge of the law and local practices, a commitment to good client service, dependability, loyalty, thoroughness, and plain hard work are all required of the successful lawyer.

But proper adoption of technology can improve the lawyer's life *and* the work product for clients.

Let's examine how one basic operation should be accomplished.

A lawyer drafting a document for a client recognizes a specific client situation that requires adding several paragraphs into the primary document and creating a new separate document. Traditionally the lawyer could search prior work for the precedent language or draft the provisions from scratch. Even when using a simple form where no customization is needed, there would be names and dates to add and other items to proofread. Then the new document would be created (hopefully from a saved form), and the information related to this client would be manually filled in by a lawyer or legal assistant. Certainly this would take billable time charged to the client.

But the aspirational goal, which is completely attainable with today's tools, would be for the drafting lawyer to recognize the situation and click on a button or item from a list to insert the needed provisions. No customization would be required, as the inserted language would either match defined terms within the document or automatically fill with required information (a/k/a data) for this client and/or transaction. The new document would also be created quickly and filled with the required data. The lawyer would then consult the firm's checklist or workflow outline to determine if additional tasks needed to be done as a consequence of these changes.

What would have taken the better part of an hour for drafting and proofing would now be done in minutes. But of equal importance is the fact that the firm has a standardized process so every client of the firm with this situation receives these additions to his or her documents. These provisions were vetted by the firm experts and reflect the state of the art (and the state of the law) as far as the firm is concerned.

Time that would have been billed to the client is saved, which results in both a better value for the client and a potential loss of revenue to the firm. This is why a discussion of law office automation should go hand in hand with a discussion of billing at least some tasks differently than by the hour. But the benefits of automation are greater: The lawyer and legal assistant avoided a part of their work that is tedious—replacing names, dates, and other data when using prior work and proofreading the same document multiple times. One goal of this process is to free the legal professionals for more creative, challenging, and valuable work. Other benefits could include quicker turnaround for client projects and fewer nights spent burning the midnight oil at the law firm.

The scary thing is how soon the above project will be handled by the lawyer saying to the computer, "Take the Jones AX50 data and create documents 43, 47, and 47B. Print the draft to my screen." Only law firms that have successfully incorporated the current improvements in process will be ready to take that next step.

All of these technology tools are just that—tools. So the smart small firm lawyer today will need to combine these tools with processes. Whether these combinations are called workflows or legal project management or some new term of techno-jargon (or management-speak) really matters not. Law firms that invest in these processes will obtain advantages over those firms that do so more slowly and incompletely—or not at all.

Some of the advantages in the service delivery to clients will include:

- using secure, encrypted client portals for delivery of information instead of completely insecure e-mail and attachments
- never asking clients for information they have previously provided because it has been misplaced or cannot be quickly located
- using digital client files that can be accessed by several lawyers or staff simultaneously and that can never be "lost" (if the firm does its data backups correctly)
- having the ability to answer routine questions from the client instantly (e.g., "What is my total bill right now?")

There are many resources and systems available on time management and efficiency. You may have adopted the late Stephen Covey's *Seven Habits of Highly Effective People*, David Allen's Getting Things Done®, or Merlin Mann's 43 Folders. I often direct lawyers to the easy-to-read book *The Checklist Manifest* by Atul Gawde.

The 2014 Solo and Small Firm Legal Technology Guide can help you purchase new tools to replace those that have become outdated or broken. But the highest and best use of the *Guide* is to use it with some of the tools profiled in it and other information to build improved processes and systems in your law office, setting your firm on a path to success and creating your own future.

James A. Calloway is the Director of the Oklahoma Bar Association Manage-ment Assistance Program, an author of several books on law practice manage-ment, and a former chair of the ABA TECHSHOW board. He co-produces the podcast Digital Edge Lawyers and Technology *with Sharon Nelson. He blogs at* Jim Calloway's Law Practice Tips *(**jimcalloway.typepad.com**) and tweets at **@jimcalloway***.

CHAPTER ONE

Computers

Desktop Computers

Personal Computers (PCs)

The Dell OptiPlex line of computers continues to offer the perfect combination of performance and business-grade hardware at just the right price. All Dell computers can be purchased with a three-, four -, or five-year warranty and offer a large selection of available options when it comes to protecting your investment. They offer both hardware and software warranty protection of varying levels, along with same-day or next-business-day response for the replacement of failed computer hardware or software. We strongly recommend the purchase of a three-year warranty—the average life span of a business computer system—with any new computer. Purchasing software technical support, in our judgment, is generally not worth the additional cost, especially when most firms have an IT provider who is familiar with their software and setup and can assist when help is needed, rather than having to rely on Dell for assistance.

Dell also offers accidental damage protection for its computer systems, which covers damage caused by spilled liquids, drops, falls, and electrical surges for a period of three to five years, at an additional cost ranging from $34 to $55. This cost is much lower than in previous editions of this book.

Another option from Dell worth noting is its Keep Your Hard Drive program. Typically, if a hard drive crashes while under warranty, Dell will take the failed hard drive and replace it with a new or refurbished one. Citing privacy concerns—with all the recent data breaches in the news— Dell now offers its users the ability to keep their hard drives, even in the event a replacement is needed, but at an additional cost. The cost for this option ranges from $14 to $21, depending on the length of the warranty, and it is a small price to pay to maintain total control over and responsibility for the sensitive and confidential data on the hard drive. For recommendations on how to securely remove data from a hard drive before disposal, check out the Utilities chapter.

Below, we provide you with our recommendations for a Dell OptiPlex business-grade computer system with all of the hardware components included.

Windows-Based Desktop Computer

<u>Hardware Component</u>	<u>Recommendation</u>
Computer Model:	Dell OptiPlex 9010 Mini Tower
Operating System:	Microsoft Windows 7 Professional 64-Bit
Processor:	3rd Gen Intel Core i7-3770 Processor (Quad Core, 3.4 GHz, 8 MB, w/HD4000 Graphics)
Memory:	8GB DDR3 Non-ECC SDRAM 1600 MHz
Video Card:	1GB AMD RADEON HD 7470 (2 DVI or 2 VGA)
Hard Drive:	500GB SATA 6GB/s with 16MB Databurst Cache
Optical Drive:	16X DVD+/–RW
Network:	Intel Gigabit LAN 10/100/1000 Ethernet
Warranty:	3-Year Basic Hardware Service with 3-Year Next Business Day Onsite Service After Remote Diagnosis
Other Notes:	No mouse and keyboard required; no out-of-band systems management; USB 3.0 ports included

The third-generation Intel Core i7-3770 Quad Core 3.4 GHz processor will provide more than enough power to support both current and future versions of business-grade software, including the next version of the Windows Operating System, throughout the life cycle of the machine. The Intel Core i7 has replaced the Intel Core 2 Duo processor and has become the standard for business-grade systems. The Intel Core i7 Quad Core processor is offered with varying levels of clock speeds, with the 3.4 GHz version currently in the upper range of processor clock speeds offered by Dell for this model of computer system. The faster the processor, the higher the premium you will pay for having cutting-edge technology. The amount of memory included in this system is enough to support your business applications, handling even "memory hungry" applications with ease. Eight gigabytes (GB) of memory has become the recommended standard for the minimum amount of memory in business-grade computers, given the low cost and high gain in performance for the upgrade. This upgrade is a must-have option when purchasing a 64-bit system, which can actually take advantage of the additional resources.

The video card included in this system provides dual digital visual inter-face (DVI) outputs or legacy dual video graphics array (VGA) outputs. By providing dual interfaces, this graphics adapter allows you to have dual monitors, an option we will never go without when purchasing a new computer system. In fact, John has recently stated that he is considering a third! (Monitors, keyboards, and other peripherals are discussed in subse-quent chapters.) A hard drive plays an important role in the configuration of your computer system because it is the hardware component where your information (files) is actually stored. In short, the better the hard drive, the faster your computer can read and write your data. This system comes with a 500GB Serial ATA (SATA) hard drive, which will provide enough storage space for the average lawyer user. The SATA (6GB/s) inter-face is the latest generation of the SATA specification (revision 3.0), allow-ing for more throughput and higher cache than the previous revisions of the SATA specification. In fact, Dell no longer offers earlier versions of SATA hard drives as an option when configuring an OptiPlex desktop or smaller capacity drives. We wouldn't be surprised if, in the near future, the usage of 3.5-inch hard drives is discontinued due to the large power requirements to operate them and their propensity to fail, especially as the cost of solid-state hard drives continues to fall. In fact, Dell now offers more choices for notebook sized (2.5-inch) drives and solid-state drives for the Optiplex model line than they do for the standard (3.5-inch) SATA drives.

When configuring an optical drive for the system, choosing the 16X DVD+/−RW drive will allow you to burn and read data from both CDs and DVDs. We used to recommend that you purchase your computer with a FireWire 400 or 800 Mbps adapter, but that is no longer the case. Newer interfaces have come out within the past two years, such as USB 3.0 and Thunderbolt, a serial data interface primarily found on Apple computer systems, and are now beginning to be offered on a small number of Windows-based computers. Now that these technologies have been out for a few years, especially USB 3.0, it might be the time to jump on board—especially if you transfer a lot of data to external hard drives. In actuality, it's becoming harder to find just USB 2.0 external hard drives, so you might as well take advantage of the added speed. The Dell OptiPlex 9010 Mini Tower now includes four USB 3.0 ports (two on front, two on back) and six USB 2.0 ports.

Dell currently offers its computers preinstalled with the Windows 7 or Windows 8 operating systems. Even for die-hard techies like us, it would be a reach to think about using Windows 8 at this time in a business envi-ronment—remember the problems with Windows Vista and hardware drivers? Windows 8 just hasn't caught fire with businesses as many industry analysts predicted it would, and given the current lack of implementation, it is considered by many to be another Microsoft failure, just like Microsoft Vista. It remains to be seen, but at this time we have no plans to upgrade our systems from Windows 7 to Windows 8 and just may wait for the next release. The exception would be for touch devices, where Windows 8 may be a better alternative.

The three-year, next-business-day onsite parts and labor warranty will cover hardware defects and failures of the computer system for three years at a relatively small cost. The cost of this warranty is built into the cost of the recommended system and should be considered a requirement when purchasing a new computer for your business or firm. Dell provides the consumer with a toll-free phone number to call for technical support, and if any hardware needs to be replaced, Dell will send a support technician to your location to replace the defective part by the next business day. The hardware replacement and labor cost is covered by the warranty, so there should be no additional out-of-pocket costs.

There are some additional pointers to consider when configuring this desktop system. First, most users already have their own wireless keyboard and mouse and don't need another basic USB keyboard and mouse taking up space in the desk drawer. This can be avoided by removing them from the default configuration of this system, and you'll save about $15. For those of you who don't have a wireless keyboard and mouse—you should be looking at upgrading immediately. Our recommendations for a wireless desktop suite can be found in the Computer Peripherals chapter.

Another tip: Dell also includes by default an out-of-band management device, which shouldn't be necessary. Again, just removing this piece of hardware can save you approximately $30.

For those users who are looking to purchase a new monitor or two, Dell does offer the ability to bundle monitors when configuring your new computer system. If you need a new monitor or two, it may be a good idea to save a few bucks and bundle them with the purchase of your new computer system. Based on a price comparison, it appears that you save about $40 per monitor when selecting them at the time of your computer purchase, and we're always looking for ways to save you money!

Keep in mind that, on average, the expected life cycle of a new computer system is three years, which is covered by the three-year warranty you purchased. The recommended Dell OptiPlex 9010 Mini Tower desktop computer can be configured and purchased from Dell's website starting at around $993.

Remember that the "sweet spot" in buying computers changes regularly. Our specs will get you close, but they will shift slightly during the life-span of this publication. You can receive a courtesy copy of our current specs (for workstations, laptop, and servers—PC or Mac) by e-mailing **sensei@senseient.com** and simply making a request. We are generally able to get our current specs to you within 24 hours during the work-week. We are happy to report that many, many readers are taking advantage of this offer, so don't be shy. We are always pleased to help.

Apple Computers (Macs)

Apple computers (Macs) are still not as widely used in law offices as Windows-based computers are, but since Apple's shift to using Intel-based processors in all of its systems, and with the continued popularity of the iPad, they are now chosen more frequently by solo and small firm lawyers. As a result of this change, Macs can now run both the Mac OS X and Windows operating systems on the same computer. In a way, it's like having two systems in one.

A Mac computer can be easily configured to connect to and function on a Windows-based network, including communicating with and authenticating a Windows domain controller. In the past, however, Macs were used primarily by businesses with a need for multimedia functions, such as video editing and graphic design—both areas in which Apple systems have always excelled. Usually, Apple's appearance in an office environment was the result of someone having a personal preference for the Macintosh operating system over the Windows-based system.

For those concerned with computer security, Mac systems are perceived to be more secure than their Windows-based counterparts since they are not targeted as often by malware, due to the overall smaller number of Mac users. Most Mac users would scoff at the suggestion that their computer should be running some kind of security software for protection. However, they would be wrong; Macs absolutely need security software. Remember, the bad guys who write browser exploits (pieces of malware that take advantage of vulnerabilities in Internet browsers such as Firefox) don't care what operating system the computer is running. In fact, security companies consistently warn that malware writers who attack browsers are increasingly becoming the real threat, as vulnerabilities in operating systems are less frequently targeted.

The Flashback virus that affected over half a million Macs early in 2012 has been the largest attack on Mac OS X to date. In an unprecedented move, Apple released two security updates/fixes addressing just this vulnerability.

In early 2013, a new Trojan virus was discovered targeting computers running Mac OS X, creating an encrypted reverse-shell connection providing attackers with potentially unfettered access to infected machines. It was dubbed "Pintsized" for the very small, yet efficient threat.

So Apple users, please don't be naive—you, too, need virus and malware protection. In 2012, Apple removed from its website the language suggesting that you didn't need this type of protection.

Apple's continuing release of security patches, even for the latest version of its operating system, is a clear sign of just how targeted this software and its applications are by the developers of malware. For years, we have recommended that security protection suites be installed on all computers, regardless of the operating system.

While they are still not commonplace, we are beginning to see Apple computers make their way into smaller law offices, especially in the solo, stand-alone environment. Now that Apple computers use Intel chipsets, users are taking advantage of the opportunity to better integrate their systems with the Windows world. Some users run Windows on their Mac computers as the primary operating system. Others use Boot Camp, a free utility provided by Apple at no charge with each system, to dual-boot between Windows and Mac OS. With Boot Camp, you can install a Microsoft Windows XP operating system or newer right alongside Apple's OS X on any Intel-based Macintosh computer. To run the Windows 7 or newer operating system, you must upgrade your version of Boot Camp to version 4.0 or newer. The most current release of Boot Camp is version 5.0.

For those users who purchased Mac OS X Mountain Lion, this updated version of Boot Camp was included. Boot Camp guides users through the processes of creating a new partition of the local hard drive on which to install the Windows operating system and also provides all of the necessary Windows drivers required for hardware functionality. As an alternative to dual-booting with Boot Camp, some users have even purchased third-party products like Parallels Workstation or downloaded Oracle's

VM VirtualBox, which allows them to run Windows, Linux, and other operating systems within the Mac OS itself. Virtual Machine (VM) software is described in more detail in a later section of this book.

The iMac desktop systems combine performance and ergonomics by putting the hardware components that make up the system in the same casing as the monitor, eliminating the need for separate components like a tower unit sitting underneath your desk. As a result, the space-saving design allows you to free up both desk and floor space without giving up performance. Below, we provide our recommendation for an iMac business-grade desktop system with all of the hardware components outlined.

Macintosh-Based Desktop Computer

Hardware Component	Recommendation
Computer Model:	21.5-inch iMac
Operating System:	Mac OS v10.8 Mountain Lion
Processor:	Intel Core i5 Quad Core 2.7 GHz (Turbo Boost up to 3.2 GHz)
Memory:	8GB 1600MHz DDR3 SDRAM
Video Card:	NVIDIA GeForce GT 640M
Hard Drive:	1 TB (5400-rpm) Hard Drive
CD/DVD-ROM:	8X SuperDrive (DVD+R DL/DVD±RW/CD-RW)
Network:	10/100/1000 Base-T Gigabit Ethernet Port, AirPort Extreme Wi-Fi (802.11a/b/g/n), Bluetooth 4.0
Warranty:	3-year AppleCare Protection Plan for iMacs
Other:	FaceTime HD Camera, Built-in 21.5-inch Monitor and Stereo Speakers, Dual Microphones, two Thunderbolt Ports, four USB 3 Ports, Mini Display-Port, Apple Wireless Keyboard and Magic Mouse, SDXC Card Slot, and Kensington Lock Slot

The 21.5-inch iMac comes with an Intel Core i5 Quad Core 2.7 GHz processor, 8GB of memory, and the Mac OS v10.8 Mountain Lion operating system. This system can be configured for up to 16GB of memory, which may be overkill for basic business usage. The 1TB 5400 RPM SATA hard drive comes standard and will provide more than enough storage space and hard drive performance for the average lawyer. However, if you feel that you need additional storage space or performance speed, the

hard drive can be configured with 256GB or 512GB of flash storage. The flash storage media will contain the files necessary to boot and load the operating system, dramatically increasing the speed with which the computer system starts up.

The hard drive can be upgraded to 3TB in size, but this option is only available to the 27-inch version of the iMac.

The standard Ethernet adapter and AirPort wireless adapter will allow your computer to connect to the business network, whether over a wired network or wireless, even if it's Windows-based. The AirPort wireless adapter is compatible with 802.11a/b/g/n wireless networks.

The other standard hardware included with the iMac is the built-in Face-Time HD camera, stereo speakers, 21.5-inch LED-backlit display with IPS technology, four USB 3.0 ports, two Thunderbolt ports, and one SDXC memory card slot. This system also includes one Mini DisplayPort, which allows users to add a second external monitor to their computer system if needed, and the standard Apple wireless keyboard and Magic Mouse. The 21.5-inch iMac computer weighs 12.5 pounds and has a depth of about 7 inches, making it very easy to find room on your desk for one of these systems.

Apple's standard warranty with a new iMac provides you with ninety days of telephone support and one year of service coverage. We recommend that you upgrade the warranty to the extended AppleCare Protection Plan for iMac, which provides you with telephone and service support for three years. The cost to extend the warranty plan is $169 and is well worth it. The 21.5-inch iMac computer can be purchased from Apple's webstore starting at $1,299 and the pricing of the 27-inch iMac starts at $1,799.

Laptops

Personal Computers (PCs)

The Dell Latitude line of laptop computers continues to combine performance and mobility in a laptop system that remains at the top of its class. These business-grade laptops are thin and extremely light, weighing less than four and a half pounds. They are a perfect fit for the mobile lawyer and provide an ideal mobile computing solution. Below, we provide you with our recommendations for a Dell Latitude business-grade laptop with all of the hardware components included.

Windows-Based Laptop Computer

<u>Hardware Component</u>   **<u>Recommendation</u>**

Computer Model: Dell Latitude E6430

Processor: 3rd Gen Intel Core i5-3340M Dual Core 2.7 GHz

Operating System: Microsoft Windows 7 Professional 64-Bit

Memory: 8GB DDR3 1600 MHz SDRAM

Video Card: Intel HD Graphics 4000

Hard Drive: 500GB 7200 RPM hard drive

CD/DVD-ROM: 8X DVD+/–RW drive

Network: 10/100/1000 Mbps Ethernet adapter, Intel Centrino Advanced-N 6205 802.11a/b/g/n Half-Mini Card

Warranty: 3-Year Basic Hardware Service with 3-Year Next-Business-Day Limited Onsite Service After Remote Diagnosis

Other: 14-Inch Wide HD LED screen, 90W AC power adapter, 9-cell/97 WHr primary battery, weighs 4.44 lbs., two USB 2.0 Ports, one USB/eSATA Combo, two USB 3.0 ports, VGA, HDMI, Memory Card Reader, Noise Cancelling Digital Array Microphone and Light Sensitive Webcam, Fingerprint reader, and contactless smartcard reader

The Dell Latitude E6430 comes with a third-generation Intel Core i5-3340M Dual Core 2.7 GHz processor and 8GB of memory, which should be sufficient to run all of the business applications of a mobile lawyer. The system also comes preinstalled with Microsoft Windows 7 Professional 64-bit.

The system's fingerprint reader provides the level of security needed to protect your personal files and confidential data. When it's enabled, you can restrict user logon access to either the biometric access or to a user name and password. A fingerprint reader keeps data on the hard drive secure through encryption, with the hardware requiring successful authentication before the data contents can be decrypted. Enabling a start-up or hard drive password in the system's BIOS is a great way to add an extra layer of protection to your system and is highly recommended if you're storing sensitive client data on your laptop.

The Intel HD graphics card supplies crisp, clear graphics to the 14-inch-wide LED display. The 500GB hard drive will provide more than enough storage space for the mobile user, with a hard drive speed that will supply faster drive performance. The DVD+/–RW drive will allow you to burn and read both CDs and DVDs without the need to attach an external burner. The Ethernet adapter will allow you to connect your laptop to your network when you're in the office, and the wireless network adapter will allow you to stay connected when on the move. The Intel wireless adapter provides connectivity to 802.11a/b/g/n wireless networks, supporting dual-band operation (2.4 and 5 GHz) with data rates up to 300 megabits per second (Mbps). The 9-cell battery is an upgrade that will supply the laptop with power longer than the standard 6-cell battery and should charge faster as well. This battery upgrade is a must-have if you plan to use the wireless network adapter when running the laptop off of the battery, although this will add some slight weight to the unit. The 9-cell battery will provide you with approximately three hours' more battery life than the standard 6-cell battery, which will save you from searching for electrical outlets wherever you go. Finally, the integrated HD video webcam and digital microphone is great for videoconferences or recording audio, such as podcasts.

For frequent travelers and those who truly want to always stay connected, the Dell Latitude E6430 has a configuration option to add an internal mobile broadband card (3G/4G) for the Verizon, Sprint, T-Mobile, AT&T, and a few additional networks for an extra $87.50.

The three-year, next-business-day onsite parts and labor warranty is the same warranty described in the Desktop Computers section. The Dell Latitude E6430 can be purchased from Dell's website starting at around $1,166.

If you are particularly clumsy or accident-prone, you may want to consider adding the CompleteCare Accidental Damage Protection Plan to your purchase. This plan covers any damage to the laptop, including such things as liquid spills (one client has used this plan multiple times to cover the unwelcome effects of spilling red wine) and dropping the device. Obviously, it does not cover intentional damage, theft, or normal wear and tear. For the additional $76.30 to $111.30, depending on the length of the warranty, you will have peace of mind when you set your coffee cup (or wineglass) on the keyboard.

Apple Computers (Macs)
The Apple MacBook Pro is perfect for the mobile lawyer who requires a powerful notebook in a compact and lightweight design. The MacBook Pro laptop comes standard with the Intel Core i7 Quad Core 2.4 GHz

processor, wide-screen Retina display, built-in FaceTime HD camera, wireless network adapter, and much more. The MacBook Pro laptop is available with 13- or 15-inch screens. Apple no longer sells a 17-inch version of this model. In prior editions of this book, Apple offered the Retina display only in the upgraded 15-inch model of the MacBook Pro. This is no longer the case. All versions of both the 13- and 15-inch MacBook Pros come standard with the Retina display. The MacBook Pro is available only in the aluminum case with glass LED display. The MacBook Pro can be fully integrated into any Windows-based network without too much overhead and configuration. Below, we provide our recommendations for an Apple MacBook Pro business-grade laptop with all of the hardware components included.

Macintosh-Based Laptop Computer

<u>Hardware Component</u>	<u>Recommendation</u>
Computer Model:	15-Inch MacBook Pro
Operating System:	Mac OS v10.8 Mountain Lion
Processor:	Intel Core i7 Quad Core 2.4 GHz
Memory:	8GB 1600MHz DDR3
Video Card:	Intel HD Graphics 4000
Hard Drive:	256GB Flash Storage
CD/DVD-ROM:	8X SuperDrive (DVD+R DL/DVD±RW/CD-RW)
Network:	10/100/1000 Base-T Gigabit Ethernet Port, AirPort Extreme Wi-Fi (802.11a/b/g/n), Bluetooth 4.0
Warranty:	3-year AppleCare Protection Plan
Other:	FaceTime HD Camera, Built-in 15.4-Inch LED-Backlit Display with IPS Technology, Stereo Speakers, two USB 3 Ports, two Thunderbolt Ports, SDXC Card Slot, and HDMI

The base 15-inch MacBook Pro laptop comes with 8GB of memory (upgradable to 16GB) and the Mac OS v10.8 Mountain Lion operating system. The Intel HD Graphics 4000 video card provides perfect high resolution to the 15.4-inch-wide Retina LED display, with a maximum resolution of 2880 × 1800 pixels. The 256GB flash storage hard drive provides enough space to store all of your documents, pictures, and music. The 8X SuperDrive will allow you to burn and play both CDs and DVDs. The built-in AirPort Extreme Wi-Fi adapter will keep you connected on the road, and it supports the 802.11n standard. The AirPort Extreme Wi-Fi adapter is also backward compatible with 802.11a/b/g wireless networks. The aluminum body MacBook is very light, weighing just 4.6 pounds.

If you need more memory or processing power, this model can be upgraded to a maximum of 16GB of memory and an i7 2.7 GHz quad-core processor—for a pretty penny!

The multi-touch scrolling trackpad gives you precise cursor control, supports two-finger scrolling, tap, double-tap, and drag capabilities. If you have been a lifelong Windows user, be forewarned: There is no right-click button on the trackpad. To right-click on a Mac, you must hold down the Control key while clicking. A tip for former Windows users: Don't want to hold down the Control key to initiate a right-click with the mouse? You can tap the trackpad with two fingers rather than holding down the Control key—you just have to enable the option within the Keyboard & Mouse settings.

Have you ever tripped over a power cord and had your laptop come flying off the desk? With the 85W MagSafe 2 power adapter, you no longer have to worry. The magnetic power connector will cleanly disengage from the side of the laptop and cause no damage to the computer or the power cord. This a great gift to those of us who are occasionally less than graceful.

The sleek and elegant design of the MacBook Pro is what sets it apart from the competition. The design and celebrated ease of use makes the MacBook Pro a smart choice when purchasing a laptop for yourself or your firm. The MacBook Pro configured above can be purchased from Apple's webstore for $2,199.

Netbooks/Ultrabooks

Netbooks and ultrabooks continue to be very popular among mobile users, including lawyers. Essentially, these devices are highly portable mini-laptops. They are much smaller, cheaper, and lighter than most traditional laptops. As with the other computer recommendations, it is impossible to mention all of the available manufacturers and models of ultrabooks and netbooks.

More recently, netbooks have taken a backseat to a new class of laptops called ultrabooks. Ultrabooks, which are becoming increasingly popular, are paper-thin laptops (nearly weightless when compared to a traditional laptop). Ultrabooks have more robust hardware specifications than netbooks, but they also command a higher price.

Apple released the MacBook Air, an ultrabook considered the first of its class, long before PC manufacturers released the first competitor. Much as the iPad has dominated Android-based tablets, in part because it was first to the market, the MacBook Air continues to be an extremely popular alternative to the regular laptop for a mobile user, and starts at a cost of $1,000 or so.

The MacBook Air is offered in both 11- and 13-inch models, with configurable internal flash storage capacity available from 64 to 256GB. The 1.7 GHz Dual Core Intel Core i5 processor is more than capable of handling web browsing and document editing, but not a lot more than that, which is perfect for the mobile lawyer. The standard 4GB of DDR3 memory is more than sufficient for everyday usage and can be upgraded to 8GB.

If you were to hold an 11-inch model, weighing just 2.38 pounds, you'd never go back to using a standard laptop. The MacBook Air is available for purchase on Apple's website starting at $999.

CHAPTER TWO

Computer Operating Systems

Microsoft Windows XP Operating System

The Microsoft Windows XP operating system was released in October 2001 and was made available in three editions: Professional, Home, and the less common Media Center. Microsoft Windows XP Home was the first consumer-oriented operating system labeled as more user friendly than previous versions of Microsoft's operating systems. Windows XP Professional Edition was specifically designed for businesses and power users, with added functionality and security. As recently as 2010, the majority of all business computers were running Windows XP Professional Edition. In the latest statistics, this has rapidly changed with the release of Windows 7—the vast majority of the business world elected to skip Vista and went straight to Windows 7. In July 2013, roughly 42 percent of all computers accessing the Internet were running the Microsoft Windows 7 operating system, 20 percent were running Windows XP, and 5 percent were running Windows 8, according to W3Counter.

Microsoft released Service Pack 3 for Windows XP in May of 2008, which was the last service pack developed for the operating system. In April 2009, Microsoft Windows XP entered the extended support period, which will be phased out by 2014.

Microsoft Windows XP should no longer be used on computer systems, whether the system is new or existing.

Microsoft Windows Vista Operating System

Microsoft Windows Vista operating system was released in January 2007 and was made available in six editions, with two editions designed for the business community—Windows Vista Business Edition and Windows

Vista Enterprise Edition. Windows Vista Business Edition included several new business features, such as file system encryption, a full version of Remote Desktop, system image backup and recovery, Windows Shadow-Copy, and the IIS web server.

When first released, it was believed that eventually Windows Vista Business Edition would replace Microsoft XP Professional Edition as the dominant player in the business desktop operating system market, but this certainly was not the case. Many companies were hesitant to upgrade their business systems because of Vista's continuing incompatibility problems with some third-party software, licensing restrictions and costs, digital rights managements, driver issues for some peripherals, and the hardware requirements necessary to run the operating system. Vista ultimately did itself in and just never took off as it was expected to.

Microsoft Vista turned out to be a complete and utter failure for Microsoft. The operating system was rejected almost immediately by both consumers and businesses and ultimately was rated as the number two all-time technology flop by InfoWorld. Wow. (Trivia question: What was number one? If you guessed "security," you'd be correct.)

Microsoft Windows 7

Windows 7 is the successor to Windows Vista and was made available to the general public on October 22, 2009. It was ready to move on from the epic failure that was Vista, and Microsoft finally got it right with the release of Windows XP. Windows 7 is more "XP-like," emphasizing performance improvements and eliminating the compatibility issues that plagued Microsoft Vista. We have been running the various versions of Windows 7 since it was first released as a beta and absolutely love it—as do many of our clients.

Windows 7 is available in six editions, but only a few of those are worth mentioning to the solo and small firm market:

Starter Edition—primarily for small notebooks, such as a netbook. The Starter Edition is 32-bit only, supports only a single processor, and does not support multiple monitors, such as dual displays. This edition was not designed for business use.

Home Premium Edition—comes bundled with Internet Explorer 9, allows for a connection to a home network, and is for home use only. The upgrade (from a previous operating system) retail cost for this edition is $149.99 per license, and the full retail cost for this edition is $199.99 per license.

Professional Edition—includes all the features of the Home Premium Edition, plus allows connection to a company network, such as a domain, and includes a backup-and-restore utility to protect your system. The upgrade retail cost for this edition is $199.99 per license, and the full retail cost for this edition is $299.99 per license.

Ultimate Edition—includes all the features of the Professional Edition, plus BitLocker encryption to help secure your data. The upgrade retail cost for this edition is $219.99 per license, and the full retail cost for this edition is $319.99 per license.

All of these editions are available for purchase and download from Microsoft's website, and for an additional $14.95, you can elect to have a physical disk shipped to you as a backup.

For your business, you will need to purchase either the Professional or Ultimate Edition to install on your computer systems. Obviously, upgrading is less expensive than purchasing a full license. If you have computer systems running Windows 2000, or even Windows XP, now is the time to upgrade.

Users may also upgrade their computer systems to Windows 7 from both Windows XP and Windows Vista. However, for users upgrading from Windows XP, you must be careful when performing an upgrade. This upgrade path actually performs a "clean" installation, and the user must back up all programs and data because the upgrade will not retain any of the information. **There isn't a prompt during the upgrade process to notify users to back up their data**, so this step must be performed before beginning the upgrade process. In other words, there is no direct upgrade path from XP to Windows 7. It is probably best to do a clean install anyway to clean up any past "sins" and remove any leftover files from applications that didn't completely uninstall in the past. You can get some advice about your hardware and software compatibility by running the free Windows Upgrade Advisor (**www.microsoft.com/downloads/ details.aspx?FamilyID=1B544E90-7659-4BD9-9E51-2497C146AF15& displaylang=en**). This utility will tell you if your hardware is compatible and what software may need to be upgraded.

If you are upgrading from Windows Vista, most of you will not have to worry about the process deleting all of your information. As was the case when upgrading from Windows XP to Windows Vista, you need only perform a clean install if you are going to a version that is lower on the food chain (e.g., Windows Vista Ultimate to Windows 7 Home Edition).

Regardless of the upgrade path you take, we always strongly recommend that you back up your system and data before upgrading.

The only other installation scenario with a clean installation is an upgrade from a 32-bit version to a 64-bit version operating system, regardless of the edition. Microsoft released the first Service Pack for this operating system (SP1) to the public in February of 2011, and at the time of its release, it was not a mandatory update. This Service Pack addressed a number of security issues and fixed a few bugs related to HDMI audio and the printing of XPS documents.

Please note that Windows 7 can no longer be purchased online at the Microsoft Store, but it is still available when configuring a new system from Dell and other third-party retailers, both online and in brick-and-mortar locations.

Microsoft Windows 8

Windows 8 is the latest version of the Microsoft Windows operating system and is the successor to Windows 7. It was released to manufacturing in mid-2012 and became available to consumers in early fall of 2012.

The Windows 8 user interface is built based on the Metro design language, featuring a new start screen, Internet Explorer 10, support for USB 3.0, and a new Windows Defender. Windows 8 has also added support for UEFI SecureBoot, which is a feature used to prevent unauthorized firmware, operating systems, or drivers from running at boot time.

There has been much controversy over the new Metro look, replacing the all-too-familiar Windows Start button. The Metro UI environment is tile-based, similar to the Start screen seen on the Windows Phone operating system. The Start button has been removed from the taskbar, which will cause many die-hard Windows users a lot of heartburn.

Windows 8 is available in four editions, three of which are focused on business-grade computers: Windows 8, Windows 8 Pro, and Windows 8 Enterprise. The Windows RT edition is built to run solely on tablet hardware.

Windows 8 has been available for about a year now, and it appears very likely that it is headed toward a fate similar to Windows Vista. The adoption of this operating system by businesses has been very slow, and even that may be a generous description. We have no plans to upgrade our systems to Windows 8, and we will continue to purchase new computers for our clients with Windows 7 preinstalled. The exception is for a touch device. The tile interface is really made for touch and is similar to the iPad. Several of our colleagues have rolled out Windows 8, but only on touch tablets. It is not very practical to be reaching across your desk to touch your monitor.

Mac OS X Version 10.5 (Leopard) Operating System

Mac OS X version 10.5 was released on October 26, 2007, and has since become a staple of the Apple movement to gain a greater market share of personal and business computers. The Mac OS X version 10.5 OS, commonly referred to as Leopard, includes a number of new features intended to make the operating system more stable and reliable than Apple's previous operating systems. Leopard supports both PowerPC and Intel x86-based Macintosh computers and is the last Mac OS to support the PowerPC. The Leopard operating system includes more than 300 changes and enhancements, including a revised desktop; an updated Finder; Time Machine, Spaces, Boot Camp preinstalled; and full support for 64-bit applications.

Mac OS X Version 10.6 (Snow Leopard) Operating System

Mac OS X version 10.6 is the successor to Leopard and was released to the public on August 28, 2009. This version, nicknamed Snow Leopard, contains many new features and performance improvements that have allowed this operating system to be a major player in the business market.

Until now, if you wanted to integrate your Mac computer with your company's Microsoft Exchange e-mail environment, you had to purchase Microsoft Office for Macs or configure your mailbox to use the POP3 or IMAP protocols. Mac users no longer have to do this. Snow Leopard includes out-of-the-box support for connecting to a Microsoft Exchange Server 2010 through the Mail, iCal, and address book programs. This allows users to access their mailbox, shared calendar, public folders, and contacts just as they would if they were using Microsoft Outlook. Some of the other features and enhancements include support for more 64-bit applications, a refined user interface, more efficient performance through better utilization of multiple processor cores, QuickTime X, and an installation footprint about 7GB smaller than Leopard's. This operating system also dropped support for the AppleTalk protocol, which most IT administrators believed should have occurred much sooner.

Current Mac users of the Leopard operating system can upgrade to Snow Leopard for $29 per license. For everyone else looking to upgrade to the latest version of Mac OS X, a Mac Box Set license costs $169 and also includes licenses for iLife '09 and iWork '09. Both the upgrade and full licenses for the Mac OS X version 10.6 operating system can be purchased online from the Apple Store.

Mac OS X Version 10.7 (Lion) Operating System

Mac OS X version 10.7 is the latest operating system from Apple and was released to the public on July 20, 2011. This release was Apple's eighth major release of Mac OS X. This version, nicknamed Lion, contains many new and changed features, such as FaceTime, AirDrop, Mac App Store, Auto Save, and Versions. As we expected, iCloud support for Mac OS X Lion is here and is included in a recent software update, v. 10.7.2.

From a security standpoint, Mac users should upgrade to Lion as soon as possible. Some of the enhanced security features include application sand-boxing that restricts the way applications can interact with other parts of the operating system and full disk encryption. Apple also increased the security of the operating system through "addition by subtraction." It no longer preinstalls Adobe Flash Player and the Java Runtime Environment on newly purchased systems.

Mac users looking to upgrade can purchase the Lion operating system from the Mac App Store for $29.99. Apple originally didn't plan to distribute physical media for this operating system, offering the product as an exclusive download from the Mac App Store, but its stance has since softened. Since August 2011, Apple has provided in-store downloads to consumers who don't have broadband Internet access and now sells OS X Lion USB Thumb Drives online from the Apple Store for $69.

Unfortunately, when OS X Lion was first released, a significant security flaw relating to passwords was discovered. Apple had changed the way it stores password hashes. This change allowed unauthorized users access to view the password hashes and crack them with ease. Apple addressed this huge security issue in a recent software update, v. 10.7.2.

Mac OS X Version 10.8 (Mountain Lion) Operating System

Released to the public on July 25, 2012, Mac OS X 10.8 is the ninth major release of Apple's OS X operating system. Many of the features included in this version of the operating system were migrated from Apple's iOS software, including Notes, Reminders, and Messages. This version also includes the latest version of the Safari web browser, Safari 6.

Some of the additional features in Mountain Lion include the Game Center, Notification Center, AirPlay Mirroring, Dictation, and full Facebook and Twitter integration within the operating system.

The general reception of Apple's latest operating system has been positive, and it's well worth the cost of only $19.99 for the upgrade. You can download the Mountain Lion upgrade from the Mac App Store on your Mac computer.

This operating system is installed in newly purchased Macs by default. If you're using a Mac that is running an older version of the Mac OS X operating system and your system meets the technical requirements to upgrade, we recommend that you do so for the added features and security improvements.

Mac OS X Version 10.9 (Mavericks) Operating System

Scheduled for release to the public in late 2013, Mavericks is slated to become the next big release of the Mac OS X software. While still in development, some of the touted new features include integration with iBooks, a new Maps application (Google Maps competitor), reworked Calendar application, updated version of Safari, the introduction of an iCloud Keychain, improved notifications, Finder Tabs, and improved battery and performance-boosting technologies.

The cost to upgrade has not yet been released, but we wouldn't be surprised if it's in line with the upgrade costs of previous editions—which makes it relatively cheap.

CHAPTER THREE

Monitors

NOW THAT YOU HAVE your brand new computer or shiny new laptop, you are ready for the task of picking out that brand new monitor—and you can have all the real estate your heart desires these days. The era of 14-inch monitors is long gone. You might even be able to reclaim some territory on your desk—and actually see some wood for a change—even if you choose to have two or three monitors. We have standardized on two monitors for clients and ourselves, although John has recently started asking for a third!

Choosing a monitor can be an overwhelming task with all the options and bells and whistles to choose from. If you don't know what you're looking for, you can be inundated with all of the technical jargon that advertisers use to get you to purchase their monitors.

Previously, we had separate sections for all the different types of monitors, but with this edition, we've grouped them all into one—because there really is only one type of monitor you should be looking for. We will walk you through the process and explain how to weed through all of the technical jargon, providing you with a solid recommendation for purchasing a monitor.

First and foremost, the days of CRT monitors are over. Charities won't even take these monitors as donations anymore, so they can only be recycled at this point. The flat panel monitor has taken over.

Flat-panel, wide-screen monitors have a flat viewing surface that provides a better viewing angle than CRT monitors used to. They are also less bulky, taking up only a fraction of the desktop space and weighing next to nothing when compared to the weight of the ancient CRT dinosaurs. Flat-panel monitors have come down significantly in price over the past few years and are very affordable.

Flat-panel monitors, like computers, come in all different sizes, resolutions, and performance. The flat-panel monitor that we recommend is the Dell P2214H 22-inch wide-screen (16:9) LED monitor. This monitor offers an optimal resolution of 1920 × 1080 at 60 Hz, which will provide you so much desktop real estate that you won't know what to do with it all. The higher resolution will enable you to view documents, images, and videos with stunning detail, vivid colors, and seamless motion. The display can be rotated and viewed horizontally or vertically, depending on your preference.

This monitor accepts video graphics array (VGA) and digital visual interface (DVI) inputs. It also includes four built-in USB 2.0 ports (three downstream ports, one upstream port) for connecting your peripheral devices, and it only weighs about 7 pounds. If needed, this device can be mounted on a wall using a standard VESA wall mount. The Dell P2214H 22-inch wide-screen monitor can be purchased online from Dell's website for $229 and comes with a standard three-year hardware warranty.

If you need a larger viewing area, you may want to consider using dual wide-screen monitors. Of course, your computer must have dual-monitor support, which most of the newer computers have by default. Usually, you will find that purchasing dual monitors, or in some cases three monitors, will be cheaper than purchasing a single large one. And anecdotally, we have found that folks who move to dual monitors never want to go back. Certainly, none of the authors would accept anything less than dual monitors—and we are all beginning to covet a third, although we would really need bigger desks, if not a special built-in shelf.

CHAPTER FOUR

Computer Peripherals

IF YOU THOUGHT PURCHASING the right computer and monitor was tough, wait until you realize how many options there are when it comes to selecting computer peripherals. Having the right computer peripherals can make your computing experience faster, more comfortable, and a better overall experience. Wireless devices have brought peripherals into a new dimension, getting rid of that Gordian knot mess of wires that we all used to struggle to untangle. Below, we provide recommendations for mice, keyboards, wireless desktops, external storage devices, and speakers. As always, bear in mind that there is a universe of choices. These are our top picks.

Mouse

The optical mouse has condemned the classic "rollerball" mouse to extinction. Many users can remember the days when if your mouse acted up, you would simply need to clean the dirt and lint off the wheels. Optical technology allows you to navigate with better speed, precision, and reliability. An optical mouse uses light-emitting diode (LED) technology that bounces light off of a surface onto a sensor. It is important to note that the surface needs some texture to work properly. It won't work on glass, for instance, so you still may need to carry a mouse pad with you in the event you're caught working on an unusable surface. In a hotel, there's usually a magazine in your room that will suffice. The sensor inside the mouse analyzes the patterns in the images and compares them with previous captured images to determine how far the mouse has moved and relays the coordinates to the computer. Who knew this technology existed with a simple computer mouse? It is really quite a scientific marvel. An optical mouse contains no moving parts and therefore does not require the maintenance and cleaning that the legacy rollerball mouse did.

Our recommendation for a simple yet reliable optical mouse is the Microsoft Comfort Mouse 3000. This optical mouse provides advanced performance, ergonomic design, and three customizable buttons. As an example, one button can be programmed for "delete" and one can be defined as the "back" button for your browser. This mouse takes performance seriously, delivering extreme movement accuracy by taking measurements up to 8,000 times per second, supporting a maximum speed of 72 inches per second, and a maximum acceleration of up to 28 Gs. The Blue-Track technology that measures the movement of the mouse uses a large blue beam and a high image sensor to track movement and speed. Microsoft even advertises that you can use this mouse on your carpeted floor, the armrest of a lobby chair, or even your pant leg. Wow.

The mouse connects to the computer using USB and is compatible with both Windows and Mac computers. It's a wired device requiring no batteries for trouble-free performance and can be used comfortably in either hand. The Microsoft Comfort Mouse 3000 sells for $19.95 and can be purchased directly from Microsoft's website.

For portability, those users who travel with laptops and want a nifty little Bluetooth travel mouse may also want to consider the excellent Microsoft Bluetooth Notebook Mouse 5000. This mouse provides transceiver free convenience to your Bluetooth-enabled computer, using a high-definition laser to smoothly track the mouse movements. This notebook mouse also includes the standard back button and scroll wheel, in an ergonomic design that we've all become accustomed to. If you are concerned about the current battery life, the mouse includes an indicator light that will glow red when the batteries need to be replaced. The batteries should last three months or more before needing replacement. Of course, you do need to look at the light periodically so that you don't end up with a dead mouse and have to scramble for new batteries. This mouse is compatible with both Windows and Mac computers and can be purchased online from Microsoft's website for $49.95.

Keyboards

Finding the right keyboard for your computer can be a tedious task, as you sift through all of the different keyboards and features to find one that truly suits you—and there are a world of choices and personal preferences at all cost points. When selecting a keyboard, you will want to choose one that is ergonomically designed so that stress placed on your wrists is minimized. Second, you shouldn't have to give up comfort to gain enhanced features, such as the My Favorites buttons or buttons that will adjust the volume level of your speakers, including the Mute button. Also, you shouldn't have to break the bank to find a keyboard that will work for you.

The keyboard we recommend is the Natural Ergonomic Keyboard 4000 from Microsoft. This keyboard provides a great blend of ergonomic design with functionality. The reverse slope keyboard has a cushioned palm rest that allows you to rest your wrists and hands when typing and provides greater comfort, promoting a more natural hand, wrist, and forearm posture. The My Favorites keys are customizable to allow you to open your most frequently used software, pictures, videos, and music.

You can even browse the Internet with the push of a button. The Multimedia keys allow you to control your media player from your keyboard, along with the volume level of your speakers. The two buttons we use most on our keyboards are the Mute and Calculator buttons, which are a must-have for any keyboard selection.

This keyboard now includes an improved number pad, relocating the equal sign, parentheses, and Backspace keys just above the numbers. The keyboard connects to your computer through the USB interface and comes with software to help you customize your keyboard's features. It can be used with either a Windows or Mac computer. The Natural Ergonomic Keyboard 4000 from Microsoft can be purchased for around $35 from your local electronics retailer.

Wireless Keyboard Desktops

With the introduction of wireless technology, wireless keyboard desktops have become extremely popular—so popular that it's becoming harder and harder to find a USB keyboard and mouse anymore. A wireless keyboard desktop is a keyboard and mouse desktop combination that connects to your computer wirelessly using radio frequency (RF) technology. The keyboard and mouse are powered with standard or rechargeable batteries and transmit their signals to a desktop receiver that is connected to the computer. It requires very little setup to install, and it eliminates the need for cables, which have plagued computer users since the first PC came into existence.

Our recommendation when purchasing a wireless keyboard desktop is the Logitech Wireless Wave Combo MK550. This wireless keyboard desktop comes with a wave key design that provides superior comfort with full-size and full-travel keys designed for quiet operation. The slight constant curve of the keyboard features consistently sized keys, which lets you type with confidence and ease. The keyboard uses the standard QWERTY layout, so you don't have to relearn how to type, as you do with some of the other curved keyboards. The height of the keyboard is adjustable, with three options for leg height allowing you to choose the position that's most comfortable for you. The keyboard uses 128-bit AES encryption to secure data as it's transmitted from the keyboard to the receiver, and both the keyboard and mouse use the 2.4 GHz wireless spectrum to connect to the receiver. Logitech claims that the keyboard can operate up to three years before the batteries need to be replaced, and if true, the batteries should last the expected lifetime of the keyboard.

Logitech's wireless laser mouse M510 should operate for up to two years before the batteries will need to be replaced. The laser mouse uses a small infrared laser instead of an LED, which increases the resolution and sensitivity of the mouse. The Logitech Wireless Wave Combo comes packaged with batteries and includes a three-year limited hardware warranty. This wireless desktop system is compatible with Microsoft XP, Vista, and Windows 7. The Logitech Wireless Wave Combo MK550 can be purchased for around $79.99 from your local electronics retailer or online at **www.logitech.com**.

External Storage Devices

External storage devices are pieces of hardware that connect to your computer using USB, FireWire, eSATA, or some other type of interface and are used to store electronic data. These devices come in all sizes, shapes, colors, and volumes of storage space. They have all but replaced the CD-ROM, DVD, and backup tapes as the leading means to store electronic data because of their portability, low cost, and vast amount of storage space. Be sure to consider some type of secure authentication or encryption for external storage, especially if confidential client information is backed up or stored on these devices. Most products now come with some sort of built-in hardware or software encryption that can be enabled at no additional cost. **Just be sure to remember your passphrase, because if you forget it, there's no way to recover your data.**

External Hard Drives

External hard drives are great storage media to store videos, pictures, and music and to back up the data from your internal hard drive. These devices are very easy to install and use. Most external hard drives are plug and play, which means you simply have to plug them in to your computer to use them. External hard drives are not as fast as internal hard drives, but they are relatively inexpensive. For the volume of information they can store, they are a very good, inexpensive backup solution. Also, lawyers who are otherwise technically challenged seem to do well with this form of backup, which can really be reduced to the push-of-a-button or an automated method that so many lawyers seem to prefer—set it and forget it.

The Seagate Backup Plus Desktop Drive is the external hard drive that we recommend for all lawyers and users. The Backup Plus Desktop Drive comes with available capacities of 1, 2, 3, and 4TBs of storage space. These capacities allow you to select the amount of storage space that best meets your requirements and may provide enough storage capacity to contain backups from more than one computer system. The Backup Plus Desktop Drive comes with backup software to automatically back up your data to the device, and it is Windows 7 compatible. All of the models should provide enough storage space to easily back up all of the data required by most lawyers. If you're looking to back up multiple computers and/or a server, then you probably will need to purchase the larger-sized drives—and make sure that you purchase more than one. We recommend that if you're using this external hard drive to back up your company data and files, then you should rotate drives on a weekly basis—keeping one onsite and the other one offsite. This will allow your firm to be able to recover its information in the event of a disaster such as a fire in the office.

These devices connect to your computer through the USB 3.0 interface (backwards compatible with USB 2.0) and can be placed flat or on their side. The drive is whisper quiet and relatively small in size, so it can sit on your desk or on top of your computer without taking away valuable space. Compatible with both Windows and Mac computers, the drive includes an NTFS driver for Mac that will allow interoperability between systems without the need to reformat the drive. The Backup Plus Desktop Drive can be purchased online at **www.seagate.com** for between $99 and $179, depending on the storage capacity, and it comes with a two-year standard warranty.

Flash Drives

USB flash drives (thumb drives) are small, portable storage devices that use flash memory to store electronic data. Currently, they are offered with storage volume sizes ranging from 4GB to 256GB. For the most part, USB flash drives with capacities of 2GB and smaller have been discontinued. USB flash drives offer many advantages over other portable storage devices, such as the floppy disk, CD-ROM, and DVD. In particular, they are smaller, more durable, faster, and can hold more data. Unfortunately, these devices can pose a great security risk for small businesses and law firms because their small size makes them absurdly easy to lose. This risk can be minimized, however, by purchasing the SanDisk Ultra USB flash drive.

This model is available with 8, 16, 32, or 64GB of storage space for your files and comes standard with AES hardware encryption to keep your data secure. Using the SanDisk SecureAccess software, a user can protect access to private files with password protection and encryption. The data is protected using 128-bit AES encryption. The software will create a file vault (protected folder) on the USB drive, creating a secure storage location for the user to place and keep all sensitive and confidential data. This flash drive is also fast, featuring read speeds up to 15MB/s and write speeds up to 10MB/s for the first 20MB of data transfer.

The SanDisk SecureAccess software is compatible with the Windows 7 and Mac OS X v.10.5+ operating systems and also gives users up to 2GB of secure cloud storage offered by YuuWaa. Just a side note regarding cloud storage—lawyers should take the decision to store their clients' data in the cloud very seriously and shouldn't make this decision in haste. Consulting your local or state bar association for recommendations and ethics opinions would be wise.

The SanDisk Ultra USB flash drives can be purchased online at **www.sandisk.com** for between $9 and $49, depending on the storage capacity, and all come with a five-year limited warranty.

For those users who require top-of-the-line security, look no further than the 4GB Personal S250 Secure Drive from IronKey, which also comes in 4, 8, 16, and 32GB versions. The D250 model does come in a 64GB version, but we prefer the more robust S250 model. A comparison of the two models is provided in Figure 4.1, from IronKey's website:

IRONKEY S250 VERSUS D250 HARDWARE COMPARISON

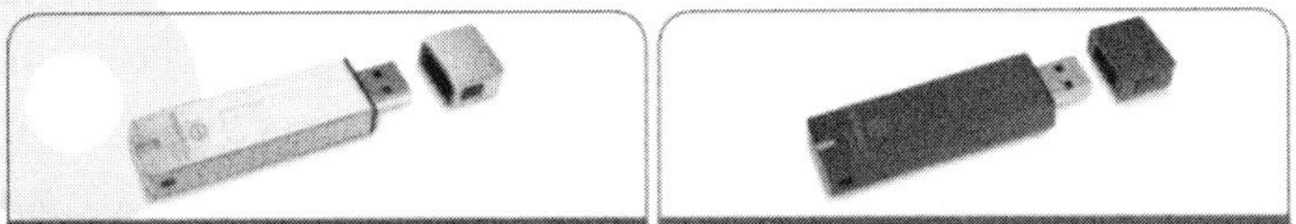

FEATURES	S250	D250
Capacity	2GB, 4GB, 8GB, 16GB, 32GB	2GB, 4GB, 8GB, 16GB, 32GB, 64GB
Speed	Up to 31MB/s read Up to 24MB/s write	Up to 29MB/s read Up to 13MB/s write
Dimensions	75mm X 19mm X 9mm	75mm X 19mm X 9mm
Weight	0.9 oz (25 grams)	.9 oz (25 grams)
Waterproof	MIL-STD-810F	MIL-STD-810F
Operating Temperature	0°C, +70°C	0°C, +70°C
Storage Temperature	-40°C, +85° C	-40°C, +85°C
Durability	Ruggedized	Ruggedized
Operating System Encryption Compatibility	Windows 7 Windows Vista Windows XP SP2+ Macintosh OS X 10.5+ Linux 2.6+	Windows 7 Windows Vista Windows XP SP2+ Macintosh OS X 10.5+ Linux 2.6+
Hardware Encryption	Data: AES Cipher-Block Chaining mode Encryption Keys: 256-bit Hardware DRNG PKI: 2048-bit RSA Hashing: 256-bit SHA FIPS Validations: 140-2 Level 3	Data: AES Cipher-Block Chaining mode Encryption Keys: 256-bit Hardware DRNG PKI: 2048-bit RSA Hashing: 256-bit SHA FIPS Validations: 140-2 Level 3
Hardware Interface	USB 2.0 high speed Section 508 Compliant	USB 2.0 high speed Section 508 Compliant

Figure 4.1 IronKey Secure Drive Comparison

As outlined in Figure 4.1, the main difference between the two models is the speed with which data can be read or written to and from the device.

This USB device is designed for the needs of sensitive military, government, and enterprise networks and includes AES hardware encryption that has been validated to meet government Federal Information Processing Standard (FIPS) requirements, specifically FIPS 140-2 Level 3. The security features require no software or drivers to enforce, with all the security being handled by the device hardware, and the features are always on. The device requires that a user authenticate with a password before encryption keys are enabled and data can be accessed. This device is even waterproof! As they tend to be inadvertently placed in washing machines while in the pocket of your pants, this is an excellent feature, though we've not yet put it to the test.

This device has a self-destruct mechanism (think *Mission: Impossible*) that will wipe (i.e., remove) the data contents if a user or thief tries to break into the IronKey and enters 10 incorrect passwords. The Password Manager and Password Generator applications are also included. The Password Generator application will generate very secure passwords of whatever length you desire. The Password Manager securely stores your passwords on the IronKey along with the associated web address. Merely insert your IronKey device in your computer and go to a website that requires a user ID and password. The IronKey will prompt you to save the credentials if it is the first time the IronKey has "seen" the website. If the logon credentials are already stored on the IronKey, a dialog box will be presented to confirm that the ID and password should be retrieved from the secure Password Manager application. Make sure you back up your password "vault" to the IronKey website in case your IronKey is lost or damaged. The password information is backed up to IronKey in a secure encrypted fashion. If you ever lose your IronKey device, just retrieve your password information from the IronKey website. The device even comes preloaded with a portable version of Firefox, which, when launched and used with the provided Secure Sessions Service, encrypts and keeps all of your Internet traffic private and secure. The IronKey Personal S250 Secure Drive can be purchased online from IronKey's website (**www.ironkey.com**) for from $109 to $599, depending on the storage capacity.

Speakers and Headphones

Lawyers (and their staff) often tell us that the most important peripheral device they need for their computer is a pair of speakers. They like to be able to listen to music while they work and are adamant about fidelity. Without breaking the bank, reasonable-quality desktop speakers can be purchased to provide the user with a clear, true sound. Logitech, a leading provider of speaker systems for computers, makes the LS21 speakers. They offer 2.1 stereo sound with a subwoofer, providing enhanced bass, and the speakers come in a slim, stylish profile. These speakers offer quality audio at a reasonable price. The speakers have a stereo headphone jack, an auxiliary input where you can connect your iPod or MP3 player, and integrated controls located on a wired remote. They even include a cable-management system to help reduce the clutter of wires. The Logitech LS21 speakers can be purchased online for around $30 from **www.logitech.com**.

If you purchase one of the recommended Dell flat-panel monitors, consider adding a sound bar. The sound bar clips onto the bottom edge of the Dell flat panel and gets its power from the monitor itself. It provides a clean installation and doesn't take up any additional desk space. The model of the sound bar will vary depending on the Dell monitor that you wish to attach the speakers to, so be sure to check out Dell's website to ensure that you select the appropriate model.

Be careful of speaker "wars" in the office as people battle for the loudest music. Consider headphones to provide a quieter office environment.

If you use a laptop, desktop computer system, or a smartphone that supports Bluetooth and wish to keep your music to yourself, a number of wireless headphone options are available. Jabra makes the BT8030 Bluetooth Stereo Headphones, a lightweight headset featuring a built-in microphone with echo cancellation for crystal-clear audio and voice reception. The device includes a rechargeable battery that lasts up to 8 hours on a single charge, provides up to 240 hours of standby time, and weighs only 10 ounces. This device only takes 3 hours to fully charge. The wireless device supports Bluetooth 2.0, including Hands Free Profile (HFP), Headset Profile (HSP), Advanced Audio Distribution Profile (A2DP), and Audio/Video Remote Control Profile (AVRCP). This headset can be purchased online or from your local electronics retailer starting at just $99.

CHAPTER FIVE

Printers

EVEN IN THE ERA of the "paperless" office, most law firms still print a lot of documents on a daily basis, probably more than any other type of business. To say that the practice of law tends to be less than green is a massive understatement—at least most firms have implemented a recycling program. Nonetheless, it is certainly critical to have a good, reliable printer to ensure that your firm is printing quality documents in the shortest amount of time. Below, we discuss and recommend printers for stand-alone systems, network systems, and multifunctional printers/copiers.

Stand-Alone Printers

The most basic type of printer is the stand-alone printer. This type of printer connects directly to a computer and is not placed on the network. It only has to be capable of handling a single user's print jobs. Even in environments where networked printers are used and recommended, there can be valid reasons to have stand-alone printers—perhaps so the bookkeeper can keep financial records from inadvertently being picked up by someone else. Senior partners may feel their information is so confidential that they want a printer in their office (though their staff often mutters that they are just too lazy to walk down the hall). Many makes and models of stand-alone printers are available to choose from, and each has different performance specifications, features, and available fonts.

The questions about whether to use an ink-jet printer are gradually declining. We highly recommend going with a laser printer. Ink-jet printers typically result in a higher cost of ownership over the long haul, with ink cartridges printing at a higher cost per page than the average laser printer. There are even studies that show a cost of $3,000–$5,000 per gallon for name-brand ink cartridges. Human blood is cheaper. Laser is better quality and more economical—case closed.

A stand-alone printer can be shared through enabling File and Print Sharing on your local computer, but we strongly counsel against this practice. It creates a host of security vulnerabilities that could compromise not only your system, but your entire network, and it causes a lot of management and configuration headaches for the IT administrator.

When discussing printers with our clients, we are frequently asked, "Should I purchase a color or a black-and-white laser printer?" You will pay a premium for a color laser printer, and in most instances it is not worth the cost when purchasing a stand-alone printer. It is usually more cost-effective to purchase a color laser printer to be placed on the local computer network and shared so that more than one user can print to it.

The Hewlett Packard (HP) LaserJet Pro P1606dn printer is the perfect solution for the stand-alone or network (up to five users) printer. The printer has a built-in Ethernet connection for network connectivity and prints in duplex (two-sided) mode by default. This printer prints as many as 26 pages per minute, comes standard with a paper input capacity of 250 sheets, and has a recommended monthly volume of up to 2,000 pages but can support a monthly duty cycle of up to 8,000 pages if needed. The printer has a first-page-out speed of 7 seconds and supports all the common page types, such as letter, legal, executive, and envelopes. This printer comes standard with 32MB of memory and connects to your computer using the USB interface. It should be noted that the printer doesn't come with a USB cable, which will have to be purchased separately. For mobile users, this printer is compatible with Apple's AirPrint service, which allows users to print to the device from their iPad, iPhone, or iPod touch.

This black-and-white printer was designed for quick business printing and offers a cost-effective solution to personal printing. The printer is both Mac and Windows compatible, including Vista, Windows 7, and Windows 8. It also comes standard with a one-year limited warranty. The HP LaserJet Pro P1606dn printer can be purchased online for around $209.99 (before discounts) from **www.hp.com**. At the time of writing, this printer was discounted to a cost of $149.99 on HP's webstore.

If you're looking for tips on how to reduce the frequency with which you have to purchase replacement laser cartridges, there are a few things you can do. First, look into software that automatically removes wasted pages from printing jobs, especially common when printing out content from websites using your Internet browser. This printer comes with software called HP Smart Web Printing that you can install on your local computer, which reduces the wasted pages and space when printing from websites.

Another great tip is to change the print quality to "Draft" if the document is just going to be discarded shortly after printing and not something official that you're going to submit to court. This alone can save you lots of toner.

Networked Printers

Networked printers are used to provide a printing resource to multiple users. Networked printers are generally installed in a central location and then shared throughout the local network. The administration and security of these printers can be integrated into your network's security infrastructure, such as through Windows Active Directory for a Windows-based network, and networking a printer is much more secure than sharing it through the File and Print Sharing service. Installation in a central location simplifies the management, administration, and security of these devices. Network printers can be shared with the various computers and users that make up your network with very little overhead and effort. There are many types of networked printers, and depending on your need—low volume, high volume, color—your options will vary. A popular request from many law offices is to have multiple trays for the printer. The capability to have multiple paper types loaded is usually available in the mid-range to higher-end printer models.

Low-Volume Network Printers

Low-volume network printers are designed for workgroups of users having a small to moderate print volume, as high as 5,000 pages per month. These printers are moderately priced and are primarily used to segment printing within offices based on user group or physical location. Network printers have more robust hardware than stand-alone printers to handle multiple jobs from different users at the same time.

The HP LaserJet Pro 400 Printer M401dw black-and-white network-based laser printer is great for a small law firm because it provides users with a highly reliable, cost-effective printer that is capable of handling the expected volume produced by an average small firm. The HP LaserJet Pro 400 Printer M401dw prints as many as 35 pages per minute and has a monthly recommended print volume of up to 3,000 pages. It comes standard with an input capacity of 300 sheets and 256MB of memory, and it handles all sizes of paper. This printer has a first-page-out speed of 8 seconds.

As an added feature, the printer allows for automatic duplexing for printing double-sided documents. The printer has an embedded gigabit Ethernet network adapter to attach the printer to your local network and a built-in Wi-Fi 802.11 b/g/n adapter for wireless connectivity. This printer also supports Apple's AirPrint service, allowing users to print directly from their iPad, iPhone, or iPod Touch device. For additional security, this printer can prevent unauthorized access with management features including 802.1x authentication and password protection. Unlike some of the other HP printers, this model does come with a USB cable.

The memory of this printer can be upgraded if desired, and the printer's drivers are compatible with both Mac- and Windows-based systems, including Vista and Windows 7. There are even drivers for Windows 8 and Windows 8.1 available for download. The printer comes with a standard one-year warranty and includes a CD-ROM with the drivers and software necessary to configure the device. The HP LaserJet Pro 400 Printer M401dw black-and-white laser printer can be purchased online for around $450 (before any discounts) from **www.hp.com**. At the time of writing, this printer was discounted to a cost of $379.99 on HP's webstore.

High-Volume Network Printers

High-volume network printers are designed for businesses that need the capacity to print a large volume of pages on a monthly basis and are usually considered when your firm needs a printer that can produce more than 5,000 pages per month. These devices contain hardware that can handle the volume load and are built to be constantly printing.

The HP LaserJet Enterprise M4555f Multifunction Printer is ideal for firms that print large volumes of documents on a monthly basis. This printer has a recommended monthly printing volume of 5,000 to 20,000 pages and prints up to 55 pages per minute. The printer comes with a standard input capacity of 1,150 sheets, three paper trays, 1280MB of memory, and an embedded gigabit Ethernet network adapter to attach the printer to your local network. This printer handles all sizes of paper and can easily be upgraded with additional paper trays or envelope feeders for a maximum capacity of 2,100 sheets. The network connectivity can be upgraded to support wireless networks, a must-have option for those firms that use a wireless infrastructure for their local network. It should be noted that the printer doesn't come with a USB or network cable, which will have to be purchased separately if you want to connect the printer directly to a computer.

For future compatibility, this printer is IPv6-ready. For added security, this printer supports network authentication (LDAP, SMTP) that lets administrators control device access and secure print jobs through user authentication.

The printer comes with a one-year, next-business-day onsite warranty. It is compatible with both Mac- and Windows-based networks, including Windows 8. A CD-ROM that contains both printer driver files and software necessary to manage and configure the device is included. The HP LaserJet Enterprise M4555f Multifunction Printer can be purchased online for around $3,499.99 from **www.hp.com**, and it comes with a standard one-year warranty. At this cost, you may want to investigate using your digital copier as a printer, depending on your anticipated monthly print volume and cost per page.

Color Network Printers

Color network printers are essential for any law firm or small business that wants to print a significant volume of documents in color. If the color printer is networked, multiple users can have access to the shared resource, which is far more cost-effective than giving everyone a color printer. HP is still the leading manufacturer of color printers in terms of value, selection, overall reliability, and performance. Its color LaserJet printers are reasonably priced and produce high-quality color documents.

For a small business or law firm, the HP Color LaserJet CP4025dn printer is perfect for everyday color printing. This printer prints up to 35 pages per minute for both black and color, has a recommended monthly volume of 2,000 to 7,500 pages. Its first-page-out speed of less than 9.5 seconds means that the color print job starts almost as soon as it has been sent to the printer. The standard input capacity is 600 sheets, and the printer supports all sizes of paper and can be upgraded with an envelope feeder.

The printer comes standard with 512MB of memory and an embedded gigabit Ethernet network adapter that enables the printer to connect to your local network. If necessary, the memory can be upgraded to a maximum of 1GB. The printer's drivers support both Mac- and Windows-based systems, including Vista and Windows 7, and the printer can be networked for easy accessibility. Windows 8 and Windows 8.1 drivers are also available for download from the HP website. The printer comes with a one-year onsite limited warranty.

The HP Color LaserJet CP4025dn printer can be purchased online for around $1,300 (before discounts) from **www.hp.com**. At the time of writing, this printer was discounted to a cost of $1,049.99 on HP's webstore. It should be noted that the printer doesn't come with a USB or network cable, which will have to be purchased separately. That shouldn't be a problem since you will most probably connect this printer to a network and not directly to a computer.

The largest operational cost for a color laser printer is the consumables. Color cartridges are not cheap, and color prints can be very expensive. One configuration point to make on all computers networked to your color printers: change the default color setting to black. This will save on the printing and subsequent waste of color cartridges for unnecessary color copies.

Digital copier manufacturers are beginning to take over the task of color printing. Investigate using a color copier for your color print needs versus a stand-alone color printer, or if you have a large-scale color print job, you may want to consider the costs of outsourcing the project to your local copier store. You might be surprised at the amount of money you could save.

Typically, lawyers lease their copiers. As you work with your copier lessor, who normally provides your supplies, make sure you negotiate a low cost per color copy and only pay for the number of pages that you print. Don't pay for the consumables (e.g., toner cartridges) or maintenance, as these should be included as part of the per-page cost.

Multifunctional Printers/Copiers

Don't you wish there was a single device that you could install on your local network that could do everything your office needs—printing, faxing, scanning, and copying? Happily for lawyers, today such devices are becoming a standard fixture. Multifunctional printers (MFPs) offer the capability to print, scan, copy, and fax from the same device, combining the functions of multiple devices into just one and eliminating the need to purchase them separately. In the long run, purchasing or leasing an MFP can save you the time and money often expended to upgrade and service multiple devices.

MFPs are very expensive and are generally leased because of the high cost to purchase. When looking at whether to buy or lease MFPs, keep some functionality questions in mind:

- Do you want the ability to print in color and black-and-white?
- Do you need duplex printing?
- Do you want to scan documents to your hard drive, user box, or e-mail?
- Do you want incoming faxes to be sent to e-mail as an image file or just printed?
- Do you want to be able to link the use of the MFP to the firm's billing program?
- What printing capacity do you need?
- Do you need any finishing capabilities (e.g., stapling, folding, 3-hole punch, etc.)?
- Do you need to implement any security on the unit, and if so, what?

The answers to these questions will give your vendors enough detail to provide you with the MFP device that best meets the firm's needs. Your digital copier may already have some of these features installed but not configured. Check with your vendor to see what capabilities your current copier has. In our office, we have a Konica Minolta Bizhub C224e MFP device. It allows us to print both in color and in black-and-white at speeds up to 22 pages per minute; scan to hard drive, user box, e-mail, or FTP; and fax documents, although we do not use that feature. We are able to download our scanned documents from a built-in secure internal website as JPG, PDF, XPS, or TIFF files, as well as scan to an internal e-mail address—which we constantly use. This device has a 3,650 sheet max capacity with dual scanning speeds up to 160 pages per minute.

The Bizhub has advanced security features such as job erase, hard drive sanitizing and lock, user authentication and account tracking, IP address filtering, and secure print and scan encryption. Plus, there are options for biometric and HID proximity card authentication, should we ever need these advanced security features. Needless to say, the Bizhub provides us with a secure MFP option. We are huge fans—as this is our second edition of one of these devices.

CHAPTER SIX

Scanners

ALMOST AS COMMON AS printers, scanners have become a necessary piece of equipment in most offices, as more paper documents are being scanned and stored electronically. The drive to a paperless office is still very much under way. The setup and operation of scanners has become simple to the point where even the most novice computer user can do it. Many of the tasks that once had to be performed manually are now automated, and in most cases the hookup entails connecting a single wire. Not often do we have to insert a CD to install software anymore, now that preloaded drivers are prevalent. Network scanners, however, are a little more complex to set up and configuring them may require the assistance of the IT staff.

Most desktop scanners communicate with the computer via the USB or FireWire interface and come with a variety of software to assist in the scanning and file-conversion process. Some models come standard with optical character recognition (OCR) software that will read the scanned image and produce a document that is editable and searchable. Fujitsu, a manufacturer of home- and business-grade scanners that have been constantly rated the best models for businesses. In the following sections, we make recommendations for both low-volume and high-volume scanners from Fujitsu.

Some law firms may already have scanning capability in their digital copier. As we previously stated, check with your vendor to see if scanning with your copier is a more cost-effective solution than purchasing a stand-alone unit.

Low-Volume Scanner

The Fujitsu ScanSnap S1500 scanner, our recommendation since the inception of this book, has finally been discontinued by Fujitsu and replaced with the iX500 Desktop Scanner, which is what we now recommend.

The Fujitsu ScanSnap iX500 Desktop Scanner is a great value for a solid automatic document feeder (ADF) scanner. This desktop scanner scans up to 25 color pages per minute, has an ADF capacity of 50 sheets, and can handle both legal- and letter-sized paper. The scanner has a maximum scanning resolution of 600 × 600 dpi and connects to the computer via the USB 3.0 interface, which is responsible for the increase in scanning speed. This scanner also comes with a built-in wireless adapter allowing you to scan directly to a computer or mobile device. This scanner is compatible with Microsoft Windows 7 and Windows 8 (32-bit and 64-bit) and Mac OSX v.10.6 or newer. This scanner comes with bundled software that includes Adobe Acrobat X Standard Edition, ScanSnap Organizer v5.0, ABBYY FineReader for ScanSnap 5.0, and CardMinder v5.0.

Adobe Acrobat X Standard software allows you to automatically convert scanned data into searchable PDF files. Some of the automatic features of this device include auto paper-size detection, auto de-skew, and auto blank-page removal. The auto blank-page removal eliminates the need to edit scanned documents because the scanner has the ability to recognize the deleted blank pages. The ABBYY FineReader software allows you to scan documents directly to applications such as Microsoft Word, Excel, and PowerPoint.

A new feature of this scanner is the ability to scan to the cloud. With the free ScanSnap Connect app, users can link their ScanSnap to their iPad, iPhone, or Android mobile device for viewing on the go. Users also have the ability to scan to Evernote, Google Docs, Salesforce, SugarSync, and Sharepoint. Again, as with all cloud services, please use caution and seek the advice of your IT staff when moving client data to the cloud to ensure that your documents are secure.

The scanner comes with a standard one-year limited warranty that can be upgraded to the Advanced Exchange Service program. The Fujitsu ScanSnap iX500 Desktop Scanner can be purchased online from Fujitsu's website (**www.fujitsu.com**) for $495 and comes with a one-year limited warranty. The inclusion of Acrobat Standard makes this a very worthwhile purchase.

High-Volume Scanner

The Fujitsu fi-5530C2 is perfect for legal professionals who need a high-speed scanner on a modest budget and are serious about scanning documents. The built-in automatic document feeder (ADF) holds 100 pages and scans up to 50 pages per minute (100 images) in 200 dpi black-and-white mode. Everything needed for creating a paperless office is included free with the fi-5530C2, including Adobe Acrobat X Standard Edition, ScandAll Pro, and Kofax VRS Professional. The scanner comes standard with 64MB of memory.

Using the Fujitsu fi-5530C2 scanner, you can convert any document to Adobe PDF using the Adobe Acrobat Standard software that is included with the scanner. The scanner can handle a vigorous duty cycle of up to 4,000 documents per day and can handle documents ranging in size from a business card to a legal document. The Ultra SCSI and USB 2.0 interface allows for simplified connectivity to your computer. The scanner is compatible with Microsoft Windows 7 systems. This scanner is not compatible with Macs. The Fujitsu fi-5530C2 scanner can be purchased online from Fujitsu's website (**www.fujitsu.com**) for around $2,500 and comes with a three-month onsite limited warranty.

This is a lot of money for a solo or small firm operation, especially to spend on a scanner. We're sure that your digital copier could provide a less expensive solution for your scanning needs, especially if you have a newer unit that will provide a convenient ability to scan to e-mail—which none of these ScanSnap devices do. Consider that before you make a purchasing decision and you might be able to save yourself a lot of money.

CHAPTER SEVEN

Servers

ONE OF THE BIGGEST, most important, and most expensive decisions you will have to make regarding technology for your firm is which server to purchase. This is the mother ship of the network, so the purchase decision should be made very carefully. This is absolutely not the time to be penny wise and pound foolish. This is a business decision—make no mistake about that—and if made with great consideration and thought, it will allow your business to run efficiently and effectively from a technology perspective.

Like workstations and laptops, servers come in every make, model, and flavor. Unlike workstations, however, servers can be very expensive and can consume a large chunk of your technology budget rather quickly. Your firm will need to plan carefully when selecting a server—including discussing future needs and goals—so that the desirable hardware and software components can be identified. Plan carefully, because you don't want to have to buy a new server every other year. Generally, the average life span of a server is four to five years—so start planning (and budgeting) well in advance!

Solo—File and Printer Sharing

The most simple and basic reason for getting a server is for file and printer sharing. By centralizing the storage of electronic files and the administration and installation of printers, you will save time, money, and headaches when it comes to maintaining and managing your network. There are servers designed specifically for the purpose of sharing files, documents, and printers. These servers come with the most basic hardware and software and are relatively inexpensive when compared to the mid-range to higher-end servers.

The Dell PowerEdge T320 server was designed for the small business to provide the most basic file- and printer-sharing capabilities. A listing of the server's hardware and software components, along with some technical specifications, is provided below.

File and Printer Sharing Server

Hardware Component	Recommendation
Chassis:	Tower
Operating System:	Microsoft Small Business Server 2011, Standard Edition, with 5 CALs
Processors:	Intel Xeon E5-2440, 2.40 GHz, 15MB Cache
Memory:	16GB RDIMM, 1333 MT/s, Low Volt, Dual Rank
Primary Controller Card:	PERC H310 Integrated RAID Controller
Hard Drive Configuration:	RAID-5
Hard Drives:	Three 600GB 15K RMP SAS Hard Drives
Network Adapter:	Onboard Dual Gigabit Network Adapters
Warranty:	3-Year ProSupport 4HR 7x24 Onsite
Other:	DVD+/-RW Drive

This Dell PowerEdge T320 was customized through Dell's website (**www.dell.com**) and contains an Intel Xeon 2.40 GHz processor with 16GB of RAM. This server comes with the Microsoft Small Business Server 2011 Standard Edition operating system with five Client Access Licenses (CALs). CALs are needed for each device or user that accesses the server.

The three SAS (serial-attached SCSI) 600GB hard drives are configured in a RAID-5 (redundant array of independent disks) hard drive configuration for increased performance and fault tolerance. In a RAID-5 hard drive configuration, if one of the hard drives were to fail, the server would continue to operate until the failed hard drive could be replaced. In most other hard drive configurations, if a server's hard drive were to fail, the server would be inoperable until the disk was repaired or replaced. The RAID-5 configuration offers both fault tolerance with the parity hard drive and better performance than most other RAID or mirrored disk configurations. RAID-5 hard drive configurations are strongly recommended for all law firm servers.

In total, there is about 1.2TB of hard drive space available for the storage of electronic data, programs, and other applications. You used to be able to save a little bit of money by reducing the number of hard drives purchased and setting up a RAID-1 hard drive configuration, but since hard drives have come so far down in price, we no longer recommend this as an option.

The onboard dual gigabit network adapters will allow clients to connect to the server at gigabit speeds, assuming the rest of your network components are gigabit as well.

One of the most important features to consider when purchasing a server is the warranty. In most cases, you will not need both the hardware and software support. At a minimum, you must include a hardware warranty that will cover the hardware and labor cost to replace any of the components that fail during the server's life cycle. This Dell PowerEdge server comes with a three-year, four-hour/same-day onsite parts and labor warranty at an included cost of about $400 when bundled with the server hardware. Having a hardware warranty for your server is critical to protecting your equipment, data, and business. This is no time to be miserly. The included warranty covers seven days a week, 24 hours a day, with a four-hour onsite response time. This means a repair person will be at your site with replacement parts within four hours of the problem being diagnosed. This Dell PowerEdge T320 server was quoted on Dell's website for approximately $4,000 at the time of this writing.

Small Firm—File and Printer Sharing/Hosting Services
When purchasing a server for your network, you must decide what function the server will have in your day-to-day business operations. In addition to file and printer sharing, it's common for small firms to host their company's e-mail. Although you can also host a website, we recommend that you outsource that to a website hosting provider because of potential security, administration, and resource issues. The added hosting services (e-mail and/or web) will require a server with upgraded hardware to be able to provide the necessary resources for the services to operate reliably.

The Dell PowerEdge T620 was designed for small firms or businesses that are looking for a cost-effective solution to hosting their own e-mail or website. The server's hardware and software components, along with some technical specifications, are provided.

File and Printer Sharing/Hosting Services

Hardware Component	Recommendation
Chassis:	Tower
Operating System:	Microsoft Small Business Server 2011, Standard Edition With 5 CALs
Processors:	Dual Intel Xeon E5-2637 3.0 GHz, 5M Cache, 8.0GT/s QPI
Memory:	32GB RDIMM, 1333 MT/s, Low Volt, Quad Rank
Primary Controller Card:	PERC H710P Integrated RAID Controller
Hard Drive Configuration:	RAID-5
Hard Drives:	Three 3TB 7.2K RPM Near-Line SAS 6 Gbps 3.5-Inch Hard Drives
Network Adapter:	Broadcom 5720 Dual Port 1GB Network Interface Card
Warranty:	3-Year ProSupport 4HR 7x24 Onsite
Other:	Redundant Power Supply, DVD+/-RW Drive

The Dell PowerEdge T620 listed here was customized through Dell's website. It contains Dual Intel Xeon 3.0 GHz processors with 32GB of memory. The server specified above was customized in a tower chassis; however, the same model is available in a rack mount chassis at no additional cost. The rack mount chassis is for those firms and small businesses that maintain their servers and networking equipment in a rack. The processors will supply more than enough horsepower to configure the server as an e-mail or web server, and the 32GB of memory will allow these services to run smoothly and will prevent the server from lagging or becoming bogged down.

The server comes with Microsoft Small Business Server (SBS) 2011 Standard Edition preinstalled, which includes the Microsoft Exchange Server 2010 software for e-mail hosting and the Internet Information Server for website hosting. Five CALs are also included, but you may have to budget for more if more than five devices or users in your firm are accessing the server.

The three 3TB SAS hard drives are configured in a RAID-5 hard drive configuration and provide about 6TB of storage space for your firm's applications and data. Again, this PowerEdge server comes with the three-year ProSupport 4HR 7x24 onsite hardware warranty, which provides three years of four-hour, same-day parts and labor warranty. The Dell PowerEdge T620 server was quoted on Dell's website for approximately $7,450 at the time of this writing.

Don't forget to consider backup software and any additional applications (e.g., antivirus, antispyware, antispam, etc.) when configuring the server, because you might get a better discount from the vendor if they are bundled and purchased with the server hardware.

Small Firm—Database/Applications Server

Your firm's software requirements, current and future, will play a big role in determining what hardware and software components your server will need to contain to adequately support your firm in the coming years. So far, we have discussed the hardware and software specifications for a server used primarily for file and printer sharing and one capable of handling basic hosting services, such as e-mail and a website. When planning to use a server to host a database application, case management software, or e-discovery software, you must look at the minimum requirements for each piece of software and then go above and beyond the specifications that vendors provide. What vendors list should be regarded cautiously as a "bare minimum." To run well and reliably, the software almost always requires more horsepower.

The recommended Dell PowerEdge T620 server is capable of handling most database and software applications, as long as it's configured with advanced hardware to handle the powerful and robust database applications. The server's hardware and software components are provided below:

Database/Applications Server

Hardware Component	Recommendation
Chassis:	Tower
Operating System:	Microsoft Windows Server 2008 R2 SP1 Enterprise Edition With 10 CALs
Processors:	Dual Intel Xeon E5-2690 2.9 GHz, 20M Cache, 8.0GT/s QPI
Memory:	128GB RDIMM, 1333 MT/s, Low Volt, Quad Rank
Primary Controller Card:	PERC H710P Integrated RAID Controller
Hard Drive Configuration:	RAID-5
Hard Drives:	Three 3TB 7.2K RPM Near-Line SAS 6 Gbps 3.5-Inch Hard Drives
Network Adapter:	Broadcom 5720 Dual Port 1GB Network Interface Card
Warranty:	3-Year ProSupport 4HR 7x24 Onsite
Other:	Redundant Power Supply, DVD+/-RW Drive

The PowerEdge T620 server was customized through Dell's website and contains Dual Intel Xeon E5-2690 2.9 GHz processors and 128GB of memory. The processor is faster than the processor included with the server discussed in the previous section.

This server comes with the Windows Server 2008 R2 SP1 Enterprise Edition operating system with Hyper-V capability for virtualized environments. The Windows Server 2008 Enterprise Edition operating system does not come bundled with Microsoft Exchange Server or Microsoft SQL Server. However, Microsoft's SBS Premium does. So, if you want a single server to do "everything," such as file and print sharing, e-mail, and database hosting, SBS Premium may be a good alternative, but that's a lot of functionality to run on a single server and is not a recommended solution. For most databases, case management software, and e-discovery applications, vendors recommend a dedicated server running an Enterprise-grade operating system to take advantage of the increased support for memory capacity.

The three 3TB hard drives are configured in a RAID-5 hard disk configuration and provide about 6TB of storage space for applications and data. If more storage space is needed, this upgrade can be made when the server is configured to meet your needs, especially if you plan to use virtualization.

The redundant power supply allows the server to stay powered on in the event that one of the power supplies fails. The server comes with dual embedded Broadcom Ethernet adapters, providing connectivity for up to two networks. The PowerEdge server comes with a three-year ProSupport 4HR 7x24 onsite hardware warranty, which provides three years of a four-hour, same-day parts and labor warranty. The Dell PowerEdge T620 server was quoted on Dell's website for approximately $13,890 at the time of this writing.

Virtual Servers
The large push within the IT industry continues to be toward virtualization bundled with cloud services. Microsoft continues to sell more licenses for virtual machines than it does for physical hardware. This is one trend that isn't going to reverse.

Simply put, virtualization means that a single piece of hardware contains and hosts multiple server or desktop images, otherwise known as machines. Virtualization enables the consolidation of data and applications onto a single physical hardware server. The reduction in hardware saves energy, management, and administration effort and reduces overall hardware and software costs, along with rack space, especially if your firm needs multiple servers. Virtualization is used to separate hosting services and applications, creating independent machines, which allows for one virtual server to be down for maintenance without affecting the others. For example, if Windows updates were downloaded onto a virtual server hosting file and print sharing services, this virtual server could be rebooted and updates applied without having to bring down or affect the entire host system, keeping other virtual servers online and available to users. It also means that you can quickly "spool up" a virtual machine for testing without investing in additional hardware.

Previously, virtualization was implemented only by larger firms due to the costs, expertise, and the large budget required, and was not typically found in a small firm environment; however, this is no longer true. We are recommending that small firms consider virtualization technologies when making server hardware and software purchasing decisions, especially in scenarios where the client is hosting services such as e-mail internally.

Is server virtualization the best choice for your network environment? Probably, but you will need to answer a number of questions before making this determination.

First, what services and applications are running on your network? If your network is running Microsoft Exchange Server, SQL Server, and a case management application, most likely you will need multiple servers to host all of these services and software. Most case management applications now require a separate server to run on. By using virtualization, you can avoid purchase of another physical hardware server by installing the case management software on its own virtual server, as long as your virtual server meets, if not exceeds, the host specifications required by the vendor of the software.

When purchasing a host system (the server hosting the virtual servers), the most critical hardware options to consider are the amount of memory, number and type of processors, and amount of storage space. For each virtual server, 4GB or more of memory must be allocated for the virtual server to operate. A larger amount of memory will be needed if the virtual server is hosting a database or other memory-hungry service. This does not account for the amount of memory that the host system will require. For example, if you have a host server running three virtual servers, you will need a minimum of 16GB (better if you have 32GB) of memory installed in the host server to supply the host and all of the virtual servers with enough memory resources to operate. To accommodate the necessary hardware, the host system must be running the Windows Server 2008 Enterprise Edition.

When running virtual servers, you will need to ensure that the host system has enough processing capability to handle the processing load. At a minimum, you will want the system to contain Intel Xeon processors with a processing speed of 2.53 to 3.6 GHz. The optimum solution is to use Intel Xeon processors with the same speed range, and in virtualization solutions, you will need to have multiple processors with multiple cores. The Xeon processors included in the servers recommended previously were designed by Intel for virtualization solutions, providing increased virtualization security, reduced storage and network latencies, and acceleration of fundamental virtualization processes throughout the system. The multicore processors combine two or more cores onto a single integrated circuit, providing multiprocessing capabilities to the chip. Multiprocessing allows the execution of multiple concurrent software processes in a system, which is vital in a virtualization solution.

The amount of storage space required to run all of the virtual servers and the host system will vary from solution to solution. When determining the amount of storage space the systems will require, you need to consider the services and applications that will be hosted. For example, a virtual server hosting Microsoft Exchange Server will require enough disk space to account for the current size and future growth of the Exchange Database stores along with the program files and operating system. The amount of storage space allocated to each virtual server can be independently configured and modified at a later time if more space is needed. For ease of configuration and setup, bearing the cost of additional hard drive storage up front makes more sense than waiting to add more hard drives later on. Plus, it's always recommended that more than enough hard drive space is available to the host system and virtual servers, so problems with low disk space can be avoided. We have clients who have terabytes of disk space available just for their File and Printer Sharing virtual server. As an alternative to purchasing host-based storage, you may want to look into a Storage Area Network (SAN) device that would provide locally attached storage over a dedicated network, usually over Fibre or iSCSI.

Microsoft offers free server virtualization solutions for Windows Server 2003, Server 2008, and Server 2012. For Windows Server 2003, Microsoft Virtual Server 2005 R2 SP2 is offered as a free download from Microsoft's website and provides support for guest and host operating systems running Windows Vista SP1 (Business, Enterprise, Ultimate), Windows XP SP3, and Windows Server 2008 (Standard, Enterprise, Datacenter, Web). The software provides centralized management and administration of virtual servers, allowing for quick deployment of virtual servers that are reliable, secure, and scalable. However, if your firm is currently running Windows Server 2003, then it's about time for an upgrade.

For host systems running Windows Server 2008 or 2012, Microsoft has included the Hyper-V virtualization system with the base installation of the operating system and it is installed through the Server Roles window. Hyper-V enables the consolidating of multiple server roles as separate virtual servers running on a single host system, allowing for different operating systems such as Linux, Windows, and others to run in parallel. For more information regarding Microsoft's Hyper-V solution, you can visit Microsoft's website at **www.microsoft.com/en-us/server-cloud/windows-server/server-virtualization.aspx**.

Hyper-V was designed with enhanced security features in mind, providing an architecture that is less vulnerable to attack. This software includes a set of management and administration tools that can be used to manage the host and virtual systems' hardware from the same interface. It even allows administrators to migrate live systems from server to server. Windows Server 2012 has an updated version of Microsoft's Hyper-V, which includes such new features as network virtualization, multi-tenancy, storage resource pools, and cloud backup. The new version of Hyper-V also increases the amount of memory and storage and the number of virtual processors that each machine can be allocated. For more information regarding Microsoft's Hyper-V 2012, you can visit Microsoft's TechNet website at **technet.microsoft.com/library/hh831531.aspx**.

Depending on the operating system of the host system, these are a few Microsoft-based software options available for server virtualization, and they are fully supported. We have observed that the free Hyper-V implementations may have some issues sharing peripheral devices across the virtual machines. As an example, you may not be able to share the USB ports of the hardware with a virtual machine, which means that you can't copy files from a USB flash drive from the host system to the virtual system.

Software licensing will also play a role in determining your firm's ability to move to a virtualization environment. When you use the Microsoft Server 2003/2008 Enterprise Edition, licensing allows up to four virtual instances of the software on the same hardware system. This is one of the reasons the cost to purchase a single license of Enterprise Edition is much higher than the Standard Edition. For every other operating system, both servers and desktops, an additional license must be purchased for each virtual server or machine desired. However, if you are planning on implementing a Microsoft virtualization environment, we strongly recommend that the host system run Microsoft Server 2008 Enterprise Edition, as Windows Server 2003 Enterprise Edition is no longer available from Microsoft and has moved into Extended Support. When purchasing Microsoft Server 2012, you will need either the Standard or Datacenter Edition, depending on the number of virtual instances you require.

There are other alternatives to Microsoft's virtualization solutions, such as VMware's vSphere Hypervisor (ESXi). If you are investigating alternative virtualization solutions, you will need to work with your IT vendor to see what other options might be available. We recommend and use the VMware solution instead of Microsoft's Hyper-V solution. VMware has been in the virtualization game a lot longer than Microsoft, and you can share those USB ports with the virtual machines. VMware Tools also offers some other useful and time-saving administration capabilities. The stability of Hyper-V continues to be a concern among several of our clients. Reliability issues with Microsoft's virtualization solution have caused us to convert from Microsoft to VMware's solution. Every client that we have converted has yet to have problems like those experienced with Hyper-V. Although, the latest version of Hyper-V is considerably more stable than previous versions, the Enterprise Edition of Windows Server is a bit pricey for most solo and small firm lawyers.

The cost to purchase the hardware and software necessary to implement a virtualization environment for your network will be significantly less than the cost of purchasing multiple servers to fill the necessary roles your applications and services require.

Peer-to-Peer

Many small firms use the built-in peer-to-peer network capabilities of their computer systems as an alternative to purchasing a server. A peer-to-peer network, in its simplest form, is two or more computers that are able to communicate with one another to share files and folders, printers, and applications without using a server to accomplish these tasks. Peer-to-peer networks are commonly used in solo or small firm offices with only two or three computers. The computers, located on the same local network and belonging to the same Workgroup, can access shared resources in the

Workgroups to which they are joined. *Workgroup* is Microsoft's name for a peer-to-peer network. Unless a computer is joined to a domain, it belongs to a Workgroup. By default, on Windows XP computers the Workgroup name is MSHOME, and in older versions of Windows the default Workgroup is WORKGROUP. Just to complicate matters, Microsoft has changed the default Workgroup name in Windows 7 back to the original WORK-GROUP.

Peer-to-peer networks may sound like a good solution for small firms that have only a few computers, but this type of network has some significant disadvantages compared to purchasing a server. First, when networking computers together, you are going to experience a slowdown and inconsistency in your system's performance. Workstations are not capable of handling concurrent access of their files by other computers. When this occurs, the system's resources are severely taxed, causing disruption to the users. Think of this as a tug-of-war for data. Your computer is trying to use data at the same time that someone else needs it. Because of the inconsistency and unreliability of the peer-to-peer network, corruption of shared files, such as case management and billing systems, occurs frequently. Since computers in a peer-to-peer network can be running different operating systems, software incompatibilities between the systems can occur. Management of user accounts, along with implementing the proper security controls to protect sensitive and confidential data, becomes a nightmare to accomplish and even more difficult should a breach occur that requires investigation.

The decentralization of critical firm data can lead to unnecessarily complex data backup scenarios, often resulting in important data not being backed up or protected. On top of all the issues above, the need to manage and administer multiple copies of the same software, such as antivirus protection on each individual computer, becomes needlessly tiresome. Software that is centrally managed is much more cost-effective to purchase and maintain, as opposed to managing each computer's software suites independently. Just figure in the added administration costs that your firm will pay its IT provider; this will more than cover the cost of a server—and then some!

There is an inaccurate perception that peer-to-peer networks save money and cost less than client/server networks. Yes, purchasing a server—even a lower-end unit—might seem expensive at first. However, in the end, this is never the case. The costs of managing and maintaining a peer-to-peer network will always be higher than the costs you would have been incurred if you had implemented a server/client network in the first place. Peer-to-peer networks can have higher licensing costs for software because you are purchasing single licenses. Software that is administered and maintained on independent computers will take more time than if it were centrally managed from a server. Technical support and consulting costs will be much higher in a peer-to-peer environment, which is usually not taken into consideration when making the initial decision to purchase and use a peer-to-peer network. For most small network environments, even those involving as few as two computers, purchasing a server to centralize applications and data can save time and money—and the number of headaches you will have to endure—in the long run.

CHAPTER EIGHT

Server Operating Systems

CHOOSING THE HARDWARE COMPONENTS is just one step in selecting the right server for your business. The next step is determining what operating system and software will be necessary to best meet both the current and future needs of the firm. There are many variations of server operating systems currently available, and they are described in detail below.

Microsoft Windows Server 2003 Standard Edition

The Windows Server 2003 operating system was produced by Microsoft as the successor to Windows Server 2000 operating systems. The Windows Server 2003 operating systems deliver better performance, is more scalable, and offers more enhanced security features than its predecessor. The Microsoft Windows Server 2003 Standard Edition was released to target small to medium-sized businesses. The Standard Edition supports file and printer sharing, centralized desktop application deployment, and enhanced security and access management through upgrades to Active Directory. Microsoft Windows Server 2003 Standard Edition supports up to four processors and 4GB of memory.

As of July 13, 2010, Microsoft Windows 2003 Server went into Extended Support and will continue to offer security updates until July 2015. This product is no longer available from Dell as an option when configuring a server on its website and shouldn't be considered when configuring a new system. We mention it here to point out the end-of-life date. If you are currently running this version of the server software, begin making plans to replace it before July 2015.

Microsoft Windows Small Business Server 2003 Standard and Premium Editions

Microsoft Small Business Server (SBS) 2003 was developed and designed to provide small businesses with an operating system that would offer a complete technology solution. The technologies integrated with Microsoft SBS include remote access, Remote Web Workplace, Terminal Services, enhanced security features, Fax Server, unified messaging console, and enhanced monitoring and logging. The Standard Edition of SBS includes Windows SharePoint Services used for work collaboration, Microsoft Exchange Server 2003 for e-mail, Active Directory, and other features. The Premium Edition of Microsoft SBS 2003 includes Microsoft SQL Server 2000, Microsoft Internet Security, and Acceleration Server 2004, as well as everything included with the SBS 2003 Standard Edition.

SBS Client Access Licenses (CALs) are more expensive than CALs for other editions of Windows. The reason for the increased cost is that the license is for bundled software—e.g., Microsoft Exchange and Microsoft SQL Server—although this is less expensive than buying licenses for each of the different products individually. The CALs can be purchased either per device or per user.

The SBS operating system bundle provides small businesses with a cost-effective, complete solution, but Windows SBS 2003 does have some disadvantages or limitations:

- Only one computer in a domain can be running it.
- It is limited to 75 CALs (user or device).
- It cannot be set up to trust any other domains.
- It is limited to a maximum of 4GB of memory.
- Terminal Services can operate only in Remote Administration mode for a maximum of two concurrent connections at once.

While you may still be able to find licenses for Small Business Server 2003, we don't recommend deploying it on any new systems. This is an aged version of the server operating system. Small Business Server 2011 is the version you should consider for current needs.

Microsoft Windows Server 2003 Enterprise Edition

Microsoft Windows Server 2003 Enterprise Edition is aimed toward medium to large-sized businesses requiring a server that can provide enterprise-level features and service—for example, when a user has applications that require more than 4GB to run efficiently.

Microsoft Server 2003 Enterprise Edition supports up to eight processors and up to 32GB of memory. Remember, Microsoft Windows Server 2003 Standard Edition and SBS support only up to four processors and 4GB of memory. The Enterprise operating system also provides Enterprise-class features, such as using Microsoft Cluster Server (MSCS) for clustering. This operating system is recommended for servers that will be hosting database applications, case management applications, or other software that requires large amounts of processing power and memory addressing—more than the Standard and SBS operating systems can support.

As with Small Business Server 2003, you may be able to find licenses for this version. However, we would not recommend using this version of the server operating system at this time on any new system. Windows Server 2012 is the current server operating system of choice for enterprise-level solutions.

Microsoft Windows Server 2008 R2

Microsoft Windows Server 2008 R2 is the successor to Windows Server 2003. It was officially launched in late February 2008 and built from the same code base as Windows Vista. However, it is not a nightmare like Vista.

This operating system includes a lot of new features and enhancements, such as native support for IPv6, new security features such as BitLocker, and an improved Windows Firewall with a more secure default configuration. Also, the manner in which this operating system handles processors and memory is different from previous versions. Processors and memory are now treated as plug-and-play devices, meaning they are "hot-swappable." They can now be removed and replaced without shutting down the server, although sticking your hands into a hot, running server is probably not a very bright idea.

Windows Server 2008 includes expanded Active Directory functionality and a major upgrade to Terminal Services. Terminal Services now supports Remote Desktop Protocol 8.0, which provides the ability to share a single application over a Remote Desktop connection rather than the entire desktop, as was the case in previous versions. It also provides additional support for multiple monitors and stronger encryption algorithms for keeping data traffic secure.

In previous versions of the Windows operating system, if corruption or errors were found on a new technology file system (NTFS) volume, the volume would have to be dismounted and taken offline for the errors to be corrected. Windows Server 2008 supports a self-healing NTFS format that can detect and fix errors while online without having to bring down the entire system. Microsoft Windows Server 2008 is offered in both 32- and 64-bit versions.

Windows Server 2008, like previous versions, is offered in the following editions:

+ Standard Edition
+ Enterprise Edition
+ Datacenter Edition
+ HPC Server
+ Web Server
+ Storage Server
+ Small Business Server
+ Essential Business Server

Most of the editions listed above would not be considered when purchasing a server solution for a small business or law firm and will not be discussed in more detail in this book. However, the Standard, Enterprise, and Small Business Server editions are described below.

In February 2011, Microsoft released Service Pack 1 for Windows Server 2008 R2, which introduced two new features and addressed a number of security issues present in this version of the operating system. The two new features, RemoteFX and Dynamic Memory, add support for 3D graphics within a Hyper-V-based virtual machine, as well as dynamic memory allocation based on the resources required at the current time by the virtual machine. It is recommended that if you're running Windows Server 2008, you download and install the latest Service Pack from Windows Updates as soon as possible.

Microsoft Windows Small Business Server 2008 Standard and Premium Editions

Windows Small Business Server (SBS) 2008 is based on Windows Server 2008 and includes Microsoft Exchange Server 2007 Standard Edition, Windows SharePoint Services 3.0, and trial subscriptions for Microsoft's new security products, such as Forefront Security for Exchange.

The SBS 2008 operating system was officially launched on November 12, 2008. Like previous editions of SBS, the 2008 version is offered in both Standard and Premium editions. The Standard Edition is regarded as a single server solution for small businesses, your all-in-one operating system. In one server, you get file and printer sharing, e-mail, web hosting, and the ability to set up a domain for up to seventy-five users and/or devices. The Premium Edition contains all of the features and software that Standard Edition has, plus a license for the Microsoft SQL Server 2008 Standard Edition. The Premium Edition requires two separate servers, one for Windows Server 2008 with Exchange and the other solely for SQL Server. This is going to be a problem for small firms on a tight budget, but it may be more affordable if used in a virtualized environment.

Windows SBS 2008 is offered only in a 64-bit version due to the requirements of Microsoft Exchange Server 2007, whose production version is 64-bit. This is an important distinction when considering your hardware purchase. Make sure you have 64-bit hardware if you are considering using these new server operating systems.

On a more positive note, Microsoft has finally changed the way CALs are purchased for SBS. In earlier editions, CALs could be purchased only in groups of 5, 10, or 20 licenses, but not anymore. CALs for SBS 2008 can now be purchased individually.

We still hold to our previous recommendation that Small Business Server 2011 should be the current version deployed in your firm. While you may find that licensing is slightly cheaper for the 2008 version, its life will be much shorter, and some of the current features will not exist.

Windows Server 2008 Standard Edition

The Windows Server 2008 Standard Edition was designed to increase the reliability of your server infrastructure while simultaneously saving time and reducing costs when it comes to server maintenance.

Standard Edition comes with enhanced security features to help protect your data and network and includes powerful tools that give you greater network control. Windows Server 2008 Standard Edition comes with IIS 7.5, a powerful web hosting and services platform. The operating system also includes Windows Server Hyper-V, virtualization software designed to support machine virtualization, and an upgraded version of Terminal Services that supports Remote Desktop Protocol 8.0.

In terms of security, Standard Edition includes tools to improve auditing and secure startup, and it enables disk encryption using BitLocker. Standard Edition supports up to 32GB of memory, four multicore processors, and up to 250 concurrent Terminal Service connections.

Windows Server 2008 Enterprise Edition

Microsoft Windows Server 2008 Enterprise Edition, like its predecessor, is an operating system that is aimed toward medium to large-sized businesses looking for a server capable of handling enterprise-level services. Microsoft Server 2008 Enterprise Edition provides mission-critical applications through such features as failover clustering, fault-tolerant memory synchronization, and cross-file replication. This edition also features the latest advancements in security and is extremely scalable to support mission-critical applications.

This operating system is recommended for servers that will be hosting database applications, case management applications, or other software that requires more processing power and memory addressing than the Standard and SBS operating systems can support.

Microsoft Small Business Server 2011 Standard and Essentials

Microsoft Small Business Server 2011 (SBS 2011) is the successor to SBS 2008 and is offered in two versions: Standard and Essentials. A separate SBS Premium add-on is available for small firms that require SQL Server.

The Standard Edition is designed for small businesses and supports up to seventy-five users and/or devices. Like the previous SBS versions, this edition provides a single server solution for small businesses that includes e-mail, remote access, and file and printer sharing. This edition includes both Microsoft Exchange Server 2010 and SharePoint Foundation Server 2010.

The Essentials Edition is designed for small businesses and supports up to twenty-five users and/or devices. This edition is integrated with Microsoft's cloud services and doesn't require the end-user to purchase any CALs. This edition, unlike the Standard Edition, does not include Microsoft Exchange Server or SharePoint Foundation Server 2010.

For those small businesses that need to deploy additional servers on their network to run SQL Server 2008 R2 Standard, the Premium Add-on license is the component that they'll need to purchase. Additional server and SQL CALs are required with this component and will add cost to the purchase, depending on the number of users and computers that need to access this system.

Microsoft Windows Server 2012

In September 2012, Microsoft released the next version of its operating system software, to coincide with the release of Windows 8. Server 2012 is offered in four editions, only three of which (Essentials, Standard, and Datacenter) would be considered when purchasing a server for a small business.

Server 2012 includes a number of new and enhanced features that IT administrators will love including:

- ♦ A newly redesigned user interface with a focus on easing server management tasks, including the administration of multiple servers from within the same window
- ♦ An updated version of Windows PowerShell with over 2,300 commands, compared to about 200 in Windows Server 2008
- ♦ A new version of Windows Task Manager
- ♦ IP Address Management (IPAM) role for discovering, monitoring, auditing, and managing IP address space used on the local network
- ♦ An updated version of Windows Active Directory, including simplified upgrading of the Domain Functional Level to Server 2012, a new graphical user interface (GUI), the ability to set multiple password policies within the same domain, and the ability to safely clone virtualized domain controllers
- ♦ An updated version of Hyper-V, which includes such new features as network virtualization, multi-tenancy, storage resource pools, cloud backup, support for an increased number of virtual processors, greater storage capacity, and more memory
- ♦ A new version of Internet Information Services (IIS) (version 8.0) used to host websites
- ♦ A new file system, Resilient File System (ReFS), that is intended for file servers and improves the features of NTFS

This version of the Windows operating system has made it through a year of testing, and we have given it our approval stamp. This is the operating system of choice when purchasing and configuring new server-based systems for our clients.

Microsoft Server 2012 R2

Windows Server 2012 R2 is the next version of Windows Server, currently in preview release at the time of writing. This server operating system will probably be released to manufacturing sometime in the fall of 2013.

Some of the confirmed changes from Windows Server 2012 that will be introduced in Windows Server 2012 R2:

- ♦ Automated tiering of frequently accessed files on fastest physical media
- ♦ Deduplication for Virtual Hard Drives
- ♦ New version of Windows PowerShell (v4)

- ◆ Integrated Office 365 support
- ◆ Return of the Windows Start Button
- ◆ UEFI-based virtual machines
- ◆ Boot from SCSI device option
- ◆ Faster VM deployment (50 percent increase in speed reported)

X64 Operating Systems

Until about six years ago, 32-bit processors dominated the commercial marketplace, and 64-bit processors were found only in supercomputers or very high-end and expensive servers. Now, however, 64-bit processors are standard rather than an option when configuring a server or a desktop computer prior to purchase. The 64-bit operating systems have been developed to run on these processors and offer many advantages over their 32-bit counterparts. In fact, the newer versions of Microsoft's server operating systems are offered only in 64-bit versions.

First, these systems process more data per clock cycle, and second, they offer direct access to more virtual and physical memory than 32-bit systems. These advantages provide for more scalable, higher performing computing solutions, which is a requirement when running a virtualized environment. There are far fewer device driver issues with X64 operating systems now than when 64-bit systems first appeared on the market; however, it's always important to make sure everything is compatible before migrating from a 32-bit environment to a 64-bit environment.

The current versions of Windows desktop-based operating systems and server-based operating systems are all offered in 64-bit versions, and with most editions, that is the only option.

Mac OS X Server 10.5 (Leopard)

The Mac OS X Server 10.5 release, code-named Leopard, was released for Mac servers on October 26, 2007. OS X version 10.5 includes applications that allow administrators to more easily manage their users and computers and host websites and e-mail, and it provides services such as file and printer sharing. The Leopard Server combines proprietary Apple applications and open-source technologies to provide administrators with a powerful tool set that rivals the features and functionality provided by Windows-based operating systems. The Leopard Server allows for groups of employees to collaborate and communicate through an internal Wiki website that comes complete with calendar, blog, and mailing-list functionality. Users can create and edit their own Wiki pages, tag and upload files and materials, and have the ability to search.

Mac OS X Server 10.6 (Snow Leopard)

The Mac OS X Server 10.6 replaced the Leopard version of the Mac OS X server operating system and included new features and software, such as iCal Server 2, Podcast Producer 2, and new Address Book server capabilities. The Snow Leopard operating system uses a 64-bit kernel, allowing for the support of greater amounts of memory and a larger number of multi-core processors. Also included is Mail for e-mail hosting services, Apache for hosting websites, and the Mobile Access Server to provide remote accessibility to clients.

Mac OS X Server 10.7 (Lion)

In keeping with the tradition of releasing a new version of its server operating system in conjunction with its latest desktop operating system, Apple released Mac OS X Server 10.7, code-named Lion.

This version includes an application called the Server app, which is a simplified configuration process for setting up and administering the most critical functions of the server, including file sharing, e-mail, contacts, backups, and remote access, to name a few. The software also includes Apple's equivalent of Microsoft's Active Directory and a new feature that provides wireless file sharing for iPad devices that allows access to documents on the server.

Lion Server also includes updated versions of the iCal Server 3, Wiki Server 3, Mail Server 3, and Xsan software. This software requires a base purchase of OS X Lion from the Mac App Store and is actually purchased as an add-on or a bundled group of apps sold as Mac OS X Lion Server. The Lion Server is available from the Mac App Store for $49.99.

Mac OS X Server 10.8 (Mountain Lion)

With the latest release of the Mountain Lion desktop software, Apple has released its server counterpart. Mac OS X Server 10.8, nicknamed Mountain Lion, has several new features that should appeal to small businesses and enterprises alike. This product, now an add-on from the Mac App Store, has new and enhanced features, including:

- Advanced administration through the Server app
- Profile Manager that provides one-stop administration of all Apple devices within an organization, including both Mac and iOS devices

- ◆ The ability for iOS users to self-enroll their devices for system management through an internal web portal
- ◆ Revamped wiki service, providing collaboration and document and project management capabilities
- ◆ Renaming of various services to match their Mountain Lion desktop equivalents, e.g., iChat Server is now Messages Server, iCal Server is Calendar Server
- ◆ iPad/iWork integration
- ◆ Push notifications
- ◆ Active Directory integration

To get this software, you must first be running Mountain Lion. Then you can purchase and download the Mountain Lion Server app from the Mac App Store for only $19.99.

Mac OS X Server 10.9 (Mavericks)

Mac OS X Server 10.9, nicknamed Mavericks, was released in the fall of 2013 as a downloadable package from the Mac App Store, just like Mountain Lion was. This Server app costs only $19.99 for the upgrade.

One of the new features in the Mavericks operating system is a new XCode Server used in iOS development—Caching Server 2, which speeds up the download and delivery of software through the App Store, Mac App Store, and iTunes Store so that copies can be downloaded faster to computers and iOS devices from the local cached resource.

Linux-Based Operating Systems

Linux-based operating systems are similar to Unix-based operating systems and are built on an open-source kernel packaged with system utilities, software, and libraries. The underlying source code of the operating system can be freely modified, used, and redistributed, and it is supported by a community of programmers and volunteers.

Linux is now packaged for different uses, primarily servers, which contain modified kernels along with a variety of software packages tailored to different requirements. Some of the commercially available distributions that are backed by corporations are Fedora (Red Hat), SUSE Linux (Novell), Ubuntu (Canonical Ltd.), and Mandriva Linux. Each of these distributions has versions specifically designed and programmed to run on server-based hardware to provide management, web and e-mail hosting services, and file and printer sharing, along with other services and functionality that are available in both Mac- and Windows-based server operating systems. There are also desktop versions for each of these versions of Linux, which only hold a microscopic fraction of the desktop operating system market share.

Unless you're a serious technologist, you don't want to go anywhere near Linux-based operating systems.

CHAPTER NINE

Networking Hardware

NETWORKING HARDWARE TYPICALLY REFERS to equipment that allows network devices to communicate with one another, but not always. Some other types of networking hardware can include server racks, cabling, and other devices that help make up the computer network. Here we provide descriptions and recommendations for the most common types of networking hardware that you will require in a solo or small firm computer network.

Switches

A switch is a piece of networking hardware that connects network segments (discrete sections of the network), allowing multiple devices to communicate with one another. For example, if two or more computers are connected into the same switch and are located within the same defined network, the switch will allow these devices to communicate. Switches inspect data packets as they are received and, based on the source and destination hardware addresses, will forward the data packet appropriately. By delivering the packet of information only to the device it was intended for, network bandwidth is preserved, as well as confidentiality, and the information is delivered much more quickly. In comparison, network hubs send the traffic to all ports, irrespective of the destination device, and are rarely seen in a production environment anymore. Unlike network hubs, switches are "intelligent" devices and can operate on more than one layer of the Open Systems Interconnection (OSI) model, such as a multilayer switch. Switches allow traffic to pass through them at speeds of 10 Mbps, 100 Mbps, 1 Gbps, or 10 Gbps, depending on the speeds of the ports.

The International Organization for Standardization created the OSI model as a way of subdividing a communications system into seven layers: Physical, Data Link, Network, Transport, Session, Presentation, and Application. We could write a whole book on the OSI model, but others already have.

Most solo and small law firms will not need expensive high-end network switches for their computer infrastructure. In the majority of situations, a switch is needed only to connect computer workstations to the server and to the router for Internet access. NETGEAR offers reasonably priced switches in a variety of configurations to meet almost any solo or small firm need. The ProSafe Unmanaged Desktop series is a good choice for the solo or small law firm because of the low cost, ease of setup, and reliability. Setup of these devices requires no configuration—just plug in the power and network cables and you're ready to go.

When purchasing a switch for your firm, you will need to determine the number of connections or ports the switch will need. Next, you will have to determine the speeds of the ports that you will require. Will all of your computers need the ability to connect to the server at gigabyte speeds, or will just a handful of devices need that kind of speed? Remember, you certainly will pay more for a 48-port switch with 48 gigabit ports than if you buy a 48-port switch with only two gigabit ports and 46 10/100MB ports. Given the bandwidth of today's networks and applications, it's almost a requirement to purchase a switch with gigabit ports, and the added speed is worth the additional cost. The ProSafe Unmanaged Desktop Switches from NETGEAR can be found on its website at **www.netgear.com**. These switches are also offered in a 1U rackmount solution that will fit standard 19-inch racks.

For those law firms that require or desire tighter security controls over their computer systems and users, a managed switch may be the solution. A managed switch, unlike an unmanaged switch, is a device that can be administered or controlled. Advanced features include the ability to limit how computer systems can "talk" with one another at the physical level (private virtual LANs), advanced performance monitoring, Layer 3–based prioritization, and increased bandwidth control. These switches also support Quality of Service (QoS), which can be used to prioritize certain network traffic over other functions, such as VoIP phones. A good cost-effective managed switch for small to medium-sized law firms is the ProSafe Gigabit Smart Switch from NETGEAR. This managed switch can be found on NETGEAR's website (**www.netgear.com**) starting at around $225 and can be purchased with differing numbers of ports and connection speeds, depending on the requirements.

As an alternative, Dell manufactures some very cost-effective switches for network connectivity. They have managed and unmanaged versions as well as multi-gigabit port models.

Entry-Level and Intermediate-Level Routers

A router is a computer-networking device that connects two or more independent networks—e.g., your firm's local computer network and your Internet Service Provider's (ISP) network. A router's job is to determine the proper path for data to travel between the networks and to forward data packets to the next device along the path—basically to get your data from point A to point B. Routers come in all shapes and sizes and can have different features. For a solo or small firm, the most basic router will often be sufficient to connect the local network to the Internet, as well as protect computers and other hardware devices on the local network from outside attacks. A basic router will require some configuration from the default values to communicate with the ISP's network, as well as to strengthen the security and protection it provides to your information systems. Most basic routers are capable of handling only broadband Internet connections, such as cable or DSL, by using the Ethernet port coming from the cable or DSL modem. If your firm has a T-1 or any variant of this Internet connection, your ISP will probably provide you with a router.

The increasing number of data breaches has created a lot of discussion recently about which router a solo or small firm should use. Whichever router your firm chooses, it must have a built-in firewall and logging capabilities. There can be no exceptions. Previously, we recommended a Linksys router as a basic routing solution for solo and small firms. When configured correctly, this device can provide adequate protection for your firm's data and information systems. However, our recommendation has changed.

Today, the bad guys have gotten so good at breaking into law firms that it's becoming increasingly hard to keep them out. When they do get in, most law firms don't realize that they've been compromised until it's too late. For this reason, there is no longer an entry-level routing solution that we can recommend with confidence. Your firm's data is just too valuable.

Given the types of data that your firm stores, such as Social Security numbers, credit card numbers, patient/medical records, and other sensitive client information, the only way to combat hackers and have a chance of keeping them out is through the implementation of a defense-in-depth security strategy. This type of information protection strategy provides security at all levels of your computer network, including the point at which your local network interfaces with the public Internet. For this reason, we recommend the Cisco Small Business RV Series line of routers, even for a solo lawyer.

The Cisco Small Business RV Series routers provide high-performance connectivity for small businesses and have built-in threat defense, including a proven stateful packet inspection firewall, intrusion detection system, and an optional content filtering subscription package to restrict a user's access to undesirable websites that may contain malware and phishing attacks. The Cisco WRVS4400N router offers a wireless option for those firms that require it. The Cisco Small Business RV Series routers start at around $200.

A Cisco device is a little more complicated to configure from the command line, although a graphic user interface (GUI) is available to assist those less familiar with the Cisco configuration syntax. Unless you are comfortable with the syntax of Cisco's IOS (yes, Apple used the iOS term after Cisco), we recommend that you not attempt to configure the device. Seek out the expertise of your IT professional or another resource that "speaks" Cisco's IOS language.

It's becoming harder to find a router for a small to medium-sized business that doesn't include wireless 802.11 capabilities. Be careful when purchasing these devices for your firm's computer network, as you may unintentionally open up your network to unwanted guests if your system is not configured properly. The majority of these devices come preconfigured with open, unsecured wireless networks—which may be OK for your guest network, but even most wireless devices now have an option to set up a separate guest network to keep your visitor's computer network separate from the firm's. You can never be too safe. Remember, you also have the ability to disable the wireless capability if you don't need it.

Make sure you consult with your IT vendor on best practices when implementing a wireless network for your law firm. And for heaven's sake, make sure all the default settings are changed. Even "script-kiddies" know all the default settings.

Firewalls/IDS/IPS Devices

An intrusion detection system (IDS) is used to detect many types of malicious network traffic and computer usage that can't be detected by a conventional firewall or router. These malicious activities include network attacks against vulnerable services (web hosting, e-mail, databases, etc.); data-driven attacks on applications; host-based attacks, such as privilege escalation; unauthorized logins; and access to sensitive files. Privilege escalation is the act of exploiting a known vulnerability in an application to gain access to resources that would have otherwise been protected. When an IDS is used in combination with an Intrusion Prevention System (IPS), they also can detect and prevent malware such as viruses, Trojan horses, and worms from entering the network.

An IDS/IPS device is commonly placed at the gateway of the computer network so that all incoming and outgoing network traffic passes through it. This allows the device to scan all incoming/outgoing traffic before it is passed on to the destination located on the local computer network, denying the entry of any malicious traffic and prohibiting the exit of any malicious traffic. A firewall has the ability to permit or deny data traffic based on port number, originating or receiving Internet Protocol (IP) address, and protocol type, to name just a few, and it is usually based on rules that are set up and configured by an administrator. An IP address is a unique address or identifier assigned to a networked device, such as a computer, that allows the device to communicate with other networked devices. Just think of an IP address as being the same as a home address, which is a unique way to identify your home's physical location.

A firewall device with these described capabilities is critical for the protection and security of your firm's computer equipment and information systems. For those users who have a broadband Internet connection at home, a router with firewall should also be used to protect your home-based computer network from outside attacks. This is especially important for those lawyers who work remotely, because you do not want your clients' data to become compromised while working offsite. According to the Internet Storm Center, which is part of the SANS Institute, it takes only twenty minutes or less for an unprotected and unpatched computer connected to the Internet to become compromised. Imagine that the computer is yours and it contains confidential client data. This is the stuff of which nightmares are made.

For this reason, we recommend the Cisco ASA 5500-X Series Adaptive-Security Appliance, which provides a good solution for solo and small firms looking to secure their local computer network from outside attacks. This appliance integrates a world-class firewall, unified communications (voice/video) security, SSL (Secure Sockets Layer) and IPSec (Internet protocol security) VPN, intrusion prevention, and content security services into a single piece of hardware. These devices offer advanced security features such as granular control of applications and micro-applications with behavior-based controls, highly secure remote access, and near-real-time protection against Internet threats. Combining all of the functionality into one piece of network hardware eliminates the need to purchase a single device for each function. This saves time in setup and configuration, eliminates complexity, and tremendously reduces the cost to adequately secure your business computer network.

The Cisco ASA 5500-X Series provides intelligent threat defense and secure communications services that stop attacks before they affect your firm's business continuity. The firewall technology is built on the proven capabilities of the Cisco PIX family of security appliances, allowing valid traffic to flow in and out of the local network while keeping out unwelcome visitors. The URL and content-filtering technologies implemented by the device protect the business as well as the employees from the theft of confidential and proprietary information and help the business comply with federal regulations, such as HIPAA and Gramm-Leach-Bliley. The application control capabilities can limit peer-to-peer and instant-messaging traffic, which often lead to security vulnerabilities and the introduction of viruses and threats to the network. The implementation of a Cisco ASA 5000-X Series device will deliver comprehensive, multilayer security to your computer network and will help you to sleep better at night knowing your electronic data and equipment are protected. The Cisco ASA 5500-X Series Adaptive-Security Appliance can be purchased from Cisco Systems online at its website (**www.cisco.com**) or through a distributor.

The cost of the Cisco ASA 5500-X Series device can range in the thousands of dollars, depending on the number of licenses, features, warranty, and support purchased with the product. When purchasing this device, we absolutely recommend that you get SmartNet maintenance. SmartNet allows you access to the excellent technical support personnel of Cisco, hardware replacement for failures, and upgrades to the device operating system.

Make no mistake about it—this is an excellent high-end firewall well worth the investment to protect your network and confidential information.

Racks

A rack unit or enclosure is a piece of hardware that is used to store, organize, and secure your networking and computing equipment. Most often, rack units are used to hold rack-mount servers and network communication equipment such as firewalls and switches. There are many types of computer and networking hardware that are offered in rack-mount sizes, due to the need to place and secure equipment within a single physical location. Rack units can be portable units mounted on caster wheels, bolted to the floor, or, if small enough, mounted on the wall. The amount of space that is available for the servers and networking equipment will greatly affect which type of rack to purchase. The leading manufacturers of rack units and enclosures are American Power Conversion (APC) and Chatsworth.

APC NetShelter SX enclosures are rack enclosures with advanced cooling, power distribution, and cable management for server and networking devices. The 19-inch rack is vendor neutral and is guaranteed to be compatible with all EIA-310 compliant 19-inch equipment, which covers nearly all rack-mountable equipment. The 19 inches refers to the horizontal distance between the mounting screws for the equipment. These enclosures offer large cable access slots in the roof to provide overhead cable egress, which is useful when cable runs come down through the ceiling. The bottom design allows for unobstructed cable access through a raised panel floor, which is common in network data centers. The enclosures are well ventilated with perforated front and rear doors to provide ample ventilation for servers and other networking hardware that require unobstructed air flow to keep systems cool. The front and rear doors can be arranged to open in either direction, depending on the layout of the room. For physical security protection, both of these doors can be locked.

The enclosure contains rear cable-management channels to assist in managing the plethora of cables that servers and network equipment require. The frame design of the NetShelter SX enclosures is made with heavy-gauge mounting rails and casters to provide support for up to 3,000 pounds of equipment. APC's NetShelter SX enclosures are offered in many different sizes (stand-alone, datacenter, colocation, etc.) and can be purchased with accessories, such as UPS battery backups, retractable keyboard, mouse pad, flip-down monitor, cable-management arms, additional fans, and power distribution centers. The APC NetShelter SX rack enclosures can be purchased online at APC's website (**www.apc.com**), and the basic enclosures start at around $1,500.

If you're hesitant to spend $1,500 on a piece of equipment just to hold your servers and networking devices, you may be able to find used racks from local businesses that are moving or have been closed, or through your local online classifieds, at only a fraction of the price.

Cabling

Now that you have all of your computer equipment selected and purchased, you will need to decide how to wire your data and voice network
and what type of network patch cables should be purchased to connect
your computers to the network drops (cables from the wall outlet to the
hub/switch location). These patch cables come in various lengths and are
primarily offered in two different types.

First, you have the category 5e cable, which is not the same as the generically termed Cat5 specification. Second, you have the category 6 cable,
more commonly referred to as Cat6, along with category 7 cables used for
networks requiring data transfer speeds of up to 10 Gbps. Each type of
cable has a different maximum throughput speed that it's capable of handling. As with computers, as time progresses, newer cable standards are
developed that can handle greater data transfer speeds. There is even a
category 8 cable that should be standardized shortly, promising a new
copper speedway for data centers in the not-too-distant future, operating
up to speeds of 40 Gbps.

The Cat6 standard cable is becoming increasingly popular as more and
more networking and computer devices operate and communicate at
gigabit speeds. Current data transfer rates and applications operating at
speeds of 1 Gps are starting to push the limits of category 5 cabling;
although category 5e cable is rated for gigabit speeds, it should be used
with caution. The trends of the past and predictions for the future indicate that data rates have been doubling every 18 months. The category 6
cables offer double the amount of bandwidth capacity of category 5
cables and a better transmission performance. The category 6 cable provides a higher signal-to-noise ratio, allowing for higher reliability for current applications and higher data rates for the future. Analysts have indicated that the majority of new wiring installations are using Cat6 cabling.
This is a fairly easy decision, because all Cat6 cabling is backward compatible with Cat5e cabling.

Category 7 cabling is only commonly seen in data centers and is not yet
widely used in local networks. If your firm is planning on wiring the
office for data and voice, it makes all the sense in the world to wire with
Cat6 cabling. Remember, once the dust has settled from the construction,
it would be extremely costly to have any type of cabling pulled out and
replaced. The approximately 10 percent premium that you currently will
pay for Cat6 cabling over Cat5e cabling is worth the added cost. As time
goes on, the premium is getting smaller and smaller.

Wireless Networking Devices

A wireless networking device allows for communication between devices without being physically connected by wires or network cables. In a solo or small firm, if the investment cost to wire an office space with data cables is too expensive, a wireless solution may be the answer. Plus, who wants networking cables all over the place? This is particularly true in older properties—and may be aesthetically desirable in historic buildings. A wireless network is extremely convenient for lawyers who use laptops, smartphones, or tablets because they can move from their office to the conference room with these devices and still stay connected to the local network and Internet. The cost to purchase a wireless networking device is extremely low, and the benefits gained are worth the small investment. However, do not implement a wireless network without taking the proper security precautions. By default, most wireless routers and access points are preconfigured not to enable encryption. This means that by default, all communications between computers and the wireless device are unencrypted and therefore insecure. How many people have connected their laptop to an unencrypted wireless network so that they could check their e-mail or perform online banking? We see this all the time—even at legal technology conferences!

Wireless networks should be set up with the proper security. First and foremost, encryption should be enabled on the wireless device. Most wireless devices come preconfigured with either an unencrypted network or a network encrypted using the wired equivalent privacy (WEP) 64- or 128-bit algorithm. Ultimately, neither of these solutions is adequate. WEP is a weak encryption algorithm and can be cracked in a matter of minutes using free open-source software. Do not use WEP! Frankly, the Federal Trade Commission and the Canadian Privacy Commissioner have both found WEP encryption insufficient to secure credit card information, so we suggest it not be used at all. Some time ago, WPA using the TKIP (temporal key integrity protocol) algorithm was cracked by a group of Japanese scientists in about a minute. So avoid WPA as well. This means that you should be encrypting using WPA2 only.

If the wireless network is for the firm only, enable MAC (media access control) filtering on the wireless device. MAC filtering essentially limits the devices that may communicate with the wireless device. If the MAC address of a computer's wireless network card does not match an authorized MAC address, then the wireless device will not communicate with the unauthorized computer. Enabling MAC filtration will also stop employees from connecting their personal smartphones to the wireless cloud without authorization, even if they know the appropriate network name and passphrase. This is an added layer of security. Most commonly, wireless routers and access points ship with default network names such as Linksys or NETGEAR. While in operation, these devices will broadcast their names so that wireless clients can locate the wireless networks. It is strongly recommended, for security reasons, that the default name of the wireless network be changed (not to something identifying who you are—such as TheSmithLawFirm) and that SSID (service set identifier, which is essentially the network name) broadcasting be disabled.

If your router doesn't come equipped with built-in wireless support, there are other wireless solutions available for the solo and small firm that provide reliable and secure network connections.

Linksys continues to be a very popular manufacturer of wireless networking devices for residential users and small- to medium-sized businesses. Its products have only gotten better since the company was purchased by Cisco a few years ago. Cisco sold the Linksys line to Belkin, but the products are still rock solid. The Linksys EA3500 Router is an all-in-one Internet sharing router with a four-port switch. Although this router can be used to connect your local computer network to the Internet, it should be implemented as a wireless access point only in coordination with another firewall/IDS/IPS device. The 802.11n wireless standard protocol is used by this device and offers data transmission speeds up to 300 Mbps. This standard is about six times as fast as the 802.11g standard, which offered data transmission speeds up to 54 Mbps. One of the benefits of the 802.11n standard is that it is backward compatible with 802.11b/g devices. This router supports the latest wireless security encryption standards, such as WPA2, to keep your data communications secure. The Linksys EA3500 Router can be purchased online from the Linksys website (**store.linksys.com**) or from your local electronics retailer for around $99.99.

Wireless device manufacturers continue their push to get consumers to purchase their 802.11n wireless products. The 802.11n standard has finally been approved, so it's fine to purchase 802.11n products. Wireless networks that use the 802.11n standard will see an improvement in connection speeds and range beyond previous 802.11 standard connections. To use the new standard, all wireless devices will have to be 802.11n compatible; otherwise, the wireless network will operate using only the same standard as the "oldest" wireless device on your network. Further, to get transmission speeds as fast as advertised, you'll have to be relatively close to the access point, and only a limited amount of devices can be connected and using the wireless network at the same time. You may also see devices that support the latest 802.11ac standard. Unfortunately, the 802.11ac standard has not been ratified yet, so we suggest that you avoid it at this time. There are wireless routers that do, in fact, support the 802.11ac standard, but it is only a draft standard at this time. This is the same thing that happened when 802.11n was introduced. Vendors began selling equipment before the standard was ratified.

If you work out of a large office space, in a building with a lot of brick or mesh metal wiring embedded within the walls, or in a cubicle next to a microwave, you can purchase a piece of hardware to extend or improve the wireless signal strength in your office. These wireless range extenders cost around $100 and can be purchased online.

CHAPTER TEN

Miscellaneous
Hardware

ASIDE FROM ALL OF the computer hardware, software, and networking equipment, many other types of hardware deserve to be discussed. These additional devices can provide mobility, security, or functionality that would benefit a solo or small firm.

Fire Safe

A fire safe is an important and often overlooked piece of hardware to have in your office to protect your backup media, software licenses, and other valuables from destruction during a fire or other natural disaster. And don't put the items in the safe and leave the door open; it is astonishing how often we see this. Let the safe serve its purpose and don't succumb to the temptation of convenience by leaving it open. Most come with a locking mechanism, so take advantage of the added security to protect your firm's information.

It is strongly recommended that you store backups, software licenses, copies of technical contracts with third parties, and other important documents in a fire safe. Purchasing a fire safe is a relatively inexpensive investment; they can be purchased from your local office supply store for a couple of hundred dollars. There are many sizes and shapes of fire safes, so you shouldn't have a problem finding one that suits your needs. The key specification is the rated internal temperature. The safe may be rated to keep the contents from burning, but it also needs to not damage the contents, such as melting a tape casing, which is why the internal rated temperature is important. If you keep important business records offsite for redundancy, make sure that this information is stored in a fire safe as well. Your ability to recover from a disaster is only as good as the weakest point in the plan.

Battery Backup Devices

A battery backup device is an electronic device that supplies secondary power in the absence of main power, such as during a power outage. Battery backup devices can also protect electronic hardware from power spikes and dirty electricity. These devices come in all sizes and power capacities, and, depending on what devices you are looking to protect, this will affect the size and capacities you choose. APC is the leading manufacturer of battery backup devices used for protecting computers, servers, and other networking hardware and equipment.

It is strongly recommended that every computer within the local network be placed on a battery backup device, such as the APC Back-UPS 350. At our office, we have our computers, printers, routers, switches, phones, and voicemail system all on battery backup devices to protect our hardware investment. This battery backup device will supply your computer system with power for up to five minutes after an outage has occurred. During this time, the battery backup device will communicate with the APC software installed on the computer (bundled with the device) and will instruct the computer to shut down properly and safely. The Back-UPS 350 supports up to 210 watts and has three NEMA 5-15R battery backup outlets and three NEMA 5-15R surge protection outlets.

Many computers and servers will experience software or hardware errors after a power outage because they did not have the opportunity to shut down properly—often referred to as a hard shutdown—which is a quick way to lose or corrupt your data. When computers and (horror of horrors) servers go down hard, the result is often not pretty—actually it's more of a catastrophe. There is a great chance for data loss or system failure in the event of an outage. By purchasing battery backup devices for your computers and other electronic equipment, you are protecting your hardware and software investment and avoiding possible IT costs to correct all the problems that might ensue from a hard shutdown. The APC Back-UPS 350 can be purchased from APC's website (**www.apc.com**) for $79.99.

We've discussed battery backup devices for workstations and laptops, but what about servers? Servers require much more power to operate than a desktop or laptop computer. Therefore, they will require more battery capacity to allow them to operate during a power outage and/or the time necessary to properly shut down. On top of that, they take much longer to shut down properly than a workstation due to the greater number of services and processes constantly running on a server. To properly shut down, the average server will take upward of 10 minutes or more if the server is hosting multiple virtual machines, so supplying the server with enough power to accomplish this task is important. Certainly, you do not want your server to experience a hard shutdown, because the risk is great for data loss or hardware failure. Battery backup devices for servers can be purchased as a tower unit or rack mountable, depending on what your firm needs to support its server configuration.

The APC Smart-UPS 1500VA is an ideal battery backup solution to protect a single server from the power outages, power spikes, or dirty electricity that can damage the server's internal hardware components. The Smart-UPS 1500VA is offered in both tower and rack-mountable forms and can supply a server with enough power to allow the server to shut down properly. Note that this unit has only enough capacity to supply power to one server and its peripheral devices. If there is a need to purchase a battery backup device for multiple servers, there are models with greater capacities that will be able to handle the load.

As with all batteries, someday they will need to be replaced. Happily, the batteries in these devices are hot-swappable, which means they can be replaced without the need to shut down the battery backup device or the devices connected to the unit. It is important to replace batteries as soon as they fail so that the systems connected to the battery backup device continue to be protected in the event of a power failure, and—trust us—you'll know when the battery needs to be replaced, because the beeping alarm is really loud. Replacement batteries for these devices can be purchased online from APC's website. Because the batteries in these units are replaceable, this is one hardware investment that you will not be replacing every one to two years. In our experience, these devices will always outlast the life of the computers, servers, or equipment connected to them.

The APC Smart-UPS 1500VA comes bundled with software that can be installed on the server itself to enable the battery backup device to communicate with the server. This is necessary so that in the event of a power outage the battery backup can alert the software installed on the server of the need to begin the shutdown process. The battery backup device connects to the server through a USB or serial cable. The APC Smart-UPS 1500VA can be purchased from APC's website for $579.

You can also purchase an optional network card for many of the larger UPS devices. The network card allows you to connect the communication over your data network and can support multiple servers. You configure the network card with an IP address, and the servers use the APC network shutdown software to "talk" to the UPS for status rather than communicating through the traditional USB or serial connection.

Fax Machines

Even though the need for fax machines has dwindled, they are still a staple in a law office and do get some use from time to time—we still receive faxes, and some clients and institutions insist that we receive information via the facsimile machine. Sometimes there just isn't enough time to scan a document and then e-mail it to a recipient, so instead the document will be faxed—or in some cases, although rare, the communicating party doesn't have access to an Internet connection. We still see plenty of solo and small firms where there is no interest in learning how to scan. The fax machine is the devil they know, and they don't want to change. So, even with all of the advancements in technology, the fax machine has a continued role. As previously stated, many digital copiers have fax transmission/receipt capabilities. Check with your vendor representative to see if using the copier is more cost-effective than purchasing a separate device.

If your firm is in the market for a fax machine, the device we recommend is the Brother IntelliFax-2940, which is a high-speed laser fax, phone, and copier. This model was designed for multiple users in a small business to easily share the benefits. Its design incorporates a high-capacity front-loading paper tray that makes replenishing the paper a task that doesn't require a degree in engineering to accomplish.

The IntelliFax-2940 is equipped with 16MB of memory, allowing multiple faxes to be stored in memory for transmission when it senses the line is free. The 33.6 Kbps SuperG3 fax modem optimizes throughput, transmitting as fast as two seconds per page. The 250-sheet capacity paper tray is front loading for easy access, which means less time spent reloading paper. The paper tray can adjust to hold either letter or legal-size paper. This fax machine also comes with a 30-page auto document feeder. Access to incoming faxes can be protected through the use of a password, ensuring that only the appropriate parties see confidential faxes. Finally, if your needs exceed or grow beyond faxing and copying, this device comes with a USB interface and can serve as a laser printer capable of printing up to

24 pages per minute. This device comes with a standard one-year limited warranty. The Brother IntelliFax-2940 can be purchased online at Brother's website (**www.brother-usa.com**) for around $300.

Backup Solutions

As hard drive sizes get larger and the volume of electronic data created increases, larger media is required to store the daily, weekly, and monthly backup files. Luckily, the days of having to purchase expensive tape drives, autoloaders, and media have long passed. The options for media to store backups have increased, while the cost continues to decline. Solo and small firms no longer need to purchase or implement an expensive backup system. Usually, a set of inexpensive external hard drives will do the trick. They offer more capacity than most tape media, are portable, have faster transfer rates, and are relatively inexpensive. And don't forget that you should keep at least one complete backup set offsite in the event that your entire office is lost—or inaccessible—during a disaster.

Depending on the backup solution that has been implemented, a lot of storage space may be necessary, especially if your firm has implemented a system where a full backup is run on a nightly basis. The Western Digital My Book adds secure high-capacity storage to your computer system and is compatible with both PCs and Mac computers. It comes pre-formatted with the NTFS file system, so if you're planning on using this device on a Microsoft Windows-based network, you will have to format the external hard drive FAT32, depending on your requirements. The USB 3.0 (USB 2.0 backward compatible) interface allows the hard drive to deliver transfer rates up to 5 Gbps and can be connected to any computer or server that supports these types of connections. The Western Digital My Books comes with built-in hardware encryption, keeping your firm's data secure.

The Western Digital My Book is offered with storage capacities ranging from 1 to 4TB in size, providing enough storage space for the average small to medium-sized firm backups. The unit also comes with a power adapter and cables to connect the device to a computer or server. If you have not yet purchased backup software, you can use the WD SmartWare backup software that comes bundled with the device. The software can be installed and used on both a computer and a server to back up your system and data files. The device comes with a three-year limited warranty. The Western Digital My Book can be purchased online or from your local electronics retailer starting at around $90 for the 1TB version.

When evaluating backup solutions for your firm, be sure to enlist the recommendations of your IT staff. Cloud-based backup solutions are becoming more popular with small businesses and might have a place in your firm. When evaluating cloud backup providers, pay attention to where your data is physically stored (we would never use a provider that stores data outside of the United States—although the actions of the National Security Agency may cause us to rethink that statement), and be sure that the data is always stored in an encrypted format, regardless of whether it's in transit or at rest, and that you hold the only key.

Some folks think data is safer in Europe because of its tough data privacy laws, but that is not necessarily true. Besides the obvious headaches that accompany cross-border data issues, some European versions of The Patriot Act make U.S. law look namby-pamby by comparison. Who knows when those laws may be invoked? For more thoughts on this issue, see this book's last chapter, "Tomorrow in Legal Tech."

CHAPTER ELEVEN

Smartphones

SMARTPHONES REMAIN THE NUMBER one tech accessory among lawyers. We all remember the time when a lawyer would carry two separate devices, a cell phone and a PDA (personal digital assistant). The cell phone was used to make phone calls, and the PDA was used to keep your notes and calendar. Some even allowed you to view your e-mail captured during your last synchronization with your work computer. Since that time, things are very different. Smartphones are like laptops—able to perform almost every function a laptop can, and in some instances, more—but at a fraction of the size. Because smartphones have so many capabilities, lawyers in firms of all sizes tend to view them as a necessity—a device they can no longer live without. Smartphones have become computers in and of themselves, with increasing functionality, and in some cases, they are more important to a lawyer than a computer system.

Among business users and especially lawyers, the smartphone debate has evolved into major warfare. Since its introduction and with its growing popularity, the Apple iPhone has grabbed the largest share of the lawyer market, and that is particularly true for solo and small firm lawyers.

According to the American Bar Association's 2013 Legal Technology Survey, the overall smartphone breakdown by platform among lawyers is as follows:

- ◆ Apple iPhone (55 percent)
- ◆ RIM BlackBerry (14 percent)
- ◆ Google Android (20 percent)
- ◆ Other/Unknown (2 percent)
- ◆ None (9 percent)

These numbers have resulted in some major changes over the past year:

♦ This is the first year that more than half of the lawyers in the United States are using an iPhone.

♦ The lack of response of lawyers using Windows Mobile devices has caused the category to be lumped in with the Other category.

♦ By this time next year, BlackBerry devices may meet the same fate as Windows Mobile devices and will be lumped in the Other category, having dropped from 40 percent usage in 2011 to 14 percent usage in 2013. That number will only continue to drop.

♦ Over the past two years, the smartphone marketplace has shrunk from five, to three, to now just two major players.

Both the Android and the iPhone continue to split the market share. We still expect to see the popularity of Androids increase. The BlackBerry is no longer a player and could become all but non-existent in the United States a year or two from now. RIM (Research in Motion), BlackBerry's manufacturer, may have been lulled into inaction by its success, but the hot new technology clearly belongs to Androids and iPhones. Because RIM is a Canadian company, Canada may keep it on life support.

A key functional requirement for any smartphone is the ability to synchronize data with your computer or server. E-mail synchronization is at the top of all lawyers' lists, followed closely by calendar synchronization. The Windows Phone 7 (previously known as Windows Mobile), Windows Phone 8, iPhone, and Android phones synchronize with Microsoft Exchange Servers via ActiveSync. This doesn't require any special hardware or software because the function is built into Exchange. However, there are some limitations, such as the inability to synchronize natively with Public Folders over the air. You may have to purchase third-party products to get all of the features you need for over-the-air synchronization of Public Folders, Personal Calendars, or Contacts. Your mailbox will synchronize without any additional software. For those firms that don't host their own e-mail, users can set up their devices to retrieve e-mail directly from their e-mail service provider.

In 2010, Apple released its new version of the iPhone (iPhone 4), replacing the third-generation iPhone with a phone that contains a greater amount of memory, increased features and functionality, and encryption. Overall, this version of the iPhone was more business friendly. In October 2011, Apple released the iPhone 4S and iOS 5. They include new functionality, including a new Voice Assistant, but do not include any announced security enhancements. Building on a strong consumer following from the earlier generation of iPhone and looking to solidify its place in the smartphone marketplace, Apple continues to support Microsoft Exchange e-mail by licensing ActiveSync from Microsoft. The latest generations of the iPhone (3GS, 4, 4S, and 5) are now "enterprise ready" and support over-the-air synchronization of e-mail, calendar, and contacts with a Microsoft Exchange Server; however, the phone lacks native support for rich-document editing and creation, requiring users to purchase or download freely available third-party software to complete these tasks.

Our continuing recommendation for any lawyer (or anybody wanting to keep his or her data secure) is to not use an iPhone. The iPhone 5 security is better but still problematic. Apple released the next generation of iPhone (5c and 5s) running iOS 7 in the fall of 2013. The 5s includes a fingerprint scanner in an attempt to improve the security of the iPhone. This form of security was compromised within two days of the new iPhone's release. Apple has released multiple fixes for various vulnerabilities as we go to press, but the fundamental insecurity of the fingerprint scanner cannot be fixed. However, it is unlikely that this will present a problem for most users, as there is some level of sophistication to the compromise. But if you are *targeted* by a professional, your data is not secure—after all, we leave our fingerprints everywhere we go.

Apple has made all kinds of marketing claims, yet there are many examples over the years of why an iPhone should not be trusted. On iPhones running certain older versions of the Apple iOS firmware, the PIN keylock code is easily replaced by a "blank" code. The iPhone also claims to store its data in encrypted form. That is true, but with some older versions of the iOS firmware you can place the phone in recovery mode and transfer the data to your computer. Apple conveniently decrypts the data as it sends it over the SSH connection, thereby negating the encryption scheme. You can remotely wipe the iPhone, but it needs to be connected to the cellular network to do it, unlike the BlackBerry and Windows Mobile phones.

This only applies to iPhones on AT&T's network and not to the Verizon and Sprint iPhones. Not much has changed in the security model, or lack thereof, of Apple's iPhone devices. There still are security problems with the current generation of the devices. Within days of each new firmware version released, a new "jailbreak" method has been discovered, although iOS 4 held up better than its predecessors., iOS 5 and 6 have both been jailbroken.

Since we know so many lawyers will (and do) ignore our advice, here's what we recommend:

(A) Only use the iPhone 4S or 5 (or the new 5c or 5s). If you're using the 3, 3G, or 4, upgrade immediately.

(B) Upgrade to the latest version of iOS 7.

(C) Enable a passphrase (not a four-digit PIN) on the device. Enable device wiping upon a set number of unsuccessful logon attempts.

As of this writing, the iPhone 5c, 5s, and iOS 7 have been released. Given the insecurity of the fingerprint scanner, make sure you configure a strong lock code and not the default four-digit PIN. There are tools available that can brute force the four-digit PIN on an iOS 4, 5, or 6 device in ten to forty minutes, even if the device is configured to wipe data after 10 invalid attempts. By the time this book is printed, we fully expect that the software will be updated to also brute force iOS 7 in a similar fashion. We are well aware that our advice is largely ignored here, as the glamour of the iPhone continues to mesmerize everyone, including lawyers. It is a very slick phone, but remember that the new ABA Model Rules adopted in 2012 require that you balance the risk of the technology you use against the security of client data!

With the introduction of iOS 5, Apple introduced the iCloud service. When enabled and configured, iOS devices use this service to backup information from your local device to the cloud. The iCloud service removes the necessity to connect your iOS device to your computer and either backup or update your device by using iTunes. All of this now takes place wirelessly, over your mobile data connection or your local Wi-Fi network. However, while convenient, there are some serious concerns with data privacy. First, consider that all information from your local device, whether the iPhone or iPad, is being sent to Apple for storage. The information may be encrypted by Apple, but it holds the decryption key and will turn the decrypted data over to law enforcement without hesitation.

For any cloud storage provider, whether iCloud, Dropbox, or some other provider, we always recommend that you encrypt the data prior to using and initiating the service. By following this process, the user holds the decryption key—not the service provider.

For iOS devices, using an app like BoxCryptor encrypts the files on your local device before the information is synchronized with the cloud storage provider. BoxCryptor encrypts files on the local device using AES-

256-bit encryption, providing the necessary security to keep your files and information secure. This also allows the user to hold and maintain possession of the decryption key, which is very important. This product can be downloaded from the App Store for free on iOS devices.

During 2013, many vendors of Android smartphones continued to release phones designed for business use. They include enhanced security and enterprise management capabilities, like encryption, support for virtual private networks, support for more ActiveSync controls, and remote locking and wiping. In October 2011, shortly after Apple's release of the iPhone 4S and iOS 5, Google announced the release of version 4 of Android, called Ice Cream Sandwich (ICS). It has since followed up ICS with the release of Android version 4.1, nicknamed Jelly Bean, in July 2012. ICS includes on-device encryption, which required third party apps on earlier Android phones. The new Motorola phones and the release of version 4 make Android a strong contender for business and law firm use. Google has announced that the next version of the Android operating system will be 4.4 and named Kit Kat. Of course Google got Nestle's blessing to use the Kit Kat trademark, so we shouldn't see any legal battles over the name. As Android matures and continues to increase in popularity, it's very possible that it may become the smartphone of choice, even surpassing the iPhone among lawyers.

For die-hard security enthusiasts, the National Security Agency (NSA) has created and released a hardened version of Google's Android operating system called Security Enhanced (SE) Android. This open source project was undertaken to limit the damage that can be done to the phone by flawed or malicious apps. It probably is only a matter of time before we see this operating system installed and running on Android phones used by government agencies. The Defense Department has already distributed many of these phones. However, given the events surrounding the release of documents by Edward Snowden, we now know that the NSA has its fingers into many sources of electronic information, including encrypted data. We would be very wary of trusting any hardened version of Android at this time and recommend protecting data with methods that you, the user, control and configure.

For those users looking for a smartphone recommendation, we strongly recommend investing in Android phones. We officially made the jump two years ago and are not looking back. We have fallen in love with the Samsung Galaxy S3 device and now wonder why we didn't switch sooner! Some of us are eager to get our hands on the Samsung Galaxy S4.

There are many Android devices to choose from. It may help to first select your cellular provider and then see what options it has. We've been to many Sprint, Verizon, and AT&T stores—nowadays, they all pretty much have the same models in store with many more options available online. For an Android, the Samsung Galaxy S3 or S4 is our current recommendation.

Over-the-air synchronization with Exchange Public Folders is a requested feature by many solo and small firm lawyers. You may require a third party server implementation such as Goodlink to perform these functions. Good Technologies, Inc., makers of Good Mobile Messaging products, provides enterprise-level messaging and control for iPhone, Android, Windows Phone 7, Symbian, and PalmOS phones. Hosted versions of Good for Enterprise are no longer available through any major cell carriers. In fact, Good has priced the software so high that it is no longer an alternative for solo or small firm lawyers. Because of the licensing costs and minimum device requirements, a Good solution would cost several thousands of dollars (not counting the server cost) just to get started. Mobile Iron used to be another alternative to manage a small population of smartphones. Like Good, Mobile Iron has increased its licensing cost to a point that only makes sense for larger firms. Believe it or not, RIM's Mobile Fusion server may be the only cost-effective solution to manage solo and small firm smartphones. Mobile Fusion can be installed on top of the free BES Express server. The license cost for each device is very reasonable, and licenses can be purchased as individual units.

Another alternative may be to install special software on your computer to synchronize with the Public Folders. Your computer must be powered up and logged into Outlook for the over-the-air synchronization to occur. As you can imagine, this is a potential security vulnerability and must be carefully considered and engineered, and it requires a lot of administration by your IT provider.

On a side note, everyone is familiar with getting spam through e-mail, but how about on the phone? Spam text messages can be costly since most carriers will charge for both text messages sent and received unless you have an unlimited plan. There is no anti-SMS-spam software available to install on cell phones to prevent receiving these messages, but there is a way to block cellular spam, and it's quite simple. The vast majority of spam text messages originate on the Internet and do not come from other cell phones. Why? Because spammers don't have to pay anything when using the Internet to send the text messages. Most carriers, led by AT&T and Verizon Wireless, offer spam SMS-blocking features. To enable this feature, just log into your online account manager and the options should be available in your account profile. Most cellular providers allow you to block SMS messages only from certain phone numbers and addresses. What are you waiting for? We've signed up.

AT&T (**mymessages.wireless.att.com**)

Verizon Wireless (**www.verizonwireless.com**)

Sprint (**www.sprint.com**)

T-Mobile (**www.t-mobile.com**)

Make sure you pay attention to smartphone updates and security notices, as the number of malware threats targeting smartphones have skyrocketed over the past year. Currently, Android devices are the most frequently targeted by malware due to their popularity, open-source operating system, the relatively lawless Android Market, and the availability of apps from multiple sources.

For Android phones, we recommend a free security product called Lookout Mobile Security (**www.lookout.com**). This free utility will scan all of your applications for malware and spyware and has a built-in "find my phone" feature on the free edition, allowing you to locate your device using the GPS if it goes missing. The free edition also includes a backup feature, which is nice if you haven't integrated your Android phone with your Google account. Some of the other features include protecting your device from malware, blocking malicious websites, seeing which apps access your private information, and preventing encounters with phishing scams. The paid version offers some additional features such as a Privacy Advisor and Safe Browsing. This product can be downloaded from the Play Store for free. Lookout also has a version for iOS devices, which alerts owners if their device may have been exposed to security vulnerabilities because of outdated software or if the device has been jailbroken. It also offers device location and backup functionality.

Even with the rising threat of malware, there are some basic steps you can take to protect yourself. First, make sure that when you're downloading an application, you do so only from Google Play or the App Store. When choosing an application to try or to purchase, be sure to carefully read through the reviews. Also, pay attention to the access permissions that an app requests when you install it, especially on an Android device. Finally, vendors of security software are now offering antivirus and antimalware products for smartphones. This is software that you should seriously consider purchasing to protect your mobile devices, especially if they contain confidential information.

Basic security measures for any smartphone should include strong passwords, passphrases or PINs, automatic logoff after a set time, encryption of the phone and storage cards, and remote wiping capability.

CHAPTER TWELVE

Productivity Software

HAVING WORKED WITH SO many solos and small law firms through the years, we know that lawyers are constantly striving to be more productive and, therefore, increase their billable time. We see a few (less than the number of digits on one hand) lawyers who still prefer to use Corel WordPerfect over Microsoft Word, but that number is continuing to drop as Corel is becoming more and more of a non-factor in the productivity software market.

Microsoft Word is what the business world uses and will continue to use for the foreseeable future. There are alternatives, but they all come with some degree of pain and a large learning curve. There are adherents of WordPerfect who are religious in their fervor, and others who are evangelical in their admiration for open-source solutions. Whether you are a fan of Microsoft or not, the reality is that Word is the preferred application of the business world, and your clients will expect you to use it. They will not appreciate any conversion problems that may occur if you are using something else. In this section, we detail the latest and greatest releases of productivity software that can help lawyers be more productive.

Microsoft Office

Microsoft's latest version of Office, Office 2013, was released about a year ago and has been taken for a test drive by many of our clients. The software was redesigned to make the most of the new Windows 8 operating system, work with mobile devices, and strongly push Microsoft's cloud services. It works and runs just fine on Microsoft Windows 7, and it is our choice for a productivity suite.

To compete with Google's cloud storage options, Microsoft designed the new version of Office as a service in which applications and files are primarily stored in the cloud and not on your local computer system. This may come as a shock to most traditional Microsoft users, and lawyers should be aware that this type of service may pose ethical issues depending on how and where their information is actually being stored. However, users also have the ability to store documents on their local computer system.

Office 2013 was released in three editions: Office Home & Student 2013, Office Home & Business 2013, and Office Professional 2013. Office Home & Student 2013 retails for $139.99, and it is designed for families and consumers. Office Home & Business 2013, which retails for $219.99, is designed for the small business market and provides e-mail, shared calendars, and web conferencing tools. Office Professional 2013 retails for $399.99; it is designed for enterprise customers and provides advanced business and cloud deployment features. Each edition includes Word, Excel, PowerPoint, OneNote, Outlook, Publisher, and Access.

To date, Microsoft Office 2010 is still the most popular and widely used version of Microsoft's productivity suite, but it will eventually be surpassed by Microsoft Office 2013. Microsoft Office 2010 contains an updated user interface and additional support for extended file formats, and it is offered in a 64-bit version for some operating systems. One of the newest features included in Microsoft Outlook 2010 is the support for e-mail message threading. As technology advocates, we subscribe to a number of mailing and support lists. In prior versions of Microsoft Office, following a conversation thread was hard, and in most instances, nearly impossible. But the latest version of Microsoft Outlook will actually group all e-mail messages belonging to the message thread, regardless of where they exist in your mailbox. This setting can be customized on a per-folder basis.

Also new to this release is the debut of free online versions of Microsoft Word, Excel, PowerPoint, and OneNote, called Office Web Apps. The online versions work in all of the popular Internet browsers, including Internet Explorer, Mozilla Firefox, and Google Chrome. The ribbon interface is continued from the 2007 version and now exists in Outlook, too.

Microsoft appears to be listening to its customers and seems to be reducing the confusion about which Office suite to buy. Office 2010 is still available in six versions, three of which are retail packages. The retail suites are Office Home & Student, Office Home & Business, and Office

Professional. The costs are $149.99, $279.99, and $499.99, respectively, and Microsoft dropped upgrade licensing with the introduction of Office 2010. Volume license and qualified organization pricing is available for Office Standard, Office Professional Academic, and Office Professional Plus.

If your firm is using Microsoft Office 2007 or older, we would highly recommend that you upgrade to Office 2010 or Office 2013 at this time.

Corel Suite

WordPerfect Office X6 is the latest version of Corel's Office Suite and is available in Standard, Professional, and Legal editions for the business user. WordPerfect Office X6, the successor to WordPerfect Office X5, was released in April 2012. New features of Corel WordPerfect Office X6 include support for multiple monitors, the ability to preview WordPerfect files in Windows Explorer and as attachments in Microsoft Outlook, Bates numbering for WordPerfect documents, and expanded find-and-replace capabilities. The components of WordPerfect Office X6 Standard Edition include:

> WordPerfect X6—word processor
>
> Quattro Pro X6—spreadsheet application
>
> Presentations X6—presentation/slideshow creator
>
> Lightning—digital notebook
>
> Mozilla Firefox—web browser
>
> Mozilla Thunderbird—e-mail client
>
> Nuance PaperPort 12 SE—document manager
>
> WinZip 16—file compression utility
>
> WordPerfect eBook Publisher—eBook creator

The Professional Edition also includes the Paradox database management program, Corel PDF Fusion PDF software, and the WordPerfect Office Software Development Kit, none of which are included in the Standard Edition. The Legal Edition also includes the Corel Perfect Authority table-of-authority creator and Corel PDF Fusion PDF software. The Standard Edition is the edition best suited for serving solo or small firm needs. Unless you need a database application, there is no reason for a solo or small firm to invest in the Professional Edition.

One of the touted advantages of WordPerfect over Microsoft Word is the Reveal Codes option, which allows users to manage document formatting with a fine-tooth comb. We are constantly amazed when lawyers mention the reveal code "excuse." Perhaps they are unaware that Word 2010 and 2013 actually have a reveal code type display, where the user can see formatting codes. However, service and support for Corel WordPerfect X5 is a bargain when compared to the costs of support for Microsoft Office. Users can request help via e-mail for free, and a toll-free support number is also provided, costing users only $20 per incident. For those who want to look for help themselves, Corel has a thorough online knowledge base that can be searched and reviewed for free.

Even with the new features included with WordPerfect Office X6, we still prefer the more seamless, although imperfect, Microsoft Office 2010 or Office 2013. Corel used to price the software suite at a much-reduced cost when compared to Microsoft Office, particularly for business-friendly packages, but that is no longer the case with the latest X6 version. Users who don't need the extensive features of WordPerfect or Microsoft Office might opt to use a product such as OpenOffice.org (described in the next section), which is free.

Corel WordPerfect Office X6 Standard Edition costs $249.99 for the full license and $159.99 for the upgrade license. Professional Edition costs $399.99 for the full license and $259.99 for the upgrade license. Legal Edition costs $379.99 for the full license, and there is no upgrade for the Legal Edition.

OpenOffice.org

Apache OpenOffice.org (formerly just OpenOffice) is a free open-source software office suite that is available for many different operating systems, including Linux, Windows, and Mac OS X. The latest release of OpenOffice.org (version 4.0) was released in July 2013 and contains many features and functions that are present in Microsoft Office and Corel WordPerfect Office. This suite was developed to reduce Microsoft Office's dominating market share by providing a free, open, and high quality alternative. Some of the new features in the latest version 4.0 include a new ODF 1.2 encryption option, new spreadsheet functions, an enhanced pivot table support in Calc, and enhanced graphics. Java has been removed from the bundle in an attempt to improve security.

OpenOffice.org can read and write most of the file formats found in Microsoft Office, including Office 2007/2010 file formats, which is important if you are going to choose to use a free utility for your productivity software. It also natively supports the standard OpenDocument file formats (ODF) and has the capability to read WordPerfect Office, Rich Text Format, Lotus, and other common productivity file types.

The components of OpenOffice.org work together to provide the features expected from a modern office suite and include:

Writer—word processor

Calc—spreadsheet application

Impress—presentation program

Base—database program

Draw—an editor used for drawing

Math—allows for creating and editing mathematical formulas

All of the components of the OpenOffice.org suite look and feel like the corresponding components in Microsoft Office and Corel WordPerfect Office. Microsoft, seeing the need for and popularity of the open-source movement, has sponsored the development of a converter from Office Open XML to OpenDocument format and vice versa. Microsoft and Corel have included add-in support for the ODF file format into their office suite products to allow reading and writing to the format.

However much we all grimace at Microsoft's domination, we do not recommend that you use OpenOffice.org as your primary productivity suite. Because it is developed and maintained by freelance programmers and other companies that make contributions to the project, such as Apache, the software is not very well supported and may not contain all of the features provided by other productivity suites. In addition, most law office staff have never seen OpenOffice.org, so the learning curve would be pretty steep.

Some of the additional features supported in version 4 include:

- Personal Information Manager
- PDF import into Draw
- OOXML support for opening documents created in Microsoft Office 2007/2010/2013
- Extensions, to add third-party functionality
- Support for multiscreen presentations

The current release of OpenOffice.org can be downloaded from the website free of charge at **www.openoffice.org**.

Adobe Acrobat

Adobe Acrobat is a family of application software developed by Adobe Systems that uses Portable Document Format (PDF) as its native file format. The PDF specification was originally a proprietary format but is now a published and approved ISO standard. The latest version of Adobe Acrobat (Acrobat XI) was released in October 2012. Like its predecessor, Acrobat XI continues to provide the ability to store and share files online by using the Adobe SendNow service. There is a free thirty-day trial that has a maximum file size of 100MB, total storage of 500MB, and 100 downloads per file. The Plus Plan costs $19.99 per year and has a maximum file size of 2GB, no file expiration date, 20GB of storage space, and unlimited downloads. Users can sign up at **acrobat.com**.

Acrobat XI is packaged differently from the prior versions. There are two retail offerings: Acrobat XI Standard and Acrobat XI Pro. The Acrobat XI family builds upon the features of the previous versions, and the feature comparisons can be viewed at **www.adobe.com/products/acrobat/matrix.html**. We would still recommend that you purchase the Pro version for the redaction, metadata removal, and Bates numbering capabilities.

The redaction and metadata removal tools can help mitigate the risk of unintended disclosure of information while submitting legal documents to clients, opposing counsel, or the courts. Bates numbering is a method of applying identifying labels to a set of related documents, where each page is assigned a sequential Bates number that uniquely identifies it while also establishing its relationship to other Bates-numbered pages.

Acrobat XI Pro contains some cool features that we're sure you'll take advantage of:

- PDF to Word
- PDF Portfolios
- Rich Media
- Action Wizard
- Version Comparison
- Extending Reader Functionality

- Streamlined Document Reviews
- Interactive PDF Forms
- Permanent Information Removal
- Standards Support (PDF/A, PDF/E & PDF/X)
- Online File Sharing

Adobe Acrobat XI allows you to combine multiple documents to create an Adobe PDF package while retaining the properties of the individual documents. With an Adobe PDF package, legal professionals can associate related project or client files, while individual files in the package can be encrypted, digitally signed, rearranged, removed, or added so that each recipient of the package can read or access only the relevant files that he or she has permission to view.

Security has been a big concern for Adobe for the past year. In an effort to minimize the impact to a user's system, Adobe has concentrated on reducing future vulnerability.

According to Adobe's website (**www.adobe.com**), "[t]he Acrobat X Family of products delivers better application security on all platforms as a result of continuing code hardening work, additional administration capabilities that provide more granular control over the execution of JavaScript, tighter integration with the Microsoft® Windows® security architecture, and other best practices in secure software development, following the Adobe Secure Product Lifecycle (SPLC) methodology."

The Adobe Reader XI PDF viewer has a Protected Mode to limit the level of access to a user's system. Effectively, this is a "sandbox" type of environment, reducing the potential security threats on a client system from persistent malware. Adobe has also removed support for Windows 2000, a highly vulnerable operating system that should no longer be in use.

Some of the noteworthy features or enhancements in the latest version of Acrobat include:

- Improved PDF editing
- Convert PDF files to PowerPoint
- Create new PDF and web forms
- Improved options for electronic signatures
- Collect form responses with FormsCentral
- Improved conversion of HTML pages to PDF

Even with some of the new features, Acrobat XI doesn't excite us as much as version 8 did. Here is our recommendation: If you currently are using Adobe Acrobat 7.0 or earlier, then the upgrade to Acrobat XI Pro is a must. The software contains added features for legal professionals that were not available in earlier versions of Acrobat, and those features alone are worth the purchase. If you are a user of Acrobat 9 or X Professional, stay with your current version unless you want to take advantage of some of the highlighted features mentioned above.

Adobe Acrobat XI Pro can be purchased online from Adobe's website (**www.adobe.com**) or from your local electronics store for $449 for the full version, which is the same price as the Acrobat X Professional version. The upgrade price is $199, which is a $40 increase from the previous upgrade pricing.

We have discovered a little trick for obtaining Adobe Acrobat XI Pro for a much lower price if you don't own any version of Acrobat (or own one prior to version 7). You should be able to buy a copy of Acrobat 9 Standard on the Internet for around $50. You then go to the Adobe site and purchase the Acrobat XI Pro upgrade for $199. This means you walk away with Acrobat XI for around $250 instead of the $449 retail price. That's a real bargain and would more than pay for this book! The audiences we speak to continue to report that this is one of their favorite tips.

Adobe, like other vendors, frequently releases security patches and updates for its products. By default, Adobe Acrobat XI products check for updates automatically. If you'd like to check for updates manually, you may do so from within the Help menu listing of your Adobe product.

OCR Software

Optical character recognition (OCR) software translates graphical images into editable text. This capability is used most commonly to edit a scanned document or image. It's widely used in law firms to convert scanned paper documents in a case file to searchable electronic files. OCR software will translate the image to text, such as a Microsoft Word document, which can be edited.

OmniPage Ultimate, by Nuance Communications, Inc., is an OCR software product enabling the conversion of paper documents and TIFF files to a text-based format for amending as needed with prominent business communications software. OmniPage Ultimate can convert scanned images to Microsoft Word, Excel, PowerPoint, Corel WordPerfect, e-mail, HTML, and even to the Amazon Kindle format. The program generates a formatted text document that preserves the layout and format, character, font, and style of the scanned image. This software boasts a 50 percent greater accuracy rate than its competitors when converting, and the updated recognition dictionaries for financial, legal, and medical specialties allow for legal-specific word recognition, which means that you will spend less time editing your legal documents.

OmniPage supports data capture from a digital camera. The software can "read" a digital photograph, which may come in handy for lawyers who use photographs as exhibits. This software is the first OCR application designed for the multicore-processor computer, taking advantage of hyperthreading to increase the conversion speed of documents. It was also the first OCR software to support Microsoft Office 2007/2010 native formats. When converting legal documents, OmniPage now has a greater ability to recognize formatting such as line numbers, Bates stamps, signatures, and more.

Some other new features included in OmniPage Ultimate worth mentioning include the ability to convert a scanned document into a readable format and send it to an Amazon Kindle, a "one click" toolbar in the Microsoft Office Suite that allows for document conversion with a simple click, and a faster load time than previous versions.

Also new in the latest version of OmniPage is the eDiscovery Assistant for searchable PDFs. eDiscovery Assistant provides the ability to safely convert a single PDF or batches of PDFs of all types into searchable documents without having to open PDF files one by one, giving the user greater flexibility when applying an OCR process to an entire group of documents.

As more and more firms look to use the features the Internet cloud provides, so do vendors. OmniPage includes the Nuance Cloud Connector application, which integrates with Evernote and Dropbox. The Cloud Connector also provides access to a number of cloud services, including Microsoft Live SkyDrive, GoogleDocs, Evernote, Dropbox, and more, allowing for users to scan and/or save their documents to the cloud.

OmniPage Ultimate can be purchased and downloaded online directly from Nuance's website (**www.nuance.com**) for $499.99 for the full version and $199.99 for the upgrade version.

Adobe Acrobat includes an OCR engine, too. We recommend purchasing Adobe Acrobat first to see if it meets your OCR needs before expending funds on another specialized product like OmniPage.

Voice Recognition Software

Arguably one of the biggest recent advances in productivity software is the continuing refinement of voice recognition software. Dragon Naturally Speaking 12 by Nuance (**www.nuance.com**) has made voice recognition software a respectable addition to your productivity arsenal. Many solo and small firm lawyers are now using Dragon as their primary composition tool. This is especially valuable for those who are not very accurate or fast typists. It takes only a short time to train Dragon to your voice, and its accuracy is astonishing. Nuance claims that version 12 is 20 percent more accurate than version 11, which is just incredible given how accurate the previous version of this product was.

Dragon can be used to compose e-mail messages, draft documents in your word processor, and even launch software applications without touching the keyboard or mouse. The software now allows users to search the Web and their computers through the use of voice shortcuts.

Along with new formatting and editing commands, the latest version also provides users the ability to post to Facebook and Twitter by voice and even allows users to use their iPhone or iPad as a wireless microphone, untethering them from their computer.

Some of the new features in version 12 include:

♦ Improved accuracy over the previous version—the new version continues to "learn" your voice and becomes more accurate the more you use the product

♦ Faster performance, by taking advantage of multicore processors

♦ Smart Format Rules—if you change the format of words, phrases, or numbers, this product will remember and make those changes for you in the future

♦ More natural text-to-speech conversion, which allows the user to fast-forward, rewind, and control speed and volume for easy proofing

♦ Enhanced Bluetooth support for wireless devices

♦ Further improvements to Google Mail and Hotmail integration, as well as built-in commands for the most frequent actions in Internet Explorer 9, Firefox 12 or higher, and Google Chrome 16 or higher

♦ Added support for Android devices to be used as remote microphones

This is a great tool and is used by many individuals with disabilities. But make no mistake—this is a mainstream product, and the able-bodied are moving to this technology in hordes!

Dragon Naturally Speaking comes in several versions. We recommend using the Legal or Professional version if you can afford it. The Legal version contains vocabulary specific to the legal profession and carries a price tag of $799.99. The Professional version is a higher-end package that allows for roaming user profiles and allows multiple custom dictionaries. The Professional version costs $599.99 and may be purchased from many webstores. The Premium package costs around $200 for physical shipment of media or $179.99 for digital download, and it may be a good alternative for some lawyers as it also supports digital recording devices, smart formatting, and text-to-speech. Dragon Naturally Speaking 12 is licensed on a per-user basis. You can install and run it on multiple computers, but you need a license for each user's voice file.

The most important tip about using voice recognition software is to proof any output from Dragon. The speech-to-text is very good, and it "learns" and improves with time, but it's not perfect. Make sure you proofread your documents, especially those that may be submitted to a court.

If you use Dragon on multiple computers, make sure you know how to move your voice files among machines. This will save on the "retraining" time when you use several computers. The process is most appropriate for those lawyers who use a computer at home and one at the office. Moving the voice files between the machines allows you to take advantage of the aggregate training time instead of each machine "learning" on its own.

A key component to the success of voice recognition is the use of a good quality USB microphone headset. We have had great success using a Plantronics 510 headset/microphone system, but they are no longer manufactured. The Plantronics Blackwire 700 Series is available for $129 from the Plantronics website (**www.plantronics.com**) and should be an excellent replacement for the older 510 model. The lightweight headphones with noise-canceling microphone connect to your computer using a standard USB connection. The wideband acoustic echo cancellation feature captures a broad range of voice signals for calls that are clearer and more natural sounding, perfect for use with Skype.

CHAPTER THIRTEEN

Security Software

COMBINED WITH NETWORK FIREWALLS or IDS (Intrusion Detection System) devices, security software provides another line of protection in the defense-in-depth information security strategy against malware, including viruses, Trojan horses, worms, and other external forces. The defense-in-depth approach to securing your network is the best way to keep your systems safe from both internal and external threats. These threats can be extremely harmful to a law firm network and very costly to remove once an infection has occurred, assuming you've been able to identify that a breach or infection has occurred. Even in a solo or small firm network, your client data is of the utmost importance and securing your computers, servers, smartphones, and information should be taken very seriously. The top security protection suites providing antivirus, anti-spyware, and antispam protection for stand-alone computers, networks, and mobile devices are discussed below, with recommendations regarding the setup and configuration of the software.

Stand-Alone

The software selections described in the stand-alone section are primarily for the computers and laptops of solo practitioners.

We no longer recommend stand-alone products for targeted protection, such as antivirus protection. This type of software is not sufficient today to keep your systems protected. The Internet security suites are the only way to go, where you get much more functionality, features, and protection for your computer at a much more affordable price.

Solos and small firms should definitely consider acquiring a single integrated product to deal with spam, viruses, and malware. Norton's security suite is a top seller for the single computer market, but we highly recommend avoiding the Norton Internet Security Suite software. We continue to find it, along with McAfee, to be a heavy load on computer processing, and it causes stability problems with many programs. It is also hard to remove once installed without causing further damage to your system.

We continue to remove McAfee from our clients' computers because of performance issues. Maybe it's our bad luck, but Norton and McAfee seem to cause our clients the biggest headaches.

For those users who want avoid the problems caused by Norton and McAfee, we recommend using Kaspersky Internet Security 2014, especially if you like your security suites to be hassle-free. This product contains firewall, antivirus, antispyware, rootkit detection, antispam protection, and much more. The antivirus engine that Kaspersky uses has been consistently highly ranked by independent testing labs.

The firewall included with this software provides two-way protection, scanning both incoming and outgoing network traffic, effectively blocking any hacker attacks against your system. The automatic exploit protection engine watches program behavior and aims to block zero-day vulnerabilities in the most commonly used software. The anti-phishing engine and URL advisor will keep you safe from drive-by malware while browsing the Internet, and the anti-banner blocks annoying banner and other advertisements on web pages. With all the bonus features included in this protection suite, purchasing this product is a very good deal. Kaspersky is available directly from **www.kaspersky.com** and costs $59.95 for one-year protection on up to three computers. This is an excellent choice for the small firm environment and it is even Windows 8 compatible.

Enterprise Versions

Enterprise versions of integrated security solutions are designed for small, medium, and large computer networks, and the software administration is performed from the server rather than on each individual computer system. The client software is installed or pushed from the central server to the local workstations with little or no effort. The server supplies the clients with program and definition updates and provides an interface to centrally manage all clients from a single console. Of course, enterprise licenses are a little bit more costly than purchasing a single license, but not by much. Even with the slight increase in cost for an enterprise license, you'll more than make up for it on the money you will not have to pay your IT consultant to manage and support the product.

Integrated Security Solutions

Kaspersky Business Space Security protects Windows, Novell NetWare, Linux-based servers (including 64-bit versions), and even Mac computers from all types of malicious programs and threats. The product provides protection from threats such as viruses, Trojans, worms, keyloggers, malware, rootkits, bots, etc. This is now the standard that we are seeing in the security product market. Former providers of antivirus software are providing protection from spyware and other malware, offering a more complete security solution to their business customers and all but eliminating the need for multiple applications to protect your systems from viruses and malware. This software provides real-time protection by scanning all files that are opened and quarantining infected files. The application can scan specified areas of the file system based on preconfigured, scheduled scans or on demand from the administrator. The scanning of critical system areas, such as running processes and startup objects, helps prevent malicious code from launching, and the ability to scan inside compound files provides an extra layer of protection.

Kaspersky Business Space Security software is a scalable security solution, allowing administrators to define the number of instances of the program they would like to run simultaneously to accelerate the processing of server requests. The software offers flexible administration through centralized installation and control. The administration tool can be used centrally to install and manage client applications and, once they are downloaded and installed, to push updates to the clients for rapid deployment of critical security updates.

Kaspersky Business Space Security, similar to other integrated security solutions, scans not only for viruses but also for other threats and malicious programs, such as spyware and keyloggers. In most instances, this solution can serve multiple functions. We use this security solution on our network systems to provide us with complete malware protection. By using an integrated solution that is capable of handling both antivirus and antispyware protection, we have one less product to purchase and renew on a yearly basis. The product also allows for different configuration settings depending on the type of network to which your computer system is currently connected, similar to the way Microsoft Windows 7 handles the different firewall settings.

As the security of smartphones is brought to the public's attention, more vendors are integrating smartphone security with their products. Kaspersky is no different. Kaspersky Business Space Security offers to protect smartphones from data leaks, malware, and viruses, and it also allows an administrator to remotely lock and wipe the device should it be misplaced, stolen, or lost. Some of the additional key features include GPS tracking, SIM card monitoring, privacy protection, and folder or device encryption. The antispam protection feature works to block both unwanted calls and text messages. Currently, Symbian, BlackBerry, Android, and Windows Mobile smartphones are supported by this product.

Notice that there is no support for iPhones. The sad reality is that Apple does not allow any access to the inner circles (kernel) of the operating system, where security software needs to be to run effectively. As a result, no vendor has a truly complete security solution for the iPhone or iPad. You'll just have to trust that Apple has secured the device appropriately, but we have our doubts. Just look at the number of security fixes and patches that are regularly released and how quickly an iOS device is jail-broken as soon as a new iOS version is issued.

There is a 10-license minimum purchase for Kaspersky Business Space Security software. Cost for the product begins at $39 per license and includes technical support and upgrades for a year. Kaspersky is priced much lower per license than its competition and is an affordable, complete security solution that is rapidly taking over the market. This software product is offered for purchase with one-, two-, and three-year subscriptions. Licenses can be obtained directly from Kaspersky's website (**www.kaspersky.com**) or from any authorized reseller.

Besides Kaspersky, we also recommend using the enterprise product from Trend Micro. Symantec has fallen from favor, especially since the introduction of its Symantec Endpoint Protection product. We have been diverting clients away from Symantec because of significant performance and stability problems and at this point no longer have any clients using this product. Independent testing has shown that Symantec is improving its product with each new version. It is getting better at detection, is less problematic with software conflicts, is more stable, and is not nearly the processor load that prior versions experienced. Even with these improvements, we are reluctant to suggest Symantec.

Trend Micro Worry-Free Business Security is a highly regarded product that is available in three editions: Advanced, Standard, and Services. We don't recommend the Services solution, as the entire configuration is set up and maintained by Trend Micro as a hosted solution.

All of the editions include antivirus and antispyware capabilities, as well as advanced security features such as the ability to limit or prohibit the insertion and usage of USB devices attached to company computer systems. The software will protect both servers and computers from malicious threats and will automatically change settings on laptops to protect employees when they are out of the office. The software will monitor active processes and applications to prevent unauthorized and harmful changes to your computers. Unlike the Standard Edition, the Advanced Edition includes antispam filtering for Microsoft Exchange Server as well as multilayered spam protection, and it offers protection for Mac clients and servers. Cost for the product starts at around $37 per license for the Standard Edition and $62 per license for the Advanced Edition, which includes technical support and upgrades for a year. This software product is offered in one-, two-, and three-year subscriptions, and licenses can be purchased directly from Trend Micro's website (**www.trendmicro.com**).

Antispam Protection

For antispam protection, we have previously recommended Google's Postini service. Google has since discontinued offering this service. We now use McAfee's SaaS Email Protection & Continuity service and love it so far.

McAfee's antispam solution is a lower-cost alternative service for e-mail antispam and antivirus without any of the headaches that come along with other products, including the products you actually need to install and run on your e-mail server. Note that your e-mail flow will be rerouted so that it goes through McAfee's servers before being delivered to your mail server or e-mail client. You can purchase the McAfee service directly from the vendor or through a reseller. McAfee's SaaS Email Protection & Continuity solution provides a web-based interface to manage the quarantine, where spam messages are held. Users receive a quarantine message in which they are provided with a summary of the e-mail messages quarantined throughout the day. From this message, a user can choose to release a quarantined message with just a simple click of the mouse. That's all you need to do to release a captured "false-positive." As the administrator of the account, you can choose when and how frequently you'd like your quarantined summary delivered, whether at the close of business or sometime overnight and whether just once a day or a couple of times throughout the day.

McAfee also has a "mail bag" feature included with this recommended solution. This feature spools your e-mail in the event you lose your Internet connection or your e-mail server goes down. Once your connection or server comes back up, McAfee will feed you the e-mail that it held during the outage, which means you won't lose any e-mail even if your server goes down for a period of time. Even while your server is down, you can access your e-mail from the McAfee portal. In other words, you will not be without e-mail even when your server goes down. Some may think that is a curse rather than a benefit, so we'll let you choose.

McAfee has a very good reputation for quality service, and clients seem to be very happy with it. Since we started using this product this past year, most of our clients have switched as well (now that Postini is defunct), and the feedback continues to be excellent. You may need to "tweak" the default rules a bit upon initial installation since McAfee is pretty aggressive in blocking messages. As an example, by default any message with the word *webinar* in it is blocked. That doesn't work for us since we attend (and give) a lot of webinars. Modifying the spam rules is easy, but your administrator should take on this task if needed.

McAfee provides 24/7 technical support; automatic maintenance and upgrades; and a monthly, annual, or multi-year subscription. This product can be purchased directly from McAfee's website and costs start at $27.90 per license for a one year subscription.

CHAPTER FOURTEEN

Case Management

IF YOU STILL LIVE in the paper world, you may not know that a case management application provides all of the case management functions that you are probably currently performing. You use a Rolodex or some other type of method to aggregate your contact information. We still see address books at the office supply store, but more and more contact information is collected in an electronic form. You have a calendar to schedule events, which may be written in a Day Planner. You have a file for each client or each client matter. We hope you use a word processor—or at least your administrative assistant does—to generate documents. You track everything you do for each client matter or should be. You probably even generate some sort of status concerning each matter. These are all functions of a case management system.

Even in a world full of smartphones and wireless devices, it amazes us that most solo and small firm lawyers still don't use a computerized case management software application. We've been making that statement for at least the last ten years. Case management is a must-have for today's modern law office. You may have heard other terms that describe the same type of software. Vendors attempt to differentiate themselves by describing their products with different names. You may hear descriptions such as practice management, contact management, litigation management, and so forth. Bottom line: They are all case management products, though they vary greatly in functionality. Arguably, the term *practice management* is more inclusive and encompasses what is termed "front office" (case/client information) and "back office" (accounting and billing).

There are several choices for case management, some of which we will cover here. The features vary by manufacturer, so make sure you understand what you're buying. Probably the feature we are asked about most is the integration of e-mail and contacts with case management. Make sure that the product will work with your e-mail system and that you understand how it needs to be configured. The synchronization is getting better, but most of our clients are less than impressed with many of the implementations of synchronization support. For example:

handwritten note in left margin: Syncing email to case mgmt software

- ♦ How does the software deal with a common firm-wide Public Folder Calendar?

- ♦ Will the product synchronize with your iPad or smartphone?

- ♦ What if you don't have an Exchange server and use hosted Exchange services?

- ♦ Can you still synchronize with a hosted Exchange environment? What e-mail clients are supported?

- ♦ Can you synchronize data with your Google account?

- ♦ Will synchronization occur wirelessly, or do you have to connect a cable and manually sync your data?

- ♦ Can you sync everything in your personal mailbox, or are you limited to a subset, such as contacts and calendar only and not the tasks?

There are two mistakes that we consistently see when firms decide to implement a case management system. The first mistake is the failure to require everyone in the firm to use the system. You will not realize the full return on your investment if only a few employees use it. In fact, it tends to cause a whole new set of problems, because sometimes there is crossover between lawyers and cases, and some operate within the case management system and some don't. The second most common mistake is the failure to invest in training. Training will allow all employees to fully use the features of the case management system, thereby becoming more efficient and properly organizing all data for a client matter. Simply dumping a case management system into a firm is worse than useless. When you price the software, price the training as well.

As with other sections of this book, we cannot mention or address every case management package or every feature of every product. We mention the most popular and widely used case management packages that we see being used by solos and small firms.

Amicus Attorney

Amicus Attorney (**www.amicusattorney.com**) from Gavel & Gown Software is a good small firm package that provides a fairly simple approach to case management. The technical requirements are very reasonable and don't require a huge and expensive computer to run. There are essentially two desktop versions available, or you can choose to select the cloud version. The Amicus Attorney Small Firm Edition should work for most solo and small law firms, and it is an on-premise solution. It is limited to a maximum of ten users. The pricing has not changed in the last five years (highly unusual, but welcome) and remains at $499 for the first user license and $399 for each additional license.

The 2013 Premium Edition uses SQL Server to achieve unlimited user and unlimited data access. The good news is that the Premium Edition includes an embedded SQL Server 2008 Standard Edition Runtime for use with Amicus Attorney, so you don't have to make a separate purchase.

For very large-scale installations, a separate SQL server is recommended. SQL Server 2008, SQL Server 2008 R2, and SQL Server 2012 are supported. Certainly a consideration is the cost of the SQL Server software and the hardware to run it on, which can add a hefty price to the implementation costs. An improvement over prior years' versions is the support for 64-bit versions of the operating system and SQL server. This means that more memory can be supported if you implement the 64-bit versions. The big price hike that took place three years ago remains unchanged for now. The first user license for the Premium Edition costs $999 and each additional user is $599, which is the same as for the past three years.

Mobility is a real focus for the majority of vendors these days. Amicus is no exception. They have changed the way they allow access to their products using mobile devices and no longer offer the Amicus Mobile add-on. If you have the Small Firm Edition, you can see and record time entries using Amicus TimeTracker during the evaluation period and if you run a licensed product that has a valid maintenance plan. Amicus Administrator must be running on a computer that has access to the Internet. The user can then log in to **www.amicustimetracker.com** using the browser from a mobile device. Supported smartphones include iPhone 5/4, Android 4.2.x/4.1.x/4.0.x, and BlackBerry 10/Torch 9860 and 9850. Supported tablets include iPad 2/1/Mini, Android 4.2.x/4.1.x/4.0.x/3.x, BlackBerry Playbook, and Windows RT Surface.

If you have the Premium Edition, you can synchronize contacts and calendar entries by using Google or Outlook as a conduit without any additional purchase. If you need more than just contact and calendar synchronization, the Amicus Anywhere product is available to provide a secure remote connection to your Amicus Premium environment using a browser. Amicus Anywhere provides you with a remote access solution and keeps your data under your control on your server and not in the cloud. Amicus Anywhere also includes TimeTracker, which was mentioned above. Amicus Anywhere is only available for the Premium Edition and not the Small Firm version. You'll have to contact Gavel & Gown for more information and pricing, as it is not available on their website (**http://www.amicus-cloud.com/welcome/**).

In addition to the on-premise solutions (Amicus Small Firm and Amicus Premium), new this year is a cloud-based implementation of Amicus. Amicus Cloud is a full-featured solution that includes matter management, calendaring, task management, global searching, billing, time entries, expense tracking, reporting, document management, and trust accounting. Amicus Cloud uses the cloud services of Microsoft Azure. It is accessible from any device using a modern browser. Supported browsers are Internet Explorer 9 and above, Firefox 9 or above, Safari 5 or above, and Chrome 16 or above. The cost for Amicus Cloud is $34.95 per user per month, or over $400 per user per year. These dollars are going to add up quickly, especially if you have more than one or two users. As with any other cloud service, make sure you understand the terms of service when placing client confidential data on a third-party server.

A trial version of Amicus Attorney (both on-premise and cloud) is available and highly recommended if you are considering purchase. Try the product first to make sure that it meets your needs and will work in your computing environment. Amicus Attorney is often mentioned in reviews as being the most user-friendly product, probably because of the graphic representation it uses as the interface.

Time Matters

LexisNexis has a couple of offerings suitable for the solo and small firm market. Time Matters (**www.timematters.com**) used to be the most popular case management package for solo and small firms (before being purchased by LexisNexis), but we are seeing lawyers jump ship at a rapid rate, just as in prior years. We are continuing to replace Time Matters with other products for our clients and have yet to do a single new installation in a long time. Time Matters is a very powerful case management application, but it can also be fairly complicated for many small firm lawyers. It is an absolute necessity to purchase training if you are considering implementing Time Matters in your firm. The learning curve is steep but well worth it because Time Matters is truly a feature-rich program.

The current version is Time Matters 12, which includes a Mobility service to keep you connected via your smartphone. The manufacturer recommendation is to install a dedicated server for Time Matters if you have five or more users. Frankly, we think you should install a dedicated server no matter how many users you have. This can significantly increase implementation costs for the solo and small firm lawyer, but it does provide for a larger and more robust case management application. Also, Time Matters is only supported in a local, directly connected environment. This means that the use of any wireless connections or WAN technologies for the application, which prevent most data center implementations, is not supported. The workstations and server need to be connected to the same local network. Peer-to-peer networks are not supported, hence the requirements for a dedicated server. Perhaps the installation requirements are why we haven't seen any new Time Matters installations for a long time.

Licensing for Time Matters is based on concurrent users. Time Matters 12 starts at $985 for the first user (a $35 increase from last year) and includes a maintenance plan for the first year. You have to contact LexisNexis to obtain costs for any additional licenses. Even if you complete the requested customer information online, pricing is not revealed until you call a sales representative. This is not a very transparent representation of the product costs. We recommend avoiding Time Matters, as there are many other good case management products that fully disclose pricing without involving a sales organization. We have also heard that Time Matters customers are not impressed with the technical support quality and the pressure to purchase maintenance. Perhaps that's another reason to look at alternative case management products.

PracticeMaster

A highly rated case management application (and our personal favorite) is PracticeMaster by STI (**www.practicemaster.com**), which is the choice of most solo and small firms in our area. Version 16 was released in early 2011 and contained some significant new features. Version 16.2 improved upon those features and is the current shipping version. PracticeMaster comes in four versions: Basic, PracticeMaster, Platinum, and SQL. The first license for PracticeMaster Basic Edition is already included if you have the Tabs3 billing software. The Basic Edition is just that—basic. The regular version of PracticeMaster contains a number of useful features that most lawyers would desire. You can view a comparison chart for PracticeMaster at **www.tabs3.com/products/practicemaster/pm_comparison.html**.

PracticeMaster introduced workflows with version 16. Workflows are essentially triggers that automate tasks within the software. In addition, PracticeMaster has one of the best e-mail integration schemes that we've seen. Smartphone support is excellent as well, especially with Tabs3 Connect.

PracticeMaster and Tabs3 licenses include the first 12 months of maintenance. This is the same as the distribution plan used by Time Matters. Perhaps it is a new trend to automatically include maintenance as a way to ensure that users pay for support. PracticeMaster Basic is no longer available as a separate purchase. The cost of the regular PracticeMaster version is $600 (including 12 months of maintenance) for the first active user license, and each additional license will set you back another $280. The pricing hasn't changed since last year.

In addition to the regular PracticeMaster version, STI offers PracticeMaster in a client server version, which scales to larger implementations. The Platinum version costs $1,320 (including 12 months of maintenance) for the first user license and $365 for each additional user. Don't forget to add the cost of the client server environment when calculating the total cost of the project. As an example, the Platinum Server Software is required for any client server implementation of Tabs3 or PracticeMaster. This Server Software could cost from $965 for eight connections up to $7,475 for 1,024 server connections. An even more robust implementation would be using Platinum SQL Server Software. Cost for the SQL version is $1,320 for eight connections up to $39,340 for 1,024 server connections.

Version 17 of PracticeMaster should be available by the time this book is published. There are several new features planned for the release. Quick-Views combines a filter, column layout, and default sort to quickly change the view on the records you see. Smart tabs allow an additional level of filtering by displaying a row of tabs at the bottom of the list. QuickViews can also be shared with other users. Another new feature is the appearance of a search box at the top right corner of the List tab on every PracticeMaster file. There are many more new features and updates to the current functionality of PracticeMaster with the new release.

Mobile access is available with the Platinum versions of PracticeMaster and Tabs3 with the maintenance contract. It is called Tabs3 Connect and is included at no extra charge. Tabs3 Connect gives you access to Tabs3 and PracticeMaster anywhere you can connect to the Internet. This means you can get to your data from your smartphone or other mobile device. You have access to your client and contact information, fee and cost entry, personal and firm wide calendar, and more. The connection is secured using SSL, and the data resides in your Tabs3/PracticeMaster environment in your office. You must have the Platinum Editions of Tabs3 and PracticeMaster to take advantage of Tabs3 Connect. The requirement for the Platinum Edition is going to put this feature out of the reach of many solo and small firm lawyers, which is very unfortunate, especially since Tabs3 Connect is the best remote access solution to practice management data we have ever seen. You can learn more about Tabs3 Connect by visiting **www.tabs3.com/products/tabs3_connect/tabs3_connect.html**.

Finally, it is highly recommended that you obtain the trial version of PracticeMaster. This will help you determine whether the product is right for your practice and your installed infrastructure. We don't think you can go wrong with this product. It is constantly being improved, and the support is among the best in the industry.

Clio

Clio (**www.goclio.com**) is a SaaS (Software as a Service) solution that is used by solo, small, and mid-sized firms. Access is via an Internet browser, which means it will work just fine on an Apple computer. Themis Solutions, the maker of Clio, is based in Vancouver, British Columbia, and has the excellent reputation of listening to its customers and is constantly enhancing Clio based on user suggestions.

Clio is a full-featured practice management platform. Features such as document management, time tracking, calendaring, tasks, billing, and so on, provide a complete solution. The billing component works well for hourly and flat fee billing. You have control over billing rates at the activity or matter level. Clio is highly customizable. Custom fields can be inserted into any matter file. These custom fields have many different formats, so lawyers can enter dates, dollar amounts, website addresses, and even full text paragraphs.

Clio can also be configured to synchronize with Outlook and Gmail to provide bidirectional syncing of calendar, contact, and task entries. Clio also integrates with many online service providers like Box, Dropbox, Google Drive, and NetDocuments. Like many other practice management products, Clio is constantly being improved, as can be seen by the increased integration with third-party products.

Clio's dedicated iOS application makes it easy to manage your law firm from your mobile Apple device. Clio also has a mobile web version of its service, making Clio accessible on Android and BlackBerry mobile phones as well as on iPads and other types of tablets.

Another key feature is the ability to use the Amazon S3 cloud for storage of your data. This means that you have complete control over your data. Your data is automatically backed up to Amazon S3 on a weekly basis. Once the data is replicated to the Amazon cloud, you then have the option of downloading the data to your own computer. There is no additional cost to use this feature other than the cost from Amazon, which is pennies per gigabyte.

Lastly, Clio provides extensive support to customers free-of-charge. In-house telephone support is available 12 hours a day. The same service is also available by e-mail and live online chat. Training classes are available online 2 days a week. Clio also offers a library of training articles and videos.

Be sure to take advantage of the free thirty-day trial to make sure Clio will work for you. The cost is $49 per month for each lawyer that uses Clio and $25 per month for each support staff user. Discounts are available as a member benefit from more than 30 state and municipal bar associations and the American Bar Association. Be sure to ask your bar association if a discount is available.

Clio is one of our favorite SaaS practice management systems, and we highly recommend it. Several of our clients have converted to Clio and never looked back.

Rocket Matter

Rocket Matter is another SaaS practice management system and has been around since 2007. Rocket Matter is a web-based practice management system designed specifically for the legal industry. It also contains a time and billing function, which provides almost all you need for your law practice. Rocket Matter is very popular among Macintosh users, as it is web-based. There really isn't any case management application that is geared toward the Apple user community, so Rocket Matter meets that need through web browser access. You can still use Rocket Matter if you are a Windows shop, since all you need is an Internet connection and a web browser.

Many practice management providers offer specific apps for the mobile market. Rocket Matter is no exception. There are specific apps for iOS and Android devices.

Rocket Matter recently introduced a new offering called Portal 2.0, which allows users to create branded portals. You have the ability to share calendar information, documents, and invoices with clients or anybody else. The portal integrates with LawPay, allowing clients to pay their invoices online. Another announced feature is the integration with Copy2Contact to add new entries to your Rocket Matter contacts.

Rocket Matter will cost you $59.99 per month for the first user, $49.99 per month for the second through sixth users. In addition, Rocket Matter offers discounts if you make a longer commitment (more than month-to-month) and pay quarterly, annually, or for a two-year term. The discounts—10 percent for quarterly payment, 15 percent for annual payment, or 20 percent for the two-year term—apply to the initial user fee of $59.99/month and the $49.99 for users two through six. Larger discounts are available, but you have to contact Rocket Matter to see what those costs would be. These dollars can add up quickly when compared to an on-premise solution. As an example, your annual costs will be over $3,000 if you have five users paid on a monthly basis. You could get that cost down to around $2,500 a year for the five users if you commit to a two-year term. There is a 30-day money-back guarantee, so you can try it out before making the financial commitment.

Rocket Matter is a SaaS implementation and carries the same issues as other providers. The data is being held by a third party even though it is transmitted on an encrypted channel. Like Clio, Rocket Matter is always working on improvements to its product. It now provides offline access to your data. You can download your billable time, matters, calendar, and contacts on demand. Those who have used Rocket Matter generally give it favorable reviews, and we recommend that solos and small firms who want a SaaS solution take a look at both Clio and Rocket Matter.

Firm Manager

LexisNexis has its version of a hosted case management system, which is called Firm Manager. It appears that Lexis has Rocket Matter and Clio squarely in its crosshairs as it competes in the SaaS market. Firm Manager is priced at $44.99 per month for the first user and $29.99 per month for each additional user. This puts it in a similar price band as the more established Clio and Rocket Matter. There may be additional discounts for some local bar associations, and LexisNexis is offering a special deal for newly admitted lawyers. Newly admitted lawyers can get Firm Manager for free through July 2014 and then for $24.99 per month through the end of 2014. We see this as an attempt to "shoehorn" into the solo/small firm market.

Frankly, we don't think Firm Manager is going to get much traction, especially since there is no billing component at the present time. LexisNexis has announced that it is working on billing functions to be available in early 2014. There is no announcement about whether the price will increase once billing is available.

MyCase

We are starting to see a lot of buzz surrounding another web-based case management product, so we decided to add it to this chapter. MyCase is similar to the other products and provides similar functions, such as shared firm calendars and reminders, tasks, contact management, document organization, time and billing, and so on. There is even an iPhone app to facilitate mobile access.

MyCase uses Amazon services to deliver its product to the end user. MyCase runs on Amazon EC2 cloud servers and is backed up using Amazon S3 storage. Data is transferred using SSL encryption, and all sensitive information is encrypted before being written to disk. We're not sure what constitutes sensitive information, but at least some amount of data is encrypted in storage. A key differentiator for MyCase is the client access portal. You have the ability to allow each client access to calendars, documents, and billing details based on permissions you set.

MyCase costs $39 per month for each lawyer and $29 per month for each paralegal or staff member. Each account includes unlimited data storage, unlimited client access, tech support, and online training. There is a free 30-day trial, which we recommend you take advantage of. We don't have any clients using MyCase, but the feedback on the listservs has been positive.

Others

There are additional products available, but some of the vendors aren't public with the cost or system requirements. We are less than impressed with companies that aren't open about their pricing and technical requirements. Products like ProLaw (Thomson Elite) and AbacusLaw (Abacus Data System Incorporated) require you to fill out a contact form so that a representative can contact you about pricing. It appears as if LexisNexis is heading down this road too, since pricing for additional licenses of Time Matters is no longer available on its website. We are not fond of this practice and recommend a relationship with more open vendors, especially when you are entering this arena and want to make an apples-to-apples comparison.

CHAPTER FIFTEEN

Time and
Billing Software

PROBABLY THE SECOND MOST important function of your law practice is billing your clients for services rendered. Practicing law is clearly the most important, but getting paid is second, thereby ensuring the continued success and sustainability of your practice. Lawyers tend to hate the billing process and are not much fonder of the software that helps them generate invoices. There are still a lot of solos and small firms generating invoices manually. We'll look at both options and try to give you some guidance.

There are a lot of options for generating your bills, from a completely manual system to the fully automatic capture and assembly of invoices. There are two components that comprise items in your bills. One is the time component. This component is calculated by taking the hourly rate and applying it to the amount of time spent on a task. You can capture this time manually or automatically while the task is being accomplished. Flat fees are also considered time components, where the dollar amount is applied irrespective of the time spent. The second component is the fixed-cost items of the invoice. This would include such expenses as postage, copier costs, filing fees, courier charges, and any other fixed fees. As with the time components, you can track these expenses manually or automatically (to some level or another) through the use of technology.

We are seeing more and more firms adopting some sort of AFAs (Alternative Fee Arrangements) for their practice. It may be flat fee only or a hybrid type of billing, where there may be a flat fee portion and an hourly portion. AFAs are more complicated to automate because of the various customized rules that may apply. The good news is that many of the software packages are sophisticated enough to handle customized rules, and they are getting better and better as time goes by. You may have to deal with some manual override techniques if the billing software can't accommodate a particular AFA scenario.

Manual Generation

Pencil and paper are the simplest way to capture time and expense. With manual generation, however, you must remember to log your time, number of copies, or whatever other chargeable component needs to be tracked. Make no mistake about it, studies have shown over and over again that this manual tracking results in a lot of lost time and expense. Because a lawyer's time equals money, many lawyers are shortchanging themselves by not moving to a technology-based solution.

Nevertheless, if this is what you do, on a periodic basis (daily, monthly, at the end of the case, and so forth) you total the charges and generate the bill. Many solo practitioners start by using a word processing package to generate their bills to save some money. They are professional enough in appearance but still require manually adding up numbers and multiplying other numbers. In addition, there has to be another method to keep track of payments made by the client and/or transfers of funds from other sources, such as the trust account. As the practice becomes more complicated, the billing process becomes more subject to mistakes.

If you must start with a manual method for generating your invoices, invest in billing software as soon as possible to improve your accuracy, maximize your income, and minimize your losses.

Accounting Software—QuickBooks

Some lawyers are actually using a financial accounting package to generate their bills. Probably one of the most popular software applications is QuickBooks by Intuit (**quickbooks.intuit.com**). Using QuickBooks to generate invoices allows the firm to have a total financial package, where all sorts of financial reports are available. However, productivity reports are not available. You won't be able to easily determine how many billable hours are attributed to a specific individual or how much money you lost due to write-offs. One advantage of using QuickBooks is the ability to generate payroll. This may not be a compelling reason for many lawyers, especially given the added cost, complexity, and reporting requirements. In general, it is more cost-effective to use a third-party service provider, such as ADP or Paychex, to handle solo and small firm payrolls. QuickBooks can also handle processing of credit card payments, thereby integrating another piece of the financials into a single product. We hear that most lawyers began using QuickBooks because their accountant told them to. Make sure your accountant sets up your chart of accounts in QuickBooks so you know where certain charges and fees should go. Your CPA should be familiar with financials for a law firm. If not, it's probably time to look for a new accountant.

QuickBooks comes in several different versions, and there is even an online version that allows access from any computer and does not require installing any software. We don't recommend using the online version, as it requires that your data be stored at Intuit. Your financial data is highly sensitive, and we recommend that you control your own data and not risk compromise by holding it at a third-party site. Consider, too, the possibly severe consequences if the third party is "down" and you can't manage the financial part of your law practice. In the last quarter of 2010, Intuit announced that it was shutting down the Quicken Online service and users could only export their data in CSV (comma separated values) format. While Quicken is a consumer-based product, we certainly wouldn't want to be stuck in the same situation if Intuit decided to shut down QuickBooks Online.

Since QuickBooks is an accounting package, some knowledge of financial principles is helpful. You will need to set up a chart of accounts for your practice. We recommend consulting with your accountant before configuring QuickBooks so that your financial categories are consistent with the accountant's needs. If you are new to QuickBooks, you may want to consider purchasing a support plan to help you learn the features of the software and get technical help. Many local community colleges also offer evening classes for QuickBooks, which would be a relatively inexpensive way to get some training in how to use the product.

The QuickBooks versions vary in cost from $249.95 up to $999.95 per user for the Enterprise version. The cost variance is due to the capabilities of the software and the number of concurrent user licenses that are needed. Most solo and small firms will find that QuickBooks Pro is more than sufficient for their needs. The cost is $249.95 for a single user. In previous years, Intuit offered a three-pack license at a reduced rate over the single user cost. That discount is no longer available, and three licenses will be three times the single user cost. Besides the Windows version, a version for Macintosh computers is also available. Accountants love it when lawyers use QuickBooks as their billing software. They can take the QuickBooks data file at the end of the year and generate tax returns with relative ease.

However, we don't recommend using QuickBooks for billing for several reasons. First, the invoices are very sterile looking and can't be made to appear more professional. The data is there and clients can understand the information, but the invoice format lacks any ability to have graphics, differing fonts, or rearrangement of how the information appears on the page. Properly showing remaining balances is an issue too. This can be a real problem for those who want to show trust account balances and transfers or automatically indicate how much evergreen retainers need to be replenished. As previously mentioned, QuickBooks won't provide you with any productivity reports either. You're going to have to find a different way to determine how many write-down hours an associate had for a month or the amount of no-charge entries by client. In spite of these limitations, we still see a lot of lawyers using QuickBooks.

Billing Specific—Timeslips

Arguably the most popular and widely used billing software among solo and small firm lawyers is Timeslips by Sage (**www.timeslips.com**). Timeslips is a billing-specific software package that generates bills, tracks receivables, and manages trust accounting. We see many Timeslips installations in solo and small firm offices, especially those that have no case management system. Even so, we are beginning to see firms going more and more with the integrated solutions that we describe later on.

Probably one of the reasons for the popularity of Timeslips is that it can be configured specifically for the legal industry and supports the LEDES (Legal Electronic Data Exchange Standard) billing format. When you first install Timeslips, you select the type of business. This configures Timeslips to use the types of tasks and expenses that are specific to the industry. As an example, when you select the legal profession, default tasks are automatically created for tasks that are performed in the law office. There will be tasks for consultations, document review, depositions, and so forth. The expense names are also automatically created and would include such costs as copier usage, courier fees, postage, and the like. Trust accounting is also built into Timeslips, which is another reason the software is very popular in solo and small firm offices. You can configure Timeslips automatically to deduct fees earned from the trust account or leave it as a manual transfer process. In addition, Timeslips can automatically create the dollar amount to place on the invoice to bring the retainer amount back to a set level. This is a very popular feature for those lawyers who have evergreen retainer arrangements.

Timeslips is licensed on a per-machine basis. Each computer that needs to access Timeslips will require the purchase of a license. In a small office, it is often the case that only one computer is used to process billing. The timekeepers (typically lawyers) may elect to manually track their time on paper and give the time sheets to the office manager or bookkeeper for entry into Timeslips. This arrangement keeps licensing costs down and allows for growth in the law firm. As the firm grows, additional licenses may be purchased and network access configured for the Timeslips database. Larger firms that may use a terminal server need licenses only for the number of concurrent users. With the expanded interest and implementation of virtual computers, this concurrent license model may be a way to control costs.

The current version is Timeslips 2014. It costs $499.99 for a single station, which is the same price as for the last three years. Additional network stations may be added up to a total of ten stations. The cost per workstation keeps getting less and less as the number of workstations goes up. With ten workstations you will pay $297.49 per computer. If you only need five workstations, then your cost will be $319.99 per computer. You'll have to contact Sage if you need eleven or more licenses. Support options are also available for Timeslips. If you have never used Timeslips, we recommend that you purchase a support plan at least for the first year of operation. After the first year, we do not recommend that you prebuy any support unless you intend to use and implement features of the newer versions. Access to the free online knowledge base is usually sufficient to work through most issues that you are likely to experience.

Two support plans are available. If you are going to purchase support, the Billing Assurance Essential Plan is recommended because it covers most incidents that you will encounter. The Billing Assurance Premium Plan is more inclusive and includes database repair services. We don't feel that the Premium Plan is worth the additional cost. You should be backing up your database on a daily basis anyway. Timeslips was notorious for data corruption issues with past versions of the software, but the recent versions of Timeslips databases seem to be much more stable. Currently, we use Timeslips for billing and haven't experienced a data corruption issue for over five years, but we do have our daily backups as well.

Timeslips can also link with QuickBooks. Setting up this integration is a manual process and can be complicated. You have to make sure that the Timeslips tasks and expenses have a corresponding QuickBooks account. Permissions (for both Timeslips and QuickBooks) also need to be considered. If you run a networked version of QuickBooks, multiuser versus single user could also cause some complications with the integration. A reader of a previous edition of this book advised us that Timeslips technical support will not help with any of the accounting aspects related to the QuickBooks link, as they feel it is giving financial advice and do not want the liability. Perhaps this is one of the reasons why our clients who use Timeslips and QuickBooks don't bother with the integration and manually input data to QuickBooks.

Some of the providers for case management software have also built links to Timeslips. Case management product links are possible for Abacus Law, Amicus Attorney, Legal Files Software, and Time Matters. Contact the provider of the case management software if you are interested in how the link would work and what the limitations are.

Billing for a Mac

There are not that many legal-specific software applications for Mac computers. Most Mac users will migrate toward web-based products for their firms. There are some native Mac applications, but like the Windows world, more and more users are moving toward the cloud.

Bill4Time

SaaS offerings are very popular in the Mac community. All you need is an Internet connection and a web browser. Bill4Time (**www.bill4time.com**) is one billing package we see used in law offices with Macs. It is a secure hosted environment that is available from any computer at any time. A free thirty-day trial will allow you to see if it fits your needs. Bill4Time now has a legal specific version, which adds ABA Activity, Expense and Task Codes; LEDES and Litigation Advisor Exports; Trust Accounting with Summaries and Reports; and Easily Check for Conflicts of Interest. Most lawyers will want to get the Legal Solo or Legal Pro version. All legal versions allow for unlimited clients and unlimited projects. The Legal Solo version limits data storage to 2GB. The Legal Pro version has a 10GB storage limit, and the Legal Enterprise version has unlimited data storage. One nice feature of Bill4Time is that it includes a mobile app. This means you can use your smartphone (Android or iPhone) to enter your time and expenses while out of the office. As we mentioned before, you need to keep track of all your billable activities—otherwise you are losing money. The mobile app feature is a great way to help maximize your revenue.

The Legal Solo version of Bill4Time is $19.99 per month and includes one user license. You can add only one additional user at a cost of $9.99 per month. This may be fine for the solo practitioner, but some small firms may need more than two users. The Legal Pro version is $39.99 per month and also includes one user license. However, you can add unlimited users at a cost of $9.99 per month for each user. Finally, the Legal Enterprise version is $99.99 per month and also includes one user license. Like the Pro version, unlimited users can be added for $9.99 per month per user. We think that $99.99 per month for unlimited storage and premium support is a bit much for a web-based billing package. At that rate, we would recommend investigating other billing alternatives to include on-premise solutions.

EasyTime

Many of the practice management implementations also include some sort of billing mechanism, so you may not need a separate software application. We'll mention a few of the billing packages that are available for the Mac, but we certainly can't mention them all. One such stand-alone package for the Mac is EasyTime. EasyTime, by BrightLight Software, runs natively on Mac OS X and does not require any third-party database packages. The current version is 2.5, released January 21, 2013. It requires Mac OS 10.6 or higher on an Intel 32/64-bit processor. The cost is $135 for a single user and $215 for a network version, which is the same price as for the last three years.

Billings Pro

Another popular package is Billings Pro (**www.marketcircle.com/billingspro/**) by Marketcircle. Billings Pro has changed its pricing and feature listing since our last edition of this book. The cost model has moved to one that identifies how many invoices, statements, or estimates you can generate per month. The Freelance plan costs $5 per month and limits you to five invoices, five estimates, and five statements per month. This plan doesn't seem to be very practical unless you only have a couple of very large clients and don't invoice all that often. The Professional plan is $10 per month and gives you unlimited invoices, estimates, and statements per month. Additional users can be added at a cost of $10 per month per user. Since there is no contract commitment with Billings Pro, we would recommend starting with the Professional plan. If it looks like Billings Pro is something that works for your firm, then convert to the Professional Yearly plan, which costs $99 for a full year. Additional users are also $99 per user for the year.

If you already have your own network and server, you can opt for hosting Billings Pro on your own equipment. The server-based version is called Self-Serve and is available for a one-time fee per user of $199.95. As with most of the products mentioned, be sure to take advantage of the free thirty-day trial before purchase.

Integrated Packages

Many of the case management products now support integration with billing packages. This means that you enter your information into the case management system and the time or expense is automatically captured for the billing process. There are advantages to using the same vendor for your case management and billing needs. The products are designed to work together and share information in a very efficient manner. However, selecting these all-in-one packages may not give you the best features of each package. If you really want a "best of breed" implementation, then make sure you investigate how the case management and billing packages share the data. Many case management applications provide links to billing packages by other vendors. Be careful to understand how to configure these links, especially if configuration is a manual process. We've seen clients who added tasks to their case management software and forgot to define the linkage to their billing software. This means that you may not bill for the effort when you use these newly defined tasks.

PCLaw

LexisNexis has several billing options to address the needs of solo and small firm law offices. A very popular package is PCLaw Version 13 (**www.lexisnexis.com/law-firm-practice-management/pclaw/**), which includes the new mobility function. PCLaw includes some features that you would expect from a case management system. You can keep track of contacts, calendar entries, phone calls, notes, tasks, and so on. This may be a good alternative for a solo practitioner to keep start-up costs down.

It appears as if Lexis is back to its old tricks. Two years ago you had the option of purchasing PCLaw without maintenance. Last year and this year, maintenance is included with each license of PCLaw. No more opting out of the annual maintenance for new purchases. You certainly have the option of not renewing your maintenance agreement, although you may not want to let it lapse. The Annual Maintenance Plan (AMP) bundles technical support, software upgrades, support, training, and access to PCLaw Mobility Service.

Transparency doesn't seem to be a hallmark of LexisNexis. If you want to know the cost of renewing your maintenance plan or add additional PCLaw users, you must already own the product or contact a LexisNexis representative. The pricing is no longer publicized on the LexisNexis website. As we've mentioned before, this is not a practice that we are fond of, and we recommend using products from vendors with transparent pricing.

Juris is another billing software application offered by LexisNexis. It is typically used by larger law firms or in integrating with Time Matters. We have never seen Juris used in a solo or small firm setting. As with some of the other products mentioned, you have to contact Lexis to get pricing information. You can't even get a single license cost like you can with Time Matters or PCLaw.

Tabs3

Another popular billing package is Tabs3 by STI. STI defines a timekeeper as someone whose time is tracked in the software. Tabs3 is the companion product to PracticeMaster, which is the case management software from STI. Tabs3 pricing is based on the number of billable entities. The solo and small firm pricing for a single-user is $415 for two timekeepers and increases to $675 for five timekeepers. You'll need to purchase the multi-user version if you need more than one person to access the data at the same time. The basic multiuser version starts at $675 for two timekeepers and is $1,340 for five timekeepers. Like LexisNexis, the first year of maintenance is included in the license cost.

The regular multiuser version is available for five, nine, and nineteen timekeepers. The cost is $1,340, $1,915, and $3,065 respectively. The Platinum version of Tabs3 costs $1,770 for five timekeepers up to $15,940 for 100+ (maximum of 999) timekeepers.

See the Case Management chapter (Chapter Fourteen) to learn about the new mobility features of Tabs3 Connect, which became available in version 16.2 Platinum Edition. Even though Tabs3 Connect is a killer application for mobile access to your data, we don't think many solo or small firms will spend the money to have Platinum versions of both Tabs3 and PracticeMaster along with the requisite maintenance plan.

Version 17 of Tabs3 should be available by the time this book is published. One of the new features is Undo Split Billing. This will let you reverse the split billing process for individual clients. Another new feature is Automatic Update Notifications, which will let you know when a critical update is available.

Unlike other billing packages, Tabs3 has separated out various financial functions and priced them as individual components. As an example, there are additional components, such as trust accounting, general ledger, and accounts payable. This means that you can expand Tabs3 from a pure billing package into a complete accounting package. You can find more information about Tabs3 at **www.tabs3.com**. Tabs3 is as highly regarded by us as its case management counterpart, PracticeMaster. It is also consistently rated highly by legal software experts.

Amicus Accounting

A less widely used billing option is provided by Amicus Attorney. Many solo and small firms use Amicus Attorney as a practice management package, but few use the billing option. Two billing packages are available, depending on which version of Amicus you are running. Use the Amicus Premium Billing application if you are running Amicus Attorney Premium Edition. If you are running Amicus Attorney Small Firm Edition, then the Amicus Small Firm Accounting software is for you.

Amicus Premium Billing 2013 adds billing, collections, and trusts to your Amicus Attorney installation. Like most billing packages, it lets you capture time and expenses for hourly, flat fee, and contingent billing. Each license is priced at $199, which makes it one of the lowest-cost billing packages. This product will not run by itself; it is an add-on to the Amicus Attorney case management software. Maintenance and technical support plans are also available. You can purchase a maintenance plan that includes unlimited technical support, Mobility, and product updates. The first license will set you back $550 a year ($130 increase over last year—ouch), but it also covers Amicus Attorney software maintenance. Each additional license is $450 ($130 increase over last year—double ouch), so the dollars will add up quickly if you have more than a couple of users. You also have the option of purchasing a technical support plan only, without product updates. Unlimited technical support for a year is $295 ($100 less than last year) for the first license (includes the required Amicus Attorney support) and $145 (same as last year) for each additional license.

Amicus Small Firm Accounting 2013 integrates with the Amicus Attorney Small Firm product. There is a major change for the 2013 version. Unlike previous versions, the Amicus Small Firm Accounting package now requires that you also have the Amicus Attorney Small Firm Classic software. This is the same requirement as the Premium version. To use the billing software, you have to have the appropriate base case management software (Premium or Small Firm). The initial license cost for Amicus Small Firm Accounting is $499 (a $100 increase over last year), and each additional license is $399 (a $100 increase over last year). Like the Premium package, the Small Firm version lets you purchase maintenance or technical-support-only plans. The maintenance plan, which includes product updates, Mobility, and unlimited technical support, is $385 (a $35 increase from last year), including support for the required base product. Each additional license is $305 (a $55 increase from last year) to include the required Small Firm maintenance. Unlimited technical support only is the same cost as the Premium version. The cost is $295 per year for the first license and $145 per year for each additional license.

One of the higher-level (expensive) billing alternatives is provided by ProLaw, which is a Thomson Elite product. ProLaw is an integrated package, and the billing component is not available as a separate function. Very few solos and small law firms have chosen this route in our experience.

Most of our clients that use stand-alone applications have chosen QuickBooks or Timeslips for billing, and they are generally quite happy with what they have chosen—though everything has a learning curve. All of these vendors are happy to let you sample their product in one manner or another, so don't hesitate to try before you buy. Also, if you aren't keen on accounting, talk to your friends who are equally numbers challenged and see what has worked for them. In many cases, the choice has been made by someone at the firm who is going to perform the accounting/bookkeeping functions, and that's fine. As long as you stay with one of the "majors," you won't be left scrambling to find someone who knows your obscure time and billing package if that person leaves.

CHAPTER SIXTEEN

Litigation Programs

SEVERAL PROGRAMS AUTOMATE CERTAIN litigation support functions, and while they offer different features, they fall into two general categories: case organization programs and courtroom presentation programs. Case organization programs are databases that are set up to analyze and manage facts and evidence. The common ones include LexisNexis Concordance (**www.lexisnexis.com/en-us/litigation/products/concordance.page**), LexisNexis CaseMap (**www.lexisnexis.com/en-us/litigation/products/ casemap.page**), Westlaw Case Notebook (**west.thomson.com/products/ services/case-notebook**), and Sanction Solutions Verdical (**www.verdict systems.com/Software/Verdical**). Summation is now a product provided by Access Data. The litigation support products many of you know, such as iBlaze, are still being offered by Access Data. Access Data is leveraging its forensic experience and merging e-discovery tools in an attempt to provide a total end-to-end solution. The Summation products are now integrated in the product offerings from Access Data. The newly named offerings are AD eDiscovery, AD ECA, and Summation. CaseMap from LexisNexis is one of the most popular packages for solo and small firm lawyers, given its lower cost and ease of use.

Trial presentation programs manage and display electronic evidence, including exhibits, video and text depositions, sound files, and more. They facilitate quick access during trials and hearings and include on-the-fly annotation, such as highlighting and call-outs. Trial presentation programs include Trial Director (**www.indatacorp.com/Products/Trial/ trialDirector.aspx**) and Visionary (**www.visionarylegal.com/products/ product.aspx?ProductsID=3**). Sanction (**sanction.com/software**) is now a product of LexisNexis. Sanction is still available as a separate product as of this writing. More maturity is now evident in the trial presentation packages for the iPad. Products such as TrialPad (**www.trialpad.com**) turn the iPad into a presentation tool for litigators. Since we are seeing so many litigators equipped with an iPad, we would highly recommend starting with TrialPad for your trial presentation software. For $89.99 you can't go wrong giving it a try. Trial Director for the iPad is a free download from the app store, but it is a much more limited version of the flagship product for the PC. Free is a good price for the solo and small firm lawyer, but reviews indicate that inData Corporation has a long way to go with its iPad application. Try it out, but we'll guess that you will end up using TrialPad instead. There are several other competitors of TrialPad, such as Exhibit A and ExhibitView. We feel that TrialPad has maintained the beachhead for iPad trial presentation software. Unless you have a compelling specific reason to use one of the other products, it appears that TrialPad is the product of choice for the majority of litigators.

Most of the mentioned products have free downloads for a trial period or online demos. Although we do not review them in detail, they should be considered by lawyers with litigation practices. Be sure to read the iWin materials from Tom Mighell and Paul Unger, which are included in Appendix A, for products that are applicable to the iPad.

CHAPTER SEVENTEEN

Document Management

DOCUMENT MANAGEMENT SOFTWARE SOLUTIONS can be relatively expensive for the solo or small firm operation, although there are some cost effective alternatives. Several of the better-known document management products tend to be used more for enterprise-size companies because of their cost and complexity. As the industry matures, vendors are merging the functions of document management, content management, and knowledge management. This is especially true as electronic files are becoming a critical component of discovery. You may see applications described as document management systems, content management systems, knowledge management systems, or even enterprise content management systems. Just because a vendor chooses to describe its product in a particular way doesn't mean there is anything unique or special about it. In general, all of the terms previously mentioned are used for applications that organize information.

The main purpose of a document management system is to organize information into a usable and searchable form. How many times have you looked for a file or document but couldn't remember the name or location? A document management system allows for fast and easy access to the data, whether in paper or electronic form. It also provides access control and enforceability of rules. As an example, perhaps one of your rules is that every document has a specific category (programmed ahead of time) tagged to it. This makes for consistency and removes the human error in typing or misspelling the category tag.

DocuShare

We will mention just a few of the products that are available, but understand that document management systems are not generally designed for small-scale operations. Xerox's DocuShare (**docushare.xerox.com**) has been around for many years. Pricing is available directly from Xerox or through partners. There is now an entry-level version of DocuShare (DocuShare Express) available for small to mid-sized office installations, which starts at a couple of thousand dollars for ten users. The current version (DocuShare 6.6) requires a 64-bit server, which would significantly increase costs if you don't have one available. DocuShare Express can run on 32-bit versions of Windows 2003 Server R2 or SP2 and Windows 2008 Server SP2. DocuShare may be a viable alternative, especially if you already have a Xerox copier that you could use for scanning documents. Be sure to take advantage of the free thirty-day trial if you are considering acquiring DocuShare.

WorkSite

It is really hard to stay current with a product that changes names and companies so many times over its life. Several years ago, we knew it as Interwoven. Then it was known as Autonomy iManage WorkSite. Today, Autonomy is an HP company and the product name is just WorkSite. (**www.autonomy.com/products/worksite**). As with DocuShare, expect to pay thousands of dollars for this system. It is a highly regarded document management environment (if you can remember the name) but is also geared more toward the intermediate to large-scale firms.

Worldox

The most popular and most used document management system for solo and small firm operations is Worldox (**www.worldox.com**). Worldox is licensed on a concurrent user basis and not per seat. There are now three versions of Worldox. GX3 Professional is the standard network client server installation that has been around for ages. It is the traditional desktop version. The next version is GX3 Enterprise, which is adapted for multi-office, remote access environments. It is typically hosted at a data center and has full communication with local applications, including Microsoft Office, Outlook, and third-party products such as case management. The final version is a SaaS hosted solution called GX3 Cloud. With the GX3 Cloud solution, your data is hosted on Worldox servers in its data center.

The cost for Worldox GX3 Professional is $425 per concurrent user, which makes it very affordable for solo and small firms, especially since there are no minimum seat purchase requirements. Annual maintenance is $88 per license and is mandatory for new orders. No separate server is required, and the indexer can be run on any workstation-class computer. The computer resource requirements for Worldox are very light when compared to other document management systems. The application is very robust and easy to use, hence its popularity within the legal community.

GX3 Enterprise is intended for multiple offices and remote access environments. It looks and acts just like the local desktop (GX3 Professional) version. You must contact Worldox to get pricing information at this time.

Worldox also offers a Web Mobile addition to the Worldox software. The mobile edition gives you access to your documents from multiple devices and locations. It currently supports a wide range of devices, including any web-browser notebook or desktop, iPads, BlackBerry smartphones, Android devices, iPhones, Treos, and smartphones. There are two pricing models for the mobile access. For $30 per user per month, you can implement the SaaS hosted solution, which installs the software on your indexer. The cost is $25 per user per month with a one year pre-payment. You can also install it on your own server, but the costs start to climb quickly. You will need a server license ($995), user licenses ($49 per named user), annual maintenance ($10 per user and $200 per server per year), a proxy server license ($600), and proxy server maintenance ($120). Doing the math, it will cost you $2,210 for five users in the first year. Years two and beyond would be $370 per year for the maintenance charges for the five user system. Installing your own Worldox/Web Mobile server makes financial sense if you plan to use it for two or more years.

Last year, Worldox released a Legal Hold feature. The Legal Hold feature will be a great benefit for firms and companies as part of the litigation process. If you are in litigation or if litigation is reasonably anticipated, you have an ethical requirement not to destroy any potentially relevant evidence. Legal Hold will let you assign rights and restrictions to files. You can even create restricted-access security groups so that only authorized employees can access the designated files. In addition, each action is tracked to create an audit trail showing who did what to which file. The key feature for Legal Hold is the ability to "lock" a file so that it cannot be changed. The best news? The Legal Hold feature is free for all Worldox GX3 Professional users. You can't ask for anything better than that. Well, perhaps you can—it is also very simple to use. We saw the demo in five minutes at ILTA's 2012 conference and that's all it took to learn how to use it. Do be forewarned that this is not litigation hold software, which includes many more features—Worldox is planning to expand its Legal Hold feature and we look forward to reviewing it.

This year, Worldox made an exciting announcement at ABA TECHSHOW in Chicago. The new product is Worldox for Mac, which includes many of the same functions as the Windows product. Worldox for Mac is not a stand-alone product. It requires an existing Worldox GX3 installation or the Worldox GX3 Cloud offering.

Case management systems (see the Case Management chapter) are also used to provide a certain level of document management. Your electronic files are referenced to a client or client matter, making them easily accessible at the click of a mouse. A key point to remember about true document management applications is their stringent enforcement of the classification rules. The user must use the system within the configured rules, and the rigid requirements sometimes frustrate people. In contrast, applications that are not specifically document management software aren't restrictive or mandatory. The danger is that data may be lost or misfiled when the rules are not stringently enforced. Worldox is an excellent choice for document management, as it integrates with almost every case management system available. It is consistently well reviewed by legal software experts.

Acrobat

Many solo and small firm offices are equipped with Adobe's Acrobat product. The latest versions of Acrobat provide the ability to manage documents. The collaboration components within Acrobat are used to organize and reference files in a manner similar to other document management systems.

Web-Based

Web-based document management systems are becoming very popular. The cost per user is typically more than purchasing a product for use within your firm, but you save on the hardware and internal support costs. The vendor provides the back-end hardware and software for the management of your documents. The nice part about web-based document management systems is that the information is accessible from any computer with an Internet connection. The bad part is that the vendor is holding your data and you are subject to the reliability of the Internet connection. If you elect to use one of the online document management systems, be aware of the security precautions for client data that is being held by a third party. At a minimum, make sure that the connection for accessing the documents is encrypted and that the data is stored in an encrypted form on the provider's equipment. You should also make sure that you have a copy of the data in your hands to avoid being "held hostage" by the third-party provider. And yes, we've seen that happen. More and more vendors now offer cloud solutions in addition to their traditional on-premise solutions.

NetDocuments

NetDocuments is a popular SaaS provider for document management. Many law firms, small to large, have had great experiences with Net Documents. We have heard lawyers say that it was very easy to install and configure. In one case, a lawyer converted his firm (tens of thousands of documents) over to NetDocuments in a weekend all by himself. NetDocuments provides all of the features you would expect in a document management system, in addition to matter-centric workspaces, e-mail management, collaboration, and mobile access.

There are three versions of NetDocuments: Basic, Professional, and Professional+. The Basic version is $20 per month per user, and the Professional version is $30 per month per user. The Professional+ version includes e-mail management and costs $38 per user per month. For all versions there is a base volume of storage allowed per user, with overage fees beyond the allowance. Your actual costs will vary depending on the selected package, since there are fees for e-mail management (except Professional+), local document storage, third-party integrations, extranet services, etc. You can see the costs for the various add-ons at **www.net documents.com/en-us/Pricing/AddOns**. We encourage you to take advantage of the thirty-day free trial before making any financial commitment.

Plain Folders

Finally, a very simple form of document management for solo and small firms is to follow a standard folder and file naming convention along with search software (see Chapter Twenty-Five, Utilities, for search tools).

Besides the cost for search software, this is a very low-cost solution. Some lawyers will use the search capabilities of Windows or Mac before even investing in supplemental search software. Typically, folders are named on a per-client or client-matter basis. Files are then given a very descriptive name, such as <client name>, followed by the file purpose and sometimes the date. As an example, *Rothburg request for admissions.doc* would be the file name for your request for admissions in the Rothburg matter. This is a very manageable method to organize data when your practice is small. As your practice grows, search software may be needed to assist in finding particular files pertaining to specific issues.

Searching

Search software such as dtSearch or X1 (see Chapter Twenty-Five, Utilities) can be used to index the files within your client folders so that you can quickly find the desired document. As an example, you may be looking for the document pertaining to the request for electronic evidence or something concerning a partner's Motorola cell phone.

If you are considering the purchase of a document management system, Worldox is an excellent first choice. We have implemented this software many times, and clients are always happy with it. No matter what product you are considering, see whether there is a trial version available, or at least participate in a demo of the product, to determine if it meets your firm's needs.

CHAPTER EIGHTEEN

Document Assembly

Essentially, DOCUMENT ASSEMBLY SOFTWARE automates the creation of legal documents that are used repeatedly. This would include such documents as wills, leases, contracts, and letters. You can think of document assembly as templates that can be used over and over. They shorten the time for document preparation and increase the efficiency of your practice. If you use flat fees, document assembly can be a godsend.

Document assembly software can be specialized for a particular industry, or it can be generic. As an example, specialized document assembly software is typically used in estate planning and tax preparation. In those situations, the user answers questions in a survey type of form and then the required documents are generated using the answers provided. If you have ever used one of the personal income tax programs (e.g., TurboTax, Tax-Cut), you've seen how document assembly works. You may see the term *document automation*, but it means the same thing as *document assembly* for our discussion.

HotDocs

In law firms, the top three document assembly packages according to the ABA's 2013 Legal Technology Survey Report are HotDocs, AIA Contract Documents, and ProLaw. HotDocs (**www.hotdocs.com**) is the most popular document assembly software by a large margin. HotDocs is a very powerful solution and has significantly matured over the years. It is composed of many different products, such as those used for template creation, cloud-based access, desktop template distribution, and centralized server-based distribution to the users. HotDocs Developer 11 (desktop based) is one of the most powerful platforms for document automation, and it allows you to convert word processing documents and PDF forms into templates. You create a template and determine what text to include or exclude, depending on the answers entered by the user. This is the survey-type entry that was described earlier. The presentation walks you through the questions to gather the data needed to generate the document. The current version supports Microsoft Word 2013 and WordPerfect 16. Hot-Docs User 11 is the other desktop product, and it is used for organizing, accessing, and running HotDocs document-generated apps. You can choose to generate a document using an existing answer file or create a new one on the fly.

As with other application software these days, HotDocs is available in a browser version, too. The product, HotDocs Server 10, allows for document assembly using a standard web browser. This is particularly helpful for remote users and means you can deploy templates via the Internet. HotDocs Server 10 must be deployed in conjunction with a web application. It shouldn't surprise you that there are two additional software packages available: HotDocs Workspace and HotDocs Workspace for SharePoint.

HotDocs must have read the 2012 edition of our book, where we criticized them for taking down the pricing for HotDocs and not making it publicly available. We are happy to say that pricing is once again publicly available. HotDocs Developer 10 costs $800, and HotDocs User is $330 per license. Online document automation begins with a base package (one to five users) costing $99/month with a twelve-month minimum. Volume discounts are available, but you will have to contact a HotDocs representative for a quote. Like many other software applications, HotDocs offers a thirty-day free trial. We always recommend the "try before you buy" process, especially if you are actually considering spending some money. Many of our friends on the lecture circuit regard HotDocs as *the* go-to document assembly software.

AIA Contract Documents

AIA Contract Documents (**www.aia.org/docs_default**) is a specialty package used for design and construction projects, so it's an excellent product for those dealing with construction law. In fact, the product was developed specifically with the law in mind. The generated documents conform to the laws in effect at the time of creation. Also, the AIA (American

Institute of Architects) documents are intended for nationwide use and are not restricted to specific states. A new single-seat license that allows for unlimited documents is $999 per year (same price as last year). You can reduce that cost to $719 ($20 increase from last year) if you are an AIA member. If you are a mid-size to large law firm, the license options range from $3,449 for an unlimited five-seat license up to $29,699 for an unlimited fifty-seat license.

There is an on demand service that will give you access to 110 of the most popular AIA Contract Documents. The price per document varies from $7.49 to $22.99. Once payment is confirmed, you are presented with a link to download the PDF file. You have 7 days from purchase to download the file. Once you've downloaded the file, just open the PDF using Adobe Reader 7.0 or above and fill in any of the optional data fields.

The limited license allows you to select document types from the entire AIA Contract Document library. The limited license plans "charge" a predetermined number of document units (DUs) when you save the final PDF. The document unit values range from 5 to 25 depending on the particular document you select. Two limited plans are available and cost from $209 per year for the Docs 100 license ($20 increase from last year; 100 DUs; must be an AIA member) to $499 per year for the Docs 300 license as a non-member ($10 increase from last year; 300 DUs; $329 as an AIA member).

ProLaw

ProLaw by Elite (**http://www.elite.com/prolaw/**) is an integrated software product designed to automate the practice of law, complete with the business functions of billing, accounting, and other financial management. It is a complete package and combines case and matter management along with its document assembly features. Smaller law firms will probably implement the ProLaw READY product. The document assembly component can create custom forms and templates with drag-and-drop fields. It can automatically convert documents to PDFs and create templates that easily merge with the elements from the ProLaw database. ProLaw's document assembly capability also integrates with Adobe Acrobat and Microsoft Word. Pricing for the system must be obtained directly from Elite. This is not a cheap alternative and requires some pretty hefty hardware to run with acceptable performance. In fairness, ProLaw is much, much more than a stand-alone document assembly product, such as HotDocs, so the cost comparison isn't apples to apples.

Final Words

HotDocs is the clear recommendation for solo and small firm lawyers wanting to embark on document assembly. As a generic package, it is very well suited for any type of law practice. HotDocs integrates with many document management and practice management packages. There are many choices for technical support, including HotDocs Wiki, HotDocs Forum, and HotDocs Documentation. HotDocs resellers are the primary method for consulting and product acquisition. Be sure to request the thirty-day trial and see if you can save some consulting expense by developing templates on your own.

CHAPTER NINETEEN

Cloud Computing

IT SEEMS LIKE EVERYBODY is talking about the "cloud." The really scary part is that many users don't know what it means to use cloud computing and believe that the weather impacts the cloud. For our discussion purposes, the cloud is generally viewed as an external computing resource that is typically accessed via the Internet. You can participate in cloud computing by putting your own equipment in a secure data center and accessing your data (and perhaps applications) via the Internet. If you don't use your own equipment and software but elect to purchase applications through third parties, then you are using a SaaS (Software as a Service) solution. To make it easy to understand, imagine that you don't own a copy of Microsoft Office; you simply go to a site on the Internet where your subscription allows you to use Office. The resulting data is held by the provider, not you. This is exactly the environment that Microsoft is pushing with its Office 365 product.

News from the ABA Legal Technology Research Center's 2013 survey of ABA lawyers:

- Web-based software is used by 30.7 percent of lawyers, up from 20.9 percent in 2012 and 1.5 percent in 2011.
- Solo practitioners were the most likely to respond affirmatively at 40.2 percent.
- Among those who had not used cloud computing, 46.3 percent said they did not intend to use the cloud in the future.

- Of those who had not used cloud computing, the top concerns they cited were:
    - 57.7 percent: confidentiality and security
    - 54.7 percent: less control of data because it's hosted by the provider
    - 54.7 percent: unfamiliarity with the technology
    - 51.7 percent: cost

The traditional client/server model puts total control in the hands of the law firm. The data is held internally, and access is controlled by the firm. You can choose to encrypt the data locally, which we recommend, or leave it in plain text. Either way, it is within the technology walls of the law firm and not directly accessible by any third party.

In contrast, the SaaS model puts your data in the hands of a third party. This is not necessarily a bad thing, but do you really know if the information is safe? Your contract with the provider may specify that the data be stored in encrypted form, but what if a disgruntled employee has access to tools that allow him or her to decrypt the data and sell it to the other side in a major litigation?

When you contract with a SaaS provider, you are required to accept the service as it is delivered to you. This means any upgrades or bug fixes will be implemented by the provider. Sound like a good thing? Just ask Ben Schorr, CEO of Roland Schorr, an information technology consulting firm with offices in Hawaii, Arizona, and Oregon, and author of *The Lawyer's Guide to Microsoft Word 2010*, *Microsoft OneNote in One Hour for Lawyers* and *The Lawyer's Guide to Microsoft Outlook 2013*, all published by the American Bar Association:

> One of my concerns about SaaS is the double-edged sword called "upgrades." A selling point of SaaS products is that the vendor just transparently updates it in the background, and you don't have to worry about it. Monday morning you log in and . . . "Oh, look, new features!" But what if you don't like those new features?
>
> What if you're on a tight deadline and Google decides to do a massive upgrade to Google Docs? Do you have time to get yourself and your staff up to speed on how the new version works? With Microsoft Office, you upgrade when you're good and ready. We do quite a bit of work with firms all over the country, in fact, helping them plan and approach that migration: training their staff, preparing for the various consequences of the rollout, and making sure their ancillary apps and add-ins are ready to support the new version. (Want some fun? Tell a managing

partner that the new version of her e-mail app is NOT compatible with her case management system . . . the day AFTER she upgrades.)

With SaaS, you don't generally get that. You may get no warning at all that features, user interface (UI), or behaviors are about to change. You certainly aren't going to get a chance to use it before your staff does so that you can get up to speed on it and be ready to answer questions when the 9:15 messenger run is waiting to go and the documents still aren't printed (unless you want to sign into the SaaS app at 3 a.m., I guess).

Hey, it's great that somebody else manages your upgrades and updates. That's usually a good thing. But it's not always. Unpredictability is not a quality I value in my mission-critical apps.

Enough said. Besides the data security and access concerns for the SaaS model, the financial stability of the provider may be a consideration, but it is becoming less of an issue as more and more vendors are providing cloud solutions. Even if you have adequate notice that the vendor will no longer provide a contracted service, the cost to migrate your data to another provider or bring it back in-house can be significant. This brings us to the topic of exit strategy. At some point, you will likely want to bring the function back within your IT control or move to another provider. The contract should provide for specific costs and timetables to facilitate the move. It should also specify what file format you will get. Will you get a copy of the complete SQL database along with the schema or just a comma delimited text file?

Another issue is the stability of the communications network. By design, you are dependent on the speed and quality of your Internet connection. Smart firms will have dual network connections to the Internet, although this will mean an increase in cost over what is normally installed at the firm. The Internet connection must be available at all times; otherwise, you will not have access to your data. There aren't many judges who are sympathetic to your problems if you miss a filing date because your Internet connection went down. And Internet connections, as we've all miserably learned, do sometimes go down—and always without notice.

To be fair, let's look at the upsides of SaaS . . . and yes, there are a few.

There can be some financial advantage to contracting service to a third-party provider. Your investment in hardware and software is minimized, since you are really only passing keyboard, mouse, and screen data over the communications link or accessing the application via a web browser. The actual processing occurs at the SaaS provider. All configuration and data hosting are external to your firm's infrastructure. Costs for the SaaS model can be based on the number of users or the amount of data storage volume. Either way, it is fairly easy to identify and budget for the cost of the service, which is a big selling point for a lot of firms. However, to get these "stable" price points, the contract terms are typically three to five years. This means that the firm must make a pretty long commitment to using the SaaS model and the specific provider.

Another advantage to the SaaS model is the rapid reaction time to changes. It is very fast to add new users or increase the amount of space for data storage. By the same measure, it is very fast to decrease the number of users or amount of storage space. This means that you are more flexible in controlling your costs. If your firm is in contraction mode, you can reduce expenses, assuming that the contract doesn't tie you to a minimum amount. Many firms like the mobility aspect of the SaaS model since they can access the applications from any machine with an Internet browser. Typically, there isn't anything special that needs to be installed on the client computer. The user needs only a browser and perhaps some type of plug-in to access the SaaS application. This means that it is easy to gain access to the firm's data from the office, home, or an Internet café in the Bahamas.

Too often, all costs and all risks are not considered when analyzing a SaaS solution. The SaaS ballyhoo has drowned out all reasonable objections. Clearly, we are not big fans at the present time, especially for law firms, but we are slowly migrating our opinion toward endorsing cloud-based services. (More on that later.) Client/server solutions can be clearly defined from implementation through the life of the solution. You control the implementation, configuration, and ongoing costs. While you can contractually specify some costs with SaaS, future upgrades and exit conversions may tip the financial decision.

You may also hear of two other cloud solutions: Platform as a Service (PaaS) and Infrastructure as a Service (IaaS). With PaaS, the client creates software using features and capabilities as available from the provider. Most law firms will not entertain the PaaS model. IaaS is where the necessary infrastructure is supplied by the solution provider. It owns and controls the equipment, operating system, network, and so on, and you load your applications onto the services. Think of it as having your data and applications running on "rented" hardware.

Hybrid Solution

We think that moving your data and applications to a secure data center is a much better solution for most solo and small firm lawyers. Think of it as the best of both worlds. It's your data and software running on equipment that you own and control. If you don't like the data center, you can always move or bring it back in-house. The costs are even more predictable because you control any upgrades. We are beginning to purchase rack space at data centers and move client equipment into the secured racks. Recent weather conditions in our area (massive snowfall and a drenching storm that had folks without power for weeks) are making more firms cognizant of business continuity solutions. Data centers have redundant power (generators, too) and Internet connections. This generally means that weather conditions will not impact your ability to access your data and applications. Data centers generally guarantee 99.999 percent uptime. Remember, though, that your own equipment could fail, and you are still dependent on your local Internet connection.

As you engineer the architecture to implement what we call a hybrid solution, be particularly aware of any software applications that contain databases, such as your case management software. Database access using the Internet as the network is extremely risky and can corrupt the data. You may have to implement a Terminal Server type connection so that you run the client software from equipment at the data center. Your IT consultant can help you determine the right connection scheme for each of your applications to achieve the greatest stability for your needs.

Bottom line: We are beginning to shift our opinion and are now actively moving clients to the cloud, though using the client's hardware rather than the cloud provider's. If you feel that you need to investigate and research SaaS vendors, we describe a few in this book. We just ask that you do it carefully and ask the right questions before making your decision.

We are listening to arguments that some SaaS providers actually offer better security than law firms themselves. There's some truth in that, to be sure, and we are moving (slowly) in the direction of recommending SaaS from proven providers with good track records for some clients. Finally, be sure to check with your bar, as several states now have opinions regarding the usage (and requirements) of cloud computing. If you're wondering how states are dealing with the cloud from an ethical perspective, the general view is that it is acceptable to use the cloud as long as you investigate the provider, particularly making sure that confidential client data will be adequately protected. Remember that ethically you are outsourcing when you contract with a cloud provider, so the ethical rules relating to outsourcing apply.

CHAPTER TWENTY

Collaboration

COLLABORATION MAY OR MAY not be at the top of your list, especially if you are a solo lawyer. However, we're sure you will have occasion to deal with other lawyers or even have a need to collaborate with your clients on a case. There are some great technology solutions to allow for collaboration—and solutions are multiplying week by week. These are just a few of the primary tools available for sharing information and working in a collaborative mode.

Social networking is a collaboration area that is gaining in popularity. Facebook has won the social networking war and is now being used extensively for business purposes. Twitter and LinkedIn are also very popular, with many lawyers preferring LinkedIn as a network for professionals. What about Google+? That's a darn good question. Google+ now has 359 million active users, which is up 33 percent from June 2012, according to GlobalWebIndex. This puts Google+ as the number two social network behind the "800-pound" Facebook. Move over Twitter and LinkedIn. So much for our previous predictions that Google+ would die a slow death. However, some experts are challenging how active Google+ is—even calling it a ghost town.

Some lawyers are getting business through social networking sites, and others are raising their visibility with potential clients or colleagues who might provide referrals. Still others have obtained opportunities to write or speak on their area of expertise. See Chapter Twenty-Six, "Social Media," for more information on how lawyers are using these new applications.

Google Drive

Probably one of the most well-known of the collaboration tools is Google Docs, which is now an offering within Google Drive. Most users know Google Docs as a web-based office suite that can create documents, spreadsheets, presentations, forms, and drawings. Not so fast. Google has repackaged its offering, and what used to be considered a suite are now separate applications known as Docs, Sheets, Forms, and Slides, all accessible within Google Drive. The popularity of this SaaS product is no doubt due to the fact that it carries the favorite price tag of all lawyers—it is completely free. The applications allow you to work on a document, spreadsheet, form, drawing, or presentation with others and see the modifications in real time. You just use the web browser on your computer with your Internet connection. There are even enhanced features, which you may not be aware of.

You do need to have a Google ID to use Google Drive. Just go to **drive .google.com** and enter your login information. You can also create an account from the main entry page. Besides creating your files from scratch, the Google apps allow you to upload files you've already created on your computer. Documents can be downloaded to your computer as .docx, OpenDocument Format, RTF, PDF, TXT, or HTML (zipped). Spreadsheets can be downloaded as .XLSX, .CSV, .TXT, and .ODS formatted data, as well as PDF and HTML files. Presentations can be downloaded as .PPTX, .XDF, and .TXT formatted data or as Scalable Vector Graphic (.SVG), .PNG, or .JPG image files.

If you are used to the way Dropbox operates, you will not have any trouble with Google Drive. The easiest way to synchronize files and work on your spreadsheets, documents, and so on, is to install the Google Drive application to your computer. Once it is installed, you will have a folder to drag and drop files into. They will then automatically get synchronized with your Google Drive storage. Google gives you 15GB of free storage when you create your account. If you need more than that, you can get 100GB or more space at a cost starting at $4.99 per month.

You can upload files to your Google Drive. The Google Drive viewer currently supports over 16 different file types:

- Google Docs
- Google Sheets
- Google Slides

- Google Forms
- Google Drawings
- Image files (.JPG, .PNG, .GIF, .TIFF, .BMP)
- Raw image formats
- Video files (WebM, .MPEG4, .3GPP, .MOV, .AVI, .MPEGPS, .WMV, .FLV, .OGG)
- Microsoft Word (.DOC and .DOCX)
- Microsoft Excel (.XLS and .XLSX)
- Microsoft PowerPoint (.PPT and .PPTX)
- Adobe Portable Document Format (.PDF)
- Tagged Image File Format (.TIFF)
- Scalable Vector Graphics (.SVG)
- PostScript (.EPS, .PS)
- TrueType (.TTF)
- XML Paper Specification (.XPS)

By default, files are not shared until you make them shareable. This is certainly the preferred security policy and keeps your data private unless you make a conscious decision to share the information. Once you've created or uploaded a file to your Google Drive, you configure how the file is shared or, as Google puts it, define your "visibility options." Google's visibility options include "Private," "Anyone with the link," and "Public on the web." "Private" is just that: private. As mentioned, this is the default visibility setting. A document set to "Anyone with the link" is like an unlisted phone number. This means the data will not be visible unless you know the URL or are just plain lucky in guessing what it is. "Public on the web" means the document is available to anyone and may get indexed by search engines.

Besides the visibility, you can also change what a user can do with the data. The creator of the document is tagged as the owner and can obviously do anything. If you define specific people to have access to the file, the choices for access are "Can edit," "Can comment," and "Can view." This gives you some level of granularity in the access and visibility options.

As a practical point, multiple people can collaborate on a file and everyone doesn't need to have the same software or version. You can go online and create a file to start the process. Once completed, perhaps you download the file as a .docx file, since you use Word as your word processor.

Another person downloads the .rtf version that he reads in an old version of WordPerfect, and a third person downloads the .odt version because she uses OpenOffice. Each person downloads the same information but in a different file format to match what's used on each computer.

The current version of Google Drive now supports mobility access. As smartphones become the computing platform of choice, Google has developed methods to get to your information. Currently, Google Drive is accessible from an Android phone or tablet running Android 2.1 or higher. For an Apple device, you need to be running iOS 5.0 or above. The Google Drive app is what facilitates access to the Google files from your mobile device. You will need to install the Google Drive app to your Android or Apple mobile device. Just access the files from your Google Drive app and the changes are synchronized across all devices connected to your Google Drive.

The caution with Google Drive is that the data is being held by a third party. Obviously, you would not want to use it to work on highly proprietary information, such as a patent application. Even though you can control who has access to the files and what they can do, Google still holds the "keys" to all of the data. Google has had some highly publicized security issues over a period of years, so it is wise to consider what data you store there.

There have also been some recent stirrings over Google's privacy policy and what data Google accesses. We remind readers to review the terms of service and privacy policies for any third-party provided service, including Google. Apparently, there were a ton of folks who never read the terms and got all upset when they heard that Google scans the data you create and deposit on their servers. This is true for the free services that Google provides, such as Gmail and Google Drive. However, Google Business Apps ($50 per user per year) does not have the same terms of service. In fact, the terms of service for Business Apps have specific confidentiality provisions, where Google will protect the data. They will also notify you if they are required by law to disclose confidential information so that you have an opportunity to challenge the disclosure.

Acrobat

Today, more and more lawyers have Acrobat (**www.adobe.com/products/ acrobat**), especially if they do e-filing of court documents. Acrobat allows for collaboration with PDF documents, so you can conduct shared document reviews that allow the participants to view one another's comments. Acrobat XI Standard and Pro allow for this type of collaboration. The free Acrobat Reader can annotate documents with the commenting tools, but it cannot manage shared reviews or other advanced features that are included in the Standard and Pro versions.

Acrobat XI Standard is currently $299 and Pro is $449. Adobe now offers Acrobat XI Pro in two subscription plans. You can purchase a month-to-month subscription for $29.99 per month or an annual subscription for $19.99 per month. Adobe also offers a free trial download from their website. As with the other products we recommend, try the trial first if you are unsure of your purchase commitment.

Lawyers should opt for the Pro version, primarily for the enhanced security, Bates stamping, and redaction ability. Acrobat XI Pro allows you to create a document that your clients may find useful. It allows users of Adobe Reader (the free reader version) to participate in reviews with complete commenting and markup tools, including sticky notes, highlighter, lines, shapes, and stamps. This means your clients (or other lawyers, for that matter) don't have to purchase Acrobat to collaborate with you.

This feature is not available with Acrobat XI Standard, hence the recommendation to purchase the Pro version. Consider purchasing Acrobat 9 Professional, especially if you can find it at a much reduced cost, since it is two versions back. Version XI is the current version, but there aren't any significant enhancements for the legal profession over those legal-specific functions that are included in Acrobat 9 Professional.

See the Acrobat section in Chapter Twelve to learn how to get the software for a lot less money.

Microsoft Word

Another collaboration tool is the "track changes" feature of Microsoft Word. With this tool, you can see the modifications of each user who modifies the document. The caveat is that the software must be configured to properly identify the user. Some preloaded Office installations have the user configured as something generic, like "Owner" or "Satisfied Customer," and not the user's name. You can see how your Office (2003 and prior) installation is configured by going to Tools > Options and selecting the User Information tab. Word 2007 users would click the

Office button in the upper left, select the Word Options button at the bottom, and see the user information in the Popular menu choice. Word 2010 and 2013 users select File and then the Options menu choice. Once this option is properly configured, the user information will show properly with the tracked changes. The user also has the ability to insert comments in addition to actually modifying the document contents. Do not strip the metadata from the document (as you might normally do for confidentiality reasons) if you are sending it to another party for collaboration. Removing the metadata also removes the tracked changes, so the recipient will not see the intended modifications. When you have the document ready and want to send it to a client, scrub the metadata at that point.

SharePoint

SharePoint is Microsoft's solution for collaboration. Basically, SharePoint is a web-based server environment that allows the end-user to collaborate on data that is managed through a SharePoint server. There is no special client software needed, as access is accomplished via a browser.

SharePoint 2013 is considered to be expensive for most solo and small firm operations, especially for new installations. Besides the cost of the server hardware, you will need the server software and Client Access Licenses (CALs). Microsoft has attempted to simplify the previously confusing licensing model for SharePoint. The on-premise solution is licensed using the server/CAL model. SharePoint Server 2013 is required for each running instance of the software, and CALs are required for each person or device accessing a SharePoint Server. There is even an option for enterprise CALs if you need a very robust and flexible SharePoint environment to take advantage of the features of Microsoft's Business Solutions or Business Intelligence for Everyone that are not available with the standard CALs. Suffice it to say that it is all very complicated and can get rather expensive. If you need the services of a full-blown SharePoint server, you may want to consider some of the hosted solutions, which should be a lot more affordable for a solo or small firm office. Microsoft offers SharePoint Online, which is licensed on a per-user basis and starts at $3 per user per month.

Microsoft is continuing to push SharePoint in a major way. It keeps threatening to remove the Public Folders function of Exchange with each new release and force users to go with a SharePoint installation to get the same features currently available with a base Exchange installation. We thought this was going to happen with the release of Exchange 2010 and then Exchange 2013, but we are happy to say that the Public Folders function is still there. Since Microsoft has been making this threat for many years, we have no reason to suspect that Public Folders will be removed from future Exchange versions.

We've written about SharePoint in the last several editions of this book. Microsoft continues to hype it, but we don't see much traction in the real world. Surveys show that 78 percent of the Fortune 500 companies are using SharePoint, but only one of our clients has it installed, and we don't see that SharePoint is worth the expense, especially for an on-premise solution. Many solo and small firm practitioners use SaaS solutions instead of investing in a complex SharePoint environment. We agree with that direction and don't think SharePoint is going to change the world, as Microsoft has often predicted.

Office 365

Microsoft has finally introduced a product that may give Google a run for its money. Office 365 is really a web-based productivity suite that also contains some collaboration capabilities. The solution is a subscription-based service, so the out-of-pocket cash flow is very reasonable. There are several subscription plans available, depending on the number of users and any advanced features that may be needed. Microsoft has changed the Office 365 offerings this year, so our recommendation is different for this edition of the book. They are trying to steer users toward a subscription model and away from the traditional retail software packages.

Solo and small firms will probably opt for Office 365 Small Business Premium, which is geared toward small businesses with up to 25 users. The cost is $15 per month per user (billed monthly) or $12.50 per month per user (annual payment of $150), which is very affordable. It includes access to business class e-mail, shared calendars, 25GB of storage space per user, the ability to use your own domain name, web conferencing, and document sharing. New is the ability to have Office on your desktop and on the go. The Office applications include Word, PowerPoint, Excel, Outlook, OneNote, Access, Publisher, and Lync. With the desktop version you can work on your files while offline. Once connected to the Internet, all of your work will automatically sync. Also included is 7GB of SkyDrive Pro storage for each user for pretty much anywhere access to the files. You can control who can see and edit each file as well as define which files sync with which device. We would recommend starting with the month-to-month plan, which can be canceled at any time without penalty.

Skype

Many users are familiar with the VoIP solution called Skype. Skype is now owned by Microsoft, and things seem to be going along fairly well. Telephone calls are free between Skype users. You can opt for pay plans if you need to call mobile or landline numbers, and the cost is very reasonable.

Unlimited calling to United States and Canada landline and mobile phone numbers is only $2.99 per month. New features with Skype make it an excellent tool for collaboration. Video conferencing is now supported within Skype. You can create a low cost or no cost video conference call in just a few seconds. Many laptops now have a video camera built into the screen case, and there are Skype apps for mobile devices such as iPhones, iPads, Windows Phone, and Android smartphones. Finally, you can share files through Skype as well. Sharing files, video conferencing, and free teleconference calls via the Internet make Skype a great low cost collaboration tool.

Beware of security issues though. We learned in 2013 that Microsoft was now routing Skype calls through its servers, contrary to previous practice. We would not recommend using Skype for confidential conversations.

Dropbox

Dropbox (**www.dropbox.com**) is not just for file synchronization between your computer and mobile devices. We have seen a tremendous increase in Dropbox being used to share files among multiple parties and even as a vehicle to deliver evidence for discovery. You can create a custom folder within Dropbox and share that folder with multiple people. Only those that you authorize can have access to the folder contents. This means you can collaborate with co-counsel, consultants, experts, and even opposing counsel.

Dropbox is free for the initial 2GB of storage. You can purchase additional storage starting at $9.99 per month. Dropbox transmits the data in a secure fashion using SSL and also stores it in encrypted form on their servers. However, Dropbox holds the encryption key and can decrypt the data should they receive a valid court order or law enforcement request. Therefore, you should consider Dropbox to be an insecure service and not used for transmitting any confidential or sensitive information. That doesn't mean you can't use Dropbox to share confidential information. Your data is safe if you encrypt it *before* you deposit it in Dropbox. That way you control the encryption key.

Desktop Sharing

There are several products that enable you to share your desktop with other people. This may be a good way to collaborate on a document or share pictures of an accident scene. Products like Webex, Teamviewer, join.me, and GoToMeeting allow for desktop sharing. If you elect to use desktop sharing products, be advised that you may not be able to determine if the remote party is recording the session. You may want to get agreement and confirmation from all parties that they are not recording the session, especially if you don't want it recorded or you want to be the only one with a record of the session. In addition, be wary if you give control over to a remote user, because that user may be able to transfer data from your computer without your knowledge. We would recommend that you "push" your desktop to the remote parties and do not let them take control.

CHAPTER TWENTY-ONE

Remote Access

MOST LAWYERS ARE ROAD warriors today. If their entire office is not on a laptop or smartphone, a good chunk of it is—and the rest is accessible through remote access. Whether in court, on vacation, traveling, or in a meeting, lawyers need access to their e-mail, calendar, appointments, and files—and they need access fast.

Many lawyers have discarded workstations entirely, using only their laptop and a docking station at work and tablets and smartphones while on the move. Others have both a workstation and a laptop. The popularity of laptops and other mobile devices has zoomed in the last decade, to the point where the lawyer without a laptop or smartphone is a relative rarity. Our new mobile lawyers are now equipped with technologies that allow them to be as productive on the road as they are in the office, minimizing downtime and keeping those billable hours (or productivity hours, in the case of the alternative billers) up. Many clients and colleagues have a strong expectation that lawyers will be constantly accessible via e-mail—even, sadly, while on vacation. We privately joke (and lament) that vacations are times when our laptops and mobile devices get a nice view of the beach. Many clients will disregard your out-of-office message and will expect a quick response. So, how do we stay in touch with the office when on the road?

Virtual Private Networking

A virtual private network (VPN) connection is a secure communications network tunneled through another network, such as the Internet. The

VPN connection allows a user to connect to the office when working remotely. The communications tunnel encrypts the data traffic between the remote user and the office network, maintaining the security of the information as it is passed back and forth. This is extremely important for law firms whose lawyers work on client files while traveling or away from the office and have to download a local copy of a client file to work on. Best of all, the VPN service software is included with Microsoft's server operating systems, and the VPN client software is included with Microsoft operating systems, at no additional cost to the user.

The average lawyer is likely to be dumbfounded when confronted with setting up a VPN, especially if third-party software and a certificate are required, so this is best left to your IT consultant. However, it is not terribly expensive, and it offers terrific security for your data. The greatest advantage of VPNs is that they are multiuser, whereas others are one-on-one solutions.

GoToMyPC

GoToMyPC is a remote connection service that allows you to connect to your work computer when you are away from the office. This service is a great alternative if you're a solo practitioner or if your law firm does not have the ability to set up a VPN-type connection for remote users (for example, if you don't have a server). Like a VPN connection, data communications between the client and the host are encrypted and secured. To connect to your work computer, software must be installed and running on the host machine (the computer you wish to connect to), and both the client and the host computers must have Internet access. The GoToMyPC website maintains contact with the host computer so the IP address of the host is always known. This is critical: This solution works even if the host has a dynamic Internet connection (dynamic IP address instead of a static one) that will not remain constant. No modifications to the configuration of your firm firewall will need to be made to get GoToMyPC up and running.

Users can even connect to their work computers from a tablet or smartphone. Apps are available for Android, iOS, and Kindle Fire devices.

GoToMyPC costs as little as $99 per year for one computer license and will need to be renewed yearly. There is a monthly plan, but the cost jumps to $10 a month. There is no limitation on how often you may connect to your host computer, and you are allowed to connect to your host computer from any device. The software requires little setup and configuration and can be purchased online from GoToMyPC's website at **www.gotomypc.com**. This software is more costly than its competitors, so be sure to check out all of your available options before selecting which remote access solution to purchase. This software also has a thirty-day free trial, so take advantage as you experiment to find which remote access solution works best for you!

LogMeIn

LogMeIn Pro is a remote access solution that is very similar to GoToMyPC. The software works the exact same way, with the service provider maintaining the IP addresses of host computers. This is another good solution for those firms with dynamic IP addresses that are constantly changing. With this service and very little effort, you can gain seamless and total access to your office PC from any computer with an Internet connection. To connect, a user logs into the LogMeIn website and the connection to the host computer is made automatically. Some of the features include remote printing, the ability to transfer and share files between the connected computers, and the ability to map network drives to your local computer. Just like GoToMyPC, this service is extremely secure, using 128- to 256-bit SSL end-to-end encryption. When compared to GoToMyPC, this remote access solution costs much less.

This service also supports connecting to your work computer from your iOS or Android device. We've used the iPad app, and it works as advertised—easy to use, great with the touch screen, and very convenient.

A LogMeIn Pro subscription costs $69.95 per year for one computer license and will need to be renewed annually. The monthly plan costs $12.20 per month, so the annual plan is recommended. This service can be purchased online from LogMeIn's website at **www.logmein.com**. We strongly recommend the use of this product for remote accessibility because of its ease of use and lower cost. Like GoToMyPC, LogMeIn offers a free trial, so we recommend taking the product for a test drive before purchasing it.

TeamViewer

TeamViewer Business Edition is a remote access solution on steroids. It contains a number of features that are not available with LogMeIn or GoToMyPC. Although it's a one-time purchase it comes with a hefty price. Just like the two remote access solutions described above, TeamViewer works flawlessly behind network firewalls and is a good solution for firms that use dynamic IP addresses. While TeamViewer not difficult to install and run, the connecting computer will need to download, install, and run the client application, which, in our experience, may be a bit more confusing and cumbersome for lawyers to perform rather than just logging into the service with the web-browser. Some of the additional features include:

- Multiplatform support, including Mac OS X, Windows 7, and Linux computers
- Communication tools that allow users to connect with each other through video chat or VoIP
- One-time charge for a lifetime license; no recurring yearly costs
- The ability to transfer files securely
- File box for common file sharing
- Microsoft Outlook calendar integration
- The ability to record meetings
- Space for up to fifteen meeting participants

Mobile device support is offered for iOS, Android, and Windows Phone 8, but users will need to purchase a separate add-on license for this feature, unlike the included mobile support offered in both of the LogMeIn and GoToMyPC alternatives to this product. TeamViewer can be purchased online from **www.teamviewer.com**, and a single lifetime business license for one computer costs $749.

Mobility Tips

Besides providing remote access solutions for the legal road warrior, we wanted to include some useful tips to think about before heading out on the road:

—Pack a surge protector. It doesn't matter what brand. You never know when you will need more than two outlets to power all of your devices and to protect your electronic devices from power surges and dirty electricity.

—Purchase a lock for your laptop. Ninety-nine percent of laptops have a Kensington security slot, and it's prudent to use it. Kensington locks, such as the MicroSaver DS Notebook Lock, can be purchased online from Kensington's website (**www.kensington.com**) for around $50—a small price to pay to keep your laptop secure.

—If you use a Bluetooth mouse, be sure to pack extra AA or AAA batteries.

—Pack a spare cell phone charger and tablet charger with an extra sync cable. You shouldn't travel without either one.

—Pack an AC extension cable. This will come in handy when you are far away from a power outlet.

—Keep an AC power adapter for your laptop in your bag. You never know when you might need one.

—If you're traveling internationally, be sure to pack multiple converters so that you can connect your devices. In the United States, we operate on a system that runs at 120 volts. Be sure to check the voltage of the country you're visiting before leaving and find out whether your power supplies will auto convert.

—It is always a good idea to have a hard copy printout of your hotel reservation and itinerary, in the event your mobile device stops working or isn't accessible right when you need it.

—Another tip for international travelers: Leave your cell phone at home. Roaming charges can be staggering and can be initiated even if you're not actively using your phone. Do you really trust putting your phone in airplane mode?

—Keep appropriate video adapters with your laptop in your laptop bag. You never know when you might need to connect your laptop or tablet to a TV or projector for a presentation.

—Pack headphones to keep the noise out. Have you ever tried to be productive on an airplane? It's hard when the person next to you can't stop talking. Just plug in your headphones and your problem is solved. You can even listen to relaxing music while you work. For those who want wireless Bluetooth headphones, check out the Jabra BT8030 headphones, costing about $150, or the Sony DR-BT101, described earlier in the book; however, you won't be able to use these on an airplane because they are transmitting devices. For music aficionados, the Bose QuietComfort 3 headphones offer top of the line headphone technology and include the noise-canceling circuitry that you hear everyone talking about. The downside, though, is the price—very, very expensive at around $315.

—Back up your data to an external hard drive or the network server. If your laptop crashes or is stolen, you will want a recent backup of your most important files.

—Encrypt your hard drive and data. There are many software tools available to do this, such as PGP, TrueCrypt, and PC Guardian. In the event your laptop is lost or stolen, your data is protected. Configure a power on or BIOS password on your computer, if available. Again, this adds another layer of data protection.

—If you have a tablet, be sure to password protect your device with a passphrase. PINs aren't as secure and can be easily cracked. On an iPad, a passphrase requirement on the Lock Screen will enable encryption of your data. On Android devices, you can encrypt your data as well through the configuration settings.

—If you have a smartphone with a data plan that allows device tethering, take advantage of the data service you have already paid for and tether your laptop or tablet with your smartphone for Internet service. Avoid paying daily hotel fees for an Internet connection if it's not provided free during the course of your stay. However, data overage charges from your wireless carrier can be expensive, so it's best not to stream the movie at the top of your Netflix queue while tethered unless you truly have an unlimited data plan.

—Encrypt your USB flash drives and external hard drives.

—Disable your wireless auto-connection feature within the Windows operating system. Most laptops with wireless cards will automatically connect to any unencrypted, open wireless network when your default connection is unavailable. If by chance your device does connect to an open wireless network, never log into any e-mail or bank account when using an unsecure connection.

—Before leaving the office, make sure that your security software has the latest updates and definitions to protect your devices while you're away. The same applies to Windows updates.

—Download and install an app to track your club membership cards so that you don't have to carry all that plastic around with you. The one that we like the most for iOS and Android mobile devices is the Key Ring Rewards Cards app. Not only does it allow you to enter and store your club card or membership numbers, but it can also generate a bar code that can be scanned should one be required. You might as well get miles points and hotel rewards while on the go!

These are just a few of the recommendations we have for the legal road warriors, all based on our own experiences traveling. We hope you can learn from our mistakes.

CHAPTER TWENTY-TWO

Mobile Security

TECHNOLOGY ADVANCES IN THIS area have come at warp speed. Gone are the days when you carried around a 50-foot phone cord, looking for an analog phone jack that could be used with the modem in your laptop and America Online. Being übergeeks, we then carried along a splitter, coupler, and additional phone cords so we could work comfortably on the bed or desk while we traveled around the nation. No more. It's even difficult to purchase a modern-day laptop with a modem these days. Wireless, whether Wi-Fi or with a 3G/4G data connection to your cellular carrier, is the preferred method of connectivity in the modern age. More and more hotels, motels, conference centers, coffee shops, bookstores, cafés, and so on, are offering wireless access solutions, many without charge.

Software

Before we jump into the boring details, let's cover some solutions that should be on your laptop no matter what other technology you use for remote connectivity. It goes without saying that you should have some sort of all-in-one security solution installed on your laptop. It should be configured to check for automatic updates and to perform a periodic full scan (we do weekly scans) to catch anything that may have "landed" before the signatures were updated. It would be just your luck to catch a virus on day one and be the first kid on the block to suffer the effects. Most of the current Internet suites also analyze the computer operation and identify activity that could be virus-like or some process trying to access something it shouldn't. This type of real time monitoring provides added protection beyond mere signature files. Normally, the all-in-one security product will contain security features like antivirus, antimalware, firewalls, spam control, and antiphishing. Don't leave home without it. There are software solutions for your smartphone and tablet, but we'll discuss those later.

Encryption

Secure mobile computing must contain some method of encryption to protect valuable personal and client data. We prefer whole disk encryption. This means everything on the hard drive is encrypted and kept secure. We don't have to remember to put files into special folders or on the encrypted virtual drive. All too often, humans are in a big hurry and may not save their data in the special protected encrypted areas, leaving the information vulnerable.

In addition, without whole disk encryption, it is possible that artifacts of the decryption passphrase would be present in various places (e.g., master file table (MFT), Page File, temp files, unallocated space). Forensics can extract these artifacts and make it probable that the passphrase can be determined. Many of the newer laptops have built-in whole disk encryption. To state the obvious, make sure you enable the encryption or your data won't be protected. Also, encryption may be used in conjunction with biometric access. As an example, our laptops require a fingerprint swipe when powered on. Failure at that point leaves the computer hard drive fully encrypted. A very comforting thought if laptop thieves, who constitute a large club these days, make off with your laptop. If you think we are being too cautious, bear in mind that a laptop goes missing every 50 seconds in the United States. In 2011, **PCWorld.com** reported that about 12,000 laptops were lost or stolen at U.S. airports per week. Where does it happen most? In Chicago, fitting for a city whose history is so steeped in criminal lore. The fact that one of ten corporate laptops will be lost or stolen over their three-year life is enough reason to take steps to protect the data. We mean it when we say, "Be careful out there." Also, don't forget to encrypt your USB flash drives. Unfortunately for us good guys, these devices are easily lost and almost always contain our most valuable data.

Wireless

What's next? We won't cover modem access in the traditional sense, since dial-up isn't desirable, effective, or even available these days for most travelers. Wireless is the norm for all the road warriors. There are two basic types of wireless access you'll encounter. The first type is generically termed a wireless hot spot and is what you find at your local Starbucks, fast food establishment, hotel, or airport. You may or may not have to pay for these wireless connection services. Many businesses are offering free wireless as a way to attract customers—heck, even McDonald's offers a free wireless hot spot. Most of these hot spots are unsecured and wide open. This means it is possible for your confidential data to be viewed by the customer at the next table or the one sitting on the park bench outside the café if you are not encrypting the traffic.

Does this mean you shouldn't use any of these wireless clouds? If you have a choice, we would say these clouds are best avoided by those who are technology averse and don't understand how to operate securely in an unsecured cloud. Read on, and determine whether you can safely be trusted to do what follows.

See if there is an option to have a secure connection to the cloud. This would be indicated if you use **https://** (note the *s*, denoting "secure") as part of the URL. Typically, website connections are unsecured and do not provide an encrypted session like the **https://** connections do. Be especially careful if you have to pay for the wireless connection. Be wary when you are at the screens that have you input your credit card and billing information. Do not enter any of this sensitive information without an **https://** connection. Once you've established a connection to the wireless cloud, be sure to use your VPN or other secure (**https://**) access to protect your transmissions. Also, when connecting to a secure website, if you're presented with an error message referencing an SSL certificate error or invalid certificate, proceed with extreme caution or don't proceed at all.

Some hotels may give you a wireless cloud that is already secured. Typically, these wireless implementations use WPA (Wi-Fi protected access) or WPA2 to secure your connection and data. The cloud will be visible to your computer, but you will be required to provide a password before your computer connects. Once connected, the data you transmit will be encrypted and secure.

One scheme we see all the time: You are in a hotel that requires you to pay for Internet access. But when you ask your computer to show "all available wireless networks," it will display something like "free public wireless" as a network name—or something else that sounds innocuous, usually using the word "free" to entice you. Beware—these are often data thieves offering up an insecure cloud for the sole purpose of making off with your data. You can get the "free Internet"—but at a terrible price. Never be tempted by these clouds.

AirCard

Another wireless connection method is commonly called an AirCard. These are cards that are used to connect to the high-speed wireless networks of cellular phone providers. We're pretty sure you've seen the cellular providers advertising their 3G/4G networks. You may see terms like EDGE or EV-DO to describe the older 3G networks and WiMAX or LTE to describe the latest 4G networks. Don't be swayed by the vendor claims for speed and availability. Make sure that you will be able to have service in those areas you travel to the most. Reliability is another consideration, as is whether you already have a cellular plan.

The AirCard itself is a hardware device that you can externally connect to your laptop or select as a built-in option when configuring a new computer system. External AirCards come in both USB and PC card formats. These cards can be used on any laptop with USB ports or PC card slots. Some laptops and netbooks have the electrical circuitry built in, so no additional hardware is required. The built-in capability means you have nothing to lose, but it is "married" to the laptop and can't be transferred between machines. Further, you would also be stuck with a single cellular vendor, as each vendor's radio is different. The external AirCards can cost several hundred dollars, but most providers offer significant discounts. As an example, Sprint currently offers a USB antenna for no cost.

The service itself can be daily, weekly, monthly, or annually by subscription. The monthly plans typically measure the amount of data you transfer over the connection and charge you for any overage usage. Unlimited data plans appear to be a thing of the past with carriers limiting data usage, especially with the tremendous number of smartphones being purchased. The exception is Sprint. They are offering unlimited plans in an attempt to grab market share. We'll have to see how long their unlimited plans last. We are also seeing a move to offer shared data access, which means all devices on your account can share the amount of data to which you subscribe. In the present market, the data plans are all over the map. Some plans are as low as 250MB per week and cap out at around 10GB per month. The cost will run between $10 and $90 per month, depending on the amount of data purchased. Be sure to read the fine print, especially on any unlimited plan. You may be surprised at the additional charges or restrictions that may be involved.

Obviously, you will want to purchase a monthly plan if you travel a lot or will use the service for more than a few days a month. The AirCard is the preferred wireless connection, as the data is secured from the very beginning. You don't have to worry about whether you have an **https://** session or not. The electronic circuitry itself and the cellular carrier provide a fully encrypted session immediately.

Also, it should be noted that if you have multiple devices that need Internet access, rather than purchasing a subscription for each device, which can be very costly, invest in something like the Verizon MiFi or other mobile hot spot. These devices create a local wireless network that can provide Internet access (over the cellular network) to up to ten devices. Similar to the Sprint AirCard antenna, Verizon offers the MiFi Jetpack free with a two-year data plan.

Public Computer Usage

A word of warning here. Be very careful about using a public computer, such as those in the library, an Internet café, or the business center of a hotel. Even if you are only accessing your web-based e-mail account, the data is temporarily written to the local hard disk. There is also the risk that some keystroke logging software is installed on the computer, thereby capturing everything that you do on the machine. Studies have shown an average of seven pieces of malware on these public computers.

Does that mean all public computers are off limits? Not at all. We are big fans of the IronKey hardware encrypted USB flash drive. Besides the drive encryption and secure management of passwords, the IronKey has portable applications intended for use with public computers. As an example, there is a specially modified version of the Firefox browser that doesn't write any data to the computer. All data stays on the IronKey, thereby making it secure and keeping it with you when you leave. Of course, this does mean that the computer has to accept the insertion of USB devices. Some business center machines are locked down and do not allow USB devices to be inserted, because it is a security risk to the business—USB devices can be used to introduce malware to the machine or network. Though we have tipped our hat to those who secure their computers this way (it's absolutely the right thing to do), it has prevented us from using our IronKey several times.

Smartphones

Want to know what the most insecure smartphone on the market is? Apple isn't going to like us, but, arguably, it's the iPhone. It's pretty clear that the iPhone was designed as a consumer phone first, with security just an afterthought. However, the latest versions of iOS on the newer iPhones have improved security to the point where it more closely approaches the other smartphones in protecting data.

At a minimum, everybody should have a PIN code programmed into the phone to prevent unauthorized access, along with a fairly short time-out period. It doesn't do much good to have an unlocking PIN and then have 30 minutes pass before the phone relocks. We know it's a pain to constantly punch in the unlock code, but that will keep your data from being accessed by prying eyes. Better yet, it will stop someone from installing spyware on your phone that can effectively trap all of your communications (voice calls, e-mail, text messages, etc.). For those devices that offer a passphrase alternative to the PIN, such as the iPad or iPhone, this would be the preferred choice to secure your device. Why, you might ask? Because a passphrase can be longer than a PIN and can contain non-numeric values, vastly increasing the strength of the protection. In fact, we do not recommend that any iPhone or iPad be configured with the very weak 4-digit PIN lock code. There are tools available to brute force a 4-digit PIN on an iPhone or iPad in less than 15 minutes, even if it is set to wipe the data after 10 attempts.

Encrypt the phone! This is easier to do than you think. Enabling a lock code on the iPhone or iPad automatically encrypts the device. To encrypt a BlackBerry device, all you have to do is enable Content Protection. The last several versions of the Android operating system have built-in encryption. Just make the selection to encrypt the device within the Security settings. You may need a third-party application if you are running an older version of the Android OS.

Besides PIN protecting your phone, make sure you encrypt any memory cards or just don't store any sensitive data on them. We're talking about the SD, micro SD, and so on, cards that you can insert into the smartphone to increase storage capacity. There are programs available for some models that allow you to encrypt the card contents if the feature is not already built into the phone. The point is, you don't want any confidential information to be accessible on the card if you lose your phone. The PIN will protect the phone access, but the bad guy will pop out the memory card and read it from his computer if it is not encrypted.

Finally, investigate the ability to remotely wipe the data from the smartphone if it is lost. You should have the phone configured to automatically wipe after a set number of invalid unlock attempts. This will clear the data even if you are not connected to a cellular network. Remotely wiping the device on demand requires that it be in communication with the cellular data network. Configure the Find my iPhone function within the iCloud settings on an iPhone or iPad. The remote wipe capability is built into the BlackBerry devices and can be invoked through the BES (BlackBerry Enterprise Server) console. Android devices can use the free Lookout application for the remote wipe function. Google has just announced that a new app called Android Device Manager will help users locate or remotely wipe their phone, and it will begin pushing out the update via the Google Play Services update. Remember that the remote wipe feature is for the memory within the phone itself and may not wipe the memory cards we spoke about earlier.

Final Words

The options and requirements for mobile security have certainly changed quickly over the years. Talk to us next year, and we're sure the world will have changed again. For now, make sure that you are aware of all the issues related to secure data transfer and that you are not relying on antique knowledge. You must assume that there is absolutely no protection of the communication stream between your laptop and your remote device. We've seen hotel networks that didn't have a firewall, so all traffic was allowed to flow through. We immediately saw probing attacks on our computers, which were stopped by the firewalls on our laptops. It's the wild, wild West out there, and you're the only marshal in town. Good luck, Wyatt.

CHAPTER TWENTY-THREE

More from Apple

APART FROM THE INFORMATION conveyed previously about Mac laptops and desktops, we want to offer you additional Apple recommendations in light of the continued interest lawyers have shown in potentially switching to Mac computers. Many lawyers may have never used a Mac, either in their personal life or for their job, but most have used one Apple product or another. Most are only familiar with the iPod or the very popular iPad. Some people may argue that Macs are ready for "prime time," to take on Windows-based PCs in the business setting. From a hardware standpoint, Macs are just as good as, if not better than, PCs. You can't really tell them apart since Macs made the switch to using Intel-based processors. The major difference now is the operating system, which is still the main obstacle for Macs gaining a greater piece of the pie in the business marketplace.

Frankly, the problem lies with software compatibility with Macs. Most law firms, no matter the size, use legal-specific software on a daily basis to do their jobs. Whether you're looking at case management, billing, trial-related or field-specific software, most vendors still do not make versions for Macs. But for lawyers who use a computer just for word processing, Internet research, filing motions, billing, and accounting, a Mac could suit these functions perfectly. In addition, centralized management is much more difficult, if not impossible, in a Mac environment. Group policies and multiple third-party tools enable a very cost effective way to distribute updates and restrict abilities in a Windows environment. The lack of centralized control and restrictions of Macs makes them less desirable (and much more costly) to deploy in an enterprise setting. This means you have to touch each individual Mac to make changes or install updates, making them more expensive to maintain. The lack of centralized control is a large reason why you see Macs in solo and small law firms and not uniformly implemented in larger firms. Below, we discuss some Mac-specific hardware and software solutions that may come in handy if you are or want to become a Mac user.

Hardware

Apple iPad

Just when you thought the fanfare for the iPad couldn't get any noisier, Apple released the next updated version, known as just the new iPad, and not the iPad 4. This upgrade brought about a few changes, but nothing requiring an immediate upgrade if you already have an iPad 2.

The arrival of very few technology devices has been met with as much excitement as the Apple iPad 2 when it was released in March 2011—and all of the new iPads since then certainly haven't received as much hype. There have been five versions of the iPad to date, including an iPad mini—which we find to be just ridiculous. The iPad mini is too similar in size to the iPhone to justify the purchase.

The most recent version of the iPad added the Apple A6X processor and replaced the 30-pin connector with an all-digital Lightning connector. The iPad runs the same iOS software as the iPhone and iPod Touch, and, like those devices, it can use iCloud for synchronization, removing the need for iTunes and a computer.

The new iPad has a 9.7-inch diagonal Multi-Touch LED-backlit IPS screen glass display, with a resolution of 2048 × 1536 pixels (264 pixels per inch). The touch screen breaks away from the previous models—devices that required a user to press the screen with a stylus, as in the old days of Palm Pilots. An embedded three-axis accelerometer is used to determine the orientation of the device—portrait or landscape mode—and some apps and games take advantage of this feature.

The new iPad comes with a built-in Wi-Fi network card, enabling the device to connect to wireless networks, and the 4G model comes with a broadband AirCard (AT&T, Sprint, or Verizon) and GPS locator. The device also includes Bluetooth capability and a 42.5 watt-hour battery lasting up to ten hours, even when continually surfing the Internet.

Some of the continuing criticisms of the iPad are the lack of Flash support, expansion capability, and alternate input/output sources. Many industry analysts say that the lack of Flash support significantly cripples Apple products since so many websites incorporate the technology. Even though the iPad comes with a fair amount of embedded memory, there are no options to add storage in the form of memory expansion cards (e.g., SD, micro SD). Finally, there are no USB ports available, which significantly limits what connections may be added. As an example, your only current printing option is to print via Bluetooth or wireless AirPrint printer, or to use a Bluetooth keyboard as an expansion device. USB printers and direct connected keyboards are not an option. Before the release of iOS 4.2, users couldn't print from these devices. It was in this iOS update that Apple provided support for wireless printing. The number of printers with AirPrint support continues to grow and includes a number of HP LaserJet and OfficeJet printer models. With the iOS 4.3 release, Apple added display mirroring, which replicates the iPad's display over the video out connection, rather than the video out feature working only with selected applications.

The latest version of the iPad has a number of features, including:

—Black and white or color options

—AT&T, Verizon, and Sprint 4G models

—1.4 GHz dual-core Apple A6X custom processor with quad-core graphics

—5 megapixel iSight camera

—1GB of processor memory

—Bluetooth 4.0 support

—1080P HD video recording

We have been pleased with the upgrades that Apple included with this model but still wouldn't recommend upgrading if you currently have the iPad 2 or the third generation version of the iPad. However, the Retina display, increased processor speed, and amount of memory make this device even faster and more responsive and to some, justify the desire to upgrade. The most current version of Apple's iOS software is version 7, which was released in September 2013.

Apple's iOS 7 is set to have an all new design, including new or improved features:

♦ Control Center—quick access to controls and apps, available with a quick upward swipe from any screen

♦ Revised Notification Center

- Updated multitasking, including intelligently scheduled updates
- New camera formats
- Airdrop sharing
- Revamped Safari web-browser
- iTunes Radio (Pandora competitor)
- iCloud Keychain—stores all your passwords in the cloud
- Updated Siri
- New security features for Find My iPhone

There hasn't been a revolutionary change to the iOS software since iOS 5. Apple's iOS 5 was released in October 2011 and included a number of new features and updates, including the introduction of iCloud, which allows users to synchronize their music, photos, apps, documents, bookmarks, calendar, contacts, e-mail, and other data between multiple iOS devices. As a cloud service, Apple will actually store this data for you in an online account associated with your Apple ID. As with many Apple products, we have determined there are a number of security and privacy concerns with using this service. If you don't believe us, just read the Terms Of Service—we did, and we will not use this service for anything business related. If you have enabled iCloud, be careful with what information you choose to synchronize with Apple. That's all we will say. We only have the Find My iPad feature configured in iCloud, so that we can locate the device if lost.

Today, lawyers frequently use the iPad for court or meetings, rather than lugging around a laptop. Originally thought to compete against e-book devices such as the Kindle or Nook, the iPad has actually established a new class of devices that compete against smartphones, netbooks, smaller laptops, and ultrabooks. Lawyers are drawn to the functionality and portability of the device, and we believe their interest will only increase as future generations are released. The iPad can be purchased directly online from the Apple Store (**store.apple.com**) starting at $499 for the 16GB Wi-Fi–only model.

Tom Mighell, lawyer and iPad expert, has three wonderful books available to assist lawyers who need help in understanding how to best use the iPad in their practice of law. The three books, *iPad in One Hour for Lawyers* (make sure you get the second edition), *iPad Apps in One Hour for Lawyers*, and *iPad in One Hour for Litigators*, can be purchased directly from the ABA's webstore and should be considered an invaluable resource for lawyers who are looking to test drive their iPads at work. You can get all three for less than $150, which is quite a deal!

Having given many lectures on the use of the iPad, we can tell you that this was the largest CLE magnet in 2013, and we expect that trend to continue. As one of our attendees said while proudly brandishing his iPad, "This is a game-changer."

Touchfire Keyboard
Some have labeled this keyboard the accessory that turns the iPad into a true laptop killer. We won't go that far, but we are impressed with this piece of hardware.

This lightweight Bluetooth keyboard is super thin and attaches to the bottom of your iPad with built-in magnets, eliminating the need to carry around heavier, bulkier keyboards. It is actually a keyboard overlay and is not a separate external device like other Bluetooth keyboards. This device provides tactile feedback when pressing the keys, enabling users to type much more quickly than on the flat keyboards often used with the iPad. If you don't use a keyboard often, you can store it in the included carrying case; otherwise, you can keep it attached to your iPad. It is compatible with and fits in the Smart Case. The downside . . . it only works in landscape mode.

In terms of compatibility, this device works with all generations of the iPad. If you want to try out this device, you can purchase one from Touchfire's website (**www.touchfire.com**) for $50.

AirPort Extreme
Apple's AirPort Extreme is its wireless solution for home, school, and business. The wireless router plugs directly into your cable or DSL modem and connects you wirelessly to the Internet. This new version of router supports the 802.11a/b/g/n protocols, including the new 802.11ac standard, which provides data rates of up to 1.3 Gbps. The wireless router supports NAT, DHCP, and VPN passthrough, allowing users the capability of connecting to their office network from home. The AirPort Extreme comes with built-in security features, such as a NAT firewall, Wi-Fi Protected Access, WPA/WPA2 and WEP encryption, and MAC address filtering. The router contains one GB Ethernet WAN port for connecting to a cable or DSL modem and three GB Ethernet LAN ports for connecting computers or networking devices.

The built-in USB port is provided to connect a printer or hard drive that is shared with other users on the local network. The AirPort Extreme is both Mac and Windows compatible, 64 percent smaller than its predecessor, and comes bundled with software, power cord, and documentation. The

AirPort Extreme can be purchased directly online from the Apple Store (**store.apple.com**) for $179.

AirPort Express

The AirPort Express Base Station is a portable wireless router, perfect for taking with you while on the road. However, this device has limited functionality in a business setting, allowing only fifty devices to connect to it at a time. The small wireless router is extremely portable, about the size of a postcard, and weighs less than 8.5 ounces. The router supports the 802.11a/b/g/n protocols and offers simultaneous dual-band 802.11n, transmitting at both the 2.4 GHz and 5 GHz frequencies at the same time. This provides 802.11n support no matter which band your wireless devices use. This wireless device is great for hotels, supplying your laptop with wireless Internet so you can surf from any location in the room.

The device has a built-in USB port for connecting a shared printer and an Ethernet port for connecting to your DSL and cable modem or your local network. The built-in wireless security supports WPA/WPA2, WEP, NAT, MAC address filtering, and time-based access control. The AirPort Express Base Station is both Mac and Windows compatible and comes bundled with the necessary software to get your computer connected to the wireless network. The AirPort Express Base Station can be purchased directly online from the Apple Store (**store.apple.com**) for $99.

AirPort Time Capsule

Looking for a solution to automatically back up your files? Time Capsule works seamlessly with Time Machine, backup software included with the Mac OS X operating system. Time Capsule is simply a wireless router with a built-in hard drive used for storing backups of your files. Using the Time Machine backup software, the application will back up your files and folders automatically, without user intervention. The data is backed up over the local wireless network to the Time Capsule hardware device.

Time Capsule can be purchased and used solely as a backup solution, or it can also provide wireless Internet connectivity to your local network. It has the same built-in features and functionality as AirPort Extreme. Time Capsule is offered in two models, with storage capacities of 2 and 3TB. Time Capsule, like the AirPort Express, supports the new 802.11ac protocol, offering data rates of up to 1.3 Gbps. This device can be purchased directly online from the Apple Store (**store.apple.com**) starting at $299 for the 2TB model.

Apple Thunderbolt Display

The Apple Thunderbolt Display is a high-definition (HD) flat-panel LCD monitor offering 27 inches of diagonal viewing area. Its wide-screen format makes this monitor a perfect display for legal professionals, providing enough real estate to display two or more documents side by side. The display is compatible with any Thunderbolt-enabled Mac notebook or desktop and supports resolutions up to 2560 × 1440 pixels.

The monitor has a 1,000:1 contrast ratio, 12 milliseconds response time, and a screen with an antiglare coating. The monitor has three USB 2.0 ports and can be purchased with an optional VESA wall mount. It also includes a built-in FaceTime HD camera with microphone and a 2.1 speaker system. The monitor even has an ambient light sensor that can automatically adjust the brightness of the LCD display. It also includes one GB Ethernet port, one Thunderbolt port, and one FireWire 800 port. The Apple Thunderbolt Display can be purchased directly online from the Apple Store (**store.apple.com**) for $999.

Apple Wireless Keyboard

The Apple wireless keyboard uses Bluetooth wireless technology, eliminating the need for obstructive and unfriendly wires to connect your keyboard to your computer. The wireless keyboard comes in a low-profile anodized aluminum frame that matches the Apple theme. The keyboard contains function keys for one-touch access to Mac features and has power management features to conserve the battery when not in use. The Apple wireless keyboard requires Mac OS X version 10.6.8 or higher, takes two AA batteries, and can also be used with the iPad. It can be purchased directly online from the Apple Store (**store.apple.com**) for $69.

Apple Magic Mouse

Like the Apple wireless keyboard, the Magic Mouse uses Bluetooth wireless technology to connect the mouse to your computer. Laser tracking allows you to use the mouse on a number of surfaces while maintaining the precision and accuracy of tracking movement. The mouse uses multitouch sensitive technology to detect both right and left clicks, and the innovative scrolling ball allows for 360-degree scrolling capabilities. The mouse is powered with two AA batteries and, when paired with the Apple wireless keyboard, allows you to work wire free at your desk. This wireless device requires Mac OS X version 10.5.8 or later to operate. Sorry, folks, but there is *no* mouse support for the iPad, so this is limited to the Apple computer. The Apple Magic Mouse can be purchased directly online from the Apple Store (**store.apple.com**) for $69.

Apple iPod

By far Apple's most successful hardware device, the iPod has sold over 350 million units since its creation in 2001. The portable digital-file-playing devices are the most popular handheld devices in use today, and some models can be used to play and shoot video, take pictures, play podcasts, and even play games. All models are capable of playing music. The iPod is available in four models: Shuffle, Nano, Classic, and Touch. The iPod Shuffle is the smallest, with no display screen, and is available in a 2GB size. The Shuffle allows you to shake the device in certain positions to change the song, play the songs in order, or shuffle the order. The newest version also includes a new VoiceOver function that will tell you the song or artist you're listening to. The iPod Shuffle costs $49 and is available in eight different colors.

The iPod Classic is the throwback to the original iPod with the circular wheel and comes in both black and silver; it's no longer offered in white. The main feature of this device is capacity. It has 160GB of storage space, which can store a vast quantity of music, video, and podcasts. This device can even be used to play games. The iPod Classic costs $249 and is available only with a 160GB storage capacity. There is actually a hard disk in this version, so it won't work well while you exercise—and no, we don't recommend that you shake it around.

The iPod Nano is one of Apple's more popular devices and has just recently had a "make over." The current version of the Nano includes a radio tuner with live pause functionality, VoiceOver, and even a pedometer. Some of the new features include a 2.5-inch multi-touch display, the ability to play video, Bluetooth, Nike+ support, and all-new EarPods. This device also gets rid of the traditional 30-pin connector and has been updated with Apple's new Lightning connector pin.

The iPod Nano is offered in seven bright colors, and it is available only with 16GB of storage capacity. The cost is just $149. Flash memory is used in the Nano, making it ideal for workouts at the gym.

The iPod Touch is probably the most versatile iPod, providing users with a way to listen to music, watch videos, and play games, as well as surf the Internet and check their e-mail. Like the Nano, the iPod Touch just went through its own refresh. The latest version is much thinner and lighter than the previous models. It comes with a 4-inch Retina display, upgraded iSight 5 megapixel camera, upgraded dual-core processor, and the all-new EarPods. The iPod Touch has a 4-inch diagonal color display and a touch-screen interface, and it is available in 16, 32, and 64GB sizes. The iPod Touch even has a built-in Wi-Fi network adapter supporting 802.11b/g/n network connections. The device also includes Bluetooth and Nike+ support. The iPod Touch costs anywhere from $229 to $399, depending on the model.

All of the iPod devices can be purchased online from the Apple Store or at your local electronics retailer. The devices are both Windows and Mac compatible, and they connect to your computer using a USB connection.

Software

Microsoft Office 2011 for Mac Home & Business
Microsoft Office for Mac 2011 is now out and includes better compatibility across platforms, improved collaboration tools, and an improved user interface. The latest version also scraps Entourage for Outlook, which will provide Mac users with the ability to import Microsoft Outlook PST files. Visual Basic support returns as well, which is a must-have for those running macro-based applications. Users can also store files online using their SkyDrive folder, which provides secure access to edit or share your work from anywhere with free Office Web Apps. Microsoft Office for Mac includes Word, PowerPoint, Excel, Outlook, Office365 support, and free tech support for one year.

Office for Mac 2011 requires Mac OS X v. 10.5.8 or later and is available only in a 32-bit version. A single license for this product can be purchased and downloaded online from Microsoft's website (**www.microsoft.com**) for $219.99.

Toast 11 Titanium by Roxio
Toast 11 Titanium is the latest version of Roxio's long-running disc-burning software for the Mac. With this software you can burn video or data to CDs or DVDs. This version gives users the ability to burn high-definition video to Blu-ray and HD-DVD. Toast even allows a user to capture streaming audio from any website and then transfer the audio to an iPod or any other iOS-based device. The software has built-in basic features, such as the ability to compress, convert, and compile video in most formats, along with backup software that can be scheduled to back up your data. Features new to this version include the ability to extract clips from any DVD video

and convert them to a format of your choice, to convert audiobook CDs for playback on iPod devices, and to build your MP3 library with the automatic capture and tagging of Internet audio. New to this version is the capability for users to even convert video recorded on their TiVo DVRs, EyeTV tuners, and Flip Video camcorders to play on their iPad, iPhone, or video game consoles. Also included with this feature is a full version of Adobe Photoshop Elements 9.

The software can be purchased online from Roxio's website (**www.roxio.com**) for $79.99.

Norton Internet Security for Mac

Every Mac user needs to protect his or her computer from viruses and other threats. Using antivirus protection on a Mac is no longer an option; it's a necessity. Norton Internet Security has an edition specifically for Mac computers that offers protection from the latest viruses, spyware, rootkits, and other web-based attacks. Norton Internet Security version 4 is compatible with OS X v. 10.4.11 and newer systems and runs natively on Intel- and PowerPC-based Mac systems, while version 5 is only compatible with systems running Mac OS X 10.7.

The antivirus protection can automatically scan and clean downloaded e-mail files and attachments and provide real-time protection and removal of viruses and other threats.

Some users still believe there are no viruses or threats for a Mac. Not so. Just look at how many systems were infected with the MacDefender or Flashback Trojan over the past two years. These were such a problem that Apple released security patches just to address these threats. There are many other documented viruses and vulnerabilities that are specific to Macs and many more that are operating system–independent. The message here is to get and install an antivirus or security solution. You should never use a computer on your business or home network without the proper security protection, even if it's a Mac. Even Apple itself removed from its website (rather late, in 2012) language suggesting that it was impervious to malware. Norton Internet Security can be purchased online directly from Symantec's website (**www.symantec.com**) for $69.99 for a one-year subscription.

For users looking for an alternative to Norton Internet Security, Kaspersky has a great product called Kaspersky Internet Security for Mac. We use Kaspersky's security software on our networks and have tried this product out on our Mac laptop, and it works as advertised. This software offers real-time protection against malware, phishing, and malicious websites, as well as antivirus protection and parental controls, and is only half the cost of Norton. The lower cost alone is a great selling point! This product can be purchased online from Kaspersky's website (**www.kaspersky.com**) for $39.95 for a one-year subscription.

Intuit Quicken Essentials and QuickBooks 2012 for Macs

Intuit Quicken for Mac offers a complete personal financial management package, providing immediate access to your accounts from a single location. By using Quicken, you can better organize your financial information and easily track your finances. Quicken Essentials provides an easy way to track and enter expenses without launching the entire application through the new QuickEntry Dashboard Widget. The software will run only on Intel-based Macs using 10.6.6 (Snow Leopard), 10.7 (Lion), or later.

Quicken Essentials is still a relatively new product, and now users can export their basic tax information to TurboTax and other applications that can read a TXF or QXF file.

If you need to switch your data files from Quicken Windows to Quicken Mac, there is a walk-through guide on Intuit's website to help you out. You can find the instructions to complete this procedure at **quicken.intuit .com/support/help/quicken-data-files-that-can-be-converted-from-windows-to-mac/GEN82214.html**.

Quicken Essentials for Mac is the latest version of the software from Intuit that is available for purchase and download on its website (**www.intuit.com**) for $39.99.

QuickBooks, another financial and accounting package from Intuit, has an edition for Macs. QuickBooks 2013 for Macs can be used to organize your business finances. This software package can be used to track and manage your business expenses, invoicing, and payroll from a single financial application. QuickBooks for Macs can synchronize your contacts directly with the Mac OS X Address Book and set reminders in iCal. This software is compatible with Mac OS X v. 10.7 (Lion), or higher.

Some of the new features of QuickBooks 2013 for Macs include:

—Redesigned sales forms that are more Mac-like

—Ability to attach key documents such as receipts or contracts in QuickBooks

—Ability to add online banking transactions in batches

—Improved Search function

—Ability to invoice for projects in phases with Progress invoicing

—Ability to create multiple time sheets with one click

QuickBooks 2013 for Macs can be purchased online from Intuit's QuickBooks website (**www.quickbooks.com**) for $249.95 for a new license. Two- through five-user versions are also available for purchase on the website.

PGP Whole Disk Encryption 10 for Mac OS X

PGP Corporation (now owned by Symantec), a leading vendor of hard disk encryption software, has released an updated version of its hard disk encryption suite compatible with Mac computers (previously called Symantec Full Disk Encryption for Macs). Symantec Drive Encryption software provides comprehensive, nonstop disk encryption for Macs, securing data on desktops, laptops, and removable devices. A user name and passphrase are required to decrypt the contents of the hard disk, protecting the data from unauthorized access. Symantec Drive Encryption requires Mac OS X v. 10.7 or v. 10.8 and only runs on Intel-based Macs. Symantec Drive Encryption can be used to provide quick, cost-effective data protection for information on hard drives and removable media. Any lawyer using a Mac laptop should definitely have this software installed to protect sensitive and confidential information. An alternative is to enable File Vault or File Vault 2, which is included as part of the operating system.

Symantec Drive Encryption software can be purchased online directly from Symantec's website (**www.symantec.com**) for $110 for a single license with one-year upgrade assurance.

Apple iTunes

If you've ever owned an iPod or older version of the iPhone or iPad, then you're certainly familiar with Apple iTunes. iTunes is Apple Software's most popular product, mainly because it used to be necessary to manage your digital music library on your iPod, iPhone, iPad, or other Apple iOS device. The newest version of iTunes allows users to download more content with their purchased songs, such as the album cover, band pictures, and even song lyrics. Using the Home Sharing feature, users can share their digital libraries with up to five authorized computers in their house, allowing them to share purchased music files across multiple computer systems. Apple now allows you to follow your favorite artists and view what music your friends are downloading and listening to. A new feature called iTunes Match lets you store all of your music in iCloud—even songs you've imported from CDs—synchronizing your music across all of your iOS devices. iCloud provides users with the ability to access their music, TV shows, apps, and books from multiple devices without the need to manually synchronize files using iTunes across multiple iOS devices.

A new feature, iTunes Radio, was introduced by Apple in 2013 as a direct competitor to Pandora and Spotify. iTunes Radio will allow users to create radio stations based on the songs/artists that they like, all for free. It's about time—but is it too late? For now, we will continue to use Pandora—which doesn't require the installation of software to run.

Using the iTunes Store, users can download apps, music, videos, podcasts, and more and then synchronize them to their devices, such as an iPad or iPhone. Users can subscribe to podcasts, and, without any user input, the iTunes application can download the latest shows as they're made available. We use this feature a lot when it comes to managing the legal technology podcasts to which we subscribe and constantly monitor. Apple iTunes is available as a free download for Mac OS X and Windows 8 from Apple's website.

CHAPTER TWENTY-FOUR

Unified Messaging and Telecommunications

THE ABILITY TO MAKE and receive phone calls is an absolute necessity for a law firm. In addition, some sort of data access is critical to the success of a firm these days. We are a very connected society, and any potential client expects to be able to contact you with relative ease, whether via voice or data transmission such as e-mail. We'll cover some of your options to provision the technology for voice and data communications.

Unified Messaging

Unified messaging is the delivery of traditional voice communications into your e-mail box. This would include the delivery of facsimile transmissions as well. Unified messaging systems began to appear around 2001 and were fairly unsuccessful for the first couple of years. They are now stable. This means that you can now monitor your communications constantly from (potentially) one location. This is a blessing and a curse, but it is now becoming a service that many clients expect you to have.

The simplest way to implement unified messaging is to have it integrated with your phone system. Some small firms may not even have a phone system, and we'll address that issue in a moment. Many of the newer PBX (private branch exchange) systems are incorporating a voicemail card directly into the telephone system chassis. Stand-alone voicemail systems are also an alternative for larger office environments.

You can even integrate unified messaging with your Exchange server or your VoIP implementation. Some outsourced providers of VoIP solutions will provide unified messaging capabilities too, which means you don't have to have any physical equipment to gain the benefits of integrating all your communication streams.

For budget purposes, plan on spending around $3,000 for a voicemail system with unified messaging. As is true for most technology solutions, your mileage may vary. There are a lot of different ways that vendors implement unified messaging. Some are better than others, and, frankly, some are nothing more than kludge workarounds to make their systems sound more robust than they really are. Our recommendation is to stick with well-known vendors of communication equipment. You really can't go wrong with suppliers such as Avaya, Cisco, NEC, Toshiba, and so on.

There are companies that resell complete unified messaging solutions, thereby saving you the investment in hardware and software. These solutions are typically available for a monthly fee, and you may have to commit to a multiyear contract to obtain the service. Also, you are stuck with whatever features and methods the vendor provides. As an example, you may not like the file format for a fax delivery into your inbox, but you'll have no choice but to accept what they give you. Another concern is that all of your communications may be going through a third party if it is not an on-premise solution. This means your phone calls actually route through the vendor's system before being delivered to your location. In that way, they can capture a voicemail message or fax and repackage it for delivery to your e-mail address. We are generally not fans of having client data move through third-party providers and would recommend that you first investigate "owned" systems that you can control. While a price tag of $3,000 isn't cheap, the value is so great that a good number of solos and small firms have made the leap, and the numbers grow monthly. We are beginning to see on-premise solutions for the small business market, which may reduce your cost and provide a more stable environment versus hosted solutions.

We'll attempt to cover some of the concerns and questions you should have when considering whether to implement a unified messaging solution. These issues are related to equipment that is provided as part of your telephone communication system. The first issue is what communications the system handles. Can it do both voice messages and fax transmissions, or just one? Even though most systems will handle both voicemail and fax, generally firms use only the voice capability and route the faxes to a dedicated fax machine or printer rather than to a specific person's inbox.

How do you want the voice messages delivered? Most firms will elect to send only an e-mail notification that a voicemail message has been received. This configuration saves bandwidth because the message itself is not transmitted to the e-mail client and stays on the voicemail server until you retrieve it. This is hardly convenient if you are traveling. In fact, some telephone systems are configured not to allow remote connections, even for voicemail retrieval, as a security measure. There are a lot of lawyers who use some type of smartphone. Sending a notification only message saves on the usage of their data plans. The other alternative is to deliver the actual message to your inbox. Obviously, this uses a lot more bandwidth, especially if you are delivering it to a cell phone that also receives your e-mail. If you elect this configuration, you'd better have an unlimited data plan for your cell phone or a data plan that can cover your traffic load. Make sure your portable device can play back the file format for your voicemail if you elect to deliver the message to your inbox. As an example, the iPad doesn't natively play back WAV files, which is the format of our unified message system. This means you'll have to purchase an app just to play attached voicemail files.

Another question for your PBX provider is how it handles the message delivery itself. Is the message forwarded to your inbox and then deleted from the voicemail system? That means there is only one copy of it, and you'll never know you received a message if it gets trapped or trashed by your spam filter. If the original stays on the voicemail system and a copy gets delivered to your inbox, does the message light stay lit on your phone? You may not want this, but then again you may want a visual indication that a voice message was delivered.

How does the vendor identify the voice message in your inbox? Is the "From: address" something that is easily recognizable as the phone system, or does it come from you? What does the subject line contain? It is particularly helpful if the caller ID is shown in the subject line, but not all vendors package messages that way. How is the voice message delivered to your e-mail system? Do you have to have a user ID and password configured on your voicemail box that is consistent with your network credentials? If so, you have the issue of constantly synchronizing your logon credentials with the telephone system. Many phone systems only accept numbers as a password, so you can't even use letters (forget capitals). This restriction may render your integration unacceptable.

Finally, how do you retrieve your messages? Are they delivered as a standard audio attachment to an e-mail message? This is certainly preferred, since you don't need any special software to listen to the message. Some of the lower cost (and kludge) solutions require that you install a software add-on to your e-mail client to listen to the voice message. This solution won't work if you are trying to deliver the voicemail to your cell phone. Another problem deals with specific software versions. You must make sure that any potential voicemail system will be compatible with your firm's e-mail solution, so if you have questions regarding what versions of Microsoft Exchange and Outlook the voicemail system is compatible with, make sure you ask your vendor before you make the investment. As you can see, having specialized software is not a recommended solution. Better to have the voice message packaged as a standard (not proprietary) audio file attachment. That way you can even retrieve your voicemail using a web browser from an Internet café while on vacation in Rio.

If all of this has given you a headache, don't worry. Make sure your IT consultant reads this chapter—he or she can answer all the questions for you. But make no mistake about it: No one who has successfully implemented unified messaging has ever discarded it. The value of unified messaging is phenomenal—being able to access your voicemail on your cell phone is a remarkable enhancement. You need never worry again about being out of touch. If you prefer not to give clients your home or cell phone number, you'll still get their messages. We cannot count the number of times that having voicemail sent to our cell phones has been worth its weight in diamonds.

Google Voice

For those lawyers constantly on the road, a free service you might find useful is Google Voice. If you'd rather not give out your personal cell phone number to your pesky clients, who always have emergencies regardless of the time, then this service might be for you. Google Voice allows you to select a phone number local to your area that forwards inbound phone calls to your other personal phone numbers. This service allows you to provide your clients with a phone number (not your personal number), screen incoming phone calls, and receive voicemails left on the Google Voice phone number in your e-mail inbox. You can specify what e-mail address you would like the voicemails forwarded to. By default, the notification is sent to the address linked to your Google account, but you can add additional e-mail addresses. Google Voice will even transcribe your voicemails to text and provide them in the body of the e-mail, allowing users to read the content before they choose to listen to the messages. The voicemail itself can be downloaded and is delivered as an MP3 file, not a WAV file as most other voicemail systems. Google Voice also allows users to receive and record phone conversations (be mindful of the laws in your state if you do this), index and search voicemails, and set up conference calls.

If you are currently a Sprint customer, you can take advantage of the Google Voice features without changing your phone number. Be sure to review the Google Voice help section (**support.google.com/voice/**) to see exactly what features you get by integrating your Sprint account with Google Voice.

Voice over Internet Protocol (VoIP)

In its most basic definition, VoIP is a family of technologies for delivery of voice communications over Internet protocol networks, such as the Internet. VoIP systems are digital and can run voice and data systems over the same network, reducing investment in infrastructure. Corporate usage of VoIP phone systems has increased dramatically over the past several years, replacing the traditional copper-wire telephone systems that we all used in the past.

VoIP systems are primarily aimed at providing users with unified communications, delivering all services (voice, fax, voicemails, and e-mail) to a single location. VoIP systems are generally more flexible and less costly to implement than your standard copper-wire systems, and they can integrate easily with most existing data network infrastructures.

Security used to be a major concern for VoIP systems. That concern has been greatly reduced. It appears that vendors have finally overcome the performance hit associated with encrypting the voice traffic. You would be hard pressed to find a current vendor that sends voice traffic in an unencrypted stream. This means you'll sleep a little better knowing that your voice traffic travels in secure encrypted channels. That doesn't mean your VoIP traffic isn't subject to hacking. In fact, security guru Bruce Schneier has published several blog posts describing how to hack a VoIP data stream. His past post discusses how it is possible to even ". . . identify the phrases spoken within encrypted VoIP calls when the audio is encoded using variable bit rate codecs." Sound scary? Given the recent news of the capabilities and actions of the National Security Agency, VoIP systems carry just as much risk of interception as traditional phone networks.

Because the underlying IP network that a VoIP system uses is unreliable, it's not uncommon to experience latency or jitteriness when making a call using a VoIP phone system, especially to offsite destinations. Once your voice packet hits the already congested Internet, you are no longer in control of how fast your data gets to where it's going, and that's what causes the delays. Using a VoIP system on the same data network as your computer system might tremendously slow down how fast you can access your server and case management applications because of all the data traffic on your local network. Be sure your existing data network and Internet connection are capable of handling the increase in load before implementing a VoIP system. If you have to upgrade existing hardware or the speed of your Internet connection, those are hidden costs that you might not be aware of and that you will have to plan for. Also, implementing an MPLS (Multiprotocol Label Switching) network gives you the option of configuring QoS (Quality of Service), where you can give the voice traffic a higher priority. MPLS networks are not cheap and tend to be used in larger firms with multiple office locations. Frankly, we think MPLS is overkill and too expensive for a solo or small firm considering VoIP. As an alternative, a large number of VoIP installations use the IP network on the local premises. They then route the external calls to the Internet and may even have some traditional phone circuits connected too. The reality is that the telephone carriers themselves are using VoIP between two IP gateways to reduce the long haul bandwidth.

Lastly, VoIP systems are susceptible to power failures and outages. Unlike analog phones that get their power directly from the copper phone lines, VoIP systems need electricity to operate, just like your computer system. You better have an analog phone line as a backup, or at least a cell phone.

VoIP phone systems have their pros and cons when compared to other digital phone systems. Be sure to ask your vendor the right questions to determine which type of system is right for you. And be wary of those vendors and check their references. We have seen a lot of VoIP installations that caused major-league heartburn for the law firms that undertook them.

Not only have hidden costs pushed their budgets far beyond the original numbers, but vendors tend not to plan for redundancy or to warn of the potential downsides of VoIP. We have had both happy and unhappy VoIP clients, so we're not saying, "Don't do it," but be aware that this may not be the right choice for everyone. As a side note, we have yet to hear of a client that wasn't happy with their Cisco VoIP installation. That has to tell you something about the quality and stability of Cisco products.

High-Speed Internet

None of our lawyers/clients ever complain that their Internet connection is too fast. We have collectively almost forgotten how slow the Internet used to be and how patiently we had to wait for our screens to load. High-speed Internet is now a requirement for solos and small law firms. High-speed Internet has all but replaced dial-up Internet connections because of the low cost and fast connection speeds, although there are still some parts of the country where dial-up is the only option. Why continue to wait for web pages to load and attachments to open if you don't have to? Few creatures are more impatient than lawyers, and virtually all of them have jumped to high-speed Internet installations.

High-speed Internet connections are available from your local Internet service provider (ISP) and usually are provided over a cable, DSL, or fiber optic connection. These high-speed connections offer download speeds in excess of 25 Mbps and varying upload speeds, depending on the provider and the service tier to which you've subscribed. If your firm hosts its own services, such as e-mail or a website, static IP addresses can be obtained from your local provider for these types of connections. The ISP may charge more to issue your business a static IP address than if you just require a dynamically leased IP address. High-speed Internet access connectivity generally will cost $75 to $200 per month.

If your firm requires a larger amount of bandwidth due to the number of users sharing the Internet connection or for web-based applications, your local ISP may be able to provide a connection type that meets your requirements. Historically, the ISPs and telco providers classified upgraded service connections as T1 or fractional T1 connections. While they may call them upgrades, they are much slower than alternate technologies and will cost hundreds of dollars more per month. These types of connections also require longer service agreements and usually include a large setup cost. They do have the advantage of a service level agreement (SLA), which means the connection must be repaired within a particular time and must be available a high percentage of the time. DSL or cable modem connections do not carry an SLA, so repair times could be several days during an outage. T1 circuits are becoming less and less popular, even though they are very reliable and guarantee bandwidth. A full T1 provides only 1.544 Mbps up and down and typically will cost $300 to $500 per month. Compare this to other broadband services (cable or DSL), where you can get 30 Mbps download and 5 Mbps upload for less than $200 a month. Do the math. Thirty is a *much* bigger number than 1.544.

If available in your area, a speedy alternative to a T1 is fiber optics. Fiber to the curb, such as Verizon FiOS, can offer business subscribers increasingly faster Internet connections at a much lower cost. Check with your local service providers to see if such a connection is currently available. In general, solos and small firms are well served by cable and DSL to meet their Internet connection needs.

Another option for Internet access is from your cellular provider. Mobile broadband Internet access has gained steam lately and is becoming a growing trend with mobile lawyers. Plus, it's a good way to avoid having to pay those outrageous prices for Internet access that hotels charge nowadays. You may have heard the terms 3G, 4G, etc., used to identify mobile broadband. For about $60 a month, your cellular provider can provide you with Internet access when on the road. If you've purchased a laptop recently, you might already have a broadband card installed. For everyone else, most providers will throw in the broadband card for no cost when you sign up for their service. We have found that it is cheaper to activate the mobile hot spot feature on our smartphones instead of acquiring a separate mobile data plan. That way you use the data plan from your phone to create the Wi-Fi "cloud" for other devices to share. You can then use the Wi-Fi only iPad (a lot cheaper) instead of one with the built-in 3G/4G capability.

CHAPTER TWENTY-FIVE

Utilities

WHAT WE ALL NEED is Batman's belt, with a full repository of tricks that we can draw upon at any moment to perform the myriad tasks associated with the practice of law. Failing that, we must acknowledge that it is impossible to list all of the utilities that a solo or small firm might find useful. There are so many great selections and just as many opinions as to what makes one utility more valuable than another.

The threshold question is, what constitutes a utility? For our purposes, we will consider a utility to be some software application that takes data and manipulates it for a specific purpose. That allows us a lot of latitude.

The challenge is to list utilities that offer a unique purpose for the solo and small firm lawyer. We have used many of these utilities ourselves and have had some great suggestions from our friends and colleagues. If you don't see your favorite utility here, just drop us a line and perhaps it will be listed in the next edition of the book.

X1

How often do you find yourself frantically searching your computer for a file only to discover that you have no clue where you saved it? It's happened to all of us, and the problem is compounded when you have copies of the same file saved in multiple locations. Which file is the right one? What a headache.

To relieve some of the stress, we recommend that lawyers use a product called X1 Search 8. X1 is a piece of software that enables users to search for and instantly find information, while keeping the resulting file in its native format. No more messy conversions. X1 allows users to search for any file, whether located within their e-mail on the local computer, a network share, removable storage drive, or even within virtual desktops. This software currently supports more than 500 file types in their native format and layout and can even search for data within multiple Microsoft Outlook PST files and Lotus Notes without having to mount the files.

The X1 program displays the search results as you type, similar to the Google Instant Search, which allows users to modify their search query in real time. The advanced searching options allow users to search multiple e-mail metadata fields, such as From, To, and Subject, as well as to sort the resulting files by any of the file properties.

The X1 program is a powerful search tool that includes a number of advanced features, such as support for searching inside compressed ZIP files and RSS feeds, as well as a number of export options, such as exporting the search results to a folder or Microsoft Outlook PST file. The product is even administrator-friendly, supporting integration with Active Directory and Group Policy, for ease of deployment and flexibility in its configuration.

Before installing, you will need to make sure that you have enough storage space for the search index this program will create, which is roughly 20 percent of the total volume of files indexed. X1 supports Microsoft Windows (32 or 64-bit) operating systems; Microsoft Outlook XP/2003/2007/2010 (32 or 64-bit); Microsoft Outlook Express 6.x; Mozilla Thunderbird 1.5/2.x/3.x; and IBM Lotus Notes and Domino 6.5x to 8.x e-mail clients.

The X1 Search 8 software costs $49.95 per license and can be purchased with varying levels of support. If you want to try before you buy, they do offer a fourteen-day trial as well. To view or purchase this product, visit **www.x1.com**.

dtSearch

dtSearch is another powerful search tool that has been used by lawyers for many years, dating back to the early MS-DOS days. This product has come a long way and remains one of our favorite and most popular searching tools—and honestly, it doesn't change much from year to year. That's how solid this product is. The dtSearch program is offered in a number of different versions, but solo and small firms should consider only the following versions:

- Desktop with Spider
- Network with Spider

The Desktop with Spider version is perfect for solo lawyers who need to be able to instantly search their client files on a single computer, although it can also be configured to index network drives. The Network with Spider version allows multiple users to search the same search index, which is a must when working in a multiuser networking environment.

The dtSearch products include support for full-text searching, the ability to search a number of common metadata fields, Unicode support, and even the ability to search within nested ZIP files. The product highlights search hits in most web-based file formats, such as XML and HTML, while maintaining the format and layout of the page, including graphics and embedded hyperlinks. dtSearch also displays search hits in other popular file types, such as documents, spreadsheets, database files, and e-mails. The built-in spider can add website content to the searchable database, including secure password-protected websites. The ability to index and search website content is a great feature for those lawyers involved in cases or matters involving e-discovery.

Like other full-text search applications, dtSearch uses a large volume of disk space to store its search index, requiring approximately one-third of the total volume of files indexed. The software states that a single index file can handle more than a terabyte of indexed text, which is a lot of files. When creating the index, the default operation is to ignore "noise" words (e.g., *the*, *a*, *and*, etc.). If you need to search phrases that include those words, make sure you override the defaults and index the "noise" words too.

dtSearch supports Windows 8 operating systems (both 32- and 64-bit versions) and even has a version for Linux. Just recently, dtSearch added support for the Microsoft Outlook 2010 64-bit e-mail client. Also new in the latest version is the ability to highlight search hits within PDF files retrieved after a search using Adobe Acrobat and Reader X. dtSearch Desktop with Spider can be purchased on dtSearch's website (**www.dtsearch.com**) for $199 per license. dtSearch Network with Spider can also be purchased at a cost of $160 per license for five to twenty-four users or $140 per license for twenty-five to ninety-nine users. Further discounts are offered for purchases of more than one hundred licenses.

Credenza

Are you looking for a way to enhance your ability to run and manage your law firm using just a single piece of software? It can be done, believe it or not, with Microsoft Outlook and a small add-in named Credenza. Surprisingly, many lawyers use Microsoft Outlook for their case management solution rather than purchasing a separate application for the job. While we don't recommend this, we have to bow to the inevitable and help those who choose to do this, even though Outlook is *not* a case management product. If you are one of those lawyers who uses Outlook for case management, you should consider Credenza.

Credenza is a legal-practice management solution that integrates with Microsoft Outlook and allows legal professionals to manage their firms more effectively. Credenza allows you to:

- Create and open a file for each client matter or case
- Track time spent on individual e-mails (it even flags messages that may have been missed or forgotten)
- Keep and make notes regarding phone calls, voicemails, and other messages
- View a complete chronology of a file
- Conflict check, automate inbox controls, and share information with other users

Previously, Credenza offered only a free trial version to its potential users. Now, it offers a Basic version of the program that is free to download and use. The Pro version can be purchased and downloaded from the Credenza Software website at **www.credenzasoft.com** and costs $24.95 per month per user. The Basic version includes all of the basic practice management features, while the Pro version is multiuser and includes collaboration tools, cloud integration, and incorporated billing along with many other more powerful features.

To determine which version of the software is right for you, you can view the Basic features here: **www.credenzasoft.com/basic.html**.

You can view the Pro features here: **www.credenzasoft.com/pro.html**.

Outlook Send Assistant

Concerned about inadvertently sending an e-mail message to an unintended recipient? If so, we have the tool for you. It is a must-have utility for every Microsoft Outlook user. Outlook Send Assistant (**www.thepayne group.com/products/outlooksend/**) is a small tool that packs a big punch.

Here are some of the features of this simple and elegant tool:

—Integrates with Microsoft Outlook 2013, Outlook 2010, and Outlook 2007

—Supports HTML and Plain Text formats

—Alerts users when the Reply All button is selected

—Warns users that the message has a blank Subject line

—Prompts the user when external recipients are detected

—Confirms with e-mail senders if they'd like to continue sending the message

—Prompts when the e-mail is addressed to a Distribution List

—Alerts users when recipient(s) are detected in the BCC field

—Inserts BCC disclosure text into the recipients' message, thus notifying them of the BCC status

—Customizes warnings when specific recipient addresses are detected

—Automatically adds Marketing, Circular 230 Disclosure, SEC, SPAM warnings, and security disclaimers to e-mail messages

Outlook Send Assistant v3 is designed for Outlook 2013, Outlook 2010, and Outlook 2007. You can get previous versions of Outlook Send Assistant that will work with prior versions of Outlook. The cost of this product is $45 per license.

GreenPrint

GreenPrint Technologies (**www.printgreener.com**) has a software product, GreenPrint, that eliminates unwanted pages from your printing jobs, saving you ink, toner, paper, money, and trees. The software intercepts your print jobs and highlights unnecessary pages that can be removed, such as blank pages. How many times have you printed a web page that prints on two pages of paper, with only a single line of text on the second page? Usually the second page contains only a URL, logo, or banner ad. No longer will these wasted pages need to be printed. The Enterprise Edition includes such additional features as the GreenPrint Advisor, a tool to help your firm select low-cost printers, and GreenPrint Analytics, a powerful reporting tool documenting your firm's true savings. If you don't already have Adobe Acrobat or another third-party PDF printer, you can also get a PDF printer from GreenPrint.

GreenPrint makes recommendations about pages that should be removed from the print job and prompts the user for approval before the job is sent to the printer. There is an edition for small business and home users and an Enterprise Edition for businesses. The Home Premium edition costs $19 per computer. You have to contact the vendor at **sales@printgreener.com** to get pricing for the Enterprise Edition. The product works with Windows XP/Vista/7 and Citrix. Support for Windows 8 wasn't currently listed on the website at the time of writing.

Winscribe for the Legal Profession

Winscribe, a leading developer of dictation software, has made a product specifically for the legal profession that allows dictations to be automatically transcribed, converting recorded words to text. Automating the process saves both time and money, increasing the efficiency of your employees. It marks the end of the "listen . . . type" era. Now your employees can spend their time doing something more productive and billable. Winscribe can even integrate with existing applications, such as your document management system, streamlining your workflow process. As the creator of the dictations, you can manage and monitor the status of your work, as well as retrieve jobs for review and editing.

Another innovative feature of this software is that it supports a wide range of input from recordings made on telephones, PCs and laptops, digital handheld devices, BlackBerrys, iPhones, Androids, or Windows Mobile devices. With the Winscribe Mobility Suite, the days of carrying around a digital recorder may be over. Now you can install mobile software on your smartphone to record dictations and transfer the files wirelessly to your firm's network. As always, client confidentiality is an extremely important issue. Winscribe protects dictations through the encryption of the files and through the implementation of a secure file transfer process. Winscribe has been vetted by the experts and found worthy. This product is available on Winscribe's website at **www.winscribe.com** and can be purchased as an in-house package or an on-demand Software as an Service (SaaS) over the Web.

Eyejot

What a slogan: "Video mail in a blink." Is video the future of e-mail? If so, Eyejot has got it right. Eyejot is a comprehensive, client-free, online video-messaging platform ideal for both personal and business communications. Eyejot is currently supported on Apple's iOS platform, with Android support expected soon. Users can sign up for the service by creating a free account, which allows an unlimited number of five-minute video e-mail messages and provides support for both RSS feeds and iTunes. If you can send an e-mail, then you can send an Eyejot.

The Free account keeps your video messages for up to one month, allows you to send a video message to any e-mail address (not just an Eyejot account), and, if needed, provides code for you to embed the Eyejot widget on your website. However, the free account is ad supported.

To send a video message, once an account has been created, a user must log into his or her account, upload the video, and then click the Send button. That's it, plain and simple. The software requires no client installation and works with all major web browsers. For those users who require more, there is a Pro account for $29.95 per year that allows you to upload videos, provides an enhanced mobile inbox, and is advertising free.

There is also a Pro+ account subscription for $99.95 per year that is advertising free and allows you to attach other documents to your video messages as well as customize your own message templates. Users can purchase and create an Eyejot account online at **www.eyejot.com**.

Hightail (formerly YouSendIt)

What a wonderful resource to transmit large file attachments without charge. There are several service packages, one of which is free. The free offering, called Lite, can transmit an attachment that is up to 50MB in size. The Lite package also provides a user with 2GB of online storage space, mobile access, and a Desktop Sync application. Since a lot of ISPs limit the size of attachments, Hightail is a great alternative to "push" the occasional large attachment. The service works by creating an account at **hightail.com** and actually uploading the file to the Hightail service. You provide the e-mail addresses for the recipient(s), and an e-mail message is sent with a hyperlink that allows for downloading the file from the Hightail site.

If you regularly need to transmit very large attachments, especially those larger than 50MB, Hightail provides several pay services to accomplish this. These services provide enhancements such as e-mail support, longer availability for file downloads, reports, advanced security options, custom branding, and more bandwidth for downloads. The Professional plan costs $15.99 per month or $159.99 per year, while the Teams and Enterprise plans cost much more. We have found this resource to be invaluable for sending conference attendees copies of our PowerPoint presentations, which tend to be quite large because of the graphics. Don't forget to encrypt your data before uploading it to Hightail's servers if it is confidential. This terrific utility may be found at **www.hightail.com**.

Copy2Contact

Copy2Contact, formerly Anagram, is a piece of software that allows you to "sweep" text from an e-mail message and create a record within Outlook. You can sweep contact information that the sender has added in his or her message footer and instantly create an Outlook contact. The software is not limited just to the creation of contacts. You can "grab" text and create calendar entries, to-do items, and even tasks. The text can originate from anywhere. Copy2Contact will create the contact, calendar entry, task, and so on, in your personal folder area, which is fine for most solos. If you have a Microsoft Exchange Server with Public Folders, records generated by this program will not go directly to the Public Folder. You will have to move the data from your personal folder if the intended destination is a Public Folder. Copy2Contact is currently available for Google Apps, Salesforce.com, Microsoft Outlook, Netsuite, iPhone, and BlackBerry. Copy2Contact is compatible with all Windows-based systems, including Windows 8. The program also has a version available for BlackBerry and iPhone devices.

The base Copy2Contact for Outlook product costs $34.95 for a single user. The Pro version is $49.95 and includes features like smart capitalization, formatting, address book selection, and extended hotkeys. There is a 14-day trial version to make sure that Copy2Contact will work on your computer and perform according to your expectations. Make sure you download and try the trial before you spend the money; however, we're sure (especially you solo lawyers) that you'll be typing in your credit card number shortly after your first use of Copy2Contact. This product can be purchased and downloaded from its website at **www.copy2contact.com**.

TwInbox

Are you a Twitter junkie? We've found a program that integrates with Microsoft Outlook that allows you to update your Twitter status directly from Outlook. TwInbox (**www.techhit.com/TwInbox/twitter_plugin_ outlook.html**), a free add-on for Microsoft Outlook, allows you to receive your follower updates and archive, manage, group, and search your tweets in the same way that you manage your e-mail. Some of the additional features of this tiny program include allowing users to search and track keywords, group tweets by sender or topic, and upload and post picture files and Outlook e-mail attachments. A newly added feature also allows users to manage multiple Twitter accounts directly from within Microsoft Outlook. This product is free—why not give it a try?

TweetDeck

If you're a Twitter user and prefer not to tweet from within Microsoft Outlook or from the Twitter website, then this program might be for you. TweetDeck, another free utility, helps you organize Twitter and those you are following. You can group people so that you can concentrate on "special" individuals whose tweets are more important to you. This helps you reduce the noise level of Twitter and focuses attention on specific tweets. It also includes a URL "shortener." TweetDeck used to require the installation of Adobe Air, which needs full administrative access to your hard disk, but since it was purchased by Twitter, the service is now offered as a web app within your Internet browser or as a desktop application that no longer requires Adobe Air. This is a wonderful "dashboard" for managing Twitter—we know because we use it. You can sign in to TweetDeck or download the desktop application at **tweetdeck.com**.

TinyURL

Have you ever wanted to give somebody a reference link only to discover that it is about 400 characters long and contains all kinds of goofy characters and non-word representations? Probably the biggest problem is the breaking up of the URL link, especially when the e-mail is viewed as text formatted. The last thing you want to do is have the recipient cut and paste the various parts of the URL back together. TinyURL stores the complete URL on its servers and provides a very small URL instead. The user selects the smaller TinyURL, which translates and redirects to the much larger one. This is a free service to make the posting of long URLs easier— especially handy for Twitter! If you're a frequent user of TinyURL, there's even a toolbar for your browser that you can install to make the service more accessible. It is available at **tinyurl.com**.

IrfanView

Do you have some graphic files for a construction case that you can't seem to view? Or a video or sound file for a wrongful termination case and don't know how to play it? IrfanView (**www.irfanview.com**) is a wonderful software application that can view a very large number of different graphic file formats and can play several audio and video formats. IrfanView is compatible with all Windows-based systems but not Mac or Linux. IrfanView is free only for home use, so you can't legally use it for your law practice unless you pay money. You will have to send an e-mail to **irfanview@gmx.net** to get the cost and payment method if you need to use IrfanView in a commercial setting.

Some of the common file types and formats that IrfanView supports include:

- —JPG
- —TIFF
- —GIF
- —MPG
- —MP3
- —AVI
- —WMA

DBAN

Darik's Boot and Nuke (DBAN) is a free program that can be used to securely wipe the contents of your hard drive. DBAN is an open-source project that can be downloaded from **www.dban.org**. DBAN will automatically and permanently delete the contents of any hard disk it can detect. DBAN also allows the wiping of multiple hard disks at the same time. We all love "free," and this program is the perfect complement to any lawyer's software tool chest. You use DBAN to wipe the data contents from your hard drives and USB flash drives so that your confidential client information cannot be recovered. We have all read stories of customer data being found on hard drives purchased on eBay. Make sure that you wipe any media that may contain information you don't want someone else to recover. Could the National Security Agency recover something wiped with DBAN? Frankly, we think that's another urban legend, and we've never—ever—seen evidence of it, even with the recent documents released by Edward Snowden. However, we continue to monitor the capabilities of the federal government in particular. DBAN is free, it's safe, and it helps you comply with your ethical duty to keep your client data confidential. When you're getting ready to donate or ditch your old computers, this is an invaluable tool. DBAN is downloaded as an ISO file that can be burned to a CD or DVD, which would then be booted from to load the DBAN program.

SimplyFile

Long ago, we realized how much time we were losing each day carefully dragging and dropping e-mail into the correct Outlook folder, often accidentally filing messages in a folder below or a folder above the intended destination. Maddening.

With the SimplyFile software, each e-mail will display the name of the folder SimplyFile believes it belongs in. After it initially indexes and "learns" your filing system (and be patient, because it may run for several hours and impact system performance), it is correct more than 90 percent of the time. If it has guessed wrong, there is a QuickPick feature. Open it, and you'll likely find that the correct folder is near the top of the list of possibilities presented. If not, you can just type in the first few letters of the folder and it will appear. Most of the time, you'll just be clicking "file" and it's done. It can also turn e-mail into a calendar or a task. Marvelous. Authors Nelson and Simek regarded this product as their "find of the year" from 2009 and don't know how they functioned without it. The current version is compatible with Outlook 2013 and Windows 8. This product does not work with Outlook Express.

The latest version, SimplyFile 3.1, includes new features such as Outlook 2010 Ribbon UI support, file thread and sender commands, the ability to batch actions, a new snooze option, and the ability to view statistics regarding your e-mail usage. SimplyFile may be purchased (or there's a thirty-day free trial) at **www.techhit.com/SimplyFile/**. The cost for a single license is $49.95.

Shred 2

PC Magazine has a free utility designed to wipe specific files or disk areas. Shred 2 "officially" runs under Windows 95, 98, 2000, ME, NT 4.0, and XP. Don't worry—we are successfully running it on Windows 7 systems, too. If you want to wipe the recycle bin, then you'll need an updated DLL file, which is discussed in the article about Shred 2 at

www.pcmag.com/article2/0,2817,13352,00.asp, but current operating systems shouldn't need anything more than the Shred 2 program itself. The software can selectively wipe files or folders and can be configured to do multiple wipes of the same area if you are particularly paranoid. This utility is especially useful in removing data remnants of files and their associated file slack, which can be forensically recovered if wiping did not occur. The nice part about having a file/folder wiping utility is that data can be selectively eradicated from your computer without having to wipe the entire hard disk and having to reload the operating system and all of the applications. Remember, though, you cannot recover the file once it is wiped, so pay attention when you're clicking that mouse.

SnagIt

No lawyer should be without a screen-capture program. SnagIt 11 is a screen-capture utility that can capture anything on your desktop. You can capture a specific window, a defined area, a specific object (e.g., the title bar), or a multitude of other things. There are more than 40 ways to capture the information you want to preserve. A screen-capture application is a great tool to "grab" images to place in a motion or brief that show exactly what is shown on the computer screen. This is particularly handy when you want only a specific area of the screen. SnagIt can output the "snagged" image to a multitude of formats as well. The latest version includes additional video capture options, new stamps, more zoom options and also makes it easier to edit and resize the captured image. SnagIt costs $49.95 for a single license version, with discounts for multiple copies. There is a thirty-day trial version available, so you can see whether it fits your needs before purchase. It is available from **www.techsmith.com/download/snagit/default.asp** and now works on all Windows 32- and 64-bit operating systems. There is a Mac version as well.

If you are using Windows 7 or Windows 8, you should try the Snipping Tool before deciding to purchase a third-party application for your screen-grabbing needs. The Snipping Tool is included by default and is Microsoft's version of a screen-grabbing utility that allows you to save the captured data to a file or copy it to the Clipboard, which is handy when creating PowerPoint slides. On a Mac, you should try the Grab app, which is Apple's equivalent screen-grabbing utility.

FavBackup 2.1.3

If you're like us, you probably have multiple browsers installed on your computer. If you're looking at upgrading your computer to Windows 7 or Windows 8, this tool provides an easy way to back up and restore your web browser settings and other data. FavBackup (**www.favbrowser.com/backup**) is a free utility and supports Internet Explorer 6–8; Firefox 2–8; Opera 9–11.6; Safari 3 and 4; Google Chrome 1–16; and Flock 2–2.5. This is definitely a tool to keep in your tool chest.

If you are a Google Chrome user, you can use the Bookmark Sync feature, which makes it easy to keep the same set of bookmarks on multiple computers. When enabled, the bookmarks or favorites will be stored online in your Google Account and will be automatically synced with each computer you use where this feature is enabled. No need to back up or transfer them manually. Again, the only potential roadblock is that a Google Mail account is required.

QuickView Plus

Spend a little more money and get a utility that can view more than 300 file formats, including Microsoft Office 2013 and Corel WordPerfect Office X5. That's what you get when you purchase QuickView Plus 13 Standard. The file support comes without the need for the native application, potentially saving you the costs of having to purchase a license for a product just to view a file. QuickView Plus maintains the formatting of the files you view, so you can view and print files as they were originally created and meant to be seen. This is a great application to view file formats, especially from your electronic discovery cases. You can handle e-mail attachments and various obscure software packages that you've probably never heard of. QuickView Plus is compatible with Microsoft Windows computer systems, including Windows 8.

At $49 for a single download license of the standard edition, it is a perfect complement to IrfanView. QuickView Plus is available for purchase and download at **www.avantstar.com**, and a fully functional evaluation copy of the product is offered for thirty days. The professional edition adds advanced viewing, searching, etc., and starts at $495 for five licenses.

Sam Spade

The name of this utility, obviously, is meant to evoke Humphrey Bogart in *The Maltese Falcon*. Indeed, this utility can perform some gumshoe functions, such as troubleshooting and dealing with Internet communications. However, the most useful function of this free utility is the ability to decode e-mail headers so anyone can decipher the cryptic entries in a readable English form. Unfortunately, the original site for Sam Spade is down and no longer active. The good news is that there are several websites that have the latest version (1.14) available for download. This product hasn't been updated since 2002 and most likely never will be again.

For instructions on how to use the application, the SANS Institute has a great white paper on the matter that can be downloaded here: **www.sans.org/reading_room/whitepapers/tools/sam-spade_934**.

As we move forward into the world of electronic evidence, having the ability to decode e-mail headers is an invaluable asset to help ascertain where an e-mail *really* came from. Mind you, there are still ways for the world's miscreants to hide, but Sam Spade can provide you with a lot of helpful information. Just do a Google search for "Sam Spade spam" and you will find several download locations on the first page of the results.

Metadata Assistant

One of our favorite metadata analysis and removal tools is Metadata Assistant by Payne Group (**www.thepaynegroup.com/products/metadata/**). Metadata Assistant integrates with your Microsoft Office installation and is particularly valuable when sending file attachments. The product will display a dialog box asking if you want to clean the attachment or just send it as is. As we mentioned previously, don't clean the metadata if you are collaborating on a document with another person, as it will remove the tracked changes. Metadata Assistant can also convert the attachment to PDF on the fly.

Metadata Assistant is extremely flexible and works with Word, Excel, and PowerPoint versions from 97 to 2013. It has e-mail integration with Outlook 2007 and higher, Office 2007 and higher, OpenText DM 5.2/5.3, Worldox GX/GX2/GX3, and Autonomy iManage 8.5 and 9.0. This product is also compatible with Windows 8. Users may purchase this product directly from Payne Group for $98 per license. Discounts are available for Enterprise-level installations involving twenty or more licenses.

No lawyer should be without a metadata scrubber to ensure removal of potential confidential data. Some states are even addressing the removal of metadata in their ethics opinions. Whether you are required to scrub metadata or not, Metadata Assistant is a possible solution for your practice.

You can also remove metadata by converting the file to PDF. This does not remove all of the metadata, but it does remove a large portion of it and leaves only what are typically considered innocuous values. Microsoft also provides the ability to analyze and remove ("clean") a document's properties in Microsoft Office 2010 and 2013. However, some values that it leaves behind are still viewable by third-party products like Metadata Assistant.

Litera Metadact and Metadact-e

If you're looking for another possible solution for metadata analysis and scrubbing, we have become very fond of Litera's Metadact program. Metadact identifies and removes all of the commonly known types of metadata, such as author and creation date, as well as many of the hidden metadata fields that are behind the scenes. This product features include:

—Profile management

—Clean and convert files

—Choose which types of metadata to clean

—View detailed reports

—Batch clean

—Clean metadata from within Microsoft Outlook

—Create custom policies and settings

—Specify safe e-mail domains

—Exclusion lists

—Seamless integration with Windows Explorer and document management systems

—Intelligent content clean

—Risk assesment

This product integrates with Autonomy iManage, DM5, DocsOpen, PowerDocs, Worldox, NetDocuments, and Microsoft SharePoint.

The Metadact-e program, which is a server-based product, adds the ability to scrub metadata from documents in Outlook, Outlook Web Access, tablets, and smartphones, as well as desktop-based documents. Whether it's a Microsoft Office, PDF, image, or ZIP file, this product will ensure that all metadata data information has been removed. No other product on the market currently has the ability to enforce metadata policies on mobile devices such as smartphones. We are huge fans of Metadact-e.

Unlike stand-alone versions, this product is centrally managed and administered, and it's suggested that this application be installed on its own server. This allows your practice to enforce its metadata policies on employees without giving them the option to "bypass" your written policies and procedures. The benefits of a server-based solution include the ability to prevent the disclosure of client-confidential and other sensitive information, transparent cleaning for the users (and no more waiting for a locally installed product to do the cleaning—you are immediately released to go to your next task while the server does the scrubbing), and compliance control through enforcing your practice's policies and procedures.

Metadact can be purchased from Litera's website at **www.litera.com** for $50 per license (user) and must be renewed on a yearly basis. Users must contact Litera directly for Metadact-e pricing.

Livescribe Echo Smartpen

The Livescribe Echo Smartpen is a device that can record a user's written notes along with the accompanying audio. The Echo Smartpen can transmit the data to a computer via USB cable, allowing a user to view digitalized notes and hear recorded audio. The pen has an infrared camera that records 75 images per second to track the spatial movement of the device on the provided sheets of dot paper, the required use of which is one of the only downsides of the product. Users can now purchase their own dot paper, notebooks, and lined and unlined journals compatible with the Smartpen.

Using the bundled Livescribe Desktop software, users can manage written notes and recordings but cannot convert notes to text because the software lacks OCR capabilities. However, using the software's PDF export capabilities, you could always OCR the exported PDF files using Adobe Acrobat.

The Echo Smartpen, just like a computer, can be updated with new firmware and software and is currently offered with 2 or 4GB of storage capacity. The Smartpen is compatible with Microsoft Windows XP SP3, Vista, and Windows 7, and also Mac OS X 10.5.5 or newer.

Livescribe also has a Sky Smartpen, which features an embedded Wi-Fi adapter that sends recorded notes and audio directly to your Evernote account. The wireless connection removes the need for access to a computer or USB cable to transfer the data.

YouMail

Tired of the standard voicemail options provided by your cellular carrier? Looking for more advanced features? YouMail (**www.youmail.com**) is like Google Voice, without the extra phone number. YouMail provides a visual voicemail client for your smartphone that offers personalization of voicemail greetings based on the caller, voicemail sharing, caller blocking, and voicemail alerts by e-mail and text. You can even organize your voicemails into folders and download them to MP3 format. YouMail is compatible with iPhone, Android, or BlackBerry smartphones.

When a call doesn't get answered, the forwarded call is transferred to your YouMail voicemail box rather than to your cellular provider's voicemail box. The Personal Edition, which allows a user to store up to 100 voicemail messages, is free but ad-supported. The Business Edition, starting at $4.99 per month, allows a user to store up to 500 voicemail messages and has no advertisements.

To view a comparison of these plans, visit YouMail's pricing page at **store.youmail.com**.

SmartDraw Business

SmartDraw Legal Edition has been merged with the VP version of the software, now called SmartDraw Business, which is a powerful software tool that allows lawyers to create sharp, professional-looking diagrams and trial exhibits with relative ease. It's a must-have for your software arsenal. The tool, more robust than Microsoft PowerPoint, can be used to create time lines, estate planning diagrams, accident reconstruction, crime scene layouts, and more. The look and feel of the software is similar to Microsoft Office, and creating diagrams from the provided templates is simple. The Business Edition provides specialized templates for the legal profession—over 1,000 of them—and if you can't find one to use, you can create your own. SmartDraw comes with more than 20,000 symbols and shapes to choose from, giving you the power to dynamically re-create that crucial event in your case. SmartDraw provides a number of export options, allowing users to save their work in a variety of formats, such as PDF, DOC, XLS, WPD, or JPG. SmartDraw does a good job as an alternative product to Microsoft Visio or Project at a fraction of the cost.

The latest update to SmartDraw Business includes a totally new user interface, powerful new print controls, new templates for brainstorming and project planning, and enhanced Visual Process Management functionality.

SmartDraw Business can be purchased directly from the website (**www.smartdraw.com**) for $197 for a single-user license. A trial edition is also available for download for those users who wish to test drive the software before purchasing.

CaseSoft TimeMap 5

Another great time line–generating utility is CaseSoft's TimeMap, which was acquired by LexisNexis several years ago. TimeMap is a time line–graphing tool that can be used to create polished time line graphs for trial exhibits, presentations, and professional documents. TimeMap can be integrated with CaseMap or used on its own. Data can be directly imported into the application from Microsoft Excel, Summation, Concordance, Microsoft Access, or almost any other spreadsheet or database program, eliminating the need to manually enter data.

As data is entered into the program, TimeMap will automatically generate a proportional time scale and allow the user to adjust it if necessary. Once your time line graph has been generated, you can present the time line using TimeMap's Presentation Mode, or you can embed the time line directly into your PowerPoint or Sanction presentation. TimeMap 5 includes new features such as vertical time lines, additional time line templates, a new PDF writer, and enhanced integration with presentation software. The latest version also includes a new Spreadsheet view, global find-and-replace option, expanded images, and improved date display tools. TimeMap 5 supports Microsoft Windows 2000/XP/Vista and Windows 7 and can be purchased directly from Casesoft's website at **www.casesoft.com**. Like the other LexisNexis products, you must register on the website before you can see product costs. This is a change from previous years, where the pricing was prominently displayed. A full-featured thirty-day trial edition is also available for download for those users who wish to give the software a test run before purchasing.

Evernote

Have trouble remembering everything? We sure do. That's why we use Evernote (**www.evernote.com**). This program makes it easy to remember things big and small, allowing you to capture everything you see when using your computer, cell phone, or mobile device. Using the program, you can clip a web page, snap a photo, or grab a screenshot and upload it to Evernote. Once uploaded, everything you capture is automatically processed, indexed, and made searchable. Of course, you can add your own tags and labels to your notes. Evernote will even scan handwritten notes and make the content searchable. There are a limitless number of ways to use this program, whether for play or work. Since all of the data you capture and tag is uploaded to your Evernote account, these files are accessible from all of your devices.

Evernote can integrate with your web browser, or you can install a small application on both Mac OS X and Windows-based computers or your iPhone/iPod Touch, iPad, BlackBerry, Android, Android tablet, or Windows Phone 7 smartphone. To sign up for a free account, visit Evernote's website at **www.evernote.com**.

WinRAR/7-ZIP

WinRAR is an application for compressing data. WinZip is a very popular program as well, but WinRAR has some distinct advantages. WinRAR is faster than WinZip and provides smaller files. It can also create compressed archives that are much larger than WinZip, so we see WinRAR used for transmitting large amounts of data. Data production as part of a discovery request would be one place to use WinRAR. This program supports all popular compression formats (RAR, ZIP, CAB, ARJ, LZH, ACE, TAR, GZip, UUE, ISO, BZIP2, Z, and 7-Zip). This is a valuable tool for sending data via the Web as well.

WinRAR is available in 32- and 64-bit versions. The cost is $29 per license, and it is available directly from the website at **www.win-rar.com**.

An alternative to WinRAR that we use often is 7-Zip (**www.7zip.com**), which is an open-source archive utility program. You can use 7-Zip to create password-protected zip files in which the contents are encrypted to securely protect your data. We use this program almost daily and don't know how we'd get by without it.

Chrometa

Track your time and bill for it without any notes or timers. Chrometa is a piece of software that plugs into Outlook or Gmail to help you keep track of time so that it can be billed to your clients. Think of it as a personal timekeeper, silently sitting in the background, recording how long you worked in a particular application, specifically noting what file or e-mail you were working on. You can have these entries categorized in a time sheet or use the keyword-based rules feature to automatically invoice clients.

There are several price plans available. The individual plans range from $19 per month for the Basic plan to $49 per month for the Premium plan.

The Premium plan holds 12 months, worth of data, allows usage on up to four devices, creates invoices, and will export data to accounting packages or legal software such as Clio, Rocket Matter, or PCLaw. You may want to consider the Plus package ($29 per month), even though it only handles two devices and 2 months, worth of data, especially if you are exporting data to another package. Chrometa is an excellent add-on, especially if you are using a web-based practice management application like Clio or Rocket Matter. Chrometa also has apps for Android, iOS, BlackBerry, and Windows Mobile devices.

eWallet

Do you have a hard time remembering all of your different passwords to your web-based accounts? We certainly do—especially since we should be using a different password for each of our accounts. Whatever you do, do not use the same password over and over for your different accounts. This is basic security 101.

To help you remember your passwords without having to write them down, we recommend a product called eWallet. eWallet is an app that is available for iOS, Android, BlackBerry, Windows Mobile 6.5, and both Windows-based (including Windows 7, 8, and RT) and Mac OS X computers that keeps your passwords safe by remembering them so you don't have to. The app stores the passwords in a vault using 256-bit AES encryption and allows you to synchronize your data across all of your devices on which the application is installed. eWallet can store website passwords, frequent flyer numbers, credit card information, membership data, and much more. This product can be purchased from your devices' app store or eWallet's website at **www.iliumsoft.com**. The price varies, depending on the device for which you're purchasing the software, but runs between $10 and $20.

LastPass

Like eWallet, LastPass is another secure password management tool. Last-Pass allows you to save your passwords and form data in a secure database and access it when needed. You no longer have to remember another password, and filling out forms and password fields is as easy as a single click. This software works on Mac, Windows, and Linux-based computer systems, as well as all of the major smartphones.

There is a new security feature called LastPass Sentry, which will alert you if your logon credentials are compromised. LastPass checks the PwnedList database (database of compromised accounts) to see if your e-mail address is on the list. If so, you receive an e-mail notifying you that your ID has been compromised. The new feature is available for all versions of LastPass.

LastPass does offer a free version available for download, as well as a paid premium version that offers a few additional features. We recommend trying the free version to see if the software meets your needs before making any purchases. You can download and take this software for a test run from its website at **www.lastpass.com**.

WordRake

WordRake fundamentally consists of a set of rules designed to cut flabby verbiage from your writing. Even good authors (and we have a club ring!) clearly can use some editing. Even our editors missed most of what WordRake found.

To be sure, it's not perfect. The founders purposely do not include an Accept All button because they know we can never tame the infinite variety and positioning of words. You have to approve each edit. Because of that, we wouldn't use it for casual writing. But for articles or any other writing that is significant, we sure would.

WordRake's creator, Gary Kinder, is a lawyer himself, and he's taught over 1,000 writing programs to firms like Sidley and Jones Day. He's also a *New York Times* best-selling author. He must use his own program!

WordRake is a Word add-on and inserts itself into Word's ribbon. It works with the 32-bit versions of Word 2007, 2010, and 2013. Support for Word 64-bit versions includes 2010 and 2013. The program is licensed on a subscription basis. The one-year cost is $99, two years is $178, and three years will cost $237. Be sure to try the free three-day trial first.

CHAPTER TWENTY-SIX

Social Media
for Law Firms—
An Overview

by Jennifer Ellis, Esq.

SOCIAL MEDIA HAS BECOME a crucial part of the average American's life. As a result, whether they want to or not, lawyers must, at the very least, appreciate the impact of social media on legal practice. Further, wise lawyers will take advantage of social media to develop their practices through the networking and marketing opportunities provided by both their own websites and the various social media sites and applications.

Many law firms have begun to embrace social media. Currently, 85 percent of leading law firms use social media, 60 percent maintain blogs, and 41 percent report that social media has resulted in new work.[1] The first and most obvious conclusion to be drawn from the numbers is that social media, in one form or another, is here to stay. It also is likely that over the next several years, the majority of social media sites will be accessed through mobile devices. This is due to the rapid increase in sale of smart-phones and the shift in movement from computers to tablets and phones.[2] Regardless of whether social media is accessed via computer or mobile device, the amount of data being shared is increasing rapidly. Frequently, that data includes information that can be helpful or harmful to a law-

---

[1] ALM Legal Intelligence, "Fans, Followers and Connections: Social Media ROI for Law Firms," 2012. The survey sought to discover how law firms use social media as well as identify costs and benefits, and "179 legal professionals took part in the survey." While the majority of responders worked for large firms, the survey did not find any "significant difference in the use of social media or social networking sites according to firm size."

[2] Amy Gahran, "Survey Says Most U.S. Cell Phone Owners Have Smartphones; So What?" CNN, March 2, 2012, **http://www.cnn.com/2012/03/02/tech/mobile/smartphones-majority-pew-gahran/**.

suit. In addition, the number of people using social media continues to increase. This means lawyers can take advantage of the number of people using these sites and applications to reach out to potential clients through networking or marketing techniques.

Attorneys who seek to begin using social media and social networking sites should keep in mind that the ethical risks involved with social media, both in terms of evidence and marketing, are very real. Therefore a proper understanding of appropriate and ethical behavior is extremely important.

It is also important to understand that in certain areas of practice, it is now verging on malpractice to fail to communicate with clients about whether and how they use social media. Failing to warn the client to halt social media use could result in that client posting material harmful to his case. Not warning the client that he may not delete posts could result in substantial sanctions for spoliation.[3] In addition, it is quite conceivable that the opposing party will post information harmful to his case, and failure on the part of the lawyer to seek out possible harmful posts can result in loss of a substantially greater bargaining position, or even loss of a case that might have been won.

Specific Sites and Applications

Social media essentially includes sites and applications that enable people to share information, pictures, videos, and the like at a rapid rate and, in return, allow other people to respond to the shared content. In some cases social media is referred to as Web 2.0, in contrast to Web 1.0, which refers to sites that serve to provide one-way communication, much like a newsletter or a book. Traditional websites are Web 1.0.

Currently, the most popular social media sites and applications in the United States include Facebook, Twitter, LinkedIn, Google+, Pinterest, YouTube, Foursquare, and Instagram. Further, blogs are sometimes considered part of social media, so they will be included in the discussion.

Marketing and Networking

It is not always easy to understand how social media can increase the potential for bringing in new clients. It is therefore important to think of social media as having uses for practice building.

---

[3]See *Lester v. Allied Concrete Co., et al.*; order dated September 1, 2011.

Advertising

Social media includes straightforward advertising. Sites such as Facebook, YouTube, LinkedIn, and others provide the opportunity to purchase small ads, which appear on the top or side of the page. These ads are controlled through varying means, demographics, keywords, areas of interest, and so on. Generally, the cost of the ads is controlled through a bidding process. The site provides a suggested fee per click. The purchaser identifies the amount he is willing to pay and competes against those who are seeking to advertise to the same individuals. Normally, the purchaser only pays when someone clicks on an ad.

Networking

Social media provides substantial opportunities for networking. It simply moves the networking from the bar association or educational program to networking online. Providing information about interests, sharing day-to-day activities, responding to the posts of others—each of these behaviors is simply a way to connect with other people. Those people, in turn, may need a lawyer or may need to refer someone else to a lawyer, just as in the offline world. Further, people tend to recommend individuals whom they know, or feel they know, and social media allows formation of that kind of relationship.

Content

Sharing useful content is a crucial part of social media for lawyers. Providing high quality content that informs about the areas of law in which a lawyer practices is an excellent way to bring attention to that attorney. The content can be as simple as commenting on a case on Facebook, sharing a useful link on Twitter, or providing a detailed analysis of a certain specific issue on a blog. This content shows potential clients that the attorney is knowledgeable in his or her area(s) of practice. Further, well-written content provides a substantial boost to search engine optimization and online reputation.

Specific Sites

Different social media sites provide different tools. In addition, some sites are better for attorneys who tend to represent businesses, while others are better for attorneys who represent individuals. It is important to target the correct site or mixture of sites for the best return on investment of time and money.

Facebook

Facebook is a consumer-oriented site. This means that the best use is for attorneys who are in the fields where they seek to communicate with or to individuals as opposed to businesses. This does not mean, however, that there is no use of Facebook for business attorneys. The networking aspects are still important in terms of communicating with the individuals who make decisions for their businesses.

Facebook has more than 1 billion users. Approximately 200 million of those users are located in the United States and Canada. Due to the number of users on Facebook, it is a site that provides substantial benefits and risks to both attorneys and their clients. Benefits include access to a substantial potential client base and potentially discoverable data that can be used in negotiation or at trial. Risks include ethical issues and data posted by clients that can hurt their own cases, as well as harm their reputation. The same risks and rewards that exist in Facebook exist in all social media sites and applications; the size simply increases the level of both.

Account v. Page

Many attorneys and businesses confuse the concept of accounts with pages on Facebook (and other social media sites). Accounts are for individuals; pages are for businesses (or firms). It is a violation of the terms of service of Facebook to create an account for anything other than an individual person.[4]

An account on Facebook can either be very public, very private, or somewhere in between. It is up to each individual attorney to determine how open she desires her communications to be. Generally speaking, it is through accounts that an attorney can engage in the kind of communication that is similar to offline networking and therefore is likely to help her learn about potential clients and allow those potential clients to learn about her. If an attorney keeps her account open, she will want to be very careful about the kind of information she shares. Many attorneys prefer to keep their accounts private to separate their business and personal lives.

Pages are for businesses. In addition to being proper under the terms of service, pages offer many tools that regular accounts do not. For example, they offer applications that add the ability to use CSS or HTML coding, as well as other features that can allow a law firm to essentially create another website on Facebook. A properly named and created page is easily found by

---

[4]"Statement of Rights and Responsibilities," Facebook, last modified December 11, 2012, **https://www.facebook.com/legal/terms**.

Facebook users and also can be cataloged by Google for search engine optimization purposes.

Figure 26.1 is a screen shot of the Facebook account for Curtis D. Ellis, an individual. Through his account, Curtis is able to share and receive information from other people. When Curtis "likes" a Facebook page, the information posted on that page shows in his Timeline. If a law firm has a page and Curtis likes it, then whatever that firm posts on its page also will appear in his timeline. Posting on a law firm page is an excellent way for law firms to provide updates about what they are doing, ethically offer details about cases they have won, share blog posts, invite followers to offline networking events, and more.

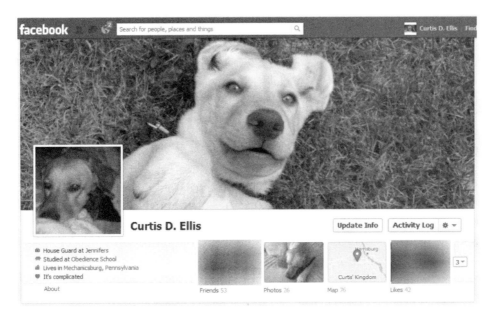

Figure 26.1 Personal Facebook Account

Figure 26.2 is the Facebook page for the American Bar Association, an organization. Through its page, the ABA can share a lot of information with its followers: upcoming events, notifications about contests, reminders to pay dues, information about leadership, and more. The image shows that the ABA is providing quick access to its Twitter account on its page, something not readily available through individual accounts.

Notice that there is an option to "Like" the ABA page. The other benefits to having a page versus an account are that anyone can see a page and anyone can like it. However, to become friends with someone, and there-

Figure 26.2 ABA's Business Facebook Page

fore be able to see that person's posts, one must first ask and receive permission. Pages by their nature are open.

Useful Applications for Pages

As mentioned, there are many applications available to increase the functionality of a Facebook page. For example, Figure 26.3 shows the tabs of my law firm's Facebook page, which include applications for customer service chat as well as easy access to the firm's blog, Google+ page, videos, and web pages containing information about various areas of practice and the firm's attorneys. The application used for the coding is Static HTML.[5] Many companies now specialize in providing robust applications to provide high level Facebook pages rapidly.

Getting Followers on Facebook

It is not easy for law firms to obtain followers on Facebook or other social media sites. This is because, generally speaking, law firms do not tend to engender the kind of interest that brands such as charities or such businesses as restaurants and clothing companies can easily command. Therefore, attorneys must first remember that they cannot expect to see the kind of results that favored brands can obtain. There are some exceptions,

---

[5]https://apps.facebook.com/static_html_plus/?fb_source=search&ref=ts.

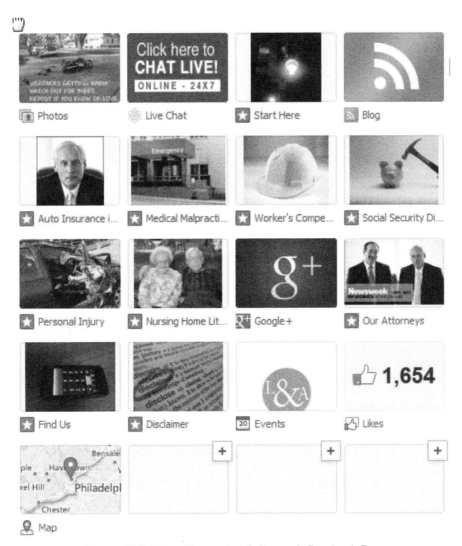

Figure 26.3 Tabs of Lowenthal & Abrams's Facebook Page

but they exist because of something about the page unexpectedly going viral. There are, however, techniques a law firm can use to attract attention and followers to its page.

The first thing a law firm needs to do is create content. That content can be anything that falls within appropriate ethical and reputational lines. Useful content that originates from blog posts, sweepstakes offering a prize such as an iPad,[6] campaigns relating to a charity—all of these tech-

---

[6]Sweepstakes laws are quite strict. Facebook has its own rules about using an application. Be sure to follow both the laws and Facebook's rules.

niques can help to increase followers. In addition, well written Facebook ads can encourage users to like a page.

The second thing the law firm must do is maintain the interest of its followers. Marketing posts on a page are not helpful and will drive followers away. Instead, provide content that maintains the interest of the firm's followers. This is where a blog can be quite useful. Sharing a bit of information from a well-written blog post can encourage visitors to the Facebook page and also to the firm's website itself.

Why a Facebook Page?

The overall goal of a Facebook page is to share enough information about a firm to educate potential clients about its attorneys, capabilities, and (when appropriate) its good works in society. The posts that the firm offers should be interesting enough that they attract the attention of followers and remind them that the law firm exists. Remember, the posts show up on the walls of the firm's followers. All of this activity, in turn, will hopefully encourage the individual followers to reach out if they need representation or to recommend the firm if they know someone who needs help.

Facebook Advertising

Facebook has two methods of advertising. One involves traditional ads, which are the items you see on the right side of the screen when you are on Facebook. The other is sponsored posts, which actually appear on the wall or timeline of Facebook users. Both types of advertising can encourage followers and activity on both a Facebook page and account and on a law firm's website.

Traditional ads are controlled by choosing location, age, interest, and so on. To set up an ad, go to **facebook.com/ads**. After you enter payment information, you will be taken to a page to create an ad as in Figure 26.4. Payment for ads is by bid. You bid the maximum you are willing to pay for each click. You are bidding against other advertisers for the same space on Facebook. You will pay only as much as is necessary to beat the other marketers for the space.

Sponsored posts are a bit controversial, and some users resent them due to the fact that they appear on the users' timeline. On the other hand, these posts result in substantially more people seeing posts as well as more activity on a Facebook page. Therefore, used with care, they can be worth

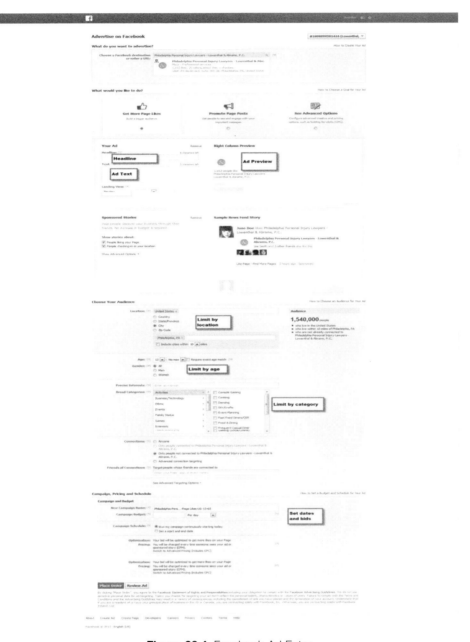

Figure 26.4 Facebook Ad Entry

the occasional upset user. In my experience, for as little as $75, a post will be seen by 10,000 people instead of 100 and receive several comments and likes instead of none. As with a regular ad, sponsored posts can be controlled by age and location, as shown in Figure 26.5.

Figure 26.5 Facebook Sponsored Post

Generally, for sponsored posts, I write a high quality blog post on my firm's website to provide useful information when people click on the link in a sponsored post. The information is not normally obvious marketing, but rather something the average person will find helpful. For example, a recent sponsored post in the late spring of 2013 talked about how to avoid Lyme disease in Pennsylvania.

For ethical purposes, I recommend limiting both your ads and sponsored posts to the jurisdictions in which you seek to represent clients. For sponsored posts, be prepared for the occasional person who is upset that Facebook allows these posts to appear on his or her wall. I generally explain that I cannot control the ads based on a specific individual. Also be prepared to respond appropriately on the wall of your own Facebook page if someone decides to vent there about your marketing. Generally if a post adds nothing constructive to the conversation, I will remove it and respond privately to the complaining individual if I believe doing so is appropriate. Sometimes I will use humor to lighten the situation. In some cases people respond back with humor, but be careful—you never know how people will respond. Regardless, have a response plan in mind. Also be certain that your spam and language settings are as high as possible to prevent people from posting foul language on your Facebook page.

Twitter

Twitter is frequently referred to as micro blogging. It enables users to share small bits of information and links. Recently, Twitter passed 500 million user accounts; however, it is believed that only about 170 million people are actually active.[7] One of the unique aspects of Twitter is that one does not need to be active to obtain useful information. It is quite conceivable that the majority of users simply read what others post. As a result, Twitter is very useful as a way for attorneys to share and re-share information that they would like to pass on to potential clients. As with Facebook, the content that individuals post on Twitter can find its way into court due to the fact that some users post harmful information through the service.

Twitter serves three general purposes. First, it is a good way to share small bits of personal information. For example, letting people know that a lawyer likes baseball and is at a game is a good way to connect with other baseball fans. Second, it is a good way to share links to information written by others that followers might find useful. Third, it is a good way to increase the sharing of content written by the lawyer and posted elsewhere, such as a blog post. Twitter is also well known as a site where people break news or share breaking information. During weather events, terrorist attacks, and even the death of Bin Laden,[8] Twitter was the premier site for information.

---

[7] Ingrid Lunden, "Twitter May Have 500M+ Users But Only 170M Are Active, 75% on Twitter's Own Clients," TechCrunch, July 31, 2012, **techcrunch.com/2012/07/31/twitter-may-have-500m-users-but-only-170m-are-active-75-on-twitters-own-clients/**.

[8] John D. Sutter, "How bin Laden News Spread on Twitter," CNN, May 4, 2011, **articles.cnn.com/2011-05-02/tech/osama.bin.laden.twitter_1_bin-tweet-twitter-user?_s=PM:TECH**.

When creating a Twitter account, the key is brevity. Use a picture that connects to the firm or the individual lawyer. Describe the firm or lawyer, and provide a link to the firm's website. In addition, consider connecting the firm's Facebook page to the firm's Twitter account.

Language of Twitter

Twitter is a bit more complicated than other sites in terms of its language and tools.[9] The tools especially are a crucial part of sharing and re-sharing information with other members and the lawyer's followers. The two most important symbols are the #, known as the hashtag, and the @, which is the symbol put before a username to identify that user. The # is used to identify a topic. So, during the ABA TECHSHOW, the ABA used the tag #abatechshow. By using this tag, everyone interested in posting about the topic or reading what other people posted could follow along simply by searching for the correct tag. In the same circumstances, if someone desired to call the ABA's attention to something, they simply used its handle in a post, @abatechshow. Figures 26.6a and 26.6b show a conversation between various users discussing the ABA TECHSHOW's new website.

First, the user @LawPracticeTips announces the new website (see Figure 26.6a).

Law Practice Mgmt @LawPracticeTips   12 Sep
#ABATECHSHOW is back with a new Website! bit.ly/yjeiVV
Explore the site and save the date for April 4-6, 2013.
Expand

Figure 26.6a Tweet Announcing ABA TECHSHOW

Next, a number of people responded, using the correct hashtag as identified by the original poster. Each of these users' followers saw the information, which drew more attention to the ABA's original announcement. Others responded by adding additional information, furthering the conversation. This interaction is a perfect example of how social media, Twitter especially, helps to share information rapidly in outward circles, as more and more people share the information with their followers.

---

[9] For a detailed glossary, see **https://support.twitter.com/entries/166337-the-twitter-glossary#**.

Beverly A. Michaelis @OreLawPracMgmt   4h
#ABATECHSHOW 2013 - new Web site unveiled. techshow.com
Expand

LegalTypist @LegalTypist   5h
@gyitsakalakis Actually, if there is #LexThink13 -
@SueAnneShirzay would be a GREAT presenter! pssst
@matthomann #ABATECHSHOW
💬 View conversation

Gwynne Monahan @econwriter5   7h
#ABATECHSHOW has a new website up already. And a newly
designed blog. ow.ly/dGYDY And social media gets its own track!
Maybe.
Expand

david_bilinsky @david_bilinsky   7h
RT @stevematthews: RT @ABATECHSHOW: We're back w/ a new
Website! bit.ly/yjeiVV Explore the site & save the date 4
#ABATECHSHOW 2013.
Expand

Figure 26.6b Responses to Tweet from @LawPracticeTips

Retweeting is also a crucial aspect of Twitter (see Figure 26.7). The general idea is that by retweeting, the user is rapidly sharing a post that she found valuable so that her own followers can see it. Sometimes the retweet is accompanied with additional information, sometimes not. The Retweet command is built into Twitter and its various applications.

Figure 26.7 Retweeting

LinkedIn

LinkedIn is the top business social media network. With over 225 million users,[10] one of LinkedIn's most impressive statistics is that it can count among its membership executives from all 500 of the Fortune 500 companies.

Due to its business nature, all lawyers should have a LinkedIn account. That account should be completed with more than just a simple résumé. It should contain a detailed profile of the lawyer, explaining her history and area(s) of practice. If at all possible, the lawyer should seek recommendations, which clients or other lawyers can put right on the site. There is no fear of harmful statements because the lawyer can choose to refuse a recommendation. Make certain that you obey the ethical rules of your jurisdiction for seeking and approving recommendations.

LinkedIn is a bit different from the other social media sites in that the users are separated by degrees. A user can seek to form a connection only to someone with whom she has a mutual connection, even a third-degree connection through other people or through a shared group. If the user does not have a connection, she can seek one if she knows the other person's e-mail address. LinkedIn's purpose is to connect professionals with one another. As such, it is an excellent networking and referral source.

As with Facebook, LinkedIn has both individual accounts and company pages. When a company has a page, an individual can connect to it through current or past employment with that company. Individuals can follow companies through their pages. Recently, LinkedIn has been making its pages more useful in terms of the content companies are able to place there, therefore increasing the import of having a LinkedIn page for the firm.[11] Law firms can include information about areas of practice, appropriate pictures, updates about the firm and its lawyers' accomplishments, videos, and other information (see Figure 26.8a). The page also provides links to the profiles of the employees of the firm, enabling potential clients to research and identify specific lawyers they might want to contact (see Figure 26.8b).

Both the pages and the accounts enable lawyers to share information and seek out business relationships. In addition, a substantial number of groups provide networking and educational opportunities.

---

[10]LinkedIn Press Center, "About LinkedIn," accessed October 21, 2013, **press.linkedin.com/about**.
[11]Mike Grishaver, "Introducing a New Look for Company Pages," LinkedIn Blog, September 6, 2012, **blog.linkedin.com/2012/09/06/new-look-for-company-pages/**.

Figure 26.8a LinkedIn Company Page

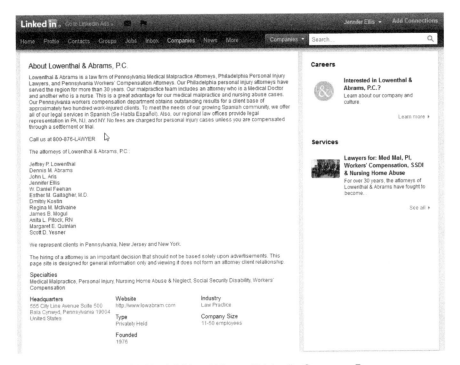

Figure 26.8b Additional View of LinkedIn Company Page

Another service at which LinkedIn excels is its job search service. Businesses can post listings, and potential applicants can see if they already are somehow connected to the business. With a complete LinkedIn profile, a user can easily apply for the job, and the business can view a much more detailed history than is normally available with a résumé.

LinkedIn has both a free and a paid version of its service. The paid version provides more information about those who have looked at an individual's profile, as well as increased networking and search capabilities.

LinkedIn has a skills option, which allows users to add their own skills to their profiles. Connections are automatically asked to endorse those users in the skills users have chosen to list. Unfortunately, sometimes LinkedIn picks skills its algorithm thinks are appropriate for you. Other people can pick skills for you as well. If you do not practice in the areas for which people endorse you, it is best (and might be ethically required) to remove those areas to prevent any confusion.

Another area of concern on LinkedIn is that it lists certain areas as "specialties." Some states do not allow lawyers to list a specialty except for specific considerations, such as certain areas of practice or approved examinations and certifications. Recently, the New York State Bar Association Committee on Professional Ethics made it clear that law firms may not list services under specialties. Nor may individuals list their practice areas under specialties unless they are appropriately certified.[12] We can only hope that LinkedIn will take notice of this problem and change the wording of its Specialties sections.

Google+

Google+ maintains a unique position among the social media networks due to its ownership by Google. Because of its relationship to Google's search engine, Google+ is integrated with search results (see Figure 26.9). This means that from a business perspective, Google+ is the most powerful of the social media networks in terms of search engine optimization (SEO). SEO means how near the top of the list a website appears in Google's search results. A firm that is not listed on Google might as well not exist in terms of its findability.

Google+'s integration with Google's search engine means if someone writes about a topic, perhaps employee benefits, on a Google+ page or account, when someone searches for employee benefits, the post from Google+ might well show up. Essentially, Google has turned search engine optimization on its head by integrating its own social media site into its search results. As a result, the wise firm or business would do well to create a Google+ page and put valuable content in that account as a

---

[12]New York State Bar Association Committee on Professional Ethics, "Listing in Social Media," Opinion 972, June 26, 2013.

Figure 26.9 Google+ Local Search

way to encourage people to find it on the Web. Individuals may choose to have accounts on Google+ as well. Sharing information on those accounts can raise the web footprint of the user through SEO.

Google also has a product called Google Places, which it is slowly changing into Google+ Local. This is a location-based search that helps users find something near a specific area. For example, a search for dog groomers in Mechanicsburg, Pennsylvania, shows a map and a list of relevant businesses in that area. Clicking on a business link brings the user to a page for the business. If the business has not filled out the page, the result is a relatively empty (and useless) page. But if the business has completed the page, it has taken advantage of the opportunity to provide a substantial amount of information to someone who is actively searching on Google for a dog groomer, or, of course, a law firm. Based on this functionality, it is important for firms to claim and create Google+ pages and connect them to Google+ Local so that users can find them when searching for a firm in a specific geographical area.

Pinterest

Pinterest is the new kid on the block as far as social media goes. What Pinterest brings to the table is that it is based on pictures instead of text (see Figure 26.10). On Pinterest, the goal is to share a picture with a related

The ABA provides the right for attorneys to share client information to effect a lateral move.

 Add a comment...

Figure 26.10 Pin on Pinterest

link and only a small amount of text. The other unique aspect of Pinterest is that it is 80 percent female. Though Pinterest is still relatively new, it has over 10.4 million monthly users. At the same age, Facebook only had 6 million users, and Twitter 3 million users.[13] It is clear that Pinterest is showing growth at an extraordinary rate.

The nature of Pinterest's users makes it a useful way to reach out to the female market. An easy way to take advantage of Pinterest is to write a blog post, include a photograph or image in that post, and then "pin" (the term used on Pinterest) that image to a Pinterest board belonging to the law firm. When someone clicks on the image, it takes her to the appropriate link.

As with other photo sharing sites, a lawyer can also upload appropriate images connected with links to the law firm or choose to share images related to her hobbies and personal life at whatever level makes her comfortable. Other users can follow the firm's boards, re-pin the lawyer's pins, and offer comments on the pins as well.

YouTube

YouTube is video sharing. The scale of that sharing has grown so large that it is practically beyond comprehension. Each month, over 800 million unique users visit YouTube. During the same time period, over 4 bil-

---

[13]David Wallace, "Pinterestingly Enough: Interesting Pinterest Stats," Search Engine Journal, June 22, 2012, **www.searchenginejournal.com/pinterestingly-enough-interesting-pinterest-stats/45328/**.

lion hours of video are watched. Thirty percent of YouTube traffic comes from within the United States: 240 million unique visitors each month.[14]

The value of video for legal marketing cannot be overstated. While many potential clients are happy to read blog posts, others prefer to watch videos. Biography videos in which lawyers introduce themselves to potential clients, interview videos in which an lawyer explains different aspects of his or her practice, short clips discussing specific issues about which clients often have questions—each of these items is extremely useful in spreading the word about the firm. The videos can be uploaded to YouTube (or other video sharing sites) and then embedded into the law firm's website and blog and shared via its various social networking sites.

YouTube is owned by Google and, like Google, is searched via keywords. As a result, it is important to use the correct title, description, and keywords when uploading a video. Figure 26.11 is a screen capture of a video

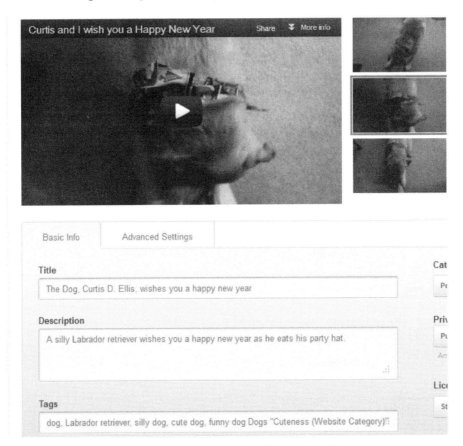

Figure 26.11 Edit Page for a Video on YouTube

---

[14]YouTube, "Statistics," accessed October 21, 2013, **http://www.youtube.com/t/press_statistics**.

uploaded about Curtis D. Ellis, a dog. The title of the video has appropriate keywords for people searching for videos about dogs. The video's description also has appropriate keywords, while explaining what occurs in the video. The tags contain relevant terms that people are likely to use while searching YouTube or Google for videos about cute dogs.

When embedding a video from YouTube on a website, blog, or social media site, it is very important to turn off related videos; leaving related videos on frequently results in marketing for the competition. For example, a video called "5 things to know about filing for a divorce in Pennsylvania" and tagged with appropriate keywords is likely to show related videos from other lawyers on similar topics. Providing valuable real estate to another lawyer on a law firm's website or social media network is exactly the opposite of what the firm wants to accomplish. Fortunately, this is easily resolved.

Access the page for the video the firm desires to share and choose the Share option. Then click on Embed. Next, make sure the "Show suggested videos . . ." option is not checked (see Figure 26.12).

Figure 26.12 Sharing a Video from YouTube

Foursquare

Foursquare represents the trend of geolocation social media. In essence, users check-in to certain locations as a way of letting others know where they are. This tool makes it easier for the network's users to find each other and get together for social events. As a way of encouraging check-ins, businesses offer discounts or rewards to those who check-in at their locations. Facebook offers a check-in feature as well. As of September 2013, Foursquare had 30 million members and over 3 billion check-ins.[15] Foursquare relies on a smartphone application. Users may check-in on the Web, but the real purpose is for members to use their phones and the app to check-in as they move around.

While lawyers will not want clients to check-in to their law firms (client confidentiality issues), lawyers can check-in when they are speaking at events, attending conferences, or engaging in other networking activities.

Instagram

Purchased by Facebook for the staggering sum of $1 billion, Instagram is a photo sharing application. As of September 2013, the application had 130 million users with over 16 billion photos uploaded.[16] Instagram is especially popular amongst "tweens," who are technically violating the application's terms of service, since users must be 13 or older.

As with Foursquare, it would not be appropriate for a lawyer to take pictures of clients or potential clients, unless under correct ethical circumstances, but that lawyer can take pictures of events at which they participate and share them via Instagram for public relations purposes. In addition, Instagram can be connected to other social media sites, allowing appropriate images to be shared throughout the lawyer's network.

Blogs

Initially blogs simply served as online diaries; but over time, many blogs have become a source of useful, high quality information. A blog is a crucial part of a law firm's online presence. Blog posts are the key way for lawyers to provide information to potential clients, showing that they know their area(s) of practice. The posts can then be used to drive the content on the firm's social media presence.

Due to the value that Google places on unique, frequently changing content, the search engine optimization value of a blog post is extremely high. Therefore, if a lawyer writes a post called "Why prenuptial agreements matter in Pennsylvania," and someone is wondering whether to have a prenuptial agreement drawn up, and that person resides in Pennsylvania, a well-written and search engine–optimized post might help bring that person to the lawyer's e-mail inbox.

---

[15]Foursquare, "About Foursquare," accessed October 21, 2013, **https://foursquare.com/about/**.
[16]**instagram.com/press/#**.

Topics

When identifying topics to write about, think through what new clients want to know when they walk through the door. Use the blog to answer those questions, because those are the questions people are searching for on the Web. Keep the blog posts concise, sharing just enough information to answer the question the reader is asking. Write the post using straightforward, non-legalese language.

A second way to identify topics is directly from the news. During the Sandusky scandal in Pennsylvania, Sandusky was offered supervised visitation. A common Google search at the time involved the terms "Sandusky supervised visitation." A blog post explaining the concept of supervised visitation and what it meant in the Sandusky case, written at that time, would have been a home run.

Creating a Blog

Create a blog using stand-alone software or through sites that allow hosting of a blog. The better choice is to make certain the domain is a branded one, meaning directly related to the area of practice or to the firm and/or lawyer. Some sites, such as **Wordpress.com**, allow for purchase of a domain, and so provide a branded option without having to handle a self-hosted blog. On the other hand, a self-hosted blog provides not only for branding but for better control of and greater use of plug-ins (tools that expand the functionality of the blog). The most popular self-hosted blog software is WordPress.[17] The most popular outside-hosted blog sites are WordPress (**www.wordpress.com**) and Google (**www.blogger.com**). Additional popular choices include TypePad (**www.typepad.com/**), Squarespace (**www.squarespace.com**), and LiveJournal (**www.livejournal.com/**).

Discovery of Social Media

Given the value of the information contained within social media accounts, it is no surprise that lawyers desire to obtain access to the information. It is not at all uncommon, for example, for an individual to say one thing in person to her lawyer or a judge and to post completely contradictory information on Facebook. An individual might claim in court or interrogatories that she cannot leave her home due to emotional harm from an injury, but in turn post a video on Facebook showing her dancing at a party. In the past, it was necessary to hire a private investigator to

---

[17] **en.wordpress.com/stats/**.

prove someone was lying about his injury for a workers' compensation claim; now the plaintiff frequently posts a picture of himself chopping wood or carrying a heavy couch, the exact evidence the defense lawyer needs to prove her case.

Privacy Settings Are Important

Privacy settings control what an individual shares on social media sites. However, many users never change their privacy settings or simply find the settings too complicated to alter. Many social media sites barely have any privacy settings at all. Twitter, for example, is either open or private.[18] Facebook's settings are extremely complicated and confusing.[19] Blogs are meant to be open, and people frequently believe they are private when they are not.[20] Since many people do not change their settings, lawyers should and do look through the social media sites in an ethical manner and view and preserve the information they can find.[21] Keep in mind, if the lawyer does the preservation and authentication becomes an issue, the lawyer could be forced to become a witness in her own case. It is best to have someone else in the firm do the preservation.

The Client's Social Media

The first step when a new client walks through the door is to ask if he uses any social media. The next step, in some cases, is to inform the client that he must stop posting immediately. Unfortunately, the addiction to and use of social media can be so great that the client will be unwilling to stop. As a result, you should also advise your client that if he does post, he should not post anything that deals with the case. You must be clear about what *deals with the case* means, since many clients will simply

---

[18]Twitter, "About Public and Protected Tweets," accessed October 21, 2013, **https://support .twitter.com/entries/14016#.**

[19]Approximately 13 million U.S. users never change their Facebook privacy settings. Of those that do, the majority are unaware that their privacy settings can be compromised by allowing additional applications access to their accounts and do not take the steps necessary to further protect their data. Emil Protalinski, "13 Million US Facebook Users Don't Change Privacy Settings," ZDNet, May 3, 2012, **www.zdnet.com/blog/facebook/13-million-us-facebook-users-dont-change-privacy-settings/12398.**

[20]Natalie Munroe was a teacher in Pennsylvania who blogged about her students. She believed her blog was only being read by a few people and was apparently unaware that it could be widely read (**tinyurl.com/8hx95c6**). Munroe was suspended, brought back, and eventually fired. She claims she was fired due to the blog. The district claims she was fired for incompetence. Munroe has since brought a lawsuit against the district. Chris Palmer and Ben Finley, "Blogging Central Bucks Teacher Is Fired," BucksInq (blog), **Philly.com,** accessed October 21, 2013, **www.philly.com/ philly/blogs/bucksinq/160413996.html.**

[21]New York State Bar Association, Committee on Professional Ethics, Opinion 843 (September 10, 2010).

think it means specifics about how the case is going, as opposed to comments about giving money to his mistress, lifting a heavy couch, attending a party, and so on. Make certain to ask the client not only about his own accounts, but his comments on other blogs and websites that might be relevant to the case. Social media and other online surprises can be very harmful. It is also important to remind the client that he may not delete any content from his account, even if it is potentially harmful to his case.

The first meeting with a client is also the time to speak with him about changing his privacy settings to make certain that his account is secure. Providing instructions on how to change privacy settings in written form or a video can be very helpful. It is also a good idea to have the client sign a document making it clear that he was told not to delete any content. This will protect you from accusations of spoliation later on. In some cases it might be wise to ask for access to the account(s). Asking to friend the client is not enough; the password is necessary for a complete review of the client's online conduct.

Also, if the client has a personal relationship with the opposing party, ask about the other side's use of social media. In addition, ask the client if any potential witnesses are using social media. Find out if the client and potential witnesses are friends and therefore has access to private areas of one another's accounts.

Opposing Party and Witnesses

Immediately view the opposing party's accounts and witness accounts if they are freely accessible. It is permissible to view the accounts if the client has access. It is also permissible to ask witnesses to provide access to their accounts, though the attorney or other individual asking for access must be honest about his or her relationship to the case.

Also send a Notice of Preservation to opposing counsel. Fortunately, the amendments to the federal discovery rules from 2006 allow for discovery of electronic data to begin very early in the litigation process. Make it clear to opposing counsel that all data must be preserved. Do not just name specific social media sites, but be clear in the preservation that it means all sites and all accounts. Unfortunately, exactly what preservation is required is not yet clear. Does preservation mean keeping the privacy settings as is, so if an account was open it remains such? Does it simply mean that data may not be deleted? Be clear about expectations and do not be surprised if the matter ends up before a judge.

Send out the interrogatories relating to social media as quickly as possible and ask the right questions. Again, do not give the opposing client a chance to wiggle out by asking simply for Facebook when the client might have a Plaxo account. Ask for everything. Ask for all e-mail addresses as well, because the opposing party might have several accounts under various e-mail addresses. Further, keep in mind that with strict privacy settings the opposing party can all but hide the existence of his account(s).

Trouble for Failure to Preserve

In the past, some have believed that it is acceptable to delete posts from social media accounts. A Virginia decision from 2011 puts the debate to rest. It is spoliation to delete relevant posts. In the case, the lawyer instructed his client to "'clean up' his Facebook because we don't want blowups of this stuff at trial." The lawyer further instructed the client to delete or deactivate the account and then responded to discovery requests by informing opposing counsel that his client had no Facebook account. The client deactivated the account instead of deleting it. Upon reactivating the account, the client deleted 16 photographs, following his lawyer's instructions. Based on the spoliation, the court held that sanctions should be granted against both the lawyer and the client. The sanctions amounted to $722,000 in legal fees, over $500,000 of which was payable by the lawyer. In addition, the judge in the case reported the lawyer to the Virginia State Bar.[22] In the end, the lawyer agreed to a five-year suspension of his license.[23]

A recent New Jersey case shows the serious consequences of deleting content from Facebook. In that case the plaintiff claimed that he deactivated his Facebook account and did not restore it quickly enough, resulting in deletion of his account. Leaving aside that this is not how Facebook deactivations and deletions actually work,[24] the result was that the court found that deletion of the account was spoliation of evidence and granted an adverse inference instruction.[25] Given the cases and the trend, it seems to

---

[22]See *Lester v. Allied Concrete Co., et al.*; order dated September 1, 2011.

[23]"On July 17, 2013, the Virginia State Bar Disciplinary Board suspended Matthew B. Murray's license to practice law for five years for violating professional rules that govern candor toward the tribunal, fairness to opposing party and counsel, and misconduct. This was an agreed disposition of misconduct charges." VSB Docket Nos. 11-070-088405,11-070-0884222.

[24]In the author's experience, when a Facebook account is deactivated it is never deleted. When the owner logs into his account again, it is restored. For a Facebook account to be deleted, specific actions requesting deletion must be taken on the part of the account owner.

[25]*Gatto v. United Air Lines, Inc., et al.*, Case No. 10-cv-1090-ES-SCM (D.N.J. Mar. 25, 2013).

be straightforward that deleting posts, pictures, or videos is unacceptable and likely to lead to serious sanctions.

Ethical Pitfalls in Research and Discovery

There are a number of relevant guidance opinions from the New York City and State Bars,[26] Philadelphia Bar,[27] and the San Diego County Bar[28] Associations surrounding issues related to performing research using social media.

General Research

First, as already noted, it is perfectly acceptable to search and access social media sites that are freely accessible. The New York Guidance Opinion states, "[an attorney] may access the public pages of another party's social networking website (such as Facebook or MySpace) for the purpose of obtaining possible impeachment material for use in the litigation."[29] On the other hand, the Philadelphia Opinion makes it clear that an effort to obtain access to the account through deception or illegal means is unacceptable.[30]

Friending a Witness

In the Philadelphia opinion, the lawyer asked whether it would be acceptable for the lawyer to have a third party request a witness to "friend"[31] the opposing client. The third party did not intend to lie, but neither did he intend to reveal his relationship to the lawyer.

The opinion noted that such behavior would violate several rules of ethical conduct. The lawyer would be "procuring conduct [and be] responsible for [that] conduct" in violation of Pennsylvania Rule 5.3 (Responsibilities Regarding Nonlawyer Assistants). Also, the lawyer would be violating rule 8.4 (Misconduct) by engaging in "deceptive" conduct. In addition,

---

[26]Google New York State Bar Association Guidance Opinion 843 to access a PDF of the opinion.

[27]Philadelphia Bar Association Guidance Opinion 2009-02, **www.philadelphiabar.org/WebObjects/ PBAReadOnly.woa/Contents/WebServerResources/CMSResources/Opinion_2009-2.pdf**.

[28]SDCBA Ethics Opinion 2011-2, May 24, 2011, **https://sdcba.org/index.cfm?pg=LEC2011-2**.

[29]New York State Bar Association Guidance Opinion 843.

[30]Philadelphia Bar Association Guidance Opinion 2009-02.

[31]*Friend* is Facebook's term for two people who are connected to each other on the service. Different social media providers use different terms. For example, LinkedIn uses *contact* and *connection*. Friending someone requires the affirmative action of a request on the part of the individual seeking the connection and an affirmative action on the part of the individual accepting the connection. See Facebook, "How do I add a Friend?" **www.facebook.com/help/?faq=12062**.

the lawyer would be encouraging a third party to violate Rule 4.1 (Truthfulness in Statements to Others) by having the third party "omit a highly material fact."[32] Based on the Philadelphia Bar Association's Guidance Opinion, it is very clear that having a third party (or the lawyer herself) friend a witness without revealing her relationship to the case would be highly inappropriate.

Communicating with a Represented Party

The San Diego County Bar Association took on the issue of communicating with a represented party. In short, because the case is offline, it is inappropriate to communicate with a represented party online. In the instant case, the lawyer did not identify himself as the lawyer, which made the effort to communicate all the more grievous. An additional issue—of concern for those involved in employee cases—includes an analysis of whether the contacted employees serve as represented parties.[33]

In 2012, the issue of friending represented parties came up in New Jersey, where two lawyers are likely to face sanctions due to their paralegal friending the opposing party in a case.[34] The issue came to light during a deposition when it became clear that the lawyers had access to the private areas of the plaintiff's Facebook account. The lawyers denied responsibility because they simply asked the paralegal to perform a general search of the Web. The issue with this defense is that lawyers are responsible for the behavior of their staff. The lawyers are charged with violating New Jersey rules 4.2 (communications with represented parties), 5.3(a), (b), and (c) (failure to supervise a nonlawyer assistant), 8.4(c) (conduct involving dishonesty and violation of ethics rules through someone else's actions or inducing those violations), and 8.4(d) (conduct prejudicial to the administration of justice). In addition, the more senior of the two lawyers is charged with RPC 5.1(b) and (c) (ethical obligation in relation to supervising another lawyer). These are all very serious charges, and regardless of the outcome, the publicity, which will spread rapidly through social media, will no doubt be very harmful to the two lawyers in question.

---

[32]Philadelphia Bar Association Guidance Opinion 2009-02.
[33]SDCBA Ethics Opinion 2011-2, May 24, 2011.
[34]Eric Meyer, "Ethics Charges for Two Lawyers over Facebook Friending a Litigant," Labor and Employment Law (blog), LexisNexis Legal Newsroom, September 13, 2012, **http://www.lexis nexis.com/legalnewsroom/labor-employment/b/labor-employment-top-blogs/archive/2012/09/13/ethics-charges-for-two-lawyers-over-facebook-friending-a-litigant.aspx**.

At this point it seems well-settled that the action of friending someone or seeking to access their accounts through some form of communication, is a form of contact. Therefore lawyers should never seek to friend or obtain access to the account of an opposing party through any form of communication with a represented party. If seeking to friend a witness, the lawyer or individual assisting the lawyer must be clear of his or her relationship to the case.

How to Obtain Access

If a lawyer believes useful information is contained within a social media account, she should seek to obtain access to the information hidden therein. There are a number of ethical ways to do so, aside from just looking to see what is freely available.

See If the Client or a Friendly Witness Has Access

In family law cases especially, the parties or witnesses might have access to each other's accounts. It is perfectly acceptable to view and use any information that is freely available through this method. Be cautious in any case, though, if it looks like a witness might be sharing the information under duress. For example, in an employer/employee case, if another employee is friends with a plaintiff on Facebook, he might feel he has no choice but to share the information. If that employee complains later and says he was forced to share the access, it is uncertain how a court will look upon it.

Ask for Access to the Account

During the discovery process, unless there is a reason not to do so, ask for access to any and all social media accounts. In terms of Facebook, it is possible to download an entire account, so request that the opposing party do so and provide a copy.[35] Be sure to ask for continuing access as well. The opposing party will likely refuse this request, and wisely so. Social media postings can provide a plethora of private information, some of which may be harmful to a case. It is possible to simply ask the opposing party to adjust privacy settings so the account is viewable, but again, it is likely this request will be refused. It is always best to ask, though, because during the discovery process the judge will certainly ask if the request was made.

---

[35]Facebook's **Download your information** tool is located under Account Settings.

Send a Subpoena to the Site

Though generally the social media sites will not cooperate with a civil subpoena, from time to time they will be surprisingly helpful.[36] As a result, it never hurts to send the subpoena. Even if the site won't provide content, citing the Stored Communications Act, it will normally provide assistance in connecting an account with an e-mail address. This can be helpful if ownership of the account will be in issue. For example, in a criminal case the prosecution's verdict was overturned when it was shown that the prosecution had failed to tie the account in question to the defendant's girlfriend.[37] Proof of ownership could have been shown with MySpace's assistance.

Compel Discovery

This is where things get tricky. Different judges tend to have different responses to the request to compel discovery of a social media account. The best approach, and the one that has shown the most results, is to capture what is already viewable (through appropriate ethical means) and to show it to the judge. If the judge can see that the account has relevant and contradictory information, she is likely to provide access to the account. If the judge has concerns about the privacy of those other than the account holder, request that the court review the data first to help resolve the issue. Some judges do not feel that there are any privacy rights in social media content.[38]

Case Law

There are a number of opinions related to discovery of social media when the account itself is not a part of the case, in other words, when opposing counsel believes that she might find useful data in the account but the online behavior is not at the center of the dispute. At this point the trend in such cases is to provide access to social media accounts only when the opposing party can show that there is relevant and/or contradictory information contained therein. For example, in *McMillen v. Hummingbird Speedway, Inc.*,[39] a review of the public areas of McMillen's Facebook page revealed information contradictory to what he was claiming in terms of

---

[36] See Won't the Social Media Provider Help, *infra*.

[37] Kashmir Hill, "Bad MySpace Detective Work Results In Overturned Murder Conviction," Forbes, May 10, 2011, **blogs.forbes.com/kashmirhill/2011/05/10/bad-myspace-detective-work-results-in-overturned-murder-conviction**.

[38] NY v. Harris, 2012 NY Slip Op 22175, June 30, 2012.

[39] **www.padisciplinaryboard.org/documents/McMillen-v-Hummingbird-Speedway.pdf**.

his injuries. The judge provided access, noting specifically that the Facebook information was not privileged.

Another case is simply the paragraph long *Piccolo v. Paterson.*[40] The judge denied access to the Facebook pages the defense desired. The judge noted that the defense already had many pictures and that no pictures or other data were freely available that showed contradictory information to what the plaintiff was claiming. It is interesting to note that the plaintiff actually changed her privacy settings early in the case, to preclude anyone other than a friend viewing her pictures.

In *Zimmerman v. Weis Markets Inc.,*[41] the judge granted discovery due to the public availability of pictures that contradicted the plaintiff's claim that he did not wear shorts due to his embarrassment about a scar. The plaintiff posted pictures on his MySpace profile that clearly showed him wearing shorts after his injury (the scar was visible). Due to the public availability of this contradictory information, the judge found that there was clearly relevant data to be found within the MySpace account and therefore access to the account was properly compelled.

A more recent case comes from Judge R. Stanton Wettick. Judge Wettick is known as a discovery judge in Pennsylvania, so his view on the discovery of social media was quite welcome. Judge Wettick denied mutual requests for access to Facebook accounts in the case of *Trail v. Lesko* because he was not going to allow a fishing expedition when there was no evidence that contradictory or useful information could be found in either Facebook account.[42] Therefore Judge Wettick used the same reasoning as in many of the other cases on this issue.

In a recent Florida case, the judge granted in part and denied in part the request by defense in a personal injury case for complete access to the plaintiff's social media network. He held that the plaintiff must provide copies of all pictures depicting her since her injury, rather than provide access to the entire social media account in question. He further held that in requesting that the plaintiff provide every device on which she accessed her social media accounts, the defense had overreached.[43] In reaching his decision, the judge noted that social media sites are "neither privileged

---

[40]Gina Passarella, "Facebook Postings Barred from Discovery in Accident Case," The Legal Intelligencer, last modified April 8, 2013, **tinyurl.com/3jhmk2e**, and **www.theemployerhandbook.com/piccolo.PDF**.

[41]*Zimmerman v. Weis Markets, Inc.*, No. CV-09-1535 (2011).

[42]*Trail v. Lesko*, No GD-10-017249.

[43]*Davenport v. State Farm Mutual Automobile Insurance Co.*, Case No. 3:110-cv-632-J-JBT, (M.D. FL, 2012).

nor protected by any right of privacy." He also noted, though, that the discovery request must be properly tailored. To support both assertions, he cited the decision in *Tompkins v. Detroit Metropolitan Airport.*[44]

In *Tompkins,* the court found that while social media is discoverable, and "generally not privileged," the opposing party still may not "have a generalized right to rummage through information that Plaintiff has limited from public view." The court required a "threshold showing that the requested information is reasonably calculated to lead to the discovery of admissible evidence." As in the other cited cases, the court wanted to see some evidence that justified the defendant "delving into the non-public section of [plaintiff's] account." The court noted specifically that if the public segment of plaintiff's account had "contained pictures of her playing golf or riding horseback," that the defendant would have had a better case to access the private portions of her account.

The conclusion to be drawn thus far about the majority of social media discovery decisions is that while courts are willing to provide access to private sections of social media accounts, they are not willing to allow fishing expeditions simply based on the view that the accounts *might* have useful information. Some evidence showing that relevant information can be found in the account must be offered before discovery will be granted.

Won't the Social Media Provider Help?
Social media providers will not provide content from a social media account in civil cases. As recently as 2007, some providers did respond to civil subpoenas with content, but now the providers state unequivocally that due to the Stored Communications Act, 18 U.S.C. § 2701 *et seq,* they may not provide content.[45] The providers will respond to a subpoena only with information about who owns the account.[46] This means the only way to get the data is to have the owner of the account cooperate. In criminal cases, most social media providers will assist when provided with an appropriate subpoena or warrant. On occasion a social media site will be surprising, go against its stated rules, and provide the evidence. Therefore, it never hurts to ask with a subpoena in a civil case. Just be prepared for a no.[47]

---

[44]*Tompkins v. Detroit Metropolitan Airport,* Case No. 10-10413, 2012 WL 179320 (E.D. MI. 2012).

[45]Facebook states, "Federal law prohibits Facebook from disclosing user content (such as messages, wall posts, photos, etc.) in response to a civil subpoena." **www.facebook.com/help/?faq=17158**.

[46]For Facebook this requires the e-mail address that the attorney desires to connect to the account. **https://www.facebook.com/help/?page=211462112226850**.

[47]See Send a Subpoena to the Site *supra.*

The various social media sites generally have details on the subpoena process and what they will provide. Review each site to learn the appropriate steps.

What Happens If the Owner of the Account Deletes the Data?

Most social media providers claim that when a user deletes information from his account, it is gone forever. Facebook, for example, explains that its deletion system works much like a recycling bin. In essence, when a user deletes data, that data is stored on Facebook's server briefly until the system writes over it; this means, unfortunately, if someone is savvy and starts deleting harmful data, there is nothing that can be done to bring it back, once it is overwritten. Facebook does state, "[i]f a user cannot access content because he or she disables or deleted his or her account, Facebook will, to the extent possible, restore access to allow the user to collect and produce the account's content. Facebook preserves user content only in response to a valid law enforcement request."[48] Of course, if there is nothing to find because it has been deleted and destroyed, then the site cannot restore the data. And outside of criminal cases, it must be the account's owner who requests the data be restored.

Authentication

Authentication is another troubling issue when it comes to social media. Facebook states that the owner or someone familiar with the account can authenticate it. The issue, however, is that it is impossible to know whether the user deleted something in the account, leaving only helpful items. This is why it is extremely important to perform research early in the process and to take screenshots of any evidence discovered immediately. Be certain to keep records as to how the evidence was preserved.

In terms of proving who owns the account, remember, it is very easy to create a fake social media account. Just because an account looks like it belongs to someone does not mean that it does. That is why it might be important at least to subpoena the account-identifying information from the social media site if there is any question as to ability to prove ownership of an account.

The case law on authentication and admissibility of social media sites is contradictory. In *State v. Bell*, the court found that the level of admissibility is low. It accepted as good enough, testimony from a witness familiar with the MySpace account and e-mail address of the party the infor-

---

[48]See Information on Civil Subpoenas, **https://www.facebook.com/help/?page=211462112226850**.

mation was to be used against. Also the evidence showed that the defendant used certain code words and that those words were contained within the account. The court also noted that the witness agreed that the provided printouts seemed to be an accurate reflection of the MySpace account in question.[49]

On the other side, in *Griffin v. State*, the court was concerned about how easy it is to create a fake account and noted that information such as birthdate, picture, and residence were not enough to prove ownership.[50]

The Other Side—Responding to Social Media Requests

It is important to be prepared to respond appropriately to requests for social media content. All businesses (including law firms) should have a social media policy that controls who may (and may not) speak on behalf of the company. The policy should also consider addressing whether supervisors may be connected to employees on the more social sites (as opposed to professional sites liked LinkedIn), and remind employees about the fact that policies online are the same as policies offline; specifically in relation to sexual harassment and other such issues. Employees should also be reminded not to discuss private information and/or litigation on their social media accounts. Employers might consider training employees on social media privacy settings to assist in security. As already explained, individuals should be warned not to post anything that can be harmful to their cases on social media.

Social media evidence needs to be preserved appropriately. For a business with a great deal of social media evidence to preserve, it is wise to involve a company that can help in the preservation process during litigation. An individual can simply print out the pages or download the account. If the account is large (and is not on Facebook where it can be downloaded) and it is likely the history of the account will enter into the lawsuit, it might be wise to arrange for preservation of the account through a third party, to avoid any accusations of spoliation later on.

In the end, it is crucial for clients—indeed for everyone—to remember that any content posted on a social media site, even back in 2004 when Facebook was first created and the client might have been in college, could come up later during litigation. Therefore everyone needs to be careful to think before posting. This does not mean that people should go

---

[49] *State v. Bell*, 882 N.E.2e (2008).
[50] *Griffin v. State*, 2011 Md. LEXIS 226, 27-28 (Md. Apr. 28, 2011).

back and clean up their accounts just because some day they might, by chance, be sued. But it does mean they might want to give some thought to their online reputations due to their past and current postings.

Ethical Issues—Advertising and Communication

Is social media advertising? Well, it depends. Clearly, purchasing an actual ad on Facebook or LinkedIn is advertising. But is writing a blog post or creating a Facebook page an ad? The answer is unclear. Perhaps consider them kindred spirits to websites, and follow the rules accordingly.

What about writing a quick post on Twitter or providing a status update on a personal Facebook account. Is that an ad? Again, the answer is uncertain, but if it is an ad, how can a lawyer possibly follow the rules given the fleeting and brief nature of the communication? One can hardly put a disclaimer on Twitter while trying to fit a post in 140 characters.

On the other hand, recently the issue of whether blogs are marketing came up in Virginia. In a controversial decision, the State Bar determined that blogs are advertising and disciplined the lawyer for failing to provide an advertising disclaimer. The lawyer disagreed and felt the blog was not advertising and did not require a disclaimer.[51] The Virginia Supreme Court agreed that the lawyer had a First Amendment right to blog about a case insofar as the facts cited were a matter of public record. It also decided that the post was advertising and required a disclaimer, which the lawyer has said he will now provide. In the end, what the decision tells lawyers is that a proper disclaimer on a blog is a good idea. And a number of ethics experts question whether a lawyer may reveal client information even when it is a matter of public record (normally, court records remain obscure). So stay tuned; other states may revisit that portion of the opinion.

Given the uncertainty, the safest approach is to assume that everything is an advertisement and to follow the ethical rules as best as possible within the confines of the technology. The reason for such caution? It is difficult to know exactly how various states will determine to handle social media, and it is best to make certain to avoid future ethical issues through current online communications. On the other hand, a good faith effort to follow the rules in such an uncertain world will probably go a long way toward appeasing any disciplinary board that becomes concerned with a

---

[51] *Hunter v. Virginia State Bar et al,* Civil Action No. 3:11-VC-216-JAG (2011).

lawyer's social media efforts. Remember also that different states have different rules. It is important for lawyers to be aware of the rules in their own states.

7.1. Honest Communication and 8.x Integrity

The first two rules for online behavior should be considered an umbrella under which all behavior is judged. First, lawyers should never be misleading in their communications in relation to their services. No communication should contain a material misrepresentation of either fact or law, nor should any statement omit facts necessary to make the statement appropriate under Rule 7.1. This concept flows throughout all communications by lawyers when discussing their services. The second set of rules, 8.x, involves maintaining the integrity of the profession; in other words, not holding the profession up to ridicule through one's behavior.

7.2. Advertising

The first rule of which lawyers need to be aware relates directly to advertising, and it is Model Rule 7.2. One of the issues that can be a problem under Rule 7.2 is that various states require lawyers to keep all ads for a certain period of time. In Pennsylvania, for example, lawyers must keep copies of ads for two years. Other states have longer requirements. It is also important to note that a specific lawyer must take responsibility for the ad and its placement, so make certain that a specific lawyer is responsible for every action, even if performed by a non-lawyer. Fortunately, the various accounts are meant to stay intact, so it is easy to keep records. If a post needs to be deleted, grab a screenshot of it and store it where it will be easily findable. Make certain to identify the lawyer responsible for the item.

Various states have other requirements, so lawyers should check Rule 7.2 in every state in which they are licensed.

Rule 7.3. Solicitation of Clients

Also implicated by use of social media for communication with potential clients is Model Rule 7.3. Attorneys may not solicit potential clients through real-time communication. This aspect of the rule does not apply to family members, current clients, or other lawyers. Real-time communication includes telephone, in-person, and real-time electronic chat. There is disagreement as to whether lawyers may solicit new clients through large chat rooms in which a large number of people are present versus instant messages, which are more personal and direct. Given this, it is safe to assume that starting a chat on Facebook is real-time communication and should be avoided. E-mail is considered written communication. To obey the rule, at a minimum, lawyers must label advertising as such and comply with Rule 7.1.

Attorneys may not solicit a client who has already made it clear he does not wish to be contacted, or if "the solicitation involves coercion, duress or harassment." This means if someone has made it clear through social media that he desires not to be contacted, it would be a violation of the rule to contact him. The tone of writing matters as well. If the content is seen as inappropriate, it violates the rule.

Multi-State Practice—Rule 8.5
An area in which it is easy to get in trouble, due to the vast and multi-jurisdictional nature of the Internet, is multi-state practice. Attorneys must comply with their home states' rules in relation to:

- Where the office is located
- Where the lawyers are admitted
- How they are seeking clients
- How they engage in advertising
- Obeying all the rules of the states in which they market

Other Ethical Issues
Aside from advertising, communication with potential clients, and inappropriate use of social media in discovery, there are other ways in which legal professionals have gotten themselves in trouble using social media.

Attorney/Client Relationship, Conflicts of Interest, and Unauthorized Practice of Law
Many sites enable direct communication with potential clients. Blogs often actively seek to encourage communication (though comments can be disabled). Answering a question by an anonymous reader in one's own state could actually cause a lawyer to help an opposing party without knowing it. Providing legal advice in a state in which a lawyer is not licensed could result in a claim of unauthorized practice of law. A person asking a question could believe he has formed an attorney/client relationship if he is not warned otherwise through a statement or disclaimer. It is best that lawyers be cautious about what questions they choose to answer and how they choose to answer them in any online medium. It is acceptable to provide general educational information. It is not OK to provide actual legal advice.

Confidentiality and Honesty

One potential area of trouble involves confidentiality, Rule 1.6. A lawyer got herself in trouble by sharing confidential information about a case in such a way as to make it possible to identify her client. She also provided information that suggested that she knew her client had lied on the stand and did nothing about it. In addition to Rule 1.6, the lawyer was accused of violating other rules involving honesty, fraud, and more.[52] In the end, the lawyer lost her job of nineteen years[53] and was suspended for ninety days by two different jurisdictions.[54, 55]

Another serious consequence the lawyer suffered is that when searching her name online, page after page of results show her disciplinary problems. Though she has since opened her own firm, it is difficult to find anything positive about her on the Web in a Google search.

While it is perfectly acceptable to discuss one's life, and even one's professional activities, it is important to obey the ethical rules while doing so. Discussing a case on a blog while it is going on, outside of appropriate PR, is a bad idea. Failing to protect a client's confidentiality is even worse. And, of course, failing to properly inform the court of inappropriate conduct by the client was a serious mistake. Judgment is a critical part of both practicing law and posting online.

Jokes and Satire

Jokes can also be a serious problem online. It is impossible to see body language or hear the tone in a person's voice. Something one person might find amusing might not be so funny to another. As a result, joking through social media can be problematic, especially on a politically charged topic. An Indiana deputy attorney general learned this the hard way when he tweeted an unfortunate joke surrounding protests in Wisconsin in 2011. His tweet led to an argument with the editor of *Mother Jones* magazine. In turn, the magazine researched the lawyer and found similar comments on his blog. In the end, the price of the lawyer's online behavior was his job.[56]

---

[52]In the Matter of Kristine Ann Peshek, Commission No. 09 CH 89, Illinois Attorney Registration and Disciplinary Commission (2009).

[53]Debra Cassens Weiss, "Blogging Assistant PD Accused of Revealing Secrets of Little—Disguised Clients," ABA Journal, September 10, 2009, **www.abajournal.com/news/article/blogging_ assistant_pd_accused_of_revealing_secrets_of_little-disguised_clie/**.

[54]Chris Bonjean, "Illinois Supreme Court Disbars 12, Suspends 26," Illinois State Bar Association, May 18, 2010, **iln.isba.org/2010/05/18/illinois-supreme-court-disbars-12-suspends-26**.

[55]*Office of Lawyer Regulation v. Peshek*, 2011 WI 47 (2011).

[56]Dana Chivvis, "Indiana Deputy Attorney General Fired Over Threatening Twitter Posts," AOL News, February 24, 2011, **www.aolnews.com/2011/02/24/indiana-deputy-attorney-general-jeff-cox-fired-over-threatening/**.

The attorney general's office stated that it chose to fire the lawyer after a "thorough and expeditious review," noting that it respects First Amendment rights but expects civility from its public servants.

Personal v. Private

Sometimes lawyers will develop both a private and public persona on the Web, believing the two will remain separate. Unfortunately, this is simply not the case. It takes very little effort to perform research on the Web and to connect the public and private behaviors of someone who has written something offensive or upsetting. In an infamous case, an assistant Michigan attorney general was fired due to his online (and perhaps offline) behavior toward the student body president of the University of Michigan. The lawyer argued that his speech was political and also had nothing to do with his work as an assistant attorney general. But in the end, the public and private became much too intertwined, and the attorney general was left with no choice but to fire him. Recently the student won a verdict of $4.5 million for invasion of privacy, defamation, abuse of process, and intentional infliction of emotional distress.[57]

The lawyer in this case did not hide who he was, but he did try to argue that his actions had nothing to do with his work. However, as a public servant and as a lawyer, it was simply impossible to separate the public employee from the (not so) private behavior, and that cost him his job. He was fired for "violat[ing] office policies, engag[ing] in borderline stalking behavior," and more. The lawyer sometimes posted his online attacks while at work and engaged in behavior that was "not protected by the First Amendment. . . ."[58] Much of his behavior was offline, but it was his online behavior that brought an incredible amount of attention to what he was doing, so much so that he ended up on TV shows, including *Anderson Cooper* on CNN.[59]

It is unwise to believe that anyone can live two separate lives online. If one engages in controversial behavior, the result will be a magnifying glass of attention. In turn, it is virtually impossible for the individual to keep his private and public online lives from colliding.

---

[57]Kevin Dolak, "Attorney Andrew Shirvell Ordered to Pay 4.5 Million for Attacks on Gay Student," ABC News, August 17, 2012, **abcnews.go.com/US/attorney-andrew-shirvell-ordered-pay-45-million-attacks/story?id=17028621**.

[58]David Jesse, "Andrew Shirvell Fired from Job at Michigan Attorney General's Office," The Ann Arbor News, November 8, 2010, **www.annarbor.com/news/andrew-shirvell-fired-from-job-at-attorney-generals-office/#.UFQIPVEQd60**.

[59]Huffington Post, "Anderson Cooper: Andrew Shirvell Responsible for His Firing, Not 'Liberal Media,'" Huffington Post, last modified May 25, 2011, **www.huffingtonpost.com/2010/11/09/anderson-cooper-andrew-sh_n_780874.html**.

Judges

Many judges enjoy having an online presence as well. This has led to questions over whether judges should be friends with lawyers, and what happens if a judge is a friend with a defendant.

In attempting to resolve the first issue, the Florida Supreme Court Judicial Ethics Advisory Committee determined that judges may not be friends on Facebook with lawyers who appear before them.[60] In turn, a defendant sought to disqualify a judge based on his Facebook friendship with the prosecutor. The trial judge denied the request, but upon appeal the motion was granted. The court held that the Facebook friendship "conveys the impression that the lawyer is in a position to influence the judge."[61] Ohio came down on the other side, noting that it is acceptable for judges to friend lawyers who appear before them. However, the judges must comport themselves properly, following all ethical rules, and must be careful to disqualify themselves should the online friendship cause a bias.[62]

Other states have seen issues arise when the judge learns he is Facebook friends with a defendant. Two cases occurred in Pennsylvania. In the first, the judge was asked to recuse himself, and eventually did so when it turned out he knew the defendant's father. He was, however, unaware of the Facebook friendship before being alerted to it. Like many people, the judge simply friended anyone who asked and thought nothing of it.[63] Another controversy arose when a judge suppressed evidence against a defendant, resulting in dismissal of the case. After the fact, the prosecution realized that the judge was Facebook friends with the defendant, though the defendant and the judge did not know each other. The prosecutor asked the judge to reverse the suppression and recuse himself. The judge decided not to recuse himself due to concern about setting a dangerous precedent.[64]

On February 21, 2013, the American Bar Association released Formal Opinion 462, Judge's Use of Electronic Social Networking Media. It offers the new acronym, ESM, meaning "electronic social media." Judges are

---

[60]Opinion Number 2009-20, November 17, 2009, **www.jud6.org/LegalCommunity/LegalPractice/opinions/jeacopinions/2009/2009-20.html**.

[61]*Domville v. State*, No. 4D12-556 (Fla. 4th DCA 2012).

[62]December 8, 2010, Advisory Opinion: Judges May 'Friend' 'Tweet' if Proper Caution Exercised. **www.supremecourt.ohio.gov/PIO/news/2010/BOCadvisoryOp_120810.asp**.

[63]Sara Ganim, "Cumberland County Judge Thomas A. Placey under Fire for Having Too Many Facebook Friends," PennLive, last modified September 20, 2011, **www.pennlive.com/midstate/index.ssf/2011/09/judges_facebook_friend_has_som.html**.

[64]Aaron Moselle, "Judge Refuses to Recuse Himself from Parker DUI Case, State Plans an Appeal," NewsWorks, November 22, 2011, **www.newsworks.org/index.php/neighborhoods/mt-airy chestnut-hill-/item/30248-hayden-denial-story-**.

allowed to participate in ESM as long as they "comply with the relevant provisions of the Code of Judicial Conduct and avoid any conduct that would undermine the judge's independence, integrity or impartiality, or create an appearance of impropriety."

In the end, the best advice for judges is that they be careful who they friend and also be aware of who they friend. Friending everyone is not a good idea for a judge, since it is easy enough, as shown above, for the judge to end up being friends with a defendant and to be completely unaware of their online relationship. Judges who have many friends on social media sites might want to take a look at who those friends are and determine whether they should remain friends. On the other hand, judges who prefer to have many friends online might find it wise to be certain they know who those friends are and at the least make both sides aware of the Facebook friendship prior to the trial beginning. If necessary, perhaps the judge could have a clerk make a quick check of his account to make certain that he is not friends with defendants who appear before him.

Jurors

These days it is extremely common to look over to the seats behind the prosecution, plaintiff, or defense and see individuals hard at work on their computers during the *voir dire* process.[65] This is because jurors, like almost everyone else, provide an immense amount of information about themselves online. Some of this information might well disqualify an individual from serving on a jury or simply show a particular side that it would be unwise to seat a potential juror.

While there are currently no conclusive decisions on the issue of researching jurors via social media, there is guidance on the subject.[66] A New York opinion, quite reasonably, makes it clear that it is acceptable to research jurors online, including viewing their social media accounts under several conditions. First, the accounts must be accessed appropriately, i.e. only looking at accounts and information that have been left freely accessible by the jurors. Also, it remains impermissible to communicate with the jurors in any fashion. That means no friending (or having a third party friend) a juror to obtain access to the private sections of an account.

---

[65]Michael Cary, "Lawyers in Murray Trial Using Facebook, Twitter to Screen Jurors," CNN, last modified September 21, 2011, **http://www.cnn.com/2011/09/20/tech/social-media/social-media-jurors-murray/index.html**.

[66]NYCLA Committee on Professional Ethics, Formal Opinion 743, May 18, 2011, **https://www.nycla.org/siteFiles/Publications/Publications1450_0.pdf**.

Of late, jurors have been engaging in social media or other Internet use that has caused serious trouble for the court system. Judges, prosecutors, and defense lawyers frequently find themselves throwing their hands up in the air due to the frustration caused by jurors who refuse to follow the instructions. While it might seem beyond belief that jurors would choose to engage in social media discussion or Internet research after being specifically told not to do so, the reality is that they do.[67] In response to juror behavior, many judges and court systems are developing instructions to provide to jurors to warn them away from social media use. For example, the Judicial Conference Committee on Court Administration and Case Management recently created "Proposed Model Jury Instructions [on] The Use of Electronic Technology to Conduct Research on or Communicate about a Case."[68] Regardless of the language, it is crucial that right at the outset of a case judges warn the jury of the serious ramifications, and potential punishments, for violating court orders on use of social media during a trial.

Conclusion

Understanding how the public uses social media is important for lawyers so they can appreciate the types of evidence they might find online to help their cases and so they can appropriately warn their clients about social media use. Knowing the benefits and risks of social media in terms of networking and marketing can help a lawyer grow her firm without harming her hard-earned reputation through improper online activities. Being aware of how judges and juries use social media and how that use might affect a case is important so lawyers can be prepared to respond accordingly.

There is no doubt that social media can be a serious minefield in terms of day-to-day practice and ethical requirements. On the other hand, the substantial benefits available in terms of evidence, research, marketing, and networking cannot be overstated. With the number of people using social media increasing every day, social media will continue to impact the legal profession in every imaginable way, and perhaps some unimaginable ways too. As a result it is crucial for lawyers to embrace the technology and determine how they can use it both in their practice of law and in their efforts to grow their client base.

---

[67]Michael Kiefer, "Social Media's Clout Worries Legal System," WFMY News website, September 13, 2012, **www.digtriad.com/news/article/245301/175/Social-Medias-Clout-Worries-Legal-System**.
[68]Proposed Model Jury Instructions [on] The Use of Electronic Technology to Conduct Research or Communicate about a Case, **www.uscourts.gov/uscourts/News/2012/jury-instructions.pdf**.

In Memoriam

ROSS KODNER
1961–2013

THANKS, ROSS, FOR BEING such a good friend over so many years. John and I will always remember that you brought us our first national speaking engagement at ABA TECHSHOW. We had a lot of fun together over the years, sharing many dinners, good-natured technology debates, and more than a few laughs. It ended too soon. Save us a place at the table, and we'll do it again—in time. We miss you, dear.

CHAPTER TWENTY-SEVEN

The Paper LESS Office: Cutting Edge Still, or is it, The Magic "Edge" for Small Firms?

by Ross L. Kodner, Esq.*

WITH THE NEW "NORMAL" legal economy well-entrenched, small firm lawyers are on a constant quest for "the Edge," that intangible *je ne sais quoi* that will separate them from the local competition and make them stand out. But is there such an edge? Something different that the guy two doors down hasn't yet stumbled upon?

The answer is an absolute, unequivocal . . . maybe. But the answer is closer than one might think. It can be found on the surfaces of every desk, credenza, and file cabinet in the small firm office. What is it, you ask?

The answer, in a Seinfeldian way, is . . . Wait for it . . . Here it comes . . . "Nothing." That is, no paper. No piles of it. No boxes of it. Smooth, neat, clean working surfaces that represent a paperless office at its best and most functional. "The Edge" turns out to be nothing more than the ability to convert otherwise wasted non-billable administrative time spent enslaved to the paper monster into billable, productive time, relying on complete and contiguous electronic case files—the essence of the paperless office.

Note: I work as an independent technology consultant for law firms. As part of this work, my firm acts as a reseller for certain technology products. However, just as the authors have stated in the preface that the book contains their objective advice, I have strived to provide unbiased advice and product recommendations in this chapter.

This is the holy grail of legal technology since the dawn of computing technology. And the good news is that every small firm can afford it, every small firm can accomplish it, and it's much, much easier than you're thinking.

> *First thing we do, let's kill all the paper.*
>
> —Will Shakespeare,
> if he were alive today

> *Paper, paper everywhere,*
> *Nor any page to find.*
> *Unless it's electronic paper in the cloud.*
>
> —Ross L. Kodner
> Continuing Thoughts on The Paper LESS Office[TM]

LAST YEAR COULD HAVE been termed the Year of the Cloud—web-based systems were shiny, new, exciting, and still largely unproven. A year later, cloud-based systems have entered the mainstream. This year, the thrill of cloud legal technology is gone and we're back to the basics—the things that really matter. Small firm lawyers are searching for "the Edge"; the competitive difference that helps them vanquish competition, maximize their profits, and at the same time, perhaps reduce the aggravation factor inherent in all types of law practice. What was "sexy" technology once—the "paperless chase" is becoming a practical necessity again.

The Edge

In the last year, as small firm lawyers came to accept the maturing cloud-computing offers as mainstream choices, and iPads and as Android tablets became commonplace fixtures in small firm conference rooms across the world, things changed—and shifted.

While the latest Apple iEverything announcements still generate a lot of buzz, we seem to have settled down and put on our big boy/big girl pants once again. More and more small firms are focused on what actually matters in their practice. New, shiny, and sexy might offer fleeting psychic rewards and feed our short attention spans; that's not likely to ever disappear. We are in a profession that craves distraction so we can maintain a semblance of sanity.

But with that said, more and more small firms are fixing their eyes on the prize—the one thing that matters if they want to succeed in their practices.

The Edge

What is "the Edge"? While it may vary from practice to practice, the Edge could be defined as "whatever it takes to get ahead." That can mean different things to different practitioners, certainly. But the most common themes among "Edge-Seekers" are finding ways to make more money (maximizing profits, not just increasing top-line gross revenue), better competing for new business, better service of and retention of existing clients, better staff retention, and better quality of life (reducing the aggravation factor of law practice while maximizing the fun factor). These are the things that matter, right?

The latest version of an iPhone doesn't really matter. How much more money will you make if you have an iPhone 5 instead of that now-obsolete iPhone 4S? The answer to that question would be . . . none.

But what kind of an Edge would a small firm gain if it were to master a technology that provably can reduce non-billable administrative time and convert it into billable time—generating more top-line revenue and more bottom-line profit without adding a single minute to a workday? A significant Edge.

One of the easiest Edges to achieve is to become Paper LESS in practice. Not getting rid of paper as much as creating a case-handling process and law practice operation environment that virtually never requires paper to be handled, searched for, filed, or even touched. The inevitable result—one that is virtually guaranteed—is more profit from reduced expenses, more profit from top-line revenue increases without any attendant increases in the monthly "nut," clients who get quicker responses, and lawyers and staff who can take their work virtually anywhere, on any device, and work anytime they choose or anytime a client needs them. Who wouldn't, in their right mind, want to accomplish these things?

So, what are the obstacles to accomplishing these things? What stands in the way of achieving this particular version of the Edge?

Piles and piles of paper that conspire to waste our otherwise productive and billable time are the problem. Piles of paper that cause untold angst as we chase around our offices and homes looking for documents that might only exist in electronic form. Exasperation when we realize that the client work we need to do at home one evening is just not going to happen because our ability to work is dependent on the physical presence of the paper client file . . . which we forgot to take home. But there's good news—there may be hope in getting out from under all that paper.

For years, lawyers have been on a quest for the paperless office, but this concept is likely the greatest lie of the technology age. Our offices never will be paperless, at least in the foreseeable future. We need to accept the fact that even if we reduce the amount of paper we generate, other people will continue to send us paper. Can you realistically walk into most court-rooms and present a paperless case to a jury? Doubt it—at least not in most jurisdictions. Are your 50-year-old eyes comfortable with proofing a 50-page contract onscreen? Perhaps "yes" for some, but likely "no" for most of us. Early technology scanning was touted as the great answer, but it is not.

I Want It NOW! Or Sooner! Life in the Age of Instancy

Lawyers and legal professionals in all walks of practice—from SmallLaw to BigLaw, in corporate and government practice—all face the reality of this "Age of Instancy" in which we practice and live. Think of it this way: Twenty-five years ago, do you remember how extraordinary it seemed when the company then known as Federal Express promised that it could deliver a hard copy document, anywhere in the world, by 10:30 the next morning? It seemed positively miraculous, didn't it? Today, 10:30 the *next* morning seems like an eternity to have to wait. How our perceptions of time and expectations of access to documents and other information have changed.

Today, while on the phone with a client across the continent, if the need to share a document arises, what do we do? Instinctively and without need for any taxing conscious thought, we say, "No problem, I'll e-mail it while we're talking." A 5-megabyte collection of attachments zips across the ether and arrives in the client's e-mail inbox, almost before we can finish the sentence. Collaboration, oral and digital, all happening virtually at the speed of light. Or even better, don't bother e-mailing it at all—use a web-based secure document repository such as Dropbox (**www.dropbox.com**), Microsoft SkyDrive (**windows.microsoft.com/en-US/skydrive/home**), Google Drive (**www.drive.google.com/start**), Box (**www.box.com**), NetDocuments (**www.netdocuments.com**), or the Worldox/Web Mobile adjunct to the Worldox legal document/e-mail management system (**www.worldox.com**). A growing number of legal ethics opinions and the ABA's 20/20 model rules and recommendations have begun to legitimize cloud computing from an ethical perspective.

If your jurisdiction doesn't yet have formal ethical guidance that permits reasonably investigated and educated choices about cloud computing, it will soon.

In the last couple of years, the rise of cloud Computing has been meteoric. The concept of cloud computing can generally be described as the ability to either run software functions or access data across the Internet, in one of many different ways. In terms of the concept of becoming "Paper LESS," one can look at several different cloud approaches, all focused on anyplace, anytime, any system access to client and firm files. We'll explore these various approaches later in this chapter.

Instant access to information changes our expectations. Clients are "trained" to expect instantaneous everything. Instant access to documents, electronically delivered. Instant responses to questions they pose to their lawyers, such as when was that deposition scheduled? Or, how much do I have left on my retainer balance? Or, do you have the contact info for that financial forensic consultant you mentioned last week? Law practices that are not able to instantly respond to such "in conversation" queries quickly become labeled as "techno-peasants." Such lawyers may be instantly branded by their clients as being both mechanically and substantively incompetent and, frankly, more of an irritant than a professional counselor to the client.

While the Age of Instancy may not be a positive development of the human experience, it is a fact of professional life. Woe to the lawyers who fail to acknowledge this issue by putting themselves in their clients' shoes and understanding how true it is that the client's perception is the only reality that counts. So, what does this have to do with managing paper in our practices? Simply . . . everything.

Paper—Endless Frustration and Expense

Even in 2013, paper is the bane of every law practice's existence. This is actually nothing new—it is one of the endlessly frustrating Great Truths of Law Practice. Paper wastes our time. Paper costs us money. Paper files get lost. Paper hides itself at the most inopportune time. Paper costs money to store. Paper costs yet more money to retrieve. Paper, used injudiciously, negatively impacts the environment. Paper tends to get coffee or lunch spilled on it in direct proportion to the importance and irreplaceability of the document. Paper isn't searchable in any efficient way compared to electronic searching abilities. In fact, there is a great corollary of life in law practice that says "the more urgently one needs a paper client file, the less likely it is where it is supposed to be." Who hasn't experienced a day when an urgently needed paper file just never turns up? Haven't we all? The toll on profitability and client responsiveness, not to mention our personal sanity and psyches, is dramatic and negative. It makes sense to find practical ways to avoid this multi-dimensional self-infliction of pain.

Saving the Planet, Saving Your Sanity— More Paper Is NOT the Way

Being environmentally conscious is no longer optional. The movement to become more "green" is now entrenched and continually sweeping across the worldwide business landscape. Clearly, generating more paper is the antithesis to being green, meaning that becoming Paper LESS in law practice is of paramount importance and can be the touchstone of a green initiative in any law firm or legal department.

Think about the environmental impact and the staggering carbon footprint involved in printing just a single sheet of paper:

- ♦ Trees are harvested, with considerable energy expended in the acquisition ("chopping it down") process, the transportation process, the process of transforming trees into logs, logs into wood chips, wood chips into wood pulp, and then eventually into paper.

- ♦ Then the paper is packaged in . . . *more paper!*

- ♦ The paper is shipped to its retail location, then shipped to the consumer.

- ♦ The paper is printed in a device—a printer or copier—that has its own significant environmental footprint and trail of anti-green shame.

- ♦ The printing system employed devours consumables—toner or ink—again, supplies carrying their own carbon imprint and anti-green burden.

- ♦ Eventually the paper is likely discarded, often bypassing a responsible recycling process and contributing to overfilled landfills.

Becoming Paper LESS in practice—generating far less paper, or, frankly, virtually no new paper—is a perfect way to jump-start a green initiative. It is a positive by-product of the Paper LESS Office process, in addition to the myriad economic, functional, and client service-related benefits.

The Cost of Being in a Paper MORE Office

Think about this question: How much time do you or your staff waste in an average workday, either (a) looking for paper client files or (b) looking for information you can only find in paper files? How many of you waste fifteen minutes chasing paper? Thirty minutes? An hour or more? How many of you have experienced days where the paper file never turns up at all? Or, even worse, a staffer starts an expedition to seek out a missing, urgently needed paper file. After fifteen minutes and no success, the lawyer then chases the staffer, who in turn is still chasing the file. So it ends up being thirty staff minutes and fifteen lawyer minutes—a phenomenal waste of otherwise billable and productive time.

We can perform some quick legal business math to calculate the value of these endless paper chases. Presume a net realized billed rate of $200 per hour—a likely average for solo and small firm lawyers in private practice. Then presume a billable value of $60 per hour for legal assistants or paralegals. Assume three lawyers wasting an average of fifteen minutes per day chasing paper, one legal assistant and one paralegal wasting thirty minutes each day (more for staff because they are often chasing paper on behalf of requesting lawyers). This common small firm scenario represents a total daily value of otherwise billable/productive time wasted of:

- ◆ $150 per day for the lawyers
- ◆ $60 per day for the staff

That translates to:

- ◆ $750 per week for the lawyers, $3,000 per month, $36,000 per year
- ◆ $300 per week for the staff, $1,200 per month, $14,400 per year

That represents more than $50,000 in otherwise billable/productive time for this firm. And make no mistake; the effect of $50,000 in revenue never coming back to this firm has precisely the same effect as writing out a $50,000+ check at the end of the year. A basic business operations lesson shows that a reduction of top-line gross revenue has precisely the same negative impact on bottom-line profit as writing a check for $50,000. A cardinal principle of business operations is that a firm does not actually have to generate a check to spend money. Money not coming in has the same effect as that check that draws down from a bank account.

That is the cost of being mired in a Paper MORE practice. A $50,000+ hit for a three-lawyer practice. Hardly inconsequential—in fact, a staggering drain of a law practice's only available "product inventory," its billable and productive time. In the current economy, where so many law practices are being squeezed to the limits of financial viability, no firm can afford to subsidize this level of uncaptured revenue.

With so much at stake in managing the paper chase, why have we heard nothing but stories about failed attempts to go "paperless"? Whether it's a law practice down the street or, more often than not, some government agency that devoured millions of taxpayer dollars in a fruitless multi-year paperless office project, the results are the same: failure, or at best, a mediocre outcome. Why is this the case? The reason is simple—no matter how much your practice or your company tries to reduce the paper it uses and generates, the rest of the "paper clueless" world (especially budget-challenged government agencies) will inundate you with paper. The reality is clear—paper will be with us for some time to come, perhaps forever. Even if you had to look at this cynically and say there are too many companies whose livelihoods are derived from paper in some way (e.g., paper companies, copier companies, printer companies, printing consumable companies, etc.), you would come to this frustrating and inevitable solution. So, is it hopeless? Are we doomed to be perpetual slaves to the printed page?

What if you never had to chase paper files around the office? What if you could find a way to have to touch the paper files less often, or virtually never? What if you could "buy back" that wasted fifteen, thirty, sixty or more minutes per day looking for paper necessary for you to serve the needs of clients? What might that mean economically? Even if you took an especially conservative posture in terms of how you viewed the conversion of "wasted paper chasing" time into billable time and cut the above recovery calculation by 50 percent, that would still represent $25,000 per year in "found money," and that's not pocket change for a three-lawyer practice.

And what if the answer to this problem cost less than $10,000 in out of pocket costs for software, hardware, and consultative guidance (approximately $3,000 for software, $3,000 for desktop scanners, and $4,000 for planning, process-streamlining, installation, and training)?

In that 50 percent discounted conservative analysis, the first year net yield is at least $15,000 ($25,000 in converted/recovered billable/productive time less $10,000 in out of pocket costs) and then at least $25,000 per year thereafter—a conservative five-year billable/productive net revenue increase of approximately $115,000 in exchange for an approximately

$10,000 front-end investment. Wouldn't it be ironic to find out that the best investment you could ever make in your life turned out to be investing in your own law practice? This is the proverbial economic "no-brainer."

Another factor, while more subjective in measurement but equally tangible in perceived value, is the positive effect on everyone's psyche and mental well-being. The endless daily paper chases take a toll psychologically on lawyers and staffers. It is just plain stressful when a paper file eludes location and wastes time, usually at the most inopportune moment. The toll of stress, frustration, and angst that missing paper files inflicts on legal professionals may be difficult to quantify. Nevertheless, it is as real as the fact that the sun rises in the east. Stress lessens our effectiveness, drives away valuable employees, and affects our well-being, especially when we take it home and inflict it on our families. Modern law practice is complicated and aggravating. Anything we can do to positively impact our stress levels while simultaneously filling our firm coffers is something we need to run to, as fast as we can.

Fragmented Client Files Defy Common Sense

Being paper-centric in practice brings another inherent anti–common sense inefficiency. One of the core problems when working on client files is that they are always split between two locations. The documents we create are located internally on our PC systems. The client documents we receive from outside sources are stored in our paper filing systems. So if you want to view all the correspondence on a client's file, you have to look in two separate places—on-screen for your own documents, and then you need to track down the paper file and rifle through it to view the externally generated letters. That is, of course, if no one happened to have that particular file in a briefcase at home. Who hasn't experienced the fallout from this irrational and illogical artificial fragmentation of our case files? This is most certainly not a "best practices" approach. It is a professional competence issue before it ever rises to the level of being a technology problem.

Stop the Madness: Become Paper LESS in Your Practice

Fine. You're still reading and slowly becoming a believer in some kind of Paper LESS Office—one where you can avoid wasting time in the paper chase that has haunted you for your entire law practice career. The next question is, how does your practice become Paper LESS? Surprisingly easily. With a combination of scanning tools, the wonders of the universally accessible and compatible PDF file format, sound but simple procedures, and a document/e-mail management system, a law practice can undergo a Paper LESS transformation overnight. Let's see how.

How many of you have had bad scanning experiences over the years? Many of you, in all likelihood—and there's a logical reason for all the scanning frustrations of the past. Since the dawn of document scanning, the term "scanning" has been synonymous with "OCR" (optical character recognition). In other words, most people equated scanning with trying to use software to identify the characters on a page and turn the page into an editable word processing document. It was a good idea conceptually, but in practice, even with the best OCR technology available, the process is still far from perfect. For example, with 97 percent OCR accuracy, three incorrect characters out of every 100 could mean as many as 66 errors per page on average. And what if any one of those errors is critical and not detected?

And then, even with the latest, greatest OCR software running on new PCs that are dripping with computing horsepower and fast new scanners, the process is about as slow as watching water boil . . . or paint dry . . . or grass grow. How can that be? It's 2014 (or beyond) after all, not 1992. The reason is that recognizing the raw text when trying to turn scanned pieces of paper into a Word document has become trivial. However, it is still very difficult to replicate the layout by applying codes, styles, and other formatting tools to produce a usable word processing document. And it is often surprisingly slow—turning that shiny new 40 page per minute scanner, effectively, into a 5 page per minute unit. Go ahead and let out that primal scream—we have all been there and have all similarly suffered.

So stop the madness. The bottom line is that modern scanning should not be equated with OCR. Instead, scanning should be looked at simply as a way to turn physical paper into electronic paper—effectively, to photocopy the documents, but not in the traditional way that copying produces a duplicate piece of paper. Rather, to photocopy a document to the computer screen, producing a precise duplicate of the scanned paper. You can then store it as a searchable (or as Adobe calls it, an "accessible") PDF file. Then use a document management system and well-thought-out document storage procedures with a smart file-naming convention to store the "electronic paper" in your electronic client file cabinet.

If the on-screen document looks precisely the same as the original piece of paper, why would you ever waste time trying to locate the paper itself? Of course, you wouldn't. You would use your document management system to rapidly navigate through your electronic file cabinet or use instant search technology to pinpoint the document and pull it up on-screen. No more "Keystone Cops" episodes of staff chasing paper, lawyers chasing staffers. No more drain of otherwise billable or productive time. Instead of those endlessly amusing games of "Who the heck has the Jones file?," just click, click and you're working—billing time, making more money—sans all the paper-chase-related stress that previously dominated your days.

Taking that a step further, what this all yields is the ability to completely portabilize (to coin a new verb) all the documents—of all types—in your practice. This is what enables the realistic ability to work any time, from any place, when clients need you to work or you choose to work. And it also brings in the practical reality of device independence. With web-based access to complete and contiguous electronic document files (securely of course), does it matter if you're using a Windows laptop/net-book, an iPad, or even an iPhone, BlackBerry, or Droid smartphone? Nope. It's such an exciting degree of flexibility in work habits, work timing, and work location that it could induce heart palpitations.

Getting Specific about Being Paper LESS

That's the essence of the Paper LESS Office process. Now let's get specific. What tools do we need? What processes make sense? How do we get from a Paper MORE Office to the Paper LESS Office?

Paper LESS Side Benefit: When you close a Paper LESS file, it's already "electronic paper": you can store it in a convenient byte-sized package (sorry, pun intended). This is a far better alternative for closed file storage than the costly, space-hungry storage requirements for physical paper files, which usually end up commandeering an area the size of a starter home.

With a concept that I developed first in 1995 and have since called the Paper LESS Office[TM], scanning is viewed as a way to turn physical paper into digital paper.[1] When documents are scanned as *images*, the process

---

[1] Kodner first put forth the Paper LESS Office[TM] concept in an article of the same name in the now defunct *Law Office Computing* magazine in September 1995.

can be as much as 20 times faster than the processing-intensive and error-ridden OCR approach. On the screen, imaged documents that have been scanned as searchable PDFs look precisely like the originals. Even handwriting, preprinted lines, and boxes scan perfectly.

One of my own clients, lawyer and litigator Dale Cottam, a partner with the firm of Hirst & Applegate in Cheyenne, Wyoming, explains how his firm uses the Paper LESS Office process:

> When staff and lawyers receive paper documents in the mail, they scan each one using a low cost and efficient Fujitsu ScanSnap S1500 scanner [a model since replaced by the newest iX500 which includes Adobe Acrobat X Standard as of this writing], which essentially is a "PDF machine." Every person at the firm—staff and lawyers—has a ScanSnap on his or her desk to make converting paper documents to electronic documents second nature.
>
> Once scanned, the electronic documents are saved in the universally readable PDF format. With a click of the mouse and a few seconds per page processing time, the text in the electronic document is converted to searchable text. The original paper document is placed in an expandable file folder and, in most cases, never is touched again. In some instances, the original is mailed to the client.
>
> The electronic documents are stored in the lawyer's electronic in-box using the Worldox document management system,[2] or they are routed directly to the lawyer via e-mail. Either way, a copy of the electronic document is saved on the firm's network server, which is backed up nightly.
>
> Attorneys read the electronic documents on their computer monitors. If they are on the road, they can access the electronic documents through the firm's VPN (virtual private network), a high-speed remote connection.

Scanning Systems—What Works?

In terms of scanners, a critical success element is the use of a combination of a centralized higher-speed scanner or multi-function copier with scanning abilities as well as distributed, decentralized individual desktop scanners. Why both? Why not just rely on that newly leased,

---

[2]Worldox is a product of World Software, Inc. (**www.worldox.com**)—one of the three leading legal-focused document/e-mail management and work product retrieval systems, in addition to Interwoven (Interwoven, Inc., formerly known as iManage) and eDOCS (Open Text Corporation, formerly known as PC DOCS Open).

monolithic, all-powerful, hulking multi-function copier/printer/scanner down the hall?

After all, you're paying for it every month, and it's a wonderfully rapid high-capacity scanner, right?

Here is why relying solely on that über-capable multi-function unit will ultimately cause your Paper LESS Office initiative to fail. Let's assume you have a wire basket next to your super-duper multi-function device down the hall. Everyone puts their documents to be scanned in the basket. Then every Tuesday and Thursday afternoon, your partner's 16-year-old daughter's boyfriend's cousin, 15-year-old Nick, comes in to scan your documents. Now think about the scenario for a moment. How would Nick, the high school scanning clerk, have any clue about where to store the documents or what to call them? You didn't have the time to clip notes to the documents indicating the precise client and matter to store the documents under and an equally descriptive file name. So the odds are, in spite of Nick's best efforts, you'll end up with a jumbled mess.

Instead, the approach that has proven itself in the field over many years places individual desktop direct-to-PDF scanners at *each* PC in the office, lawyers and staff alike. The idea is that inbound paper is distributed to the people who are familiar with the documents and who are familiar with the cases to which they belong. These people know where to store the documents and what to call the documents because these are the cases they actually work on. Lawyers and staff will likely scan different types of documents. Lawyers may scan a few business cards collected at the Rotary Club meeting that represent prospective clients and possible referral sources. The same lawyers might scan a pertinent article from the latest issue of the *ABA Journal* or their local state bar magazine. Staff are likely to scan case-related documents—incoming correspondence, pleadings received in the mail, and so on.

With each person doing his or her own case-related scanning, the overall scanning burden is distributed, and it is accomplished contemporaneously. This yields electronic case files that are made whole in real-time or near real-time, which means any lawyer or staff looking at the electronic file on-screen can count on the file being current and complete. This encourages further reliance on the electronic file by maximizing trust in the new approach.

Of course, when a larger volume of paper comes in, such as several banker's boxes in response to a discovery request, no one will want to scan 10,000 pages at a 20 page per minute desktop scanner with the 25-sheet paper feeder. That is when the staffer trots down the hall and scans using that monster multi-function machine, equipped with a high-capacity paper feeder and blistering 60 page per minute scanning speed. But in this case, the key is that the person scanning is the staffer who is actually familiar with the case and knows where to store and how to name the electronic paper.

This combination of centralized and decentralized scanning resources is an approach that has proven itself. Throw into the mix using the right lawyer or staff resource to scan the documents—the people who best know their own files and their own documents. This works. One approach to the exclusion of the other has inevitably failed in firms that tried the centralized approach alone.

In terms of USB port–connected desktop scanners, there are a variety of capable products. A consistent favorite over the last several years has been the ScanSnap series from Fujitsu, a well-respected and entrenched producer of scanning systems. With 25 page per minute scanning speed for the current iX500 and duplex capability (scans both sides in a single pass), this color-capable printer includes a 50-page feeder with an adjustable guide that can handle stock as small as a business card. The attraction of the ScanSnap series has been a combination of reliability, incredible ease of use via the famous "big green button," the inclusion of a full copy of Adobe Acrobat Standard X edition, and a reasonable price—in the $450 range. While the current version of Acrobat is Acrobat XI (the roman numeral for 11), Acrobat 10 is still highly functional, and if you wish to be more current, Adobe will let you upgrade from the bundled version to the current X Pro version (think: lots of legal-focused features like Bates stamping and secure redaction) for $199 directly from the Adobe website.

Other capable desktop scanners include models from Fujitsu and Visioneer, from Xerox with its fast 50 page per minute Documate series, from Canon and Kodak, and from Hewlett-Packard with its venerable ScanJet product line.

It's possible to take your Paper LESS Office totally mobile as well. Fujitsu extended its popular ScanSnap series to include the very portable model 1100 scanner (**tinyurl.com/ScanSnapS1100**). This is a tiny Windows-focused device, about the length of an egg carton but about one-third its depth. It weighs in at about 12 ounces and is powered by a USB cable connected to your computer of choice, so no bulky power brick. Unlike the desktop model, there is no document feeder to stack a pile of paper to scan. Rather, it is in the "high-touch" category, requiring you to insert one page at time. The ScanSnap Manager software controlling the scanner is smart enough to keep asking you to insert pages of any given document until you tell it you're finished. Like its big brother ScanSnap models, the 1100 will show the newly scanned document in Adobe Acrobat, ready to organize and make part of your electronic client file. Perfect for toting in one's laptop bag and using at a deposition, will signing, real estate closing, or at counsel's table.

Paper LESS Quick Tip: A common misconception is that if one scans at a higher resolution, the text recognition results will improve. In fact, often the opposite is true. Lower scanner resolution settings can yield better recognition. At higher resolutions, modern scanners have such capable optics that they can actually become "confused" by the fibers of the papers, which are incorrectly interpreted as characters. Set the resolution to 150–300 dpi for better text recognition results, whether you're using OCR software or producing searchable PDF files.

Document Management Systems: The Electronic Glue Holding It Together

The critical element in the Paper LESS Office process is the use of document management technology. A dedicated legal-focused document management software application or document management capability is the "digital glue" that holds the Paper LESS Office together.

There are four "traditional" legal document management systems (or perhaps five?) available as of this writing:

♦ Worldox GX3 from World Software, an update to the product released in January 2012 (**www.worldox.com**, available since the late 1980s after starting its life as a DOS application called Extend-a-File). While suitable for large firms and deployed in a number of BigLaw organizations, Worldox has traditionally dominated the small and mid-sized law practice marketplace. This has been the result of several factors, including the lower cost to acquire and implement because it doesn't require a pricey underlying SQL Server database infrastructure and is relatively simple to implement and to maintain compared to its BigLaw-oriented rivals. It integrates tightly with Microsoft Outlook for e-mail management and to many practice management systems, including Amicus Attorney (**www.amicusattorney.com**), PracticeMaster (**www.tabs3.com**), and LexisNexis Time Matters and Total Practice Advantage (**www.timematters.com**).

♦ Autonomy iManage Worksite (**www.autonomy.com**), traditionally a larger-firm oriented document management system that relies on a SQL Server database. This more expensive and more complex infrastructure is an impractical choice for SmallLaw.

♦ PC Docs from OpenText (formerly known as Hummingbird Docs) (**www.opentext.com**) is very similar to the Autonomy system as a BigLaw-oriented, SQL Server–based application. It is quite prevalent in large firms and virtually never seen in small firms.

♦ NetDocuments (**www.netdocuments.com**). A SaaS product (Software as a Service—in other words, an application that runs in a web browser with documents either stored on a third-party hosted storage system or on the firm's own web-accessible servers). The NetDocuments team brings tons of document management street cred—the founders were principals with the venerable SoftSolutions, the long defunct original pioneering document management product that Novell killed in the 1990s. SaaS brings its own range of questions and holds promise, but this product is not oriented to smaller firms in terms of pricing or its relative inability to directly integrate with SmallLaw practice management systems. NetDocuments has recently made inroads into the smaller firm marketplace with a $20 per user per month Basic membership for 10GB of base storage plus 1GB of additional storage for each user.

There are also approaches focused on using web-based secure document repositories—examples of cloud computing or SaaS offerings. These tend to be much more minimal in functionality compared to actual document/e-mail management software. Rather, they are focused more on universality of accessibility and device independence, storing documents in password-protected web folder systems for authorized users to share. Perhaps the best-known service of this type is Dropbox (**www.dropbox.com**) (2GB free, 100GB for $10 per month, 200GB for $200 per year, or the group-oriented Dropbox Team plan for $795 per year, which includes five user licenses and 1TB of shared storage. Additional Dropbox Team user licenses are available for $125 per year with 200GB of storage included with each additional user). Google and Microsoft are in the game as well with Drive and SkyDrive. One of the pluses of this approach is that someone else takes care of backing it up for you. A downside is that if your Internet access is down, your access to your documents can be compromised (although some web document services will sync your cloud-stored documents to your local hard drive to deal with this possibility).

For that matter, you can use a device like PogoPlug to create your own cloud storage (**pogoplug.com**). This $30 device attaches to your Internet router and any USB hard drive. Through the vendor's web portal, all Windows and Mac systems and all iOS and Android devices can store and access files on your own hard drive, accessible through the cloud from anywhere, any time. It is effectively a private access cloud—the data is on your hard drive in your office or in your own home. Slick and worth considering, with the primary downside being that the data *is* in your home or office and subject to loss if something happens, such as a fire or theft. Also, no one is backing it up.

As for the traditional locally installed systems, the Worldox GX3 (**www.worldox.com**) document management system is the most suitable of the above-listed applications for SmallLaw. It organizes paper documents received in the mail and scanned as searchable PDFs, e-mails received with attachments (when used with Microsoft Outlook, even e-mails with multiple attachments can be organized by Worldox in one step, rather than the daunting series of steps usually required), and documents created within the office, regardless of which software program was used to create them (for example, Word, WordPerfect, Excel, Adobe Acrobat/PDFs, digital photos, voicemail files, etc.). The same Worldox interface is common to all file-saving processes, simplifying the approach and cutting the learning curve. Your electronic filing system can be set up and organized to precisely parallel your file cabinet/red-rope brown expandable file/manila folder–based paper system, making it easy for all to understand, regardless of whether they are legal techno-pros or techno-peasants. There is an adjunct module called Worldox/Web Mobile that extends the accessibility of Worldox-managed documents and e-mails to the Web, securely, on Windows PCs, Macs, iPads, and smartphones.

Most practice management software, such as Amicus Attorney, Practice-Master, ProLaw (from Thomson-Reuters), and Time Matters (from Lexis-Nexis), as well as cloud systems such as Clio (**www.goclio.com**), Rocket Matter (**www.rocketmatter.com**), MyCase (**www.mycase.com**), and others, incorporates some degree of document and e-mail management. Alternatively, some leading practice management systems integrate with leading legal document management systems. Which approach is best? The internalized document management functionality of a practice management application of the third party, or a separate but integrated dedicated document manager? The answers are specific to the unique document management approaches of each practice management system, but the bottom line for most firms is that the more robust features and the mandatory must-save-it-the-document-management's-way approach of third party tools tends to prevail. Built-in document management segments of practice management systems often do not require documents to be saved to client case files. Experience shows that the failure to make this an automatically mandatory process results in people lazily taking shortcuts and creating incomplete case files that cannot be relied on.

In essence, the document management system takes the scanned document-turned-PDF and organizes it in this manner:

When one clicks the ***File Save*** or ***File Save As*** function in Acrobat, instead of the software's native file-management dialogue boxes appearing, the Worldox document management system pops up.

To save the file, one selects the appropriate **File Cabinet** (or in Worldox-speak, the "profile group"). Examples commonly include Client Documents, Forms & Templates, Firm Administration, and Personal Files.

Then one is presented with a **Profile** screen that allows the user, instead of having to navigate through an often mystifying and inconsistent Windows folder tree, to complete a set of fill-in-the-blanks with information such as the **Client Name**, the **Matter Name**, the type of document (e.g., correspondence, contracts, pleadings, etc.), who authored the document, and sometimes the historical date of the document or a notation as to whether the document has been reviewed by a responsible party in the firm. These pieces of information are accessible very rapidly from quick-pick lists or even in a single-click approach that calls up a template called a Quick Profile for oft-accessed client matters or subject files. All in all, it is much more concise and faster than common Windows navigation.

Fill in a plain-English name for the document, ideally following a logical file-naming convention agreed upon and consistently used by everyone in the firm, and click OK. The scanned electronic paper is now organized and connected to a cohesive, contiguous, and complete electronic matter file, as are all the internally generated word processing files, spreadsheets, presentations, digital photos, downloaded PDFs, and e-mails with their attachments—a complete electronic case file.

Later, documents can be found by simply "checking the electronic file cabinet"—clicking to the Client, the Matter, and then an electronic version of the manila folder. If it is not possible or efficient to locate the desired document by viewing the electronic file cabinet and scanning the list of plain-English file names, the document can be nearly instantly found by searching for key text within the document itself, using a word or phrase search similar to a query in Google, Lexis, Westlaw, Fastcase, or CaseMaker. Worldox searches are infinitely faster than the brain-dead File, Find function in the Windows XP operating system and every bit as fast as the modern desktop search products such as Windows Desktop Search, Copernic, X1, and Google Desktop. Note that the Windows 7 and Windows 8 operating systems (available when you read this book) have an "instant search" function built in, a carryover from their not-lamented, long-dead Vista predecessor (and frankly, one of the only positive aspects of Windows Vista). Mac users have long benefited from instant searching via the Spotlight feature of the Mac operating system.

Even a scanned document, which is otherwise just an "image," like a digital photo, can be located using key terms, provided that when it was scanned the image was converted to searchable text using Adobe Acrobat (version 7 and up to the current version XI, Standard/Professional edition) or an equivalent product that does automated batch conversions of scanned "image" PDFs into "searchable" PDFs, such as Aqua Forest's Autobahn DX (**www.aquaforest.com**), which can be set to find all new "image" PDFs stored during the day and convert them in an automated fashion into "searchable" PDFs.

Okay, Now Let's Get to Our Documents from Anywhere, Any Time: The Paper LESS Cloud

It is impossible to overstate the nearly all-pervasive emphasis on cloud, or Internet-based, computing today. It's a revolution that has swept through all aspects of legal technology and the choices and options available to small firms, as well as practices of all sizes. But the challenge is defining what the cloud is and how it might meet (or not meet) the needs of any given practice.

The first step is demystifying the cloud computing concept. What exactly is it? Well, it's not an "it," it's a whole raft of "its." There are many different ways of accessing law practice information over the Internet—even more than the types of clouds that meteorologists categorize. Let's explore some of these approaches, looking at the Paper LESS suitability of each for small law practices.

1. **Web-Based Software (a/k/a SaaS—Software as a Service, or cloud systems):**

   ◆ The idea here is that the software you use isn't installed on your own computer hardware. Rather, it's installed on a remote system somewhere else (that someone else owns), and you access its functionality and your firm's data via a web browser. Some purists consider this the "real" cloud approach since it has the least software impact on your own hardware. In fact, it doesn't matter what hardware you use—Windows or Mac, iPad or other tablet—if you have a high-speed Internet connection, you can work from any device, any time.

   ◆ **Paper LESS Connection:** Some SaaS products, including Clio, Rocket Matter, Advologix, Houdini, Esq., and MyCase, include document management to varying degrees. Online document management such as NetDocuments and online document storage such as Dropbox, Box, SpiderOak, Google Drive, Microsoft SkyDrive, and SugarSync are examples of web services with Paper LESS connections.

      ◆ There are some potential disadvantages of the SaaS approach. Your ability to work depends on your ability to find a high-speed Internet connection. No connection generally means no work.

2. **Rent-a-Cloud:**

   ◆ Under this approach, you can use all the software you'd normally use on your own systems—practice managers like Tabs PracticeMaster, Amicus Attorney, and Time Matters, as well as document managers like Worldox. But instead of these programs running on your own network server, you can rent a server maintained by a third party and access it across the Internet cloud. This approach has all the benefits of running the more fully featured software that you may already own, plus the benefit of not having to maintain your own server hardware—including having someone else back up your information and update the server's operating system software.

      ◆ As with SaaS, there are some potential disadvantages of this approach. Your ability to work depends on your ability to find a high-speed Internet connection. No connection generally means no work under this approach as well.

♦ There are also potential ethical issues related to giving control of confidential client information to a third party. These are likely a red herring since there are long-standing accepted precedents for this approach; in particular, storing client files at third-party document warehouses.

♦ In the short run, start-up costs are lower than buying one's own new server. There is little upfront cost, other than possibly an IT consultant's assistance in migrating information from a traditional local system to a new web-based server. As an example, one could use a third-party server host, such as the well-known **GoDaddy.com** offering, where a dedicated Windows 2008 Server with 500GB of storage space costs about $300 per month and then about $6 to $10 per month per user for hosting a Microsoft Exchange Server to handle mail and calendars with Outlook. Over time, these costs add up and are more expensive in most cases than the third option below—having your own cloud.

♦ **Paper LESS Connection:**

   ♦ Works just like your present internal systems connecting to a Windows server, as is so commonly the case. So there are no changes in your present software; the only difference is that the server is somewhere else and you use something called Windows RDS (Remote Desktop Services) to access the information. This means that Macs can access the information also—an added benefit.

3. **Build Your Own Cloud:**

   ♦ Under this approach, you would still have your own server, but if you're a Windows-using firm, as so many are, you can access all your firm's information and software across the Internet cloud by using something called Windows Terminal Services (TS) or the more modern iteration of it, Windows RDS. Under this approach, anyone outside of the office can click an icon, get an office "desktop," and then work as if they were sitting in the office. This works even better with a relatively inexpensive piece of more capable remote access software, Citrix XenApp Fundamentals—considered the "king of remote access tools." For all intents and purposes, most readers can view Citrix as a layer on top of Windows RDS or Windows TS that just plain works faster and better and supports remote access by Windows and Mac computers, iPads, other tablets, and smartphones.

♦ Advantages are numerous—you maintain total control of your own systems but extend the reach of your Paper LESS practice to any authorized users, any time, any place they can get a high-speed Internet connection from many types of devices. This is a relatively low cost addition to an existing Windows system: five users can access their system remotely via Citrix XenApp Fundamentals for about $1,245 in software cost with no ongoing subscription fees (**store.citrix.com/store/citrixus/en_US/pd/ ThemeID.9505600/productID.194911600**).

♦ Disadvantage: You own the hardware, so you have to maintain it. That means backing it up, updating the software systems, and paying for IT support when there are specific operational problems.

4. Scattered Cloudiness—Being Partly in the Cloud:

♦ One option is to put part of your practice, Paper LESS–wise, in the cloud. One way to do this is to outsource your mail server functions. Small firms that use Microsoft Outlook can very cost-effectively outsource the underlying Microsoft Exchange Server functions to a third party. Microsoft Exchange Online (**www.microsoft.com/exchange/en-us/exchange-online-hosted-email.aspx**), **GoDaddy.com**, and **Rackspace.com** are three large and proven providers of these services. Users can use Outlook just as they currently do—integrating with a legal document manager such as Worldox GX3 to organize inbound/ outbound e-mail and attachments to electronic case folders. From the technical end, the Exchange Server software—which isn't trivial to configure, support, and maintain—is provided by the third party host. This is a very workable and usually very cost-effective situation for firms of all sizes.

♦ Based on Microsoft's own Exchange Hosting options, a five-person law practice can avail itself of this service for $20 to $40 per month, receiving a very generous 25GB per user in mailbox storage (or unlimited storage with the $8 per user per month plan) and full Microsoft ActiveSync functionality for syncing with smartphones, iPads and other tablets, and so on, for lawyers on the go.

5. **Have Your Cloud and Eat It Too—Wholesale Line-Blurring in Progress:**

    ♦ Sorry about that uncalled for torture of a perfectly good analogy. But the idea here is that "terrestrial" software products, like segment standard-bearers Tabs3 and Tabs PracticeMaster, are adding cloud access to their traditional locally installed systems. With the release of Tabs3 Connect in September 2012, the development team at publisher Software Technology, Inc., added impressive and elegant cloud access to the Platinum Edition of its Tabs3 financial system and Tabs PracticeMaster practice management system. With information and screen views at **www.tabs3.com/products/tabs3_connect/tabs3_connect.html**, Tabs3 Connect offers true web-browser-access-securely-from-anywhere, from-any-device access to its systems. With an interface that is familiar to Tabs users and, at the same time, artfully simplified for the browser-preferring crowd, this approach brings all the advantages of cloud accessibility (e.g., any browser, any device, anytime, from anyplace) but with access to a much more powerful and fully featured set of financial and practice management tools than any of the solely cloud-based systems.

        ♦ Is this the perfect approach for small firms? Is there a catch? Yes and yes would be the answers. Perfect in terms of functionality. Tabs3 Connect keeps your data on your system—you run the Tabs programs in your office (or on your hosted server) exactly the way you always have. Nothing changes when you're in the office. When outside the office, you log in via a browser and Internet connection like any cloud system. But the difference is that it's *your* cloud—Tabs3 Connect creates it for you so your confidential client and firm data never leave your control and are never in the hands of a third party—arguably not running afoul of any ethics rules. It's your data, all the time. So what's the catch? Cost. The Platinum Edition of Tabs3 and Tabs PracticeMaster run on a robust SQL-like client/server database. Great for performance and reliability when compared to the company's standard Premier and Basic editions, but they come more dearly.

♦ Figure 27.1 outlines the comparative software license and maintenance costs, as of the fall of 2012, for Tabs3 and Tabs PracticeMaster Premier (which does *not* include Tabs3 Connect) for a two-lawyer/one-staffer practice and the Platinum Edition (which includes Tabs3 Connect at no additional charge).

Program	Tabs 3 Premier w/o Tabs 3 Connect	Tabs 3 Platinum with Tabs 3 Connect
Tabs 3 billing for 2–5 networked timekeepers	$675[†]	$1,770[†] Note: This is for 5 timekeepers since there is no 2-timekeeper version of Platinum.
Tabs PracticeMaster for 3 networked users	$1,160[†]	$1,685[†]
Tabs Platinum Server Software (for up to 8 connections)	N/A	$965
TOTAL FIRST YEAR	$1,835[†]	$4,420[†]
TOTAL RECURRING SOFTWARE MAINTENANCE AFTER FIRST YEAR (optional, but recommended)	$475[‡]	$890[‡]

[†]Software maintenance costs are included for the first 12 months and are renewable, optionally, thereafter. Software maintenance includes all updates/upgrades and unlimited technical support from the publisher.
[‡]Annual maintenance after the first year is optional, but strongly recommended so the software doesn't fall behind in compatibility with other systems, such as Windows, document managers, Microsoft Office, etc.

Figure 27.1 Tabs3 Premier v. Tabs3 Platinum

♦ Firms need to look carefully at the extra utility that cloud access brings and the likelihood that additional time would be captured from tablets or smartphones at times when it isn't otherwise practical to record time. This could translate into a strongly positive return. For example, if an iPad user captures .25 additional hours of billable time per day at $200 per hour, that translates into approximately $12,000 of additional top-line revenue captured every year, clearly outweighing the additional cost of the Platinum Edition in the first year and every year thereafter.

The Real World: Comments from the Trenches in the Paper Wars

Dale Cottam further observes from his perspective as a busy commercial litigator:

In today's fast-paced technology world, many clients expect their lawyers to be at least at the same technical level of capability and proficiency as they are. With the relatively low cost of available scanning hardware and document management software, firms can keep up with their clients. Part of the cost of this technology will be offset by decreased expenses for postage and long-distance phone calls associated with faxing and increases in productivity. The level of stress involved in searching for lost files and documents is reduced dramatically.

Figure 27.2 demonstrates the real-world and practical advantages of electronic versus paper files. If you are considering moving from paper to electronic files but aren't sure how to start, here are a few suggestions:

Factor	Paper Files	Electronic Files
Active Case and Archival Storage	Paper is expensive to file, route, and store.	Electronic documents are cheap and convenient to store. If paper files are shredded after closure of a case, physical storage costs are cut dramatically, yet lawyers have all old file information accessible instantly via electronic searches. Archiving on the firm's server(s) takes the place of physical storage. Electronic paper can always be reduced to physical paper if needed.
Finding Lost Documents	Finding lost documents takes significant time, sometimes many hours, including discussion with other lawyers and staff. If a document has been misfiled, it may never be found.	Searching for electronic documents is nearly instantaneous using a search engine contained within document management systems. A lawyer who previously wasted fifteen minutes per day looking for paper files can easily recover valuable billable time by immediately locating "electronic paper" and not chasing paper files around the office. If this fifteen minutes can be converted into billable time v. wasted non-billable time, the financial effect can be an additional $12,000 per year for a lawyer who bills an average of $200 per hour.
File Sharing	Collaborating on paper documents is cumbersome—copies must be made and routed at significant cost in terms of staff time and consumables, not to mention the negative environmental impact.	Collaboration, revisions, remote access, and sharing of important information are very convenient when documents are stored electronically.

Figure 27.2 Advantages of Electronic versus Paper Files

Factor	Paper Files	Electronic Files
Remote Access	Paper documents must be mailed or faxed offsite, or lawyers who need to work on files must remember to bring boxes of paper with them.	Electronic documents are available to lawyers and staff over secure remote connections or can be received via e-mail, effectively providing instantaneous access to every single document on a single matter, without regard to the location of the physical paper file. With device-independent approaches, documents of all types can be securely accessed from devices ranging from laptops to netbooks (Windows *or* Mac systems), iPads, and smartphones.
Protecting Client Files from Disaster	Irreplaceable paper documents are at risk of being destroyed by fire and natural disasters.	Electronic files are easily backed up and stored offsite and can be restored to the firm's network in little time. As "electronic paper," this is the first realistic way to protect paper files from damage by fire and natural disasters.
Brief Banking	Tedious filing and organization must be used so people can quickly find relevant briefs in paper format—most firms fail to keep it updated, so few people would ever trust it.	Electronic versions of briefs and memos can be located quickly using search engines and indexers that look for specific words or phrases. Finally, the mythical "brief bank" becomes usable, current, and reliable.
E-mail Management	To make a "complete" paper file, you would need to print every e-mail and attachment that is sent and received. Sheer inefficient insanity.	The Paper LESS Office™ approach, using the Worldox (or other) document management system, allows you to save (via "profiling") a stand-alone e-mail or one with multiple attachments in a single step, for both inbound and outbound messages. The result is a nearly miraculous answer to a spiraling issue of e-mail chaos that plagues so many law practices today. E-mails are merely correspondence, and they belong connected to the complete electronic case file, as opposed to being eternally buried in the bottomless hole that is the inbox of most people.
Environmental Impact	Obviously, using more paper has a significant negative impact on the environment from several perspectives. More paper used = more dead trees = not a good thing for the planet. More paper printed = more chemical consumables (toner) and more electricity used = also not good things. More paper stored = more floor space required for your office = more cost to your firm = also not a good thing.	Obviously, less paper printed has benefits to the environment and economic benefits to the firm. Paper LESS = Environment More.

Figure 27.2 Advantages of Electronic versus Paper Files—*(Continued)*

Make the commitment to the process of moving toward the Paper LESS goal. Give up on the pipe dream of being paperless; it's simply not realistic and will lead to inevitable disappointment. You're not going to rid your practice entirely of paper. The key is dedication, an emphasis on standardized and consistent procedures, and a commitment to educating your team about the "whys" and not merely the "hows" for making the shift to viewing electronic matter files as the primary, "sacred," and complete client file.

Ensure your hardware is up to the demands of the increased amount of scanning, processing, and storage. This would be the ideal time to send your six-year-old PC stations to a virtual "assisted living center" and replace them with a set of contemporary desktop and laptop systems. Dual monitors (or even three displays) are very helpful for simultaneously scanning, storing, and viewing multiple programs. With a practice management system, your word processor(s), Acrobat, Outlook or another e-mailer, a time entry input application, and one or more web browsers, the productivity payoff is normally instantaneous. Network servers need the ability to store 1GB to 5GB per lawyer per year. Having a reliable multiple level backup system and testing it often with "mini test restores" is critical, as are all the normal recommended elements of a sound data backup process.

SIDENOTE: A Paper LESS Peripheral Benefit: Protecting Your "Paper"

One of the great weaknesses of any paper-centric system is the vulnerability of the medium. It is simply impossible, in any practical or realistic sense, to back up paper client and administrative files. If a hurricane's fury tears through a community as Hurricane Isaac did in in the Gulf regions in August 2012, if an earthquake rends the ground beneath a law firm's building, if a wildfire like those that marauded across wide swaths of Colorado in the summer of 2012 incinerates a practice, paper client and administrative files, which may have no alternative media counterparts, are gone forever.

One of the unintended, yet extraordinarily valuable, by-products of the Paper LESS Office process is the protection of what would otherwise be at risk paper files. Paper LESS electronic documents can be backed up. They can be protected and stored offsite, and even online, in a geographically distant location. Lawyers have an ethical responsibility to practice competently. It takes no great intellectual leap to see that deploying a Paper LESS approach, combined with essential and sound data backup techniques that protect paper files and the ability of lawyers to serve their clients, is part of the core definition of "competency" in law practice—at least, so said the ABA House of Delegates in August 2012.

Factor in cloud storage and incorporate a degree of automated data backup that could be tough for a small practice to achieve at the same level of reliability and sophistication.

Plan and test. Spend time planning as well as "pilot" testing systems and procedures to avoid fits and starts before the Paper LESS concept is rolled out firm wide.

The Paper LESS Bottom Line . . .

Focus on finding "the Edge" for your practice. It will pay off in spades with more money in your firm's coffers, which translates to more money for the things that matter in your life. Happier clients, happier staff, happier partners, happier family—all positive things that make law practice infinitely more satisfying. Becoming Paper LESS in your practice is one of the least costly and most immediate ways to gain such an Edge.

A truly paperless office is never going to happen while any of us are alive. No matter how diligently you try to reduce or even eliminate the paper you generate, other people will send you paper for years to come. But to be sure, being Paper MORE in your practice is a one-way ticket to diminished profitability, diminished client responsiveness, and diminished sanity. The good news for everyone is that a Paper LESS Office is rapidly and practically attainable. You can use less paper, have to find less paper, and touch paper less often, thereby becoming significantly more efficient, more profitable, more responsive to your clients, more relaxed, and more environmentally responsible in your practice. Consideration of "cloud concepts" can allow your people to access your Paper LESS files anywhere they might be working, any time of the day and can open secure access to clients, co-counsel, and experts in an ethically compliant and secure manner. By employing a creative and common sense approach to scanning, turning physical paper into searchable electronic paper, and leveraging anti-paper PDF tools, you can transform your practice—and even the rest of your life—in every possible way. It's an Edge you can gain today.

CHAPTER TWENTY-EIGHT

Tomorrow in Legal Tech

"I will keep working until about five years after I die, and I've given the directors a Ouija board so they can keep in touch."

—Warren Buffet

As most readers know, this chapter belongs to me (Sharon).

I had to include that wonderful quote above from Warren Buffet. It made me laugh because it is so old school. Where are the holograms, Warren? Or the companies whose wizardry allows you to keep tweeting when you're dead (LIVESON's motto: You'll keep tweeting when your heart stops beating)? Lawyers could profit by carefully reading some of what Warren has written; he knows how to run a business—something that is foreign to most lawyers.

The economy, still rather unstable, is making more and more lawyers think about the business of law. Business isn't all that great for most lawyers. If you've been following the ups and downs of the legal economy, we're seeing a fair number of staff and associate layoffs. The joyride that was law practice twenty-five years ago has crashed and burned.

That is one reason that I developed a presentation on the Future of Law, which has rapidly become one of our most popular presentations. Lawyers are searching for answers—how do they future-proof their firms? While I don't claim to have all (indeed, or most of) the answers, folks who have attended these seminars tell me that they went away with a lot of things to think about, some of them brand new thoughts.

As I am fond of saying, "Don't predict the future—invent it." There's a lot to be said for that in the practice of law. If we just meet our futures with the same old methodologies and systems lawyers have always used, we're likely to make ourselves obsolete. But if we reinvent ourselves and the practice of law, who knows what heights we may achieve?

One thing that looks to be a near certainty in the future: We may be looking at two-year law schools where the third year is all clinical (or perhaps optional) so that students come out of law school and some sort of clinic or internship ready to actually practice law. Don't scoff—even President Obama came out in favor of having two years of law school rather than three. And one law school (New York Law School) has now made two years a reality—without increasing the annual price.

It begins there, but what about after law school? We are still seeing law school graduates struggling to find a job, competing against those who are recent graduates (still looking for a job) and laid-off associates. Lawyers are applying for paralegal jobs in record numbers.

A lot of folks are talking about established lawyers bringing newly minted lawyers into their practices as interns. The value of shadowing a real lawyer is beyond words—and if there is mentoring involved too, so much the better. There are more and more experimental programs popping up across the country.

One article that got a lot of water cooler conversations going was "The Law Convenience Store" by my friend Jim Calloway, who was kind enough to write the introduction to this book. As Jim noted, the title of the article might be deemed offensive by some people, but more and more potential legal consumers are going to look at law firms in part for the convenience that they afford.

- ♦ Do they have nighttime or weekend hours?
- ♦ Can appointments be via telephone or videoconference?
- ♦ Are all client documents digitized? This sure would make it easier for a lawyer to talk in the evening to a client.
- ♦ Can the lawyer share documents easily via Dropbox or some similar solution?
- ♦ Is it possible to have an actual store at which one can receive legal help without an appointment? This is a stretch on one prototype experiment in (where else?) California where there are "legal concierges" who guide people to resources rather than dispensing legal advice.
- ♦ Can the lawyer offer screen sharing as a way to collaborate on documents?

Well, you get the idea. Times are changing and we must evolve with them. Some of what is written above is about the business of law, and some is more focused on technology. What we know for sure is that the two are now irrevocably intertwined. Nothing has been as disruptive to the traditional practice of law as technology—and there is no going back. At least until a future Doc Brown invents a DeLorean time machine.

Let's talk about the new generation of lawyers. They were born in the digital age, so they bring some level of legal tech sophistication. They were all weaned on free legal research tools at law school. Perhaps what surprises me most is that, beyond legal research, so many of them are actually found wanting in legal tech skills. Yes, they can do legal research. Yes, they all know how to use their smartphone. But what do they spend their tech time doing? Facebook, Twitter, Instagram, Google+, Pinterest, playing games, watching movies and videos, texting, e-mailing, and so on. Their actual knowledge of legal technology is frequently pretty low.

One of the more interesting developments this year came from Kia Motors, which does, as it motto suggests, have "The Power to Surprise." They sure surprised a lot of law firms! Here's what happened.

In June 2013, Kia Motors instituted an audit to test the competency of outside law firm associates with technology. Nine audits produced nine failures.

The audit involved four mock assignments that a law firm associate must complete using standard software (e.g., Word, Excel, and Acrobat). Done efficiently, the first assignment should have taken less than twenty minutes. Done inefficiently (not using the software correctly), it would take more than five hours to complete.

Not a single tested associate came anywhere close to the twenty-minute mark on the first assignment. They approached the assignment inefficiently, in ways that required five to fifteen times longer than necessary. At $200 to $400 per associate hour, that's one heck of a price to pay for inefficiency.

The tested associates came from different firms. Some were auditioning for work and failed to get it. Others were long-time outside counsel, and their firms agreed to rate reductions (5 percent) after their associates failed the audit, with a proviso that the rate would be restored if they subsequently passed an audit.

So what can't associates do? They can't use Excel's Sort and Filter features and need to go line by line to take a provided spreadsheet and generate discrete lists of exhibits associated with witnesses on specific topics. They cannot manipulate PDFs. We have even seen associates, confronted with a Word document and told to PDF it, send it to a printer and then scan the document manually—apparently completely unaware of the Save as PDF option.

I was unsurprised at the failures. All consultants sing the same "training, training, training—and oh, did I mention training?" as critical to law firm survival.

The audit should be a wake-up call for law firms since it is such a clear example of how inefficiencies are becoming known to corporate clients, who will then take appropriate "sweeping the stable" actions. While you can quibble with the audit's particular structure, as the author (Casey Flaherty) notes wryly, "My audit is a prototype and, like its creator, not without patent shortcomings."

I have no doubt that in-house counsel will welcome a coming development that was an outgrowth of this audit. Flaherty is now working with the Suffolk University School of Law on a project headed by Professor Andy Perlman to automate the audit so it can be done online rather than in person as KIA's original audit was. Suffolk is crowdsourcing ideas for the audit and hopes to have it available in 2014. Boy oh boy, if there was ever a time for law firms to take seriously the need to train lawyers on technology, this is it. Ultimately, if this audit is widely adopted and demanded by corporate clients, work will be taken from the inefficient (therefore usually more costly) law firms and given to those who are indeed efficient—and less costly.

One big issue this year was passwords. They are all but dead—the power of supercomputers and the long nose of the National Security Agency has ensured that. In September 2013, Heather Adkins, Google's manager of information security, said that the "game is over for" any start-up that relies on passwords as its chief method to secure users and their data. "Passwords are dead," she said, announcing that Google is done with passwords for the future.

She talked about Google's use of two-step authentication and about how it is working to innovate on non-standard password security. Google is experimenting with hardware-based tokens as well as a Motorola-created system that authenticates users by having them touch a device to something embedded, or held, in their own clothing. "A hacker can't steal that from you," she said.

Can I tell you for sure where passwords are going? No. I only know that we are going beyond passwords. Google has one solution with undoubtedly more under development. Apple announced in September that its new phone can be unlocked by scanning the owner's fingerprint. All of the authors of this book will be watching tech developments in this area closely over the coming year—for now, we only know that the race is on to develop alternatives to passwords. We were already at the breaking point trying to manage strong 12-character passwords for multiple sites—and now it appears that breaking 12-character passwords is child's play if enough supercomputers are brought to bear. Again, we must evolve. It is a no-brainer to say that there will be many developments on this subject in the next year, and hopefully we'll have clear answers for you next year. We hope.

As I write this, the National Security Agency (NSA) appears to be as much of a threat to law firm data as the Chinese hackers, at least potentially. We now know that many technology providers have built in back doors for the NSA. We know that the NSA is building a data center outside of Salt Lake City that can hold five years of all the electronic communications of American citizens. We know that the NSA is using supercomputers to break encryption schemes—and that some encryption schemes have a back door just for the NSA. We know that the NSA has access to 75 percent of all Internet communications within the United States and an unknown number of access points abroad. As I write, the revelations are coming day by day.

So many lawyers use Skype—but now that Microsoft owns it and has rerouted traffic through Microsoft's servers, it is no longer secure. And it has been proven that Microsoft saves the content of Skype communications—and has assisted the NSA in getting access to that content. Next year, we will write copiously about the implications of all we are learning. It's just too new right now.

Lest I seem overly paranoid, let me quote George Washington—who better than the father of our country? "Government is not reason; it is not eloquent; it is force. Like fire, it is a dangerous servant and a fearful master."

I certainly am afraid of what the future might hold. While the government says it is only collecting ponds of data and must demonstrate (to a secret court!) good reason to go fishing in them, the government's statements about what it is and isn't doing have been proven incorrect time and again—the government has lost all credibility with me on the issue of surveillance.

Enough of that gloomy subject.

Let us turn to smartphones, which virtually all lawyers now carry. While BlackBerrys may not disappear entirely, their market share has dropped precipitously. RIM (now known only as BlackBerry) has been way behind in the "touch" world and seems unable to come up with the slick features that consumers demand. Web surfing on the BlackBerry is an exercise in Zen patience.

According to the 2013 ABA Legal Technology Survey Report, BlackBerry used to command 45 percent of the legal market, falling this year to 16 percent. That's a precipitous drop. One BigLaw partner wrote that he had ditched his BlackBerry but was still suffering from "BlackBerry leg" and having phantom vibrations. But he was very glad he switched.

iPhones, according to the study, now represent 62 percent of the market, and 22 percent belongs to Android phones. We know a number of lawyers who are ditching their iPhones for Androids, so I'll throw the dice and predict a marked shift upward next year in the number of lawyers using Android phones. The larger size makes reading (and everything else) easier, and they have become very slick in appearance and functionality. The more we use our smartphones as computers, the more such things matter.

The rise of the tablet computer was noted last year, and the ABA's latest report continues to bear that out, with 48 percent of lawyers now using tablets, the majority of them using the iPad. Interestingly, in the 2013 ILTA/Inside Legal Technology Purchasing Survey, there was much more "tablet diversity" in larger law firms.

With respect to cloud computing, some of the resistance is eroding. Most lawyers are either using the cloud in some form or thinking about it. Curiously (and it's scary too), less than half of the lawyers who store data in the cloud take any of the standard precautionary measures listed in the ABA survey that are generally recommended by security experts. It looks like the "it won't happen to me" mentality is alive and well in the legal community.

I listened recently to an edition of the Kennedy-Mighell podcast on Legal Talk Network talking about the ILTA and ABA surveys, and I agree that the year didn't hold a lot of revolutionary legal tech developments. I also agree with Tom and Dennis that the single most striking development was that the use of the file-syncing software Dropbox exploded in one year from 4 percent in 2012 to a whopping 58 percent in 2013.

This is a form of cloud computing, of course. And the growth of Dropbox probably is spurred in part by all those tablets. The preferred method of moving files to and from the iPad by lawyers is Dropbox, which owns the beachhead in the file syncing arena, though, of course, there are other products that do the same thing. Dropbox holds a master decryption key, so don't rest on your laurels believing that you can rely on Dropbox's own encryption to protect your documents. An emerging new product to ensure security of Dropbox files is Boxcryptor. With that software you can encrypt your data in Google Drive, Microsoft SkyDrive, SugarSync, Box, and many more cloud providers. It is highly recommended that you check that solution out—I anticipate that we'll see a lot more of Boxcryptor in the coming year.

Windows 8 rather unexpectedly proved a bust. It's a great operating system if you have a tablet. If you don't, muscles in your arm that you didn't know you had will ache miserably from touching your monitors (assuming it is touch sensitive). I've never seen so many people (well, since Vista) detest an operating system—and they are quick to attempt to disable the Metro interface (designed for touch—and legally, Microsoft has had to abandon the term *Metro*), only to find it "reactivated" to perform certain functions. The feeling of many lawyers is that there was too much change all at once, some of it not well thought out. Everyone hated the absence of the Start button.

In general, Windows 8 fell on its face. Some complained that it didn't go far enough and didn't offer an option to discard the desktop. The larger audience of traditional PC users complained vociferously that Microsoft was forcing the mobile/touch environment on them.

What we're doing for clients (and what many other law firms are doing) is paying a modest premium to downgrade new computers to Windows 7. Everyone seems to compare Windows 8 to the New Coke debacle several years ago. By the time you read this, Windows 8.1 will have been rolled out, reportedly with Microsoft making several significant nods to consumers who hated Windows 8. Interesting that Windows 8.1 is not being called Service Pack 1. Some say it will offer a genuine operating system shift. Since Windows 8 was regarded largely as a failure, it will be interesting to see whether Windows 8.1 can undo some of the damage of its predecessor. More on that next year.

Social media usage continues on the upswing at law firms, though it seems as though many law firms have no idea what to do with it. Still, virtually all of the major law firms have established one or more social media outposts, and they are exploring the possibilities of each platform. LinkedIn and FB ads are on the rise, with FB making sure that we see "promoted" or "sponsored" posts (which seem to be the same thing) every time we pick up our phone to check Facebook. More and more lawyers are reporting that they have actually gotten business through social media. Personally, I believe videos and blogs are the most compelling forms of social media for bringing in new business. Blogs are "Google juice" and since Google owns YouTube, videos are even better "Google juice."

One bite of crow pie (salted) that I must take: I was wrong about the growth of virtual law firms. In fact, the ABA's Annual Legal Tech Survey Report showed that fewer lawyers identified themselves as having a virtual law firm. The number of self-identified virtual lawyers was 7 percent last year and fell to 5 percent this year. My friend and legal tech guru Bob Ambrogi speculated that the business model of virtual lawyering might not be viable for most lawyers and that people still want to look their lawyers in the eye. While lawyers certainly use elements of virtual law practices, it may be that the percentage of people who regard themselves as virtual lawyers will remain rather flat, at least for a while.

Alternative fee arrangements (AFAs) have become standard fare for large firms, though there is some cynicism about whether what looks like an AFA is really an hourly rate in disguise. In-house counsel continues to pressure firms of all sizes to become more efficient and to lower the overall cost of legal services.

In the e-discovery world, predictive coding continued to dominate. Though it has become mainstream in many places and has received a number of court opinions endorsing it, it remains too expensive for smaller cases. Vendors will tell you otherwise, but sometimes what they call predictive coding (or technology assisted review—or a host of other names) bears little relation to full blown and full-featured predictive coding.

Perhaps most surprising to me was one of the results of the ABA's Legal Tech Survey, which probably has more solo/small respondents than the ILTA survey. Forty percent of the ABA respondents said they had never received an eDiscovery request, and 45 percent said they had never sent an eDiscovery request. That truly astonished me after all this time.

Perhaps you have heard about the new proposed e-discovery rules. With a hat tip to NextPoint's Discovery Cloud, here is a brief summary of what the rules would do.

Proportionality

Unless otherwise limited by court order, the scope of discovery would be as follows: "Parties may obtain discovery regarding any non-privileged matter that is relevant to any party's claim or defense and *proportional to the needs of the case considering the amount in controversy*, the importance of the issues at stake in the action, the parties' resources, the importance of the discovery in resolving the issues, and whether the burden or expense of the proposed discovery outweighs its likely benefit." (italics added)

If this rule stands, it could go a long way to helping make eDiscovery affordable to more parties. Today, parties may be asked to spend $50,000 for eDiscovery when the entire case is worth less than that. These rules would ensure that lawyers have to find a way to keep eDiscovery costs lower than the "amount in controversy."

Cooperation

The Cooperation Proclamation has been integrated into the proposed new rules. The Sedona Conference's Cooperation Proclamation was once considered a high-minded but impractical document, which encouraged lawyers to be less adversarial and more cooperative in litigation. However, as the proposed amendments read now, language has been adopted from the Proclamation to "secure the just, speedy, and inexpensive determination of every action and proceeding."

If you'd like to see the proposed Federal Rules of Civil Procedure amendments that apply *only* to eDiscovery, lawyer and e-discovery expert Ralph Losey did a nice job of putting them together at **e-discoveryteam.com/ 2013/08/16/proposed-amendments-to-the-rules-the-easy-to-read-e-discovery-only-version/**.

Final Thoughts

Reinvention of the practice of law—the business of law and the technology it uses—has certainly been a recurring theme this year and is sure to remain at the forefront for some time to come. And yet, many lawyers seem afraid to innovate, to move away from what they've always done. So perhaps it is fitting that I close my fortune-teller's booth this year with a line I saw on the Internet: "Don't be afraid to take a chance. Remember that amateurs built the ark—and professionals built the Titanic."

Here's to all of you who are building arks—especially those who have learned to use technology to reinvent the practice of law.

APPENDIX

iWin:
iPad for Litigators

by Tom Mighell, Esq., and Paul Unger, Esq.

Introduction and Tour of iPad

In the three years since it was released, the iPad has quickly become a very useful tool for lawyers, and one of the biggest innovations in legal technology, to come along in some time. The iPad's design is ingenious and handsome. Its functionality is equally as nice and continues to improve as legal software developers rush to create apps for lawyers. Indeed, the iPad remains the tablet of choice for legal app developers, far outpacing Android and Windows tablets in the number of legal apps available.

Tablets have integrated themselves into the workflow of lawyers, irrespective of firm size or practice area, and nowhere has that been more apparent than at trial. Whether you need to take notes, mark and handle exhibits, or manage deposition transcripts, these little computers can supercharge your litigation practice. We will discuss how to use tablet computers to enhance your day in court and will give a general overview on using the iPad (see Figure A.1) in your practice.

Figure A.1 An iPad

Why Use an iPad in Your Practice?

We like to describe the iPad as an "instant-on" computer that you can control with your finger. There's no booting-up process, and no keyboard is needed. It provides instant access to information traditionally accessed from your desktop computer or laptop.

Although the iPad's initial purpose was thought to be as a "consumption" device—a tablet used primarily for reading and accessing information and very light typing—its ease of use and big screen is so addicting that it evolved into a tool that can do so much more, especially for lawyers.

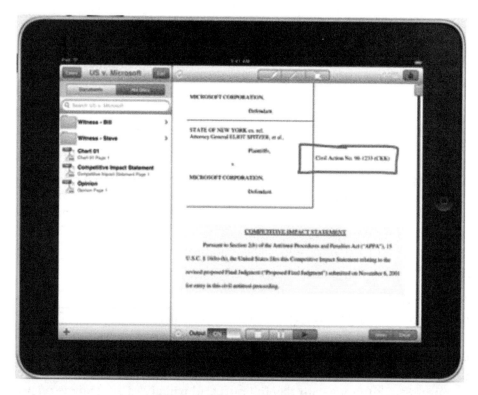

Figure A.2 Viewing Documents

If you carry around a legal pad and a lot of paper in a legal file or Redweld, the iPad can become your legal pad and digital folder. It is truly redefining the idea of the "paperless law office." For courtroom work, the iPad can be used to access exhibits, pleadings, legal research, depositions, and just about any document you might need in hearings or at trial (see Figure A.2).

Trial presentation apps are available for the iPad that make it easy to display those exhibits on projectors or monitors (wired or wireless) in the courtroom.

Overview

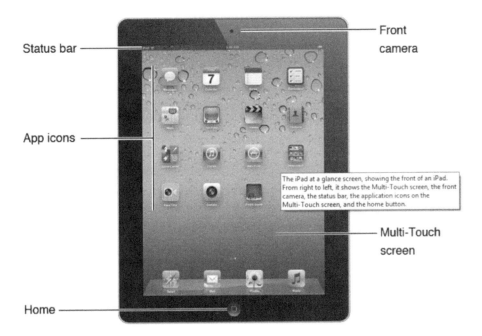

Front camera

Status bar

App icons

The iPad at a glance screen, showing the front of an iPad. From right to left, it shows the Multi-Touch screen, the front camera, the status bar, the application icons on the Multi-Touch screen, and the home button.

Multi-Touch screen

Home

Figure A.3 Front View

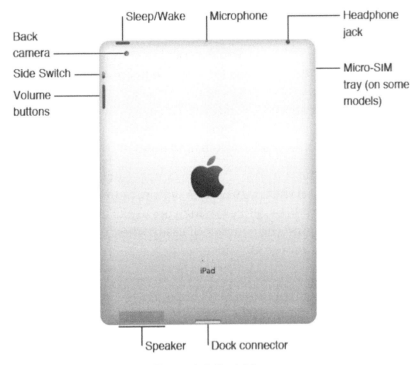

Sleep/Wake   Microphone   Headphone jack

Back camera

Side Switch

Volume buttons

Micro-SIM tray (on some models)

Speaker   Dock connector

Figure A.4 Back View

If you want to learn more about using the iPad, check out Tom's book *iPad in One Hour for Lawyers* (2nd edition), *iPad Apps in One Hour for Lawyers*, and *iPad in One Hour for Litigators*, all published by the ABA and available in the ABA webstore.

Why Use an iPad in the Courtroom?

Certainly, most of you have seen an iPad at this point (see Figures A.3 and A.4). The iPad has some drawbacks as a computing tool that make it unsuitable as a complete replacement for your desktop or laptop; however, we believe it is ideal for courtroom use because it is so light and easy to hold and operate. It is very easy to understand and use, with little training required. (In fact, if you already use an iPhone, you'll be able to start working with an iPad right away.)

Among the often-cited negatives of the iPad are (1) that it has no USB port for plugging the tablet into other devices and (2) that the battery is not removable or replaceable. One of the reasons that the lack of a USB port is not troubling is that the iPad comes with Bluetooth capability, so keyboards, printers, and other devices can be connected wirelessly to the device. Also, a number of cloud providers (Dropbox, Box, and SpiderOak, among others) make it easy for you to access all of your documents online, without needing to connect your iPad to anything.

The iPad has a 10.1-inch display, while most of its competitors have 7-inch displays. The iPad Mini, which was first released in 2012, features the smaller 7-inch screen and has become very popular for its compact design and ease of use. Because lawyers need to work with documents during trial, however, we believe that the larger 10-inch display is far preferable and will make working with documents, legal research, and notes in court much easier.

In our opinion, the main reason iPads are rapidly catching on with trial lawyers is ease of use in the courtroom. A laptop, netbook, or even the "traditional" convertible tablet PCs, which are useful at counsel table, cannot be carried around the courtroom easily when the lawyer is standing at the podium or addressing the jury.

Essentially, the iPad is just a little heavier than a paper legal pad and not nearly as heavy as the lightest netbook or laptop.

When selecting a jury, it doesn't make sense to question a jury pool while keyboarding your responses into a traditional computer; there's probably no better way to get jurors to clam up and give them the impression that the lawyer is transcribing their personal information. (This is true even though the court reporter may be quietly transcribing it in many cases.) The iPad, however, is ideally configured to take notes on your jury panel, either within a jury selection app or your favorite note-taking application.

Let's take a look at some of the ways a litigator would benefit by using an iPad, from initial receipt of a lawsuit all the way through jury verdict.

Deadline Calculators

Court Days Pro
($2.99, bit.ly/yT171w)

Court Days Pro is a rules-based legal calendaring app for the iPhone and iPad. It provides legal professionals with the ability to calculate dates and deadlines based on a customizable database of court rules and statutes. Once the rules are set up in the application, you can perform date calculations using a customizable list of court holidays. It comes with California's Superior Court rules pre-installed; however, if you do not live in California, you will need to add your own local court rules for the jurisdiction in which you practice. Unfortunately, Court Days Pro has not been updated in some time, which typically means the developers have lost interest in supporting it. We still believe it is a worthwhile app because it is currently the only one that will allow you to input your own deadlines and reuse them over again.

Once you choose a triggering event (e.g., a motion hearing date or receipt of a complaint), the application will display a list of all events and corresponding dates and deadlines based on the triggering event (e.g., last day to file moving papers, opposition, reply briefs). Icons on the screen show the number of calendar days and court days from the current date for all resulting events (see Figure A.5).

Date results can be added to the device's native calendar app, and all results can be e-mailed to your client or others straight from the application.

The app is preprogrammed with a list of all federal holidays but is fully customizable to allow the addition or removal of any court holiday to the list.

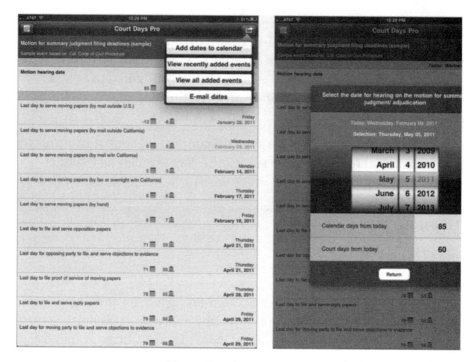

Figure A.5 Court Days Pro

If you would like a calendaring app that provides regular updates from the jurisdictions in which you practice, try DocketLaw (Free, **bit.ly/PmiBlW**) or Smart Dockets (Free, **bit.ly/URZGmj**). Both apps are free to download, but DocketLaw currently charges a subscription to access court deadlines.

Lawyer's Professional Assistant
($4.99, bit.ly/x5j7Fq)

The Wolfram Lawyer's Professional Assistant (see Figure A.6) is a reference tool that takes advantage of the company's "Computational Knowledge Engine" to help lawyers with calculations that may be relevant in their practice. Some of the features include:

♦ Calendar computations

♦ Legal dictionary

♦ Statutes of limitations for each U.S. state (see Figure A.7)

♦ Visa types, including basic requirements, common issues, and extensions and limits

♦ Financial computations, including fee calculator, settlement calculator, current interest rates, historical value of money, and federal U.S. tax rates

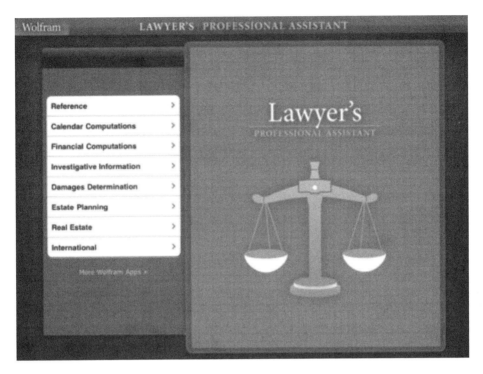

Figure A.6 Lawyer's Professional Assistant

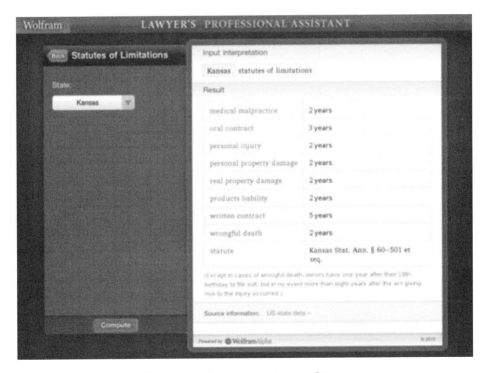

Figure A.7 Statute of Limitations Screen

- Crime rates and history for specific crimes, as well as state and national average comparisons
- Demographics of population and economy for a specific city
- Investigative information, including weather, company information, IP lookup, and blood alcohol calculator
- Damages and estate planning computations for occupational salaries, cost of living, life expectancy, and present or future value

Depositions

The Deponent
($9.99, bit.ly/warTWI)

The Deponent is a deposition question and exhibit outline application for lawyers. There are 150+ preprogrammed deposition questions by categories, but you can add your own questions as well. The app allows you to organize the order of questions and customize the questions for witnesses. Each question can be linked to an exhibit.

Exhibits can be loaded into the app from iTunes and Dropbox as PDF files, so you can view the exhibits while you are asking questions, or show them to the witness during the deposition (see Figure A.8).

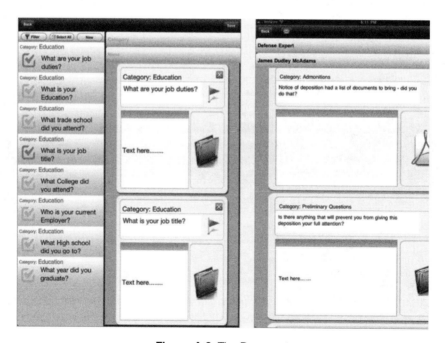

Figure A.8 The Deponent

TranscriptPad
($89.99, bit.ly/w7JGHt)

Once you have taken your depositions, you can load all of the transcripts into TranscriptPad to review them and create designations. The app only accepts text transcripts, so be sure to ask your court reporter for the deposition in TXT format. Once it's loaded, you can easily highlight testimony and code the designations with the issues you want to include (see Figure A.9).

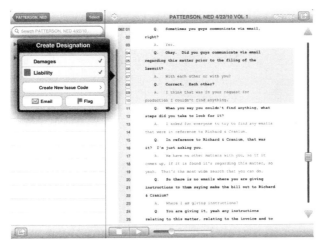

Figure A.9 TranscriptPad

Once you complete your designations, you can easily e-mail them to co-counsel, the judge, your client, or others (see Figure A.10). If you use TrialDirector or Sanction for evidence presentation, you can also import your designations directly into those tools from TranscriptPad.

Figure A.10 TranscriptPad e-mail

Jury Selection/Tracking

iJuror
($19.99, bit.ly/xJFlOT)

iJuror is an app developed to assist with jury selection (see Figure A.11).
Features include:

- Tap the seats to add juror information
- Track patterns
- E-mail the jury information to any e-mail address
- Configure seating arrangements for up to ninety-six jurors
- Get easy access to popular social networks to conduct quick research on potential jury members
- Add notes as the trial goes along, and score jurors based on their answers to *voir dire* questions
- Name view provides quick access to names and notes.
- Drag and drop to choose jurors
- Drag and drop to choose alternates
- Drag and drop to dismiss jurors

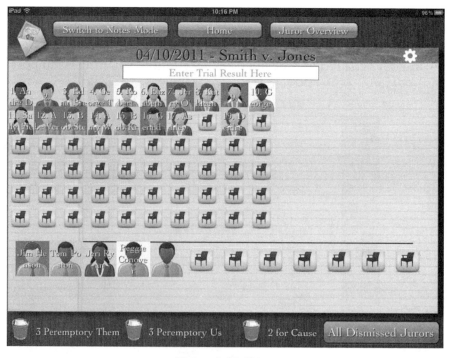

Figure A.11 iJuror

Honorable Mentions

- ♦ JuryPad ($24.99, **bit.ly/WdSP7T**) Nicely designed, this app is not quite as intuitive as iJuror, but has much of the same functionality.

- ♦ JuryStar ($39.99, **bit.ly/S38DSJ**) Similar to iJuror and JuryPad, but it requires you to manually enter a lot more information.

- ♦ iJury ($14.99, **bit.ly/ymg87i**) This nice jury selection tool has pre-populated questions and a system for ranking jurors based on their answers (see Figure A.12). However, you can only enter twelve people, which is not very helpful if you have a larger *voir dire* panel. (Note: It has not been updated since early 2012.)

- ♦ JuryTracker ($4.99, **bit.ly/xpvyuO**) This app goes to work after you have selected your jury; it works as your "personal jury consultant" to help track the reactions of jury members throughout the trial. (Note: It has not been updated since late 2011.)

Figure A.12 iJury

Evidence Presentation

TrialPad
($89.99, bit.ly/ApMDjM)

TrialPad is a legal document and exhibit management and presentation tool originally developed for lawyers to use in the courtroom. Lawyers and other legal professionals also are finding other great ways to use the app, including client presentations and law school lectures. With Trial-Pad, you can organize, manage, annotate, and store your documents and video while leveraging the portability of your iPad. It is designed to work like full-featured tools such as Sanction or Trial Director; however, because the iPad is not as powerful as your laptop, TrialPad does not offer all the functionality of traditional trial presentation software. But for many types of trials and hearings, TrialPad is the ideal presentation tool.

TrialPad differs from programs like PowerPoint or Keynote in that the presenter can present documents, images, and video in any order. It's possible to jump around, zoom, magnify, or annotate an exhibit on the fly. TrialPad is not really a competitor to PowerPoint or Keynote because it was designed to handle different situations; PowerPoint and Keynote are designed for more rehearsed linear presentations (opening and closing), where TrialPad works in more spontaneous situations like witness examination. Unlike PDF readers, it lets you create separate case folders, organize and sort important documents, and dynamically annotate and present documents via its flexible output options.

TrialPad cannot handle huge amounts of data as well as Sanction or Trial Director, and its video editing tool is not as powerful, but it works very well for hearings and most cases with manageable volumes of records. Features include:

- Organize and present evidence electronically (see Figure A.13).
- Import process via Dropbox, e-mail, or iTunes.
- No Internet connection is needed once files are loaded.

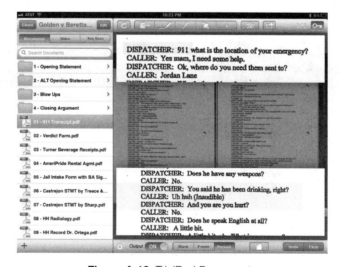

Figure A.13 TrialPad Documents

- Present wirelessly with Apple TV (requires iPad 2 and above).
- Highlight, annotate, redact, and zoom in on your documents (see Figure A.14).
- Make multiple callouts from documents or depositions.
- View documents side by side, comparing pages.
- Edit video clips or take snapshots of frames of surveillance video.
- Create Key Docs with saved annotations, and then print or e-mail them with the annotations.
- Have your expert mark up an exhibit and save it as a Key Doc for closing.
- Use the whiteboard tool to draw freehand.
- Create separate case and witness folders.
- File formats supported: Adobe Acrobat PDF, JPG, PNG, TIFF, multi-page TIFF, and TXT (Also imports DOC, DOCX, XLS, XLSX, PPT, PPTX, Keynote, Pages, and Numbers. *Please note:* Our best practices recommendation is to convert these files to Adobe Acrobat to maintain the formatting and look of the original document.)
- Video formats supported: All formats supported by iPad, such as .m4v, .mp4, and .mov

Figure A.14 TrialPad Photo

Honorable Mentions

- **ExhibitView** ($49.99, **bit.ly/zUwFnq**) This app is a worthy competitor to TrialPad. It offers a "Witness View," where you can hand the witness your iPad to view an exhibit without showing any of your other case files.

- **Exhibit A** ($14.99, **https://itunes.apple.com/us/app/exhibit-a/ id392621180?mt=8**) Although this app is less full-featured than the other two apps, it performs basic document display and annotation. It's a good choice if you're looking for something less expensive.

Legal Research

When you go to court, how many rulebooks do you bring with you? During trial or a hearing, it's important to have access to the case law, codes, and rules that are applicable in your case. Tools like the iPad now make it easy to have access to your entire law library, no matter where you happen to be. Here are a few of the tools we like:

- **Fastcase** (Free, **bit.ly/ysOcTY**) It's the companion to the legal research service.

- **WestlawNext** (Free, **bit.ly/z5pKRs**; requires Westlaw subscription)—A great tool for the courtroom, it allows you to conduct legal research, annotate the results, and e-mail case law to the judge or others.

- **Lexis Advance HD** (Free, **bit.ly/vo7wzp**; requires Lexis subscription)—This Lexis version of WestlawNext provides the same features for accessing your Lexis account.

- **LawBox** (Free, **bit.ly/y36FeU**) This app provides free access to all federal law—rules, codes, and the Constitution. You can also purchase rules for certain jurisdictions at $4.99 each.

- **FedCtRecords** ($9.99, **bit.ly/yb7gav**) This is an iPhone app, but completely worth the purchase for your iPad. The app provides access to your PACER account, so you have anywhere access to records on just about any federal case (for bankruptcy records, try FedCtBank, $9.99, **bit.ly/18iFoFx**).

- **ProView** (Free, **bit.ly/wVrUZc**; requires purchase of rulebooks)—If you practice in a jurisdiction that has rules published by Thomson Reuters, you can access the full version of those rulebooks on your iPad with this app.

- **My Legal Projects** ($1.99, **bit.ly/yVypHi**) Originally designed for summer associates or new lawyers, this app can be useful to anyone who likes to keep track of legal research. You can track research questions (issue, jurisdiction, deadlines, etc.) and connect to your WestlawNext account to do research on the particular project.

Courtroom Chatting

BT Chat HD
(Free, bit.ly/xE16tG)

If you have ever had the need to pass a note discreetly in the courtroom, you will completely understand the need for this app (see Figure A.15). With BT Chat HD, you can chat with other iPad users via Bluetooth or Wi-Fi (Wi-Fi is better if sitting at a distance).

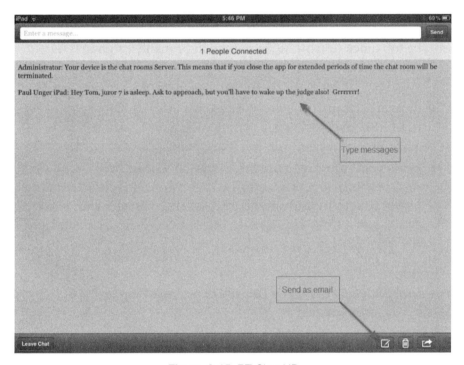

Figure A.15 BT Chat HD

Other Must-Have iPad Apps

So Many Apps . . . Which One Is Best?

There are many incredible apps for the iPad. In fact, there are so many that you will probably be overwhelmed about which ones to select, especially if you are new to the iPad.

We have listed our picks below, and we also have some honorable mentions. Some of our honorable mentions may end up being your top picks. Don't let this overwhelm you. With so many fantastic apps out there, it is hard to go wrong. In deciding which apps are best for you, follow these guiding principles:

- There are probably a dozen apps that accomplish the same thing. Review legal app blogs, consumer reviews, and ask trusted people what they recommend.

- Your workplace may prefer one app over another. Consistency and uniformity at the office is typically a good thing.

- If your co-workers or friends use the app, they can provide you with a support network to better learn and use the app.

- If a new app is released from a competing software company, don't be too quick to switch! Your app will probably catch up pretty fast and may have features the other app doesn't have yet. Remember your time invested in the app you already own.

- Apps are cheap; if you are curious, just buy it. Most apps are less than $10. The most expensive app cited in these materials is $129.99.

- If you want more recommendations, check out Tom's book *iPad Apps in One Hour for Lawyers*—he lists 200+ of his choices for the best productivity, document creation and management, legal, travel, and leisure-time apps in the App Store. It's available from the ABA webstore.

1. Dropbox
(Free app, bit.ly/z54Tpv; Free Dropbox account up to 2GB at www.dropbox.com)

Paul and Tom's Top Pick

If you have an iPad, Dropbox is almost mandatory. Setting aside debates about security, Dropbox has become the gold standard for storing files and getting them to the iPad. Most software developers are building their apps to integrate with Dropbox because it has become so widely used.

Dropbox sets up a local folder on your computer that allows you to create any subfolder structure. These subfolders synchronize into the cloud and can be shared with other people (clients, co-counsel, co-workers, etc.), if desired. The iPad can also connect to your Dropbox account so it can see and access everything that you can see on your PC (see Figure A.16).

If you can create a folder, copy and paste, and drag and drop, you can use Dropbox.

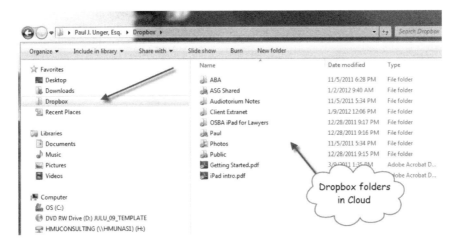

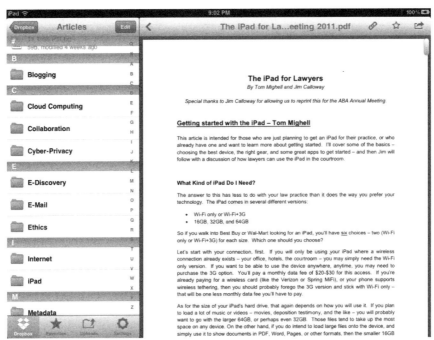

Figure A.16 The iPad's View of a Dropbox Account

2. Dictamus Dictate & Send
($16.99, bit.ly/wuv1Mq)

Paul's Top Pick

Dictamus is a dictation application for your iPhone or iPad (see Figure A.17). Like a traditional digital recorder, it allows you to rewind, overwrite, and insert anywhere. Download recordings, send as e-mails, upload to Dropbox, iCloud, FTP, or WebDAV.

Figure A.17 Dictamus Dictate & Send

3. GoodReader
($4.99, bit.ly/xb99kc)

Paul and Tom's Top Pick

Since documents are the lifeblood of the legal profession, it makes sense that one of the best uses of the iPad in a law practice is to read and annotate documents. GoodReader is best described as a universal document viewer, although it arguably works best with the PDF file format (see Figure A.18).

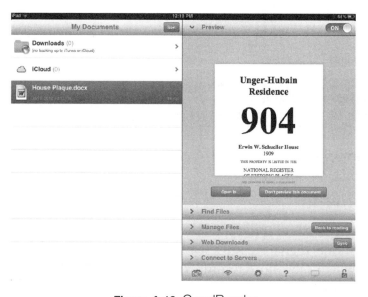

Figure A.18 GoodReader

It provides excellent annotation tools for PDF files, including the ability to highlight text, insert text boxes, post "sticky notes" comments, compose freehand drawings, and add lines, arrows, rectangles, and so on (see Figure A.19). These tools are extremely useful when you're reading a court opinion or law review article.

Popup note	Highlight	Line
Typewriter	Underline	Arrow
Add bookmark	Squiggly underline	Rectangle
Lookup (Dictionary, Google, Wikipedia)	Strikeout	Oval
	Text insertion mark	Freehand drawing
	Text replacement mark	

Figure A.19 GoodReader Annotations

GoodReader also has a robust file manager and has the ability to sync directly with your accounts from Dropbox, Box.net, Google Drive, and many other similar services (see Figure A.20).

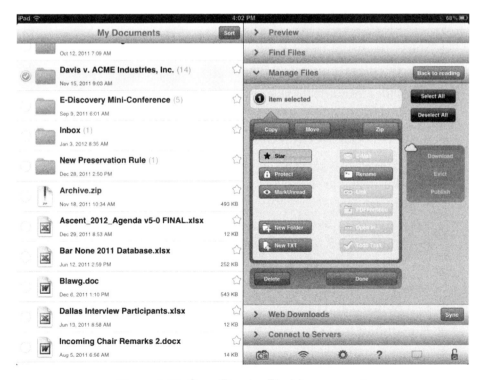

Figure A.20 GoodReader File Management

4. Quickoffice Pro HD
($19.99, https://itunes.apple.com/us/app/quickoffice/id578386521?mt=8)

Paul and Tom's Top Pick

There are a handful of office suites for the iPad that can perform the core features found in Microsoft Office on your computer. One of the top choices for legal professionals is Quickoffice, which allows you to view and edit Microsoft Word, Excel, and PowerPoint files. Quickoffice was recently purchased by Google, so now the app features direct integration with your Google Drive documents.

None of the iPad office suites have the same number of features that you'll find in the desktop version of Microsoft Office, but Quickoffice does provide a substantial amount:

- Create, edit, and share Microsoft Word, Excel, and PowerPoint files.
- Get continuous and convenient mobile access to remote storage services.
- Access and manage e-mail attachments with the most popular file formats.
- Get to your files remotely via cloud storage services (Dropbox, Google Drive, Egnyte, Box, Huddle, SugarSync, Evernote, and Catch).
- Share files using Docstoc, Slideshare, and Scribd.
- Transfer files through Wi-Fi or iTunes using USB.
- Open attachments from your native iPad e-mail client.
- Use Find and replace function.
- Multi-edit toolbox allows fast and convenient edits.
- Edit in page-layout mode, retaining full format print view.
- Use the scroll bar to preview page thumbnails and jump to any page in any size document.
- Extensive text formatting is available, including bold, italic, and underline, along with font sizes and styles (from a style sheet)
- Use Track Changes to see redlines, comments, and other changes to documents.
- Edit bulleted and numbered lists.
- File support for DOC, DOCX, TXT.
- Create, edit, view, and save PowerPoint 2003 files.

- ◆ View PowerPoint 2007 files.
- ◆ View presentations in slide show mode and on external monitors.
- ◆ Use the built-in laser pointer for presenting.

Honorable Mention
Documents To Go Premium ($16.99, **bit.ly/A5LPMq**)

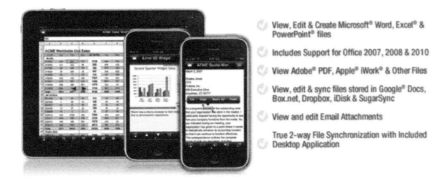

View, Edit & Create Microsoft® Word, Excel® & PowerPoint® files

Includes Support for Office 2007, 2008 & 2010

View Adobe® PDF, Apple® iWork® & Other Files

View, edit & sync files stored in Google® Docs, Box.net, Dropbox, iDisk & SugarSync

View and edit Email Attachments

True 2-way File Synchronization with Included Desktop Application

Featured on CNN: One of the Best Apps of 2009! See video

One of Apple's Best Selling Apps of 2009

2009 "Productivity App of the Year" - The iPhone Blog.com, Read here

2009 "Best App Ever Awards" Finalist - 148Apps.com

Download
Documents To Go
Desktop Application

Figure A.21 Documents To Go Premium Features

5. Notability
($2.99, bit.ly/wZT4wD)

Paul and Tom's Top Pick

Very few note-taking apps perform *all* three functions of handwriting, typing, *and* audio. We have found that Notability provides a great writing experience. You can change the thickness of the point and the width of lines and add lines and gridlines—all important to simulate an experience similar to writing on a piece of paper (see Figure A.22).

You can use your finger to write notes on the iPad, but I would highly recommend investing in a stylus so the writing experience is as similar as possible to writing on paper with a pen.

The audio feature not only records your meetings, conferences, or other gatherings but also synchronizes the recording to your notes so that you can simply tap a word or picture and hear what was being said at that moment.

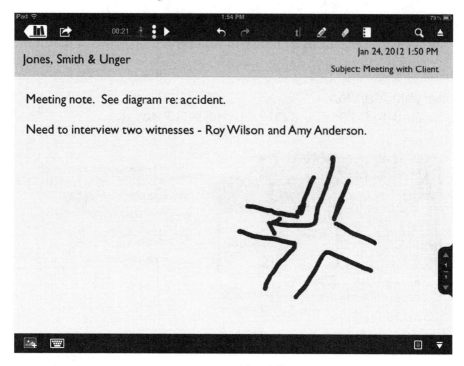

Figure A.22 Notability

Paul finds the ability to record a meeting, lecture, and so on, to be immensely helpful in certain situations. He absolutely loves this feature, does *not* want to have a separate notes program to do this (like Auditorium), a separate typing program, and a separate audio recorder. Notability provides all three functions.

6. Noteshelf
($8.99, bit.ly/y73OZd)

Tom's Top Pick

For pure handwritten note-taking, Noteshelf is one of the highest-ranking and most popular apps. You can create notebooks for your clients, cases, or projects and see them at a glance on your Noteshelf bookshelf (see Figure A.23). You can e-mail notebooks to yourself or others, or they can be exported to a PDF file and saved in Dropbox or Evernote. Tom recommends this app because it has just enough features that lawyers need to take notes without being overwhelming. It just works, and works well.

 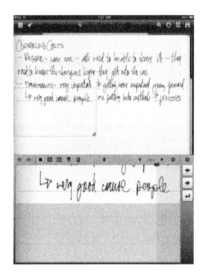

Figure A.23 Noteshelf

7. Keynote for iOS
($9.99, bit.ly/z6C1R9)

Paul's Top Pick

Keynote for the iPad or Mac is the equivalent of PowerPoint in the PC world (see Figure A.24). Keynote truly is an excellent presentation tool, and Apple has ported the software to the iPad iOS.

Figure A.24 Keynote for iOS

Keynote on the iPad can certainly be used to give presentations on a large screen with a projector. But many lawyers use Keynote as a way to share a set of images and information with a small group, such as at a client meeting. Keynote is a beautiful app on the iPad, and you can easily manipulate the slides and images.

If you have an iPhone, you might want to download **Keynote Remote** ($0.99, **bit.ly/xfceWA**), which turns your phone into a remote for the iPad's Keynote app. You can control your slides from the phone and even view any notes you might have included as part of the presentation.

8. SlideShark
(Free, bit.ly/LiHrxo)

Tom's Top Pick

I still live in the PowerPoint world, and unfortunately Keynote does not do a very good job of converting PowerPoint files for the iPad. Fonts are often missing, tables or charts are skewed, and animations just don't look quite right. With SlideShark, you can use PowerPoint on your iPad the way you designed it the first time (see Figure A.25).

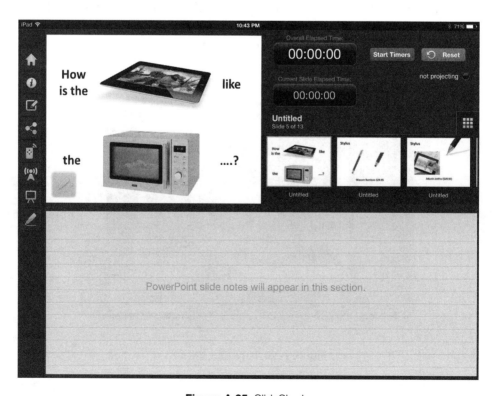

Figure A.25 SlideShark

Simply take your PowerPoint file and upload it to SlideShark; you can do this in a web browser on your computer or within the SlideShark app itself using Dropbox. SlideShark will convert your PowerPoint file to a format that can be viewed on the iPad and download the presentation to your device. The presentation tools are quite powerful and allow you to annotate on the screen as you give your presentation. Because the PowerPoint file is converted, you cannot edit your presentation on the iPad, so if you still want the ability to edit your presentation on the fly, then Keynote might be a better option for you.

SlideShark is free to use for up to 100MB of space, with subscription pricing available if you want more online storage.

9. PDF Expert
($9.99, bit.ly/hm00bi)

Paul and Tom's Top Pick

Many lawyers use PDF Expert because (1) clients can sign documents that can then be e-mailed back to the office and (2) form-fillable PDFs can now be "mobile" and filled out on the go (see Figure A.26).

Figure A.26 PDF Expert

Similar to GoodReader, PDF Expert will let you read and annotate PDF files. But PDF Expert offers a few additional features that appeal to legal professionals and are hard to find in other apps.

PDF Expert supports PDF forms and allows you to fill them in using text fields, check boxes, radio buttons, and other form elements. You can create a PDF form on your computer and transfer it to your iPad when you need to complete the form away from the office.

10. LogMeIn/LogMeIn Ignition
(Free, bit.ly/ws9m3y and $129.99, bit.ly/wOUNlw)

Paul's Top Pick

As much as the iPad can do, there will inevitably be a time when you need to work on your office computer or need to access a file that is only located on your home computer.

To access a computer from your iPad, you'll need to install the LogMeIn software client on the computer you want to access and that computer will need to be running. When you need to access the computer from the iPad, you'll simply launch the LogMeIn Ignition app and put in your credentials (see Figure A.27). Controlling and manipulating your computer

Figure A.27 LogMeIn Ignition

from the iPad can be a little tricky due to the small(er) size of the iPad's screen. But when you need access to your office computer from the road, the LogMeIn Ignition app can be your saving grace.

If you need access to multiple computers or advanced features like HD video, file management, and cloud storage, then you can pay either the one-time $129.99 fee or $39.99 per year. If you only need to access one computer and don't need any advanced features, then you can use the free LogMeIn app.

11. Find My iPhone (for the iPad)
(Free, bit.ly/xbwDkm)

Paul and Tom's Top Pick

The Find My iPhone/Find My iPad service is part of the free iCloud service. Because there is so much personal information and confidential client data stored on iOS devices today, we urge every legal professional with an iPad to sign up for a free iCloud account and enable the Find My iPad service. When you misplace or lose your iPad, you are able to either use the Find My iPhone app installed on another iPhone or iPad, or log on to any computer at **icloud.com/find** to geographically locate the iPad (see Figure A.28). From there, you can lock your iPad, send a message to the person who might have it, or erase the data that's on it.

Figure A.28 Find My iPhone Desktop Display

Since this service is free and the risk of losing so much information on an iPad is so high, many leading experts, like Brett Burney, argue that setting it up should be mandatory for any legal professional. See "Free Security for Your iPhone & iPad That Should Be Mandatory" at **www.macsinlaw.com/ find-my-iphone-free-security/**.

12. CloudOn
(Free for now, bit.ly/AAEh3H)

Paul and Tom's Top Pick

For those of you who need more functionality than tools like Quickoffice and Documents To Go provide, CloudOn is the app for you (see Figure A.29). It provides you with virtual access to Microsoft Word, Excel, and PowerPoint. You can actually create, review, and edit Office documents using real Office tools—including Track Changes!

To use CloudOn you will need to create an account and link it to your Dropbox account. When your document opens, you will be working in a modified version of Microsoft Office; almost all of the features are there, but the toolbars are adjusted for ease of use. The major drawback to CloudOn is that you must be online to use it. Because it connects to a vir-

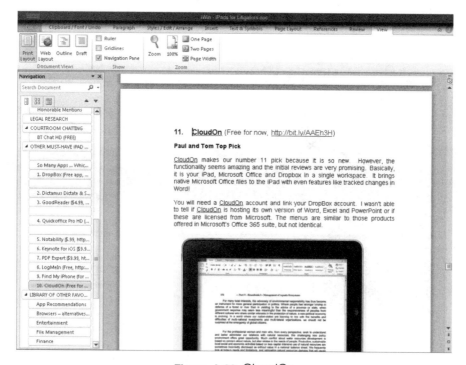

Figure A.29 CloudOn

tual version of Office, you cannot simply download a file to work on
when you are on a plane or at the beach. But for now, CloudOn is the best
option for working in a Microsoft Office environment on the iPad.

Library of Other Favorite Apps

We couldn't mention all of the apps we like in detail here, so we've listed
the names of some of our favorite apps in several categories. To find out
more about them, go to the App Store in iTunes or on your iPad or simply
type "[app name] iPad app" into your favorite search engine.

App Recommendations
- AppAdvice

Browsers—alternatives to the iPad's Safari Browser
- Atomic Web
- Google Chrome
- Skyfire—allows you to view Flash-based content

Entertainment
- Flixster—great app for buying movie tickets
- HBO Go—subscribers can watch all HBO content for free
- Hulu+—for watching television shows
- IMDb
- Netflix

File Management
- Berokyo
- Dropbox—probably the best-known cloud-based file management tool
- GoodReader

Finance
- Bank of America
- Chase Mobile

Food
- Food Truck Fiesta
- OpenTable—make reservations online

Games

- Angry Birds
- Crosswords
- Infinity Blade
- Plants vs. Zombies (1 and 2)
- Scrabble
- Words with Friends

Legal-Specific

- Black's Law Dictionary
- CFR Live Lite—access to all CFR regulations
- Court Days Pro—deadline calculator
- Deponent—conduct an entire deposition from your iPad
- Fastcase
- iJuror
- JuryPad
- Jury Tracker
- TranscriptPad
- TrialPad

Meetings and Calendars

- Calvetica Calendar
- Fuze Meeting
- GoToMeeting
- WebEx

News

- AP News
- CNN
- News 360
- NPR
- USA Today

Photos

- Photogene—photo editor
- PhotoSync—transfer photos from iPhone to iPad
- Pro HDR—improved HDR photography

Productivity

- Documents To Go—document creation/editing
- DocuSign—sign documents on the iPad
- Dragon Dictation—fantastic voice recognition/transcription tool
- Elements—note-taking
- Evernote—a fantastic repository for notes
- iThoughts HD—mind-mapping app
- iType2Go Pro—text editor and camera viewer
- JotNot Scanner Pro—document scanner
- Keynote—the best presentation app for the iPad
- MindMeister—mind mapping
- Note Taker HD—note-taking
- Noted—note-taking
- Notes Plus—note-taking
- Office2 HD—document creation/editing
- Outliner—organize your thoughts
- Pages—document creation/editing
- PDF Expert—document editor
- Penultimate—note-taking
- PlainText—text editor
- Prezi—great alternative app for conducting presentations
- Prizmo—scan and OCR
- QuickOffice—document creation/editing
- SignMyPad—have clients sign documents on your iPad
- SmartNote—note-taking
- UPAD—note-taking
- WritePad—note-taking

Reading

- Feedly—probably the best news reader/RSS feed reader currently available
- Flipboard—creates magazine-style layout of Facebook/Twitter feeds
- GoodReader—best file reader, period
- iAnnotate PDF
- Instapaper—save articles to read later

- Kindle for iPad
- Mr. Reader—imports RSS feeds from just about anywhere
- NextIssue—"Netflix for Magazines"—for a low monthly price, subscribe to over 100 magazines
- Reeder—another great choice for reading newsfeeds/RSS feeds
- Text'nDrive Pro—read text messages and e-mails
- WordPerfect Viewer—view .wpd files
- Zinio—read magazines on your iPad
- Zite—creates magazine-style layout of latest news on many topics

Social Networking and Communications

- Facebook
- HootSuite—social media aggregator
- IM+—multi-platform instant messaging client—Skype, Google Talk, etc.
- Imo.im—another good multi-platform instant messaging client
- Skype—VoIP calls and video
- TextNow—send texts for free from your iPad
- Tweetbot—the best Twitter client for iOS
- TweetDeck—a Twitter client
- Twitter

Travel

- FlightBoard
- FlightTrack
- GateGuru—airport information
- Kayak—fantastic travel search engine
- Orbitz
- Taxi Magic
- TripAdvisor
- TripIt

Utilities

- Air Display—create a second monitor with your iPad
- Appzilla—over 100 utility-type apps
- Citrix Receiver—remote access
- Digits Calculator

- Eye Glass—magnifying glass
- Google Translate—voice translation
- Google Voice—phone service
- GoToMyPC—remote access
- Jibbigo—voice translation
- LogMeIn Ignition—remote access
- Satchel—client for Backpack service
- Siri—your personal assistant
- Text Expander—macro utility
- Word Lens—translation

Navigation Tips & Settings

Add apps and folders to the iPad's dock. Out of the box, the iPad features four apps on the Dock, which is the always-visible bar at the bottom of the screen (see Figure A.30). You can add up to six apps in the Dock, and you can also add folders containing multiple apps in the Dock.

Figure A.30 iPad Dock

Launch apps from the Spotlight Search screen. While the Spotlight Search screen (accessed by swiping to the right from the first Home screen) can be used to search Notes, E-mail, Calendar Appointments, and more, you can also search for an app and tap to launch it (see Figure A.31).

Figure A.31 Spotlight Search Screen

Double-tap space bar to add a period and a space. You can quickly add a period and a space to the end of a sentence by double-tapping the spacebar. You can turn this option off in the Settings menu if you prefer.

Use the side switch to lock rotation. The Side Switch on the right side of the iPad (above the volume rocker) can be used to either mute the sound on the iPad, or to "lock" the rotation of the screen. You can change the setting in the Settings menu of the iPad.

Turn on battery percentage indicator. While the iPad by default shows you a graphical representation of the battery level, you can also turn on the percentage indicator under **Settings** > **General** > **Usage** > **Battery Usage** (see Figure A.32).

Undo typing. Many people aren't aware that there is an Undo option for the iPad. When you want to undo your most recent typing, you simply (and carefully!!) shake the iPad back and forth. A small window will appear, allowing you to undo your most recent typing.

Disable the clicking sound for typing and other sounds. You can turn off the clicking sound for typing by going to **Settings** > **General** > **Sounds**.

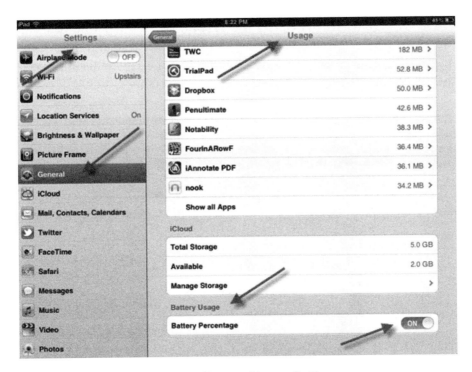

Figure A.32 Battery Usage Settings

Take a screenshot. You can take a screenshot from your iPad by simply holding down the **Home** button (front-center of device) and **Wake/ Sleep** button (top of the device) at the same time. You'll see the screen flash once and the image will be saved in your iPad's Photo app.

Use your iPad as a second monitor. You can use apps such as Air Display (Mac) and MaxiVista (Windows) to turn your iPad into a second monitor. This probably won't be your standard setup, but it can be helpful when you're traveling and need the convenience of a second monitor (see Figure A.33).

Figure A.33 iPad as Second Monitor

Save an image while browsing the Web. If you see a picture you want to save while browsing the Web on your iPad, simply tap and hold your finger on the image, and you'll be prompted to save the image into your iPad's Photo app (see Figure A.34).

Figure A.34 Save Web Image

Passcode Lock

It is very important to become familiar with the security settings of the iPad so that you can keep information stored on your tablet safe.

You can access the security settings through **Settings** > **General**.

At a minimum, lawyers and their agents should assign a passcode lock in conjunction with the auto-lock function. This will auto-lock your iPad after a set number of minutes and require a passcode to regain access to the iPad (see Figure A.35).

The iPad defaults to a "Simple Passcode," which is a 4-digit number similar to your ATM PIN. We recommend that you turn "Simple Passcode" off and set a longer passcode—at least ten to twelve numbers, letters, or characters. You should also set a time for the iPad to be idle after which the iPad will then require the passcode. Lastly, you should enable the option that erases data after ten failed passcode attempts.

Figure A.35 Passcode Lock

Resources

There are a number of good resources for lawyers using an iPad.

- *iPad 4 Lawyers* by Tom Mighell (**ipad4lawyers.squarespace.com**)
- *iPhone J.D.* by Jeff Richardson (**www.iphonejd.com**)
- *TabletLegal* by Josh Barrett (**tabletlegal.com**)
- *iPad Notebook* by Justin Kahn (**ipadnotebook.wordpress.com**)
- *Legal iPad* by Niki Black (**legal-ipad.tumblr.com**)

- *Walking Office* by Rob Dean (**www.walkingoffice.com**)
- *Macs in Law* by Brett Burney (**www.macsinlaw.com**)
- *The Mac Lawyer* by Ben Stevens (**www.themaclawyer.com**)

Another fantastic app to use for app recommendations and information is App Advice. It provides access to hundreds of articles and reviews of new iPad apps.

About the Authors

Tom Mighell, Esq.
Contoural, Inc.
tmighell@gmail.com

Tom Mighell is a Senior Consultant with Contoural, Inc., where he helps companies deal with their information governance, eDiscovery, and sensitive information control issues. Before becoming a consultant, Tom was a litigator for eighteen years in Dallas, Texas. He is a frequent speaker and writer on the Internet and legal technology and is the author of several books: *iPad in One Hour for Lawyers* (2nd edition), *iPad Apps in One Hour for Lawyers, iPad in One Hour for Litigators,* and *The Lawyers' Guide to Collaboration Tools and Technologies: Smart Ways to Work Together* (with Dennis Kennedy). He has published *Inter Alia* (**www.inter-alia.net**), a legal technology blog, since 2002. He and Dennis Kennedy are the co-hosts of *The Kennedy-Mighell Report,* a legal technology podcast. Tom is Past Chair of ABA TECHSHOW 2008, past Chair of the ABA Law Practice Division and current Chair of the Law Practice Division Publications Board.

Paul J. Unger, Esq.
Affinity Consulting Group, LLC
punger@affinityconsulting.com

Paul J. Unger is a lawyer and founding principal of Affinity Consulting Group, a nationwide consulting company providing legal technology consulting, training, and continuing legal education. His professional memberships include the American Society of Trial Consultants, American Bar Association (Law Practice Division; Chair, ABA TECHSHOW 2011), Columbus Bar Association, Ohio State Bar Association, Ohio Association for Justice, and Central Ohio Association for Justice. He specializes in trial presentation and litigation technology consulting, document and case management software, paperless office strategies, and legal-specific software training for law firms and legal departments throughout the Midwest. Mr. Unger has provided trial presentation consultation for over 300 cases. He is an Adjunct Professor for Capital University Law School's Paralegal Program. Mr. Unger is a national speaker and frequent lecturer for CLE programs.

Glossary*

Active Directory

Active Directory (AD) is an implementation of Local Automatic Data Processing (LADP) directory services by Microsoft for use primarily in Windows environments. Its main purpose is to provide central authentication and authorization services for Windows-based computers. Active Directory also allows administrators to assign policies, deploy software, and apply critical updates to an organization. It stores information and settings in a central database. Active Directory networks can vary from a small installation with a few hundred objects to a large installation with millions of objects.

ActiveSync

ActiveSync is a synchronization program developed by Microsoft. It allows a mobile device to be synchronized with either a desktop PC or a server running Microsoft Exchange Server, PostPath Email and Collaboration Server, Kerio MailServer, or Z-Push.

Adware

Adware is any software package that automatically plays, displays, or downloads advertising material to a computer after the software is installed on it or while the application is being used. Some types of adware are also spyware and can be classified as privacy-invasive software.

AppleCare Protection Plan

Apple's warranty with a new product is ninety days' complimentary telephone support and a one-year hardware guarantee. These can both be

*This glossary was compiled from definitions available online at Wikipedia (**www.wikipedia.org**).

extended to a three-year (for computers) or two-year (for iPods and iPhones) warranty and telephone support (inclusive of the initial support) through the AppleCare Protection Plan packs, which can be purchased separately within the initial one-year warranty or simultaneously with new Apple products, mainly Macs, iPods, and iPhones.

ATA

Advanced technology attachment (ATA) is a standard interface for connecting storage devices such as hard disks and CD-ROM drives inside personal computers. The standard is maintained by X3/INCITS committee T13. Many synonyms and near-synonyms for ATA exist, including abbreviations such as IDE and ATAPI.

Auto Document Feeder

Auto document feeder (ADF) is a feature in single-function and multi-function (all-in-one) printers, fax machines, photocopiers, and scanners that allows several pages to be loaded and fed one at a time into the scanner, allowing the user to scan (and thereby copy, print, or fax) multiple-page documents without having to manually replace each page.

Boot Camp

Boot Camp is a utility included with Apple's Mac OS X v10.5 Leopard and higher operating systems that assists users in installing Microsoft Windows XP or Windows Vista on Intel-based Macintosh computers. Boot Camp guides users through nondestructive repartitioning (including resizing of an existing HFS+ partition, if necessary) of their hard disk drive and using the Mac OS X Leopard disc to install Windows drivers. In addition to device drivers for the hardware, the disc includes a control panel applet for selecting the boot operating system while in Windows.

Byte

A byte is a unit of measurement of information storage, most often consisting of 8 bits. In many computer architectures it is a unit of memory addressing.

Category 5e Cable

Category 5e cable (Cat5e) is an enhanced version of Cat5 that adds specifications for far-end crosstalk. It was formally defined in 2001 in the TIA/EIA-568-B standard, which no longer recognizes the original Cat5 specification. Although 1000BASE-T was designed for use with Cat5 cable, the tighter specifications associated with Cat5e cable and connectors make it an excellent choice for use with 1000BASE-T. Despite the stricter performance specifications, Cat5e cable does not enable longer cable distances for Ethernet networks: Cables are still limited to a maximum of 328 ft. (100 m) in length (normal practice is to limit fixed ["horizontal"] cables to 90 m to allow for up to 5 m of patch cable at each end). Cat5e cable performance characteristics and test methods are defined in TIA/EIA-568-B.2-2001.

Category 6 Cable

Category 6 cable (Cat6), commonly referred to as Cat6, is a cable standard for gigabit Ethernet and other network protocols and is backward compatible with the category 5/5e and category 3 cable standards. Cat6 features more stringent specifications for crosstalk and system noise. The cable standard provides performance of up to 250 MHz and is suitable for 10BASE-T/100BASE-TX and 1000BASE-T (gigabit Ethernet). It is expected to suit the 10GBASE-T (10 gigabit Ethernet) standard, although with limitations on length if unshielded Cat6 cable is used.

Cathode Ray Tube

A cathode ray tube (CRT) is an evacuated glass envelope containing an electron gun (a source of electrons) and a fluorescent screen, usually with internal or external means to accelerate and deflect the electrons. When electrons strike the fluorescent screen, light is emitted.

CD-ROM

A CD-ROM is a compact disc that contains data accessible by a computer. While the CD format was originally designed for music storage and playback, the format was later adapted to hold any form of binary data. CD-ROMs are popularly used to distribute computer software, including games and multimedia applications, though any data can be stored (up to the capacity limit of a disc).

Central Processing Unit

A central processing unit (CPU), or sometimes just "processor," is a certain class of logic machines that can execute computer programs. This broad definition can easily be applied to many early computers that existed long before the term ever came into widespread usage. However, the term and its acronym CPU have been in use in the computer industry since at least the early 1960s. The form, design, and implementation of CPUs have changed dramatically since the earliest examples, but their fundamental operation has remained much the same.

Client Access License

A Client Access License (CAL) is a kind of software license distributed by Microsoft to allow clients to connect to its server software programs.

Code Division Multiple Access

Code division multiple access (CDMA) employs spread-spectrum technology and a special coding scheme (where each transmitter is assigned a code). In communications technology, there are only three domains that can allow multiplexing to be implemented for more efficient use of the available channel bandwidth, and these domains are known as time, frequency, and space. CDMA divides the access in signal space.

Computer Monitor

A computer monitor is a piece of electrical equipment that displays viewable images generated by a computer without producing a permanent record. The word *monitor* is used in other contexts, in particular in television broadcasting, where a television picture is displayed to a high standard. A computer display device is usually either a cathode ray tube or some form of flat panel, such as a thin film transistor liquid crystal display (TFT-LCD). The monitor comprises the display device, circuitry to generate a picture from electronic signals sent by the computer, and an enclosure or case. Within the computer, either as an integral part or a plugged-in interface, there is circuitry to convert internal data to a format compatible with a monitor.

Computer Virus

A computer virus is a computer program that can copy itself and infect a computer without permission or knowledge of the user. However, the term *virus* is commonly used, albeit erroneously, to refer to many different types of malware programs. The original virus may modify the copies, or the copies may modify themselves, as occurs in a metamorphic virus. A virus can only spread from one computer to another when its host is taken to the uninfected computer—for instance, by a user sending it over a network or the Internet, or by carrying it on a removable medium, such as a floppy disk, CD, or USB drive. Additionally, viruses can spread to other computers by infecting files on a network file system or a file system that is accessed by another computer.

Contrast Ratio

Contrast ratio is a measure of a display system, defined as the ratio of the luminosity of the brightest color (white) to that of the darkest color (black) that the system is capable of producing. A high contrast ratio is a desired aspect of any display, but with the various methods of measuring a system or its part, remarkably different values can sometimes produce similar results.

DAT72 Backup Tapes

DAT72 stores up to 36GB uncompressed (72GB compressed) on a 170-meter cartridge. The Digital Audio Tape (DAT) 72 standard was developed by HP and Certance. It has the same form-factor and is backward compatible with DDS-3 and -4.

Database Application

A computer database is a structured collection of records or data that is stored in a computer system. A database usually contains software so that a person or program can use it to answer queries or extract desired information. The term *database* refers to the collection of related records, and the software should be referred to as the database management system.

DDR2 SDRAM

DDR2 SDRAM, double-data-rate two synchronous dynamic random-access memory, is a random access memory technology used for high speed storage of the working data of a computer or other digital electronic device.

Digital Copier

In recent years, all new photocopiers have adopted digital technology, replacing the older analog technology. With digital copying, the copier effectively consists of an integrated scanner and laser printer. This design has several advantages, such as automatic image quality enhancement and the ability to "build jobs," or scan page images independently of the process of printing them. Some digital copiers can function as high-speed scanners; such models typically have the ability to send documents via e-mail or make them available on a local area network.

Digital Subscriber Line

Digital subscriber line (DSL) is a family of technologies that provides digital data transmission over the wires of a local telephone network.

Digital Visual Interface

Digital visual interface (DVI) is a video interface standard designed to maximize the visual quality of digital display devices such as flat-panel

LCD computer displays and digital projectors. It was developed by an industry consortium, the Digital Display Working Group (DDWG). It is designed for carrying uncompressed digital video data to a display.

Display Resolution
The display resolution of a digital television or computer monitor typically refers to the number of distinct pixels in each dimension that can be displayed. It can be an ambiguous term, especially since the displayed resolution is controlled by different factors in CRT and flat-panel or projection displays using fixed picture-element (pixel) arrays.

Domain Controller
On Windows Server systems, the domain controller (DC) is the server that responds to security authentication requests (logging in, checking permissions, etc.) within the Windows Server domain.

Dots Per Inch
Dots per inch (dpi) is a measure of printing resolution, in particular the number of individual dots of ink a printer or toner can produce within a linear one-inch (2.54 cm) space.

DVD
DVD (also known as digital versatile disc or digital video disc) is a popular optical disk storage media format. Its main uses are video and data storage. Most DVDs are of the same dimensions as compact discs (CDs) but store more than six times the data.

E-mail Spam
E-mail spam is unwanted e-mail messages, frequently with commercial content, sent in large quantities to an indiscriminate set of recipients.

Encryption/Decryption
Encryption/decryption is the process of transforming information (referred to as plaintext) using an algorithm (called cipher) to make it unreadable to anyone except those possessing special knowledge, usually referred to as a key. The result of the process is encrypted information (in cryptography, referred to as ciphertext). In many contexts, the word *encryption* also implicitly refers to the reverse process, decryption (e.g., "software for encryption" can typically also perform decryption), to make the encrypted information readable again (i.e., to make it unencrypted).

Enhanced-Definition Television

Enhanced- or extended-definition television, or EDTV, is a Consumer Electronics Association (CEA) marketing shorthand term for certain digital television (DTV) formats and devices. EDTV generally refers to video with picture quality beyond what can be broadcast in NTSC or PAL but not sharp enough to be considered high-definition television (HDTV). A DVD player with progressive output is considered the lower end of this class when playing a progressively encoded disc. (The maximum EDTV frame rate of 60 per second is not possible from a DVD.) The common implementations of EDTV are 480- or 576-line signals in progressive scan, as opposed to 50 to 60 interlaced fields per second (see NTSC or PAL and SECAM). These are commonly referred to as "480p" and "576p," respectively. In comparison, a standard-definition television (SDTV) signal is broadcast with interlaced frames and is commonly referred to as "480i" or "576i." EDTV can also refer to a display device that has a maximum resolution of 480p or 576p.

Extensible Markup Language

Extensible Markup Language (XML) is a general-purpose markup language. It is classified as an extensible language because it allows its users to define their own elements. Its primary purpose is to facilitate the sharing of structured data across different information systems, particularly via the Internet. It is used to encode documents and serialize data.

FireWire

FireWire is Apple's brand name for the IEEE 1394 interface (although the 1394 standard also defines a backplane interface). It is also known as i.LINK (Sony's name). It is a serial bus interface standard for high-speed communications and isochronous real-time data transfer, frequently used in a personal computer (and digital audio/digital video).

FireWire 400

FireWire 400 can transfer data between devices at 100, 200, or 400 Mbit/s data rates.

FireWire 800

FireWire 800 (Apple's name for the nine-pin "S800 bilingual" version of the IEEE 1394b standard) was introduced commercially by Apple in 2003. This newer 1394 specification (1394b) and corresponding products allow a transfer rate of 786.432 Mbit/s via a new encoding scheme termed beta mode. It is backward compatible to the slower rates and six-pin connectors of FireWire 400. However, while the IEEE 1394a and IEEE 1394b standards are compatible, FireWire 800's connector is different from FireWire 400's connector, making the legacy cables incompatible. A bilingual cable allows the connection of older devices to the newer port.

Gigabyte

A gigabyte (derived from the SI prefix giga-) is a unit of information or computer storage equal to either exactly 1 billion bytes or approximately 1.07 billion bytes, depending on context. It is commonly abbreviated as Gbyte or GB.

Global System for Mobile Communications

Global System for Mobile Communications (GSM) is the most popular standard for mobile phones in the world. Its promoter, the GSM Association, estimates that 82 percent of the global mobile market uses the standard. GSM is used by over 2 billion people across more than 212 countries and territories. Its ubiquity makes international roaming very common between mobile phone operators, enabling subscribers to use their phones in many parts of the world. GSM differs from its predecessors in that both signaling and speech channels are digital call quality, and so it is considered a second generation (2G) mobile phone system. Data communications were built into the system using the 3rd Generation Partnership Project (3GPP).

Hard Disk Drive

A hard disk drive, commonly referred to as a hard drive, hard disk, or fixed disk drive, is a nonvolatile storage device that stores digitally encoded data on rapidly rotating platters with magnetic surfaces. Strictly speaking, *drive* refers to a device distinct from its medium, such as a tape drive and its tape or a floppy disk drive and its floppy disk.

Hash Function

Hash function is a reproducible method of turning some kind of data into a (relatively) small number that may serve as a digital "fingerprint" of the data. The algorithm "chops and mixes" (i.e., substitutes or transposes) the data to create such fingerprints. The fingerprints are called hash sums, hash values, hash codes, or simply hashes.

High-Definition Multimedia Interface

High-definition multimedia interface (HDMI) is a licensable compact audio/video connector interface for transmitting uncompressed digital streams.

High-Definition TV

High-definition TV (HDTV) is a digital television broadcasting system with greater resolution than traditional television systems (NTSC, SECAM, PAL). HDTV is digitally broadcast because digital television (DTV) requires less bandwidth if sufficient video compression is used.

Hub

A hub is a device for connecting multiple twisted pairs or fiber optic Ethernet devices, making them act as a single network segment. Hubs work at the physical layer (layer 1) of the OSI model, and the term *layer 1 switch* is often used interchangeably with *hub*. The device is thus a form of multi-port repeater. Network hubs are also responsible for forwarding a jam signal to all ports if they detect a collision.

IEEE

The Institute of Electrical and Electronics Engineers, or IEEE (read: *i* triple *e*), is an international nonprofit professional organization for the advancement of technology related to electricity. It has the most members of any technical professional organization in the world, with more than 360,000 members in around 175 countries.

Intel Core 2 Duo Processor

The Core 2 brand refers to a range of Intel's consumer 64-bit dual-core and MCM quad-core CPUs with the x86-64 instruction set and based on the Intel Core microarchitecture, which derived from the 32-bit dual-core Yonah laptop processor.

Intel Corporation

Intel Corporation (Intel) is the world's largest semiconductor company and the inventor of the x86 series of microprocessors, which are found in most personal computers.

Internet Information Services

Internet Information Services (IIS) is a set of Internet-based services for servers using Microsoft Windows. It is the world's second most popular web server in terms of overall websites, behind Apache HTTP Server.

Internet Protocol Address

An Internet protocol (IP) address is a unique address that certain electronic devices currently use to identify and communicate with each other on a computer network utilizing the Internet protocol standard—in simpler terms, a computer address. Any participating network device—

including routers, switches, computers, infrastructure servers (e.g., NTP, DNS, DHCP, SNMP), printers, Internet fax machines, and some telephones—can have its own address that is unique within the scope of the specific network. Some IP addresses are intended to be unique within the scope of the global Internet, while others need to be unique only within the scope of an enterprise.

Intrusion Detection System

An intrusion detection system (IDS) is a piece of hardware that detects unwanted manipulations of computer systems, mainly through the Internet. The manipulations may take the form of attacks by hackers. An IDS is used to detect several types of malicious behaviors that can compromise the security and trust of a computer system. These include network attacks against vulnerable services; data-driven attacks on applications; host-based attacks such as privilege escalation, unauthorized logins, and access to sensitive files; and malware (viruses, Trojan horses, and worms).

IPsec

IPsec (IP security) is a suite of protocols for securing Internet protocol (IP) communications by authenticating and/or encrypting each IP packet in a data stream.

iSight Camera

The iSight camera is a webcam developed and marketed by Apple. The iSight is sold in retail outlets as an external unit that connects to a computer via FireWire cable and comes with a set of mounts to place it atop any current Apple display, laptop computer, or all-in-one desktop computer. The term is also used to refer to the camera built into Apple's iMac, MacBook, and MacBook Pro computers.

Keyboard

In computing, a keyboard is a peripheral partially modeled after the typewriter keyboard. Physically, a keyboard is an arrangement of rectangular buttons, or keys. A keyboard typically has characters engraved or printed on the keys; in most cases, each press of a key corresponds to a single written symbol. However, to produce some symbols requires pressing and holding several keys simultaneously or in sequence; other keys do not produce any symbol but instead affect the operation of the computer or the keyboard itself.

Laser Printer

A laser printer is a common type of computer printer that rapidly produces high-quality text and graphics on plain paper. Like photocopiers, laser printers employ a xerographic printing process but differ from analog photocopiers in that the image is produced by the direct scanning of a laser beam across the printer's photoreceptor.

Light-Emitting Diode

A light-emitting diode (LED) is a semiconductor diode that emits incoherent, narrow-spectrum light when electrically biased in the forward direction of the p-n junction, as in the common LED circuit. This effect is a form of electroluminescence.

Linear Tape-Open

Linear tape-open (LTO or LTO2) is a magnetic tape data storage technology developed as an open alternative to the proprietary digital linear tape (DLT). The technology was developed and initiated by Seagate, Hewlett Packard, and IBM. The standard form-factor of LTO technology goes by the name Ultrium.

Liquid Crystal Display

A liquid crystal display (LCD) is a thin, flat display device made up of any number of color or monochrome pixels arrayed in front of a light source or reflector. It is often used in battery-powered electronic devices because it uses very small amounts of electric power.

Macintosh AirPort

AirPort is a local area wireless networking brand from Apple based on the IEEE 802.11b standard (also known as Wi-Fi) and certified as compatible with other 802.11b devices. A later family of products based on the IEEE 802.11g specification is known as AirPort Extreme. The latest family of products is based on the draft-IEEE 802.11n specification and carries the same name.

Macintosh/Mac

Macintosh—or, for newer models, Mac—is a brand name that covers several lines of personal computers designed, developed, and marketed by Apple, Inc. The original Macintosh was released on January 24, 1984; it was the first commercially successful personal computer to feature a mouse and a graphical user interface (GUI) rather than a command line interface. Apple consolidated multiple consumer-level desktop models into the 1998 iMac, which sold extremely well. Current Mac systems are mainly targeted at the home, education, and creative professional markets. They are the aforementioned (though upgraded) iMac and the entry-level Mac mini desktop models; the workstation-level Mac Pro tower; the MacBook, MacBook Air and MacBook Pro laptops; and the Xserve server.

MagSafe Power Adapter

The MagSafe power adapter is a power connector introduced in conjunction with the MacBook Pro at the Macworld Expo in San Francisco on January 10, 2006. The MagSafe connector is held in place magnetically. As a result, if it is tugged on—for instance, by someone tripping over the cord—it comes out of the socket safely, without damage to it or the computer or pulling the computer off its table or desk.

Media Access Control Address

A media access control (MAC) address is a quasi-unique identifier attached to most network adapters. It is a number that acts like a name for a particular network adapter, so, for example, the network interface cards (NICs, or built-in network adapters) in two different computers will have different names, or MAC addresses, as would an Ethernet adapter and a wireless adapter in the same computer and as would multiple network cards in a router.

Megabyte

A megabyte is a unit of information or computer storage equal to approximately 1,000,000 bytes, depending on context.

Message-Digest Algorithm 5 (MD5)

Message-digest algorithm 5 (MD5) is a widely used cryptographic hash function with a 128-bit hash value. As an Internet standard (RFC 1321), MD5 has been employed in a wide variety of security applications and is also commonly used to check the integrity of files. An MD5 hash is typically expressed as a 32-character hexadecimal number.

Microsoft Exchange Server

Microsoft Exchange Server is a messaging and collaborative software product developed by Microsoft. It is part of the Microsoft Servers line of server products and is widely used by enterprises using Microsoft infrastructure solutions. Exchange's major features consist of electronic mail, calendars, contacts and tasks, and support for the mobile and web-based access to information. The software also supports data storage.

Microsoft SQL Server

Microsoft SQL Server is a relational database-management system (RDBMS) produced by Microsoft. Its primary query language is Transact-SQL, an implementation of the ANSI/ISO standard Structured Query Language (SQL) used by both Microsoft and Sybase.

Microsoft Windows

Microsoft Windows is the name of several families of software operating systems by Microsoft. Microsoft first introduced an operating environment named Windows in November 1985 as an add-on to MS-DOS in response to the growing interest in graphical user interfaces (GUIs). Microsoft Windows eventually came to dominate the world's personal computer market, overtaking Mac OS, which had been introduced previously. At the 2004 IDC Directions conference, IDC vice president Avneesh Saxena stated that Windows had approximately 90 percent of the client operating system market. The most recent client version of Windows is Windows 8.

Modem

A modem (from modulator-demodulator) is a device that modulates an analog carrier signal to encode digital information and also demodulates such a carrier signal to decode the transmitted information. The goal is to produce a signal that can be transmitted easily and decoded to reproduce the original digital data.

Mouse

In computing, a mouse (plural, *mice* or *mouses*) functions as a pointing device by detecting two-dimensional motion relative to its supporting surface. Physically, a mouse consists of a small case, held under one of the user's hands. It has one or more buttons and sometimes has other elements, such as wheels, which allow the user to perform various system-dependent operations, or extra buttons or features that can add more control or dimensional input. The mouse's motion typically translates into the motion of a pointer on a display.

MP3

MPEG-1 audio layer 3, more commonly referred to as MP3, is a digital audio encoding format. This encoding format is used to create an MP3 file, a way to store a single segment of audio, commonly a song, so that it can be organized or easily transferred between computers and other devices, such as MP3 players.

Network Address Translation

Network address translation (NAT) is a technique of transceiving network traffic through a router that involves rewriting the source and/or destination IP addresses and usually also the TCP/UDP port numbers of IP packets as they pass through.

Network Card/Adapter

The network adapter, LAN adapter, or NIC (network interface card) is a piece of computer hardware designed to allow computers to communicate over a computer network.

Optical Character Recognition

Optical character recognition, usually abbreviated OCR, is the mechanical or electronic translation of images of handwritten, typewritten, or printed text (usually captured by a scanner) into machine-editable text.

Peripheral Devices

In computer hardware, a peripheral device is any device attached to a computer to expand its functionality. Some of the more common peripheral devices are printers, scanners, disk drives, tape drives, microphones, speakers, and cameras.

Portable Document Format

Portable Document Format (PDF) is the file format created by Adobe Systems in 1993 for document exchange. PDF is a fixed-layout document format used for representing two-dimensional documents in a manner independent of the application software, hardware, and operating system.

Private Branch Exchange

Private branch exchange (PBX) is a telephone exchange that serves a particular business or office, as opposed to one that a common carrier or telephone company operates for many businesses or for the general public.

Radio-Frequency Identification

Radio-frequency identification (RFID) is an automatic identification method that relies on storing and remotely retrieving data using devices called RFID tags or transponders. An RFID tag is an object that can be applied to or incorporated into a product, animal, or person for the purpose of identification using radio waves. Some tags can be read from several meters away and beyond the line of sight of the reader.

RAID 5
RAID (redundant array of independent disks) 5 uses block-level striping with parity data distributed across all member disks. RAID 5 has achieved popularity due to its low cost of redundancy. Generally, RAID 5 is implemented with hardware support for parity calculations. A minimum of three disks is generally required for a complete RAID 5 configuration.

Random Access Memory
Random access memory (usually known by its acronym, RAM) is a type of computer data storage. Today it takes the form of integrated circuits that allow the stored data to be accessed in any order—i.e., at random. The word *random* thus refers to the fact that any piece of data can be returned in a constant time, regardless of its physical location and whether or not it is related to the previous piece of data.

Redundant Arrays of Independent Disks
Redundant arrays of independent disks (RAID) is the most common definition of RAID. Other definitions of RAID include "redundant arrays of independent drives" and "redundant arrays of inexpensive drives." RAID is an umbrella term for computer data storage schemes that divide and replicate data among multiple hard disk drives. RAID's various designs balance or accentuate two key design goals: increased data reliability and increased I/O (input/output) performance.

Remote Desktop Protocol
Remote desktop protocol (RDP) is a multichannel protocol that allows a user to connect to a computer running Microsoft Terminal Services. Clients exist for most versions of Windows (including handheld versions) and other operating systems such as Linux, FreeBSD, Solaris, and Mac OS X. The server listens by default on TCP port 3389. Microsoft refers to its official RDP client software as either Remote Desktop Connection (RDC) or Terminal Services Client (TSC).

Revolutions Per Minute
Revolutions per minute (abbreviated rpm, RPM, r/min) is a unit of frequency: the number of full rotations completed in one minute around a fixed axis. It is most commonly used as a measure of rotational speed or angular velocity of some mechanical component.

Rootkits

A rootkit is a program (or a combination of several programs) designed to take fundamental control (in Unix terms, "root" access; in Windows terms, "administrator" access) of a computer system without authorization by the system's owners and legitimate managers. Access to the hardware (i.e., the reset switch) is rarely required, as a rootkit is intended to seize control of the operating system running on the hardware. Typically, rootkits act to obscure their presence on the system through subversion or evasion of standard operating system security mechanisms. Often they are Trojans as well, thus fooling users into believing they are safe to run on their systems. Techniques used to accomplish this can include concealing running processes from monitoring programs or hiding files or system data from the operating system.

Router

A router is a piece of hardware that connects two or more different networks (e.g., LAN to WAN) to route data between them.

Scanning Resolution

Scanning resolution describes the detail of the scanned image. The term applies equally to digital images, film images, and other types of images. Higher resolution means more image detail.

Secure Sockets Layer

Secure Sockets Layer (SSL) is a cryptographic protocol that provides secure communications on the Internet for such things as web browsing, e-mail, Internet faxing, instant messaging, and other data transfers.

Serial Advanced Technology Attachment

A serial advanced technology attachment (SATA) is a computer bus primarily designed for transfer of data between a computer and storage devices (like hard disk drives or optical drives). The main benefits are faster transfers, the ability to remove or add devices while operating (hot-swapping), thinner cables that let air cooling work more efficiently, and more reliable operation with tighter data integrity checks than the older Parallel ATA interface.

Serial-Attached SCSI

Serial-attached SCSI (SAS) is a computer bus technology primarily designed for transfer of data to and from computer data storage devices such as hard drives, CD-ROM and DVD tape drives, and similar devices.

SAS is a serial communication protocol for direct attached storage (DAS) devices. It is designed for the corporate and enterprise market as a replacement for parallel SCSI, allowing for much higher-speed data transfers than previously available and is backward compatible with SATA drives.

Server

A server is an application or device that performs services for connected clients as part of a client-server architecture. A server application, as defined by RFC 2616 (HTTP/1.1), is "an application program that accepts connections in order to service requests by sending back responses." Server computers are devices designed to run such an application or applications, often for extended periods of time, with minimal human direction. Examples of d-class servers include web servers, e-mail servers, and file servers.

Service Set Identifier

Service set identifier (SSID) is a name used to identify the particular 802.11 wireless LANs to which a user wants to attach. A client device will receive broadcast messages from all access points within range that advertise their SSIDs and can choose one to connect to based on preconfiguration or by displaying a list of SSIDs in range and asking the user to select one.

SHA Hash Functions

SHA hash functions are five cryptographic hash functions designed by the National Security Agency (NSA) and published by the NIST as a U.S. Federal Information Processing Standard. SHA stands for secure hash algorithm. Hash algorithms compute a fixed-length digital representation (known as a message digest) of an input data sequence (the message) of any length. The five algorithms are denoted SHA-1, SHA-224, SHA-256, SHA-384, and SHA-512. The latter four variants are sometimes collectively referred to as SHA-2. SHA-1 produces a message digest that is 160 bits long; the number in the other four algorithms' names denotes the bit length of the digest they produce.

Shadow Copy

Shadow Copy (also called Volume Snapshot Service, or VSS) is a feature introduced with Windows Server 2003 and available in all releases of Microsoft Windows thereafter that allows taking manual or automatic backup copies or snapshots of a file or folder on a specific volume at a specific point in time. It is used by NTBackup and the Volume Shadow Copy service to back up files. In Windows Vista, it is used by Windows Vista's backup utility, System Restore, and the Previous Versions feature.

Small Computer System Interface

Small computer system interface (SCSI) is a set of standards for physically connecting and transferring data between computers and peripheral devices. The SCSI standards define commands, protocols, and electrical and optical interfaces. SCSI is most commonly used for hard disks and tape drives, but it can connect a wide range of other devices, including scanners and CD drives. The SCSI standard defines command sets for specific peripheral device types; the presence of "unknown" as one of these types means that in theory it can be used as an interface to almost any device, but the standard is highly pragmatic and addressed toward commercial requirements.

Smartphone

A smartphone is a mobile phone offering advanced capabilities beyond a typical mobile phone, often with PC-like functionality.

Spyware

Spyware is computer software that is installed surreptitiously on a personal computer to intercept or take partial control over the user's interaction with the computer without the user's informed consent. While the term *spyware* suggests software that secretly monitors the user's behavior, the functions of spyware extend well beyond simple monitoring. Spyware programs can collect various types of personal information but can also interfere with user control of the computer in other ways, such as installing additional software, redirecting web browser activity, accessing websites blindly that will cause more harmful viruses, or diverting advertising revenue to a third party. Spyware can even change computer settings, resulting in slow connection speeds, different home pages, and loss of Internet or other programs.

SuperDrive

SuperDrive is a term that has been used by Apple for two different storage drives: from 1988 to 1999, to refer to a high-density floppy disk drive capable of reading all major 3.5-inch disk formats, and from 2001 onward to refer to a combined CD/DVD reader/writer. Once use of floppy disks started declining, Apple reused the term to refer to the (originally Pioneer-built) DVD writers built into its Macintosh models, which can read and write both DVDs and CDs. As of December 2006, SuperDrives are combination DVD ±R/±RW and CD-R/RW writer drives offering speeds of 4x to 36x and supporting the DVD-R, DVD+R, DVD+R DL, DVD±RW, DVD-9, CD-R, and CD-RW formats along with all normal read-only media.

Switch

A switch is a computer networking device that connects network segments. Low-end network switches appear nearly identical to network hubs, but a switch contains more "intelligence" (and comes with a correspondingly slightly higher price tag) than a network hub. Network switches are capable of inspecting data packets as they are received, determining the source and destination device of the packets, and forwarding them appropriately. By delivering each message only to the connected device it was intended for, a network switch conserves network bandwidth and offers generally better performance than a hub.

Tagged Image File Format

Tagged Image File Format (TIFF) is a container format for storing images, including photographs and line art. Originally created by the company Aldus for use with what was then called desktop publishing, it is now under the control of Adobe. The TIFF format is widely supported by image-manipulation applications; publishing and page layout applications; and scanning, faxing, word processing, OCR, and other applications.

Tape Drive

A tape drive is a data storage device that reads and writes data stored on a magnetic tape. It is typically used for archival storage of data on hard drives. Tape generally has a favorable unit cost and long archival stability.

Terminal Services

Terminal Services is a component of Microsoft Windows (both server and client versions) that allows a user to access applications and data on a remote computer over any type of network, although normally best used when dealing with either a wide area network (WAN) or local area network (LAN). Ease and compatibility with other types of networks may vary. Terminal Services is Microsoft's implementation of thin-client terminal server computing, where Windows applications, or even the entire desktop of the computer running Terminal Services, are made accessible from a remote client machine.

Time Machine

Time Machine is a backup utility developed by Apple that is included with Mac OS X v. 10.7.

Universal Serial Bus

Universal serial bus (USB) is a serial bus standard to interface devices. USB was designed to allow peripherals to be connected using a single standardized interface socket and to improve plug-and-play capabilities by allowing devices to be connected and disconnected without rebooting the computer (hot-swapping). Other convenient features include providing power to low-consumption devices without the need for an external power supply and allowing many devices to be used without requiring manufacturer-specific individual device drivers to be installed.

Unix

Unix is a computer operating system originally developed in 1969 by a group of AT&T employees, including Ken Thompson, Dennis Ritchie, and Douglas McIlroy, at Bell Labs. Today's Unix systems are split into various branches developed over time by AT&T as well as various commercial vendors and nonprofit organizations.

USB Thumb Drive

USB thumb (flash) drives are NAND-type flash memory data storage devices integrated with a USB connector. They are typically small, lightweight, removable, and rewritable.

Video Card/Graphics Adapter

The video card/graphics adapter, also referred to as a graphics accelerator card, display adapter, graphics card, and numerous other terms, is an item of personal computer hardware whose function is to generate and output images to a display.

Video Graphics Array

The term *video graphics array* (VGA) refers either to an analog computer display standard (the 15-pin D-subminiature VGA connector, first marketed in 1988 by IBM) or the 640 × 480 resolution itself. While this resolution has been superseded in the computer market, it is becoming a popular resolution on mobile devices.

Virtual Private Network

A virtual private network (VPN) is a communications network tunneled through another network and dedicated for a specific network. One common application is secure communications through the public Internet, but a VPN need not have explicit security features, such as authentication or content encryption. VPNs, for example, can be used to separate the traffic of different user communities over an underlying network with strong security features.

Web 2.0

Web 2.0 is a trend in web design and development and can refer to a perceived second generation of web-based communities and hosted services—such as social networking sites, wikis, and folksonomies—which aim to facilitate creativity, collaboration, and sharing between users. The term gained currency following the first O'Reilly Media Web 2.0 conference in 2004. Although the term suggests a new version of the World Wide Web, it does not refer to an update to any technical specifications, but to changes in the ways software developers and end users use webs.

Wi-Fi

Wi-Fi is a wireless technology brand owned by the Wi-Fi Alliance and intended to improve the interoperability of wireless local area network products based on the IEEE 802.11 standards. Common applications for Wi-Fi include Internet and VoIP phone access, gaming, and network connectivity for consumer electronics, such as televisions, DVD players, and digital cameras.

Wi-Fi Protected Access

Wi-Fi protected access (WPA) is a class of systems to secure wireless (Wi-Fi) computer networks. It was created in response to several serious weaknesses researchers had found in the previous system, wired equivalent privacy (WEP). WPA implements the majority of the IEEE 802.11i standard and was intended as an intermediate measure to take the place of WEP while 802.11i was prepared.

Windows Recycle Bin

Windows Recycle Bin is temporary storage for files that have been deleted in a file manager by the user but not yet permanently erased from the physical medium. Typically, a recycle bin is presented as a special file directory to the user (whether or not it is actually a single directory depends on the implementation), allowing the user to browse deleted files, undelete those that were deleted by mistake, or delete them permanently (either one by one, or by the Empty Trash function).

Windows SharePoint Services

Windows SharePoint Services, or Windows SharePoint, is the basic part of SharePoint, offering collaboration and document management functionality via web portals by providing a centralized repository for shared documents, as well as browser-based management and administration. It allows creation of document libraries, which are collections of files that can be shared for collaborative editing. SharePoint provides access control and revision control for documents in a library.

Wired Equivalent Privacy

Wired equivalent privacy (WEP) is a deprecated algorithm to secure IEEE 802.11 wireless networks. Wireless networks broadcast messages using radio, so they are more susceptible to eavesdropping than wired networks. When introduced in 1999, WEP was intended to provide confidentiality comparable to that of a traditional wired network.

Index

The Lawyer's Guide to Microsoft® Excel 2013
By Ben M. Schorr
Product Code: 5110756 • LP Price: $41.95 • Regular Price: $69.95

Did you know Excel can help you analyze and present your cases more effectively? This hands-on manual will show you how to take advantage of the software you already have. Bestselling author Ben M. Schorr has produced a guide uniquely designed to help lawyers improve their efficiency and increase their productivity with the most common spreadsheet software on the market. Designed for beginners as well as advanced users.

The Lawyer's Guide to Microsoft® Word 2013
By Ben M. Schorr
Product Code: 5110757 • LP Price: $41.95 • Regular Price: $69.95

Maximize your use of Microsoft® Word with this essential guide. Fully updated to reflect the 2012 version of the software, this handy reference includes clear explanations, legal-specific descriptions, and time-saving tips for getting the most out of Microsoft® Word—and customizing it for the needs of today's legal professional.

LinkedIn in One Hour for Lawyers, Second Edition
By Dennis Kennedy and Allison C. Shields
Product Code: 5110773 • LP Price: $39.95 • Regular Price: $49.95

Since the first edition of LinkedIn in One Hour for Lawyers was published, LinkedIn has added almost 100 million users, and more and more lawyers are using the platform on a regular basis. Now, this bestselling ABA book has been fully revised and updated to reflect significant changes to LinkedIn's layout and functionality made through 2013. LinkedIn in One Hour for Lawyers, Second Edition, will help lawyers make the most of their online professional networking. In just one hour, you will learn to:

- Set up a LinkedIn® account
- Create a robust, dynamic profile--and take advantage of new multimedia options
- Build your connections
- Get up to speed on new features such as Endorsements, Influencers, Contacts, and Channels
- Enhance your Company Page with new functionality
- Use search tools to enhance your network
- Monitor your network with ease
- Optimize your settings for privacy concerns
- Use LinkedIn® effectively in the hiring process
- Develop a LinkedIn strategy to grow your legal network

Facebook® in One Hour for Lawyers
By Dennis Kennedy and Allison C. Shields
Product Code: 5110745 • LP Price: $24.95 • Regular Price: $39.95

With a few simple steps, lawyers can use Facebook® to market their services, grow their practices, and expand their legal network—all by using the same methods they already use to communicate with friends and family. *Facebook® in One Hour for Lawyers* will show any attorney—from Facebook® novices to advanced users—how to use this powerful tool for both professional and personal purposes.

Blogging in One Hour for Lawyers
By Ernie Svenson
Product Code: 5110744 • LP Price: $24.95 • Regular Price: $39.95

Until a few years ago, only the largest firms could afford to engage an audience of millions. Now, lawyers in any size firm can reach a global audience at little to no cost—all because of blogs. An effective blog can help you promote your practice, become more "findable" online, and take charge of how you are perceived by clients, journalists and anyone who uses the Internet. Blogging in One Hour for Lawyers will show you how to create, maintain, and improve a legal blog—and gain new business opportunities along the way. In just one hour, you will learn to:

- Set up a blog quickly and easily
- Write blog posts that will attract clients
- Choose from various hosting options like Blogger, TypePad, and WordPress
- Make your blog friendly to search engines, increasing your ranking
- Tweak the design of your blog by adding customized banners and colors
- Easily send notice of your blog posts to Facebook and Twitter
- Monitor your blog's traffic with Google Analytics and other tools
- Avoid ethics problems that may result from having a legal blog

The Electronic Evidence and Discovery Handbook: Forms, Checklists, and Guidelines
By Sharon D. Nelson, Bruce A. Olson, and John W. Simek
Product Code: 5110569 • LP Price: $99.95 • Regular Price: $129.95

The use of electronic evidence has increased dramatically over the past few years, but many lawyers still struggle with the complexities of electronic discovery. This substantial book provides lawyers with the templates they need to frame their discovery requests and provides helpful advice on what they can subpoena. In addition to the ready-made forms, the authors also supply explanations to bring you up to speed on the electronic discovery field. The accompanying CD-ROM features over 70 forms, including, Motions for Protective Orders, Preservation and Spoliation Documents, Motions to Compel, Electronic Evidence Protocol Agreements, Requests for Production, Internet Services Agreements, and more. Also included is a full electronic evidence case digest with over 300 cases detailed!

Android Apps in One Hour for Lawyers
By Daniel J. Siegel
Product Code: 5110754 • LP Price: $19.95 • Regular Price: $34.95

Lawyers are already using Android devices to make phone calls, check e-mail, and send text messages. After the addition of several key apps, Android smartphones or tablets can also help run a law practice. From the more than 800,000 apps currently available, Android Apps in One Hour for Lawyers highlights the "best of the best" apps that will allow you to practice law from your mobile device. In just one hour, this book will describe how to buy, install, and update Android apps, and help you:

- Store documents and files in the cloud
- Use security apps to safeguard client data on your phone
- Be organized and productive with apps for to-do lists, calendar, and contacts
- Communicate effectively with calling, text, and e-mail apps
- Create, edit, and organize your documents
- Learn on the go with news, reading, and reference apps
- Download utilities to keep your device running smoothly
- Hit the road with apps for travel
- Have fun with games and social media apps

Twitter in One Hour for Lawyers
By Jared Correia
Product Code: 5110746 • LP Price: $24.95 • Regular Price: $39.95

More lawyers than ever before are using Twitter to network with colleagues, attract clients, market their law firms, and even read the news. But to the uninitiated, Twitter's short messages, or tweets, can seem like they are written in a foreign language. Twitter in One Hour for Lawyers will demystify one of the most important social-media platforms of our time and teach you to tweet like an expert. In just one hour, you will learn to:

- Create a Twitter account and set up your profile
- Read tweets and understand Twitter jargon
- Write tweets—and send them at the appropriate time
- Gain an audience—follow and be followed
- Engage with other Twitters users
- Integrate Twitter into your firm's marketing plan
- Cross-post your tweets with other social media platforms like Facebook and LinkedIn
- Understand the relevant ethics, privacy, and security concerns
- Get the greatest possible return on your Twitter investment
- And much more!

Virtual Law Practice:
How to Deliver Legal Services Online
By Stephanie L. Kimbro
Product Code: 5110707 • LP Price: $47.95 • Regular Price: $79.95

The legal market has recently experienced a dramatic shift as lawyers seek out alternative methods of practicing law and providing more affordable legal services. Virtual law practice is revolutionizing the way the public receives legal services and how legal professionals work with clients. If you are interested in this form of practicing law, *Virtual Law Practice* will help you:

- Responsibly deliver legal services online to your clients
- Successfully set up and operate a virtual law office
- Establish a virtual law practice online through a secure, client-specific portal
- Manage and market your virtual law practice
- Understand state ethics and advisory opinions
- Find more flexibility and work/life balance in the legal profession

Social Media for Lawyers: The Next Frontier
By Carolyn Elefant and Nicole Black
Product Code: 5110710 • LP Price: $47.95 • Regular Price: $79.95

The world of legal marketing has changed with the rise of social media sites such as LinkedIn, Twitter, and Facebook. Law firms are seeking their companies attention with tweets, videos, blog posts, pictures, and online content. Social media is fast and delivers news at record pace. This book provides you with a practical, goal-centric approach to using social media in your law practice that will enable you to identify social media platforms and tools that fit your practice and implement them easily, efficiently, and ethically.

iPad Apps in One Hour for Lawyers
By Tom Mighell
Product Code: 5110739 • LP Price: $19.95 • Regular Price: $34.95

At last count, there were more than 80,000 apps available for the iPad. Finding the best apps often can be an overwhelming, confusing, and frustrating process. iPad Apps in One Hour for Lawyers provides the "best of the best" apps that are essential for any law practice. In just one hour, you will learn about the apps most worthy of your time and attention. This book will describe how to buy, install, and update iPad apps, and help you:

- Find apps to get organized and improve your productivity
- Create, manage, and store documents on your iPad
- Choose the best apps for your law office, including litigation and billing apps
- Find the best news, reading, and reference apps
- Take your iPad on the road with apps for travelers
- Maximize your social networking power
- Have some fun with game and entertainment apps during your relaxation time

The Lawyer's Essential Guide to Writing
By Marie Buckley
Product Code: 5110726 • LP Price: $47.95 • Regular Price: $79.95

This is a readable, concrete guide to contemporary legal writing. Based on Marie Buckley's years of experience coaching lawyers, this book provides a systematic approach to all forms of written communication, from memoranda and briefs to e-mail and blogs. The book sets forth three principles for powerful writing and shows how to apply those principles to develop a clean and confident style.

iPad in One Hour for Lawyers, Second Edition
By Tom Mighell
Product Code: 5110747 • LP Price: $24.95 • Regular Price: $39.95

Whether you are a new or a more advanced iPad user, *iPad in One Hour for Lawyers* takes a great deal of the mystery and confusion out of using your iPad. Ideal for lawyers who want to get up to speed swiftly, this book presents the essentials so you don't get bogged down in technical jargon and extraneous features and apps. In just six, short lessons, you'll learn how to:

- Quickly Navigate and Use the iPad User Interface
- Set Up Mail, Calendar, and Contacts
- Create and Use Folders to Multitask and Manage Apps
- Add Files to Your iPad, and Sync Them
- View and Manage Pleadings, Case Law, Contracts, and other Legal Documents
- Use Your iPad to Take Notes and Create Documents
- Use Legal-Specific Apps at Trial or in Doing Research

30-DAY RISK-FREE ORDER FORM

ABALAW
PRACTICE
DIVISION
The Business of Practicing Law

Please print or type. To ship UPS, we must have your street address. If you list a P.O. Box, we will ship by U.S. Mail.

Name

Member ID

Firm/Organization

Street Address

City/State/Zip

Area Code/Phone (In case we have a question about your order)

E-mail

Method of Payment:
☐ Check enclosed, payable to American Bar Association
☐ MasterCard   ☐ Visa   ☐ American Express

Card Number   Expiration Date

Signature Required

MAIL THIS FORM TO:
American Bar Association, Publication Orders
P.O. Box 10892, Chicago, IL 60610

ORDER BY PHONE:
24 hours a day, 7 days a week:
Call 1-800-285-2221 to place a credit card order. We accept Visa, MasterCard, and American Express.

EMAIL ORDERS: orders@americanbar.org
FAX ORDERS: 1-312-988-5568

VISIT OUR WEB SITE: www.ShopABA.org
Allow 7-10 days for regular UPS delivery. Need it sooner? Ask about our overnight delivery options. Call the ABA Service Center at 1-800-285-2221 for more information.

GUARANTEE:
If–for any reason–you are not satisfied with your purchase, you may return it within 30 days of receipt for a refund of the price of the book(s). No questions asked.

Thank You For Your Order.

Join the ABA Law Practice Division today and receive a substantial discount on Division publications!

Product Code:	Description:	Quantity:	Price:	Total Price:
				$
				$
				$
				$
				$

Shipping/Handling:			
$0.00 to $9.99	add $0.00		
$10.00 to $49.99	add $6.95		
$50.00 to $99.99	add $8.95		
$100.00 to $199.99	add $10.95		
$200.00 to $499.99	add $13.95		

*Tax:
IL residents add 9.25%
DC residents add 5.75%

Subtotal:	$
*Tax:	$
**Shipping/Handling:	$
Yes, I am an ABA member and would like to join the Law Practice Division today! (Add $50.00)	$
Total:	$